Three Aces

OTHER BOOKS BY REX STOUT

Novels

HOW LIKE A GOD • GOLDEN REMEDY • SEED ON THE WIND
O CARELESS LOVE! • MR. CINDERELLA • FOREST FIRE
THE PRESIDENT VANISHES

Nero Wolfe Mysteries

FER-DE-LANCE • THE LEAGUE OF FRIGHTENED MEN
THE RUBBER BAND • THE RED BOX • SOME BURIED CAESAR
OVER MY DEAD BODY • BLACK ORCHIDS
WHERE THERE'S A WILL • NOT QUITE DEAD ENOUGH
TOO MANY COOKS • THE SILENT SPEAKER
TOO MANY WOMEN • AND BE A VILLAIN
TROUBLE IN TRIPLICATE • THE SECOND CONFESSION
THREE DOORS TO DEATH • IN THE BEST FAMILIES
CURTAINS FOR THREE • MURDER BY THE BOOK
TRIPLE JEOPARDY • PRISONER'S BASE • THE GOLDEN SPIDERS
THREE MEN OUT • THE BLACK MOUNTAIN
FULL HOUSE: A NERO WOLFE OMNIBUS • BEFORE MIDNIGHT
THREE WITNESSES • MIGHT AS WELL BE DEAD
THREE FOR THE CHAIR • IF DEATH EVER SLEPT
AND FOUR TO GO • ALL ACES: A NERO WOLFE OMNIBUS
CHAMPAGNE FOR ONE • PLOT IT YOURSELF
THREE AT WOLFE'S DOOR • TOO MANY CLIENTS
FIVE OF A KIND: THE THIRD NERO WOLFE OMNIBUS
HOMICIDE TRINITY: A NERO WOLFE THREESOME
THE FINAL DEDUCTION • GAMBIT • THE MOTHER HUNT
TRIO FOR BLUNT INSTRUMENTS • A RIGHT TO DIE
THE DOORBELL RANG
ROYAL FLUSH: THE FOURTH NERO WOLFE OMNIBUS
DEATH OF A DOXY • THE FATHER HUNT
KINGS FULL OF ACES: THE FIFTH NERO WOLFE OMNIBUS
DEATH OF A DUDE

Tecumseh Fox Mysteries

DOUBLE FOR DEATH • THE BROKEN VASE • BAD FOR BUSINESS

Mysteries

THE HAND IN THE GLOVE • MOUNTAIN CAT
ALPHABET HICKS • RED THREADS

Three Aces

A NERO WOLFE OMNIBUS

Rex Stout

THE VIKING PRESS / NEW YORK

First published in 1971 by The Viking Press, Inc.
625 Madison Avenue, New York, N.Y. 10022

Published simultaneously in Canada by
The Macmillan Company of Canada Limited

SBN 670–14907–1
Library of Congress catalog card number: 70–151262

Printed in the United States of America

Contents

Too Many Clients

CHAPTER 1

WHEN HE HAD got deposited in the red leather chair I went to my desk, whirled my chair to face him, sat, and regarded him politely but without enthusiasm. It was only partly that his $39.95 suit didn't fit and needed pressing and his $3.00 shirt was on its second or third day; it was more him than his clothes. There was nothing wrong with his long bony face and broad forehead, but he simply didn't have the air of a man who might make a sizable contribution to Nero Wolfe's bank balance.

Which at that moment, that Monday afternoon in early May, was down to $14,194.62, after deducting the checks I had just drawn and put on Wolfe's desk for him to sign. That may look fairly respectable, but. What with the weekly wages of Theodore Horstmann, the orchid valet, Fritz Brenner, chef and house steward, and me, the handy man; and with grocery bills, including such items as the fresh caviar which Wolfe sometimes stirred into his coddled eggs at breakfast; and with the various needs of the orchids in the plant rooms up on the roof of the old brownstone, not to mention new additions to the collection; and with this and that and these and those, the minimum monthly outgo of that establishment averaged more than five grand. Also, the June 15 income-tax installment would be due in five weeks. So, with no prospect of a fat fee in sight, it was beginning to look as if a trip to the safe-deposit box might be called for before the Fourth of July.

Therefore, when the doorbell had rung and, going to the hall for a look through the one-way glass of the front door, I had seen an adult male stranger with no sample case, it had seemed fitting to open the door wide and give him a cordial eye. He had said, "This is Nero Wolfe's house, isn't it?" and I had said yes but Mr. Wolfe wouldn't be available until six o'clock, and he had said,

"I know, he's up in the plant rooms from four to six, but I want to see Archie Goodwin. You're Mr. Goodwin?" I had admitted it and asked him what about, and he had said he wanted to consult me professionally. By then I had sized him up, or thought I had, and it didn't look very promising, but time could be wasted with him as well as without him, so I had taken him to the office. Another point against him was that he had no hat. Ninety-eight per cent of men who can pay big fees wear hats.

Leaning back in the red leather chair with his chin lowered and his intelligent gray eyes aimed at me, he spoke. "I'll have to tell you who I am, of course."

I shook my head. "Not unless it's material."

"It is." He crossed his legs. The tops of his socks, gray with little red dots, were down nearly to his shoes. "Else there was no use coming. I want to consult you in the strictest confidence."

I nodded. "Naturally. But this is Nero Wolfe's office, and I work for him. If you get a bill it will be from him."

"I know." Apparently that was a triviality. His eyes *were* intelligent. "I expect a bill and I'll pay it. I can speak in assured confidence?"

"Certainly. Unless you're loaded with something too heavy for me to hold, like murder or treason."

He smiled. "Other sins only speak; murder shrieks out. Treason doth never prosper. I am loaded with neither. None of my crimes is statutory. Then in confidence, Mr. Goodwin, my name is Yeager, Thomas G. Yeager. You may possibly have seen or heard it, though I am no celebrity. I live at Three-forty East Sixty-eighth Street. My firm, of which I am executive vice-president, is Continental Plastic Products, with offices in the Empire State Building."

I did not blink. Continental Plastic Products might be a giant with three or four floors, or it might have two small rooms with the only phone on the executive vice-president's desk. Even so, I knew that block in East 68th Street, and it was no slum, far from it. This character might wear a $39.95 suit because he didn't give a damn and didn't have to. I know a chairman of the board of a billion-dollar corporation, one of the 2 per cent, who never gets his shoes shined and shaves three times a week.

I had my notebook and was writing in it. Yeager was saying, "My home phone number is not listed. It's Chisholm five, three-two-three-two. I came at a time when I knew Wolfe would be busy, to see you, because there's no point in explaining it to him since he would merely assign you to it. I think I am being followed, and I want to make sure, and if I am I want to know who is following me."

"That's kindergarten stuff." I tossed the notebook on my desk. "Any reputable agency will handle that for you at ten dollars an hour. Mr. Wolfe has a different approach to the fee question."

"I know he has. That's unimportant." He waved it away. "But it's vitally important to find out if I'm being followed, and quickly, and especially who it is. What agency at ten dollars an hour would have a man as good as you?"

"That's not the point. Even if I'm only half as good as I think I am it would still be a pity to waste me on spotting a tail. And what if there's no tail to spot? How long would it take to convince you? Say ten days, twelve hours a day, at a hundred dollars an hour. Twelve thousand bucks plus expenses. Even if you—"

"It wouldn't be ten days." He had lifted his chin. "I'm sure it wouldn't. And it wouldn't be twelve hours a day. If you'll let me explain, Mr. Goodwin. I think I am being followed only at certain times, or that I will be. Specifically, I suspect that I shall be followed when I leave my house this evening at seven o'clock to go crosstown, across the park, to an address on Eighty-second Street. One-fifty-six West Eighty-second Street. Perhaps the best plan would be for you to be at my house when I leave, but of course I shall leave the tactics to you. I don't want to be followed to that address. I don't want it known that I have any connection with it. If I am not followed, that would end it for today, and I would call on you again only when I intend to go there again."

"When would that be?"

"I can't say definitely. Possibly later in the week, perhaps some day next week. I could notify you a day in advance."

"How will you go, your car or a taxi?"

"Taxi."

"Which is more important to you, not to be followed to that address, or to know whether you're followed or not, or to identify the tail if you have one?"

"They're all important."

"Well." I screwed my lips. "I admit it's a little special. I mentioned a hundred dollars an hour, but that's for routine. The shoe would have to fit the foot, with Mr. Wolfe doing the fitting and you the footing."

He smiled. "There will be no difficulty about that. Then I'll expect you around seven. A little before?"

"Probably." I got my notebook. "Will the tail be someone you know?"

"I don't know. It might be."

"Man or woman?"

"I couldn't say. I don't know."

"An operative or a do-it-yourself?"

"I don't know. It could be either."

"Spotting him will be simple. Then what? If he's an operative I might recognize him, but that wouldn't help much. Of course I can pull him off whether I recognize him or not, but I can't squeeze his client's name out of him."

"But you can pull him off?"

"Sure. How much would the client's name be worth to you? It might come high."

"I don't think . . ." He hesitated. "I don't believe I would care to do that."

That didn't seem to fit, but I skipped it. "If it's someone on his own, of course I'll pull him off, and what else? Do you want him to know he's been spotted?"

He considered it for three seconds. "I think not. Better not, I think."

"Then I can't snap a picture of him. I can only give you a description."

"That will suffice."

"Okay." I dropped the notebook on my desk. "Your address

on Sixty-eighth Street, that's not an apartment building, is it?"

"No, it's a house. My house."

"Then I shouldn't enter it and I shouldn't get too near it. If it's an operative he would probably recognize me. This is how it will be. At seven o'clock on the dot you will leave the house, walk to Second Avenue—don't cross it—and turn left. About thirty paces from the corner is a lunchroom, and in front—"

"How do you happen to know that?"

"There aren't many blocks in Manhattan I don't know. In front of the lunchroom, either at the curb or double-parked, a blue and yellow taxi will be standing with the driver in it and the flag down. The driver will have a big square face and big ears. You will say to him, 'You need a shave,' and he will say, 'My face is tender.' To make sure, when you get in look at his name on the card. It will be Albert Goller." I spelled it. "Do you want to write it down?"

"No."

"Then don't forget it. Give him the address on West Eighty-second Street and sit back and relax. That's all for you. Whatever the driver does, he'll know what he's doing. Don't keep looking back; that might make it a little harder."

He was smiling. "It didn't take you long to set the stage, did it?"

"I haven't got long." I glanced up at the clock on the wall. "It's nearly five." I stood up. "I'll be seeing you, but you won't be seeing me."

"Wonderful," he said, leaving the chair. "Measure your mind's height by the shade it casts. I knew you would be the man for it." He moved and offered a hand. "Don't bother to show me out, I know the way."

I went along, as always for some years, ever since the day a visitor left the door unlatched, sneaked back in, and hid behind the couch in the front room, and during the night went through everything in the office he could open. At the door I asked him what the name of the hackie would be, and he told me. Returning, I went on past the door of the office to the kitchen, got a glass from the shelf and a carton of milk from the refrigerator.

Fritz, at the center table mincing shallots, gave me a look and spoke.

"That is an insult. I pull your nose. My shad roe *aux fines herbes* is a dish for a king."

"Yeah, but I'm not a king." I poured milk. "Also I'm leaving soon on an errand and I don't know when I'll be back."

"Ah? A personal errand."

"No." I took a sip. "I'll not only answer your question, I'll ask it for you. Having noticed that we haven't had a client worth a damn for nearly six weeks, you want to know if we have one now, and I don't blame you. It's possible but not likely. It looks like more peanuts." I took a sip. "You may have to invent a dish for a king made of peanut butter."

"Not impossible, Archie. The problem would be to crack the oil. Not vinegar; it would take too much. Perhaps lime juice, with or without a drop or two of onion juice. I'll try it tomorrow."

I told him to let me know how he made out, took the milk to the office, got at the phone at my desk, dialed the number of the *Gazette,* and got Lon Cohen. He said he was too busy to spare time for anything but a front-page lead or an invitation to a poker game. I said I was out of both items at the moment but would put them on back order, and meanwhile I would hold the line while he went to the morgue to see if they had anything on Thomas G. Yeager, executive vice-president of Continental Plastic Products, residing at 340 East 68th Street. He said he knew the name, they probably had a file on him, and he would send for it and call back. In ten minutes he did so. Continental Plastic Products was one of the big ones; its main plant was in Cleveland, and its sales and executive offices were in the Empire State Building. Thomas G. Yeager had been its executive vice-president for five years and was in the saddle. He was married and had a daughter, Anne, unmarried, and a son, Thomas G. Junior, married. He was a member of . . .

I told Lon that was all I needed, thanked him, hung up, and buzzed the plant rooms on the house phone. After a wait Wolfe's voice came, gruff of course.

"Yes?"

"Sorry to interrupt. A man named Yeager came. He wants to know if he is being tailed and by whom. He expects to be soaked and doesn't mind because no one but me is good enough. I have checked on him and he can stand it, and I might as well earn a couple of weeks' pay. I'll be gone when you come down. His name and address are in my notebook. I'll be back before bedtime."

"And tomorrow? How long will it last?"

"It won't. If it does we'll get Saul or Fred. I'll explain later. It's just a chore."

"Very well." He hung up, and I took the phone and dialed a number that would get me Al Goller.

CHAPTER 2

TWO HOURS LATER, at twenty minutes past seven, I was sitting in a taxi parked on 67th Street between Second and Third Avenues, twisted around for a view through the rear window. If Yeager had left his house at 7:00 sharp, he should have been in Al Goller's cab by 7:04, and Al should have turned the corner into 67th Street by 7:06. But it was 7:20, and no sign of him.

It was useless trying to guess what the hitch was, so I did. By 7:30 I had a collection of a dozen guesses, both plain and fancy. At 7:35 I was too annoyed to bother to guess. At 7:40 I told Mike Collins, the hackie, who was no stranger, "Nuts. I'll take a look," got out, and walked to the corner. Al was still there in his cab in front of the lunchroom. When the light showed green I crossed the avenue, went on to the cab, and asked Al, "Where is he?"

He yawned. "All I know is where he isn't."

"I'll ring him. If he comes while I'm inside, have trouble starting your engine until I come out and go. Give me time to get back to Mike."

He nodded and started another yawn, and I went into the lunchroom, found the phone booth in the rear, and dialed CH5-3232. After four rings I had a male voice in my ear. "Mrs. Yeager's residence."

"May I speak with Mr. Yeager?"

"He's not available at the moment. Who is this, please?"

I hung up. Not only did I know the voice of Sergeant Purley Stebbins of Homicide West, but also it was I who some years back had informed him that when one answers the phone at the home of the John Does one says not "Mr. Doe's residence" but "Mrs. Doe's residence." So I hung up, departed, signed to Al Goller to stay put, walked to the corner of 68th Street and turned right, and proceeded far enough to see that the dick behind the wheel of the PD car double-parked in front of Number 340 was the one who usually drove Stebbins. Whirling, I went back the way I had come, to the lunchroom and the phone booth, dialed the number of the *Gazette,* asked for Lon Cohen, and got him. My intention was to ask him if he had heard of any interesting murders recently, but I didn't get to.

His voice came. "Archie?"

"Right. Have you—"

"How the hell did you know Thomas G. Yeager was going to be murdered when you called me three hours ago?"

"I didn't. I don't. I merely—"

"Balls. But I appreciate it. Thanks for a page-one box. NERO WOLFE SCOOPS THE COPS AGAIN. I'm writing it now: 'Nero Wolfe, private eye extraordinary, was plunging into the Yeager murder case more than two hours before the body was discovered in an excavation on West Eighty-second Street. At five-five p.m. his lackey, Archie Goodwin, phoned the *Gazette* office to get—' "

"You'll eat it. The whole world knows I'm not a lackey, I'm a flunky, and the idea of Nero Wolfe plunging. Besides, this is the first time I've phoned you for a month. If someone called and imitated my voice it was probably the murderer, and if you had been smart enough to keep him on while you had the call traced you might have—"

"Okay. Start over. When can you give me something?"

"When I have something to give. I always do, don't I? Pretend I didn't know Yeager had been murdered until you told me. Where is the excavation on West Eighty-second Street?"

"Between Columbus and Amsterdam."

"When was the body found?"

"Ten after seven. Fifty minutes ago. Under a tarp at the bottom of a hole dug by Con Edison. Boys climbed in to retrieve a ball that had rolled in."

I took a second. "The body must have rolled in since five o'clock; that's when Con Ed men usually quit if it's not an emergency. Didn't anyone see it roll in and pull the tarp over it?"

"How do I know? We got it only half an hour ago."

"How sure is the identification?"

"Positive. One of the men we sent knew him. He phoned just five minutes ago."

"How do you know he was murdered?"

"That's not official yet, but there's a hole in the side of his head that he didn't make with his finger. Look, Archie. His file from the morgue was here on my desk when the flash came. Within an hour everybody here will know that I sent for it two hours in advance. I don't mind being mysterious, but it could be a nuisance if this gets big. So I mention that I sent for the file because of a call from you, and someone who likes to do favors mentions it to someone at Homicide, and then?"

"Then I cooperate with the cops as usual. I'll be there in twenty minutes."

"Fine. It'll be a pleasure to see you."

I went out to the sidewalk, got into Al's cab, and told him to roll around the corner to Mike. As he pulled away from the curb he said his instructions were to accept only a passenger who told him he needed a shave, and I told him all right, he needed a shave. There was no space at the curb on 67th Street near Mike, so we stopped alongside, and I got out and stood between the two cabs, at the open front windows.

"The party's off," I told them. "Circumstances beyond my control. I mentioned no figure to you because of unknown factors, such as how long it would take, but since you have only had to sit around a while, maybe twenty apiece would be enough. What do you think?"

Mike said, "Yeah," and Al said, "Sure. What happened?"

I got out my wallet and took out six twenties. "So we'll make it three times that," I said, "because you are not dumb. I haven't told you the name of the client, but I described him, and you know he was coming from around the corner on Sixty-eighth Street, and he was going to West Eighty-second Street. So when you read in the paper tomorrow about a man named Thomas G. Yeager who lived at Three-forty East Sixty-eighth Street, that his body was found at seven-ten this evening in a hole on West Eighty-second Street, with a hole in his head, you will wonder.

When a man wonders about something, he likes to talk about it. So here's sixty bucks apiece. What I want is a chance to satisfy my curiosity without being bothered by cops wanting to know why I arranged this setup. Why the hell did he go on his own instead of sticking to our program? I will add that he didn't say or hint that he expected or feared any violence; he only wanted to find out if he was being tailed, and if so he wanted the tail pulled off and identified if possible. That's what I told you and that's how it was. I haven't the faintest idea who killed him or why. You know all I know. I would just as soon have nobody else know it until I look around a little. You guys have known me —how long?"

"Five years," Mike said.

"Eight years," Al said. "How did you find out he got it? If his body was found only an hour ago—"

"When I rang his house I recognized the voice that answered, a Homicide sergeant, Purley Stebbins. When I went around the corner I recognized the driver of a PD car parked in front of Number Three-forty. When I phoned a newspaperman I know and asked for news I got it. I am saving nothing; you have it all. Here's your sixty bucks."

Al reached to get a corner of one twenty with a finger and thumb and slipped it out. "This'll do," he said. "This is enough for my time, and keeping my lip buttoned is just personal. I'll enjoy it. Every cop I see I can think, You bastard, what I know and you don't."

Mike, grinning, took his three twenties. "I'm different," he said. "Just as apt as not I'd tell everybody in reach, including cops, but now I can't because I'd have to give your forty bucks back. I may not be noble but I'm honest." He put the bills in a pocket and extended a paw. "But we'd better shake on it just to be sure."

We shook, and I got back into Al's cab and told him to take me to the *Gazette* building.

If Lon Cohen had a title, I didn't know what it was and I doubt if he did. Just his name was on the door of the little room on the twentieth floor, two doors down from the corner office of the publisher, and in that situation you would think he would be out of the dust stirred up by the daily whirlwind of a newspaper, but he always seemed to be up, not only on what had just happened but on what was just going to happen. We kept no account of how we stood on give and take over the years, but it pretty well evened up.

He was very dark—dark skin stretched tight over his neat little face, dark brown deep-set eyes, hair almost black, slicked back and up over his sloping dome. He was next to the best of the poker players I occasionally spent a night with, the best being Saul Panzer, whom you will meet later. When I entered the little room that Monday evening he was on the phone, and I took the chair at the end of his desk and sat and listened. It went on for minutes, and all he said was "No" nine times. When he hung up I said, "Just a yes man."

"I have to make a call," he said. "Here, pass the time." He picked up a cardboard folder and handed it to me and returned to the phone.

It was the file on Thomas G. Yeager. Not bulky—a dozen or so newspaper clippings, four typewritten memos, tear sheets of an article in a trade journal, *Plastics Today,* and three photographs. Two of the photographs were studio jobs with his name typed at the bottom, and one was of a gathering in the Churchill ballroom, with a typed caption pasted on: "Thomas G. Yeager speaking at the banquet of the National Plastics Association, Churchill Hotel, New York City, October 19, 1958." He was at the mike on the stage with his arm raised for a gesture. I read the memos and glanced through the clippings, and was looking over the article when Lon finished at the phone and turned.

"All right, give," he demanded.

I closed the folder and put it on the desk. "I came," I said, "to make a deal, but first you should know something. I have never seen Thomas G. Yeager or spoken with him or had any communication from him, and neither has Mr. Wolfe. I know absolutely nothing about him except what you told me on the phone and what I just read in that folder."

Lon was smiling. "Okay for the record. Now just between you and me."

"The same, believe it or not. But I heard something just before I phoned you at five o'clock that made me curious about him. For the time being I would prefer to keep what I heard to myself—for at least twenty-four hours and maybe longer. I expect to be busy and I don't want to spend tomorrow at the DA's office. So it's not necessary for anyone to know that I rang you this afternoon to ask about Yeager."

"It may be desirable. For me. I sent for his file. If I say I dreamed something was going to happen to him people might talk."

I grinned at him. "Come off it. You haven't even got a pair. You can say anything you damn please. You can say someone told you something off the record and you're hanging on to it. Besides, I'm offering a deal. If you'll forget about my curiosity about Yeager until further notice, I'll put you on my Christmas card list. This year it will be an abstract painting in twenty colors and the message will be 'We want to share with you this picture of us bathing the dog, greetings of the season from Archie and Mehitabel and the children.'"

"You haven't got a Mehitabel or any children."

"Sure, that's why it will be abstract."

He eyed me. "You could give me something not for quotation. Or something to hold until you're ready to let go."

"No. Not now. If and when, I know your number."

"As usual." He raised his hands, palms up. "I have things to do. Drop in some day." His phone rang, and he turned to it, and I went.

On my way to the elevator and going down, I looked it over. I had told Wolfe I would be back before bedtime, but it was only nine o'clock. I was hungry. I could go to a soda counter for a bite and decide how to proceed while I bit, but the trouble was that I knew darned well what I wanted to do, and it might take all night. Besides, although it was understood that when I was out on an errand I would be guided by intelligence and experience, as Wolfe had put it, it was also understood that if things got complicated I would phone. And the phone was no good for this, not only because he hated talking on the phone about anything whatever, but also because it had to be handled just right or he would refuse to play. So I flagged a taxi and gave the driver the address of the old brownstone on West 35th Street.

Arriving, I mounted the seven steps to the stoop and pushed the bell button. My key isn't enough when the chain bolt is on, as it usually is when I'm out. When Fritz opened the door and I entered, he tried not to look a question at me but couldn't keep it out of his eyes—the same question he hadn't asked that afternoon: Did we have a client? I told him it was still possible, and I was empty, and could he spare a hunk of bread and a glass of milk? He said but of course, he would bring it, and I went to the office.

Wolfe was at his desk with a book, leaning back in the only chair in the world that he can sit down in without making a face, made to order by his design and under his supervision. The reading light in the wall above and behind his left shoulder was the only one on in the room, and like that, with the light at that angle, he looks even bigger than he is. Like a mountain with the sun rising behind it. As I entered and flipped the wall switch to cut him down to size, he spoke. He said, "Umph." As I crossed to my desk he asked, "Have you eaten?"

"No." I sat. "Fritz is bringing something."

"Bringing?"

Surprise with a touch of annoyance. Ordinarily, when an errand has made me miss a meal and I come home hungry, I go to the kitchen to eat. The exceptions are when I have something to report that shouldn't wait, and when he is settled down for the evening with a book he is in no mood to listen to a report, no matter what.

I nodded. "I have something on my chest."

His lips tightened. The book, a big thick one, was spread open, held with both hands. He closed it on a finger to keep his place, heaved a sigh, and demanded, "What?"

I decided it was useless to try circling around. With him you have to fit the tactics to the atmosphere. "That slip I put on your desk," I said. "The bank balance after drawing those checks. The June tax payment will be due in thirty-seven days. Of course we could file an amended declaration if someone doesn't turn up with a major problem and a retainer to match."

He was scowling at me. "Must you harp on the obvious?"

"I'm not harping. I haven't mentioned it for three days. I refer to it now because I would like to have permission to take a stab at digging up a client instead of sitting here on my fanny waiting for one to turn up. I'm getting calluses on my rump."

"And your modus? A sandwich board?"

"No, sir. I have a possible target, just barely possible. About that man who came to hire me to spot a tail, Thomas G. Yeager. I got two cabs and had them waiting at seven o'clock, one for him to take and one for me to follow in. He didn't show up. I got tired waiting and rang his house, and Purley Stebbins answered the phone. I went around a corner and there was a car with Purley's driver in it, in front of Yeager's house. I rang Lon Cohen and he wanted to know why I had phoned him to ask about Thomas G. Yeager two hours before Yeager's body was found in a hole on West Eighty-second Street. With a hole in his head. So our client was gone, but it occurred to me that his going might possibly get us another one. He was a big shot in his field, with a big title and a nice house in a nice neighborhood, and it could be that no one but me knew of his suspicion that he was being tailed or was going to be. Also the address that he thought he was going to be tailed to was One-fifty-six West Eighty-second Street, and it was in that block on that street that his body had been found. So I spent some of your money. Besides paying the two hackies for their time, I gave them an extra forty bucks to forget where they had been—that is, I gave it to Mike Collins. Al Goller preferred to do his forgetting for personal reasons."

Wolfe grunted. *"Your* initiative. They may already have the murderer."

"Then you're out forty dollars in addition to the fifty-three dollars and sixty cents spent on behalf of a client from whom we won't collect because he's dead. But it's not as simple as that. Actually our client is not dead. Or, putting it another way, we didn't have a client. On my way home I stopped in at the *Gazette* to ask Lon Cohen to forget that I had phoned to ask him about Thomas G. Yeager, and there was a folder on his desk with some items about Yeager, including three pictures of him, which I looked at. The man who came this afternoon to hire me to spot his tail was not Yeager. No resemblance. So I suppose it's more accurate to say we didn't have a client."

CHAPTER 3

NATURALLY I EXPECTED to get a strong reaction, and I did. Wolfe straightened up to reach to the desk for his bookmark, a thin strip of gold which he used only for books he considered worthy of a place on the shelves in the office. As he inserted it in the book Fritz appeared with a tray and brought it to my desk. Seeing that Wolfe was putting his book down, he winked at me approvingly, and I swiveled to get at the tray. There was a bowl of chestnut soup, a cucumber-and-shrimp sandwich on toast, a roast-beef sandwich on a hard roll, home-baked, a pile of watercress, an apple baked in white wine, and a glass of milk.

A question of etiquette. When we are at table in the dining room for lunch or dinner, any mention of business is taboo. The rule has never been formally extended to fill-ins, but Wolfe feels strongly that when a man is feeding nothing should interfere with his concentration on his palate. Having disposed of the book, he leaned back and shut his eyes. After a few spoonfuls of soup I said, "I'm too hungry to taste anyway. Go right ahead."

His eyes opened. "Beyond all doubt?"

"Yes, sir." I took in a spoonful and swallowed. "His name was typed on the pictures. Also there was a picture of him in a magazine. A face like a squirrel with a pointed nose and not much chin. The man this afternoon had a long bony face and broad forehead."

"And, calling himself Yeager, he said that he expected to be followed to a specified address on West Eighty-second Street, and Yeager's body was found near that address. How long had he been dead?"

"I don't know. Give them time. Besides what I've told you, all Lon knew was that the body was in a hole in the street dug

by Con Edison men, it was covered with a tarp, and it was found
by boys whose ball rolled in."

"If I approve of your proposal to explore the possibility of
getting a client and earning a fee, how do you intend to proceed?"

I swallowed soup. "First I finish these sandwiches and the
apple and milk. Then I go to Eighty-second Street. Since the
body was found in a hole in the street, it's quite possible that
there is nothing to connect it with that neighborhood or that particular address. He could have been killed anywhere and taken
there and dumped. The blocks in the Eighties between Columbus
and Amsterdam are no place for a big shot in a big corporation.
The Puerto Ricans and Cubans average three or four to a room. I
want to find out what business Yeager had there, if any."

"You would go now? Tonight?"

"Sure. As soon as I empty this tray."

"Pfui. How often have I told you that impetuosity is a virtue
only when delay is dangerous?"

"Oh, six thousand."

"But you are still headlong. In the morning we shall get many
details that are lacking now. There may be no problem left, except the identity of the man who came here in masquerade, and
that may no longer be of interest. Now, of course, it is. How long
was he with you?"

"Twenty-five minutes."

"We may need a record of what he said. Instead of dashing
up to Eighty-second Street you will spend the evening at the
typewriter. The conversation verbatim, and include a complete
description." He picked up the book and shifted to his reading
position.

That took care of the rest of the evening. I still would have liked
to take a look at 156 West 82nd Street before the cops got interested in it, if they hadn't already, but Wolfe did have a point,
and it was his money I had given Mike Collins. Typing my talk
with the bogus Yeager was no strain, merely work. I have reported orally many conversations much longer than that one, with
more people involved. It was a little short of midnight when I
finished. After collating the sheets, original and carbon, and put-

ting them in a drawer, removing the orchids from the vase on Wolfe's desk and taking them to the garbage pail in the kitchen—he wants them gone when he brings fresh ones in the morning—locking the safe, seeing that the front door was bolted, and turning out the lights, I mounted two flights to my room. Wolfe was already in his, on the second floor.

Usually I get down to the kitchen for breakfast around eight-thirty, but that Tuesday morning I made it earlier, a little after eight. I wanted to go straight to the little table where Fritz had put my copy of the *Times* on the reading rack, but impetuosity is a virtue only when delay is dangerous, so I made myself exchange greetings with Fritz, get my glass of orange juice, stir it, and take a couple of sips. Then I went and got the paper. Would the headline be YEAGER MURDER SOLVED?

It wasn't. It was EXECUTIVE SHOT AND KILLED. I sat down and took another sip.

With my orange juice, buckwheat cakes and sausage, blackberry jam, and two cups of coffee, I read it in both the *Times* and the *Gazette*. I'll skip such details as the names of the boys who found the body. They got their names in the papers, and that ought to last them, and anyway I doubt if they read books. He had been shot once, above the right ear, at close range, and had died instantly. He had been dead sixteen to twenty-four hours when the body was examined at 7:30 p.m., so he had been killed between 7:30 p.m. Sunday and 3:30 a.m. Monday. The autopsy might make it more definite. There had been no workmen in the excavation on 82nd Street all day Monday because needed repair items were not at hand, so the body could have been put in the hole Sunday night. The tarpaulin had been left in the hole by the workmen. No one had been found who had seen Yeager alive in the neighborhood or who had heard a shot fired in the vicinity, so he had probably been killed elsewhere and the body transported there.

Yeager's daughter, Anne, was at college, Bennington. His son, Thomas G. Junior, was in Cleveland, employed at the plant of Continental Plastic Products. Yeager and his wife had left New York Friday evening to spend the weekend visiting friends in the country; he had returned to town Sunday afternoon, but his wife hadn't returned until Monday morning. There had been no one at the Yeager house on 68th Street Sunday afternoon. Nothing was known of Yeager's movements after he boarded a train for New York at Stamford at 5:02 p.m. Sunday.

No one was being held by the police, and the District Attorney would say only that the investigation was in progress.

In the picture of him in the *Times* he was grinning like a politician. There were two in the *Gazette*—one a reproduction of one I had seen in Lon's office, and one of him stretched out at the edge of the hole he had been found in. I clipped the one in the *Times* and the live one from the *Gazette* and put them in my pocket notebook.

At 8:51 I put down my empty coffee cup, thanked Fritz for the meal and told him I might or might not be home for lunch, went to the hall, mounted the flight to Wolfe's room, and entered. His breakfast tray, with nothing left on it but empty dishes, was on the table by a window, and beside it was his copy of the *Times*. He was standing before the mirror on the dresser, knotting his four-in-hand. Since he always goes from his room to the roof for his morning two hours in the plant rooms I don't know why he sports a tie—maybe being polite to the orchids. He grunted good morning, got the tie adjusted, and turned.

"I'm off," I said. "Instructions?"

"*Your* initiative," he said.

"No, sir. That was yesterday. Are you sending me or aren't you? Apparently it's wide open, unless they're saving something. He had been dead at least fourteen hours when that bozo came yesterday. What he said is in my desk drawer. How much do I have along for possible needs?"

"Enough."

"Any limit?"

"Certainly. The limit dictated by your discretion and sagacity."

"Right. Expect me when you see me."

Descending to the office, I opened the safe, got five hundred dollars in used fives, tens, and twenties from the cash reserve, closed the safe, and twirled the knob. Removing my jacket, I unlocked the bottom drawer of my desk, got my armpit holster and put it on, loaded the Marley .32, and slipped it in the holster. Ever since an unpleasant experience some years ago I never go on an errand connected with a murder with only my pocket-knife. I put on my jacket and went to the hall. Coat and hat? I hate to bother with them. There was no sun outside; the 7:30 radio had said possible showers. What the hell, live dangerously. I left, walked to Tenth Avenue and flagged a taxi, and told the driver 82nd and Broadway.

Of course I had no script; it would have to be ad lib, except the obvious first step, to find out if the city scientists had finished their research. Many of them knew me by sight, and they knew I wouldn't be nosing around the scene of a murder just to pass the time. So, walking east from Broadway and crossing Amsterdam Avenue, I stopped at the corner for a survey from a distance, from the uptown side of 82nd Street. I have good eyes at any distance, and I could make out the "156" on a house about thirty paces from the corner. Parked cars were bumper to bumper along the curb on both sides except where barriers guarded the hole in the pavement, but there was no police car, marked or unmarked.

Begging the pardon of the tenants of the block, it was a slum. Fifty or sixty years ago, when the stone was new and clean and the brass was shiny, the long row of five-story houses might have been a credit to the city, but no more. They looked ratty and they were ratty, and it was a bet that they would crumble any minute if they hadn't been jammed together. There weren't many people on the sidewalk, and no kids, since it was school hours, but there was quite a gathering around the barriers surrounding the hole, which was some fifteen yards beyond Number 156. There was a cop there riding herd on them, but he was merely a flatfoot. There was no sign of a Homicide or DA man.

I crossed the street and walked along to the barriers. Over the shoulder of a woman in a purple dress I could see two workmen down in the hole, so the scientists had finished with it. While I stood looking down at them my sagacity came up with five conclusions:

1. Yeager had had some connection with someone or some-

thing at Number 156. Whoever the guy was who had come and hired me, and whatever his game was, and whether he had killed Yeager or not, he certainly hadn't just pulled that address out of a hat.

2. If Yeager had been killed elsewhere and the body had been brought to this spot deliberately, to impress someone at 156, why hadn't it been dumped on the sidewalk smack in front of 156? Why roll it into the hole and climb down and put a tarp over it? No.

3. If Yeager had been killed elsewhere and the body had been brought to this spot not deliberately, but accidentally, merely because there was a hole here, you would have to swallow a coincidence that even a whale couldn't get down. No.

4. Yeager had not been shot as he was entering or leaving 156. At any time of night the sound of a shot in that street would have brought a dozen, a hundred, heads sticking out of windows. So the shooter runs or steps on the gas pedal. He does not drag the body to the hole and roll it in and climb down and put a tarp over it. No.

5. Therefore Yeager had been killed inside Number 156, some time, any time, after 7:30 p.m. Sunday, and later that night, when there was no audience, the body had been carried to the hole, only fifteen yards, and dropped in. That didn't account for the tarp, but no theory would. At least the tarp didn't hurt it. It could have been to postpone discovery of the body until the workmen came.

In detective work it's a great convenience to have a sagacity that can come up with conclusions like that; it saves wear and tear on the brain. I backed away from the barrier and walked the fifteen yards to Number 156.

Some of the houses had a sign, VACANCY, displayed at the entrance, but 156 didn't. But it did have a sign, hand-printed on a piece of cardboard fastened to the pillar at the foot of the steps going up to the stoop. It said SUPERENTENDANT, with an arrow pointing to the right. So I went right and down three steps, then left and through an open doorway into a little vestibule, and there in front of my eyes was evidence that there was something special about that house. The door had a Rabson lock. You have a Rabson installed on a door only if you insist on being absolutely certain that anyone who enters must have either the right key or a sledgehammer, and you are able and willing to shell out $61.50.

I pushed the bell button. In a moment the door opened, and there facing me was one of the three most beautiful females I have ever seen.

I must have gaped or gasped, from the way she smiled, the smile of a queen at a commoner. She spoke. "You want something?" Her voice was low and soft, without breath.

The only thing to say was "Certainly, I want you," but I managed to hold it in. She was eighteen, tall and straight, with skin the color of the wild thyme honey that Wolfe gets from Greece, and she was extremely proud of something, not her looks. When a woman is proud of her looks it's just a smirk. I don't think I stammered, but if I didn't I should have. I said, "I'd like to see the superintendent."

"Are you a policeman?"

If she liked policemen the only thing to say was "Yes." But probably she didn't. "No," I said, "I'm a newspaperman."

"That's nice." She turned and called, "Father, a newspaperman!" and her voice raised was even more wonderful than her voice low. She turned back to me, graceful as a big cat, and stood there straight and proud, not quite smiling, her warm dark eyes as curious as if she had never seen a man before. I knew damn well I ought to say something, but what? The only thing to say was "Will you marry me?" but that wouldn't do because the idea of her washing dishes or darning socks was preposterous. Then I became aware of something, that I had moved my foot inside the sill so the door couldn't close, and that spoiled it. I was just a private detective trying to dig up a client.

Footsteps sounded, and as they approached she moved aside. It was a man, a chunky broad-shouldered guy two inches shorter than her, with a pug nose and bushy eyebrows. I stepped inside and greeted him. "My name's Goodwin. From the *Gazette*. I want to rent a room, a front room."

He said to his daughter, "Go, Maria," and she turned and went, down the dark hall. He turned to me. "No rooms."

"A hundred dollars a week," I said. "I'm going to do an article on the scene of a murder after the murder. I want to take pictures of the people who come to look at it. A window on your second floor would be just the right angle."

"I said no rooms." His voice was deep and rough.

"You can shift someone around. Two hundred dollars."

"No."

"Three hundred."

"No."

"Five hundred."

"You're crazy. No."

"I'm not crazy. You are. Snooting five hundred bucks. What's your name?"

"It's *my* name."

"Oh for God's sake. I can get it next door or from the cop out front. What's wrong with it?"

He half closed one eye. "Nothing is wrong with it. My name is Cesar Perez. I am a citizen of the United States of America."

"So am I. Will you rent me a room for one week for five hundred dollars in advance in cash?"

"But what I said." He gestured with both hands and both shoulders. "No room. That man out there dead, this is a bad thing. To take pictures of the people from this house, no. Even if there was a room."

I decided to be impetuous. Delay could actually be dangerous, since Homicide or the DA might uncover a connection between Yeager and this house any moment. Getting my case from my pocket and taking an item from it, I handed it to him. "Can you see in this light?" I asked.

He didn't try. "What is it?"

"My license. I'm not a newspaperman, I'm a private detective, and I'm investigating the murder of Thomas G. Yeager."

He half closed an eye again. He poked the license at me, and I took it. His chest swelled with an intake of air. "You're not a policeman?"

"No."

"Then get out of here. Get out of this house. I have told three different policemen I don't know anything about that man in the hole, and one of them insulted me. You get out."

"All right," I said, "it's your house." I returned the license to the case and the case to my pocket. "But I'll tell you what will happen if you bounce me. Within half an hour a dozen policemen will take the house over, with a search warrant. They'll go over every inch of it. They'll round up everybody here, beginning with you and your daughter, and they'll nab everyone who enters. The reason they'll do that is that I'll tell them I can prove that Thomas G. Yeager came to this house Sunday evening and he was killed here."

"That's a lie. Like that policeman. That's insult."

"Okay. First I call to the cop out front to come in and stand by so you can't warn anyone." I turned. I had hit it. With the cops of course he had been set, but I had been unexpected and had caught him off balance. And he wasn't a moron. He knew that even if I couldn't prove it I must have enough to sick the law on him and the house.

As I turned he reached and got my sleeve. I turned back, and he stood there, his jaw working. I asked, not hostile, just wanting to know, "Did you kill him?"

"You're a policeman," he said.

"I am not. My name is Archie Goodwin and I work for a private detective named Nero Wolfe. We expect to get paid for investigating this case, that's how we make a living. So I'll be honest; we would rather find out for ourselves why Yeager came here instead of having the police do it, but if you won't cooperate I'll have to call that cop in. Did you kill him?"

He wheeled and started down the hall. I moved, got his shoulder, and yanked him around. "Did you kill him?"

"I've got a knife," he said. "In this house I've got a right to have it."

"Sure. I've got this." I pulled the Marley from the holster. "And a permit for it. Did you kill him?"

"No. I want to see my wife. She thinks better than I do. My wife and daughter. I want—"

A door ten feet down the hall swung open, and a woman's voice said, "We're here, Cesar," and there they were. The one coming was a tall grim-faced woman with an air of command. Maria stayed at the door. Perez started reeling off Spanish at his wife, but she broke in.

"Stop it! He'll think it's secrets. With an American talk American." She focused sharp black eyes on me. "We heard you. I knew this would come, only I thought it would be the police. My husband is an honest man. He did not kill Mr. Yeager. We call him Mr. House because it's his house. How do you know?"

I returned the Marley to the holster. "Since I do know, Mrs. Perez, does it matter how?"

"No, I am a fool to ask. All right, ask questions."

"I'd rather have your husband answer them. It may take a while. If there's a room with chairs?"

"I'll answer them. We sit down with friends. You after my husband with a gun."

"I was only showing off. Okay, if your legs can stand it mine can. What time did Mr. Yeager come here Sunday?"

"I thought you knew."

"I do. I'm finding out how you answer questions. If you answer too many of them wrong I'll try your husband, or the police will."

She considered it a moment. "He came around seven o'clock."

"Did he come to see you or your husband or your daughter?"

She glared. "No."

"Whom did he come to see?"

"I don't know. We don't know."

"Try again. That's silly. I'm not going to spend all day prying it out of you bit by bit."

She eyed me. "Have you ever been up there?"

"I'm asking the questions, Mrs. Perez. Whom did he come to see?"

"We don't know." She turned. "Go, Maria."

"But Mother, it's not—"

"Go!"

Maria went, back inside, and shut the door. It was just as well, since it's a strain to keep your eyes where they ought to be when they want to be somewhere else. Mother returned to me.

"He came around seven o'clock and knocked on the door. That one." She pointed to the door Maria had shut behind her. "He spoke to my husband and paid him some money. Then he went down the hall to the elevator. We don't know if someone was up there or if someone came later. We were looking at the television, so we wouldn't hear if someone came in and went to the elevator. Anyhow we weren't supposed to know. The door in front has a good lock. So it's not silly that we don't know who he came to see."

"Where's the elevator?"

"In the back. It has a lock too."

"You asked if I have ever been up there. Have you?"

"Of course. Every day. We keep it clean."

"Then you have a key. We'll go up now." I moved.

She glanced at her husband, hesitated, glanced at me, went and opened the door Maria had closed and said something in Spanish, and started down the hall. Perez followed, and I brought up the rear. At the far end of the hall, clear back, she took a key from a pocket of her skirt and inserted it in the lock of a metal door, another Rabson lock. The door, either aluminum or stainless steel, slid open. That door certainly didn't fit that hall, and neither did the inside of the elevator—more stainless steel, with red enameled panels on three sides. It was small, not even as large as Wolfe's at home. It ascended, silent and smooth, I judged, right to the top floor, the door slid open, and we stepped out.

For the second time in an hour I must have either gaped or gasped when Perez turned on the lights. I have seen quite a few rooms where people had gone all out, but that topped them all. It may have been partly the contrast with the neighborhood, the outside of the house, and the down below, but it would have been remarkable no matter where. The first impression was of silk and skin. The silk, mostly red but some pale yellow, was on the walls and ceiling and couches. The skin was on the girls and women in the pictures, paintings, that took a good third of the wall space. In all directions was naked skin. The pale yellow carpet, wall to wall, was silk too, or looked it. The room was enormous, twenty-five feet wide and the full length of the house, with no windows at either end. Headed to the right wall, near the center, was a bed eight feet square with a pale yellow silk coverlet. Since yellow was Wolfe's pet color it was too bad he hadn't come along. I sniffed the air. It was fresh enough, but it smelled. Air-conditioned, with built-in perfume.

There weren't many surfaces that would hold fingerprints—the tops of two tables, a TV console, a stand with a telephone. I turned to Mrs. Perez. "Have you cleaned here since Sunday night?"

"Yes, yesterday morning."

That settled that. "Where's the door to the stairs?"

"No stairs."

"They're boarded up below," Perez said.

"The elevator's the only way to come up?"

"Yes."

"How long has it been like this?"

"Four years. Since he bought the house. We had been here two years."

"How often did he come here?"

"We don't know."

"Certainly you do, if you came up every day to clean. How often?"

"Maybe once a week, maybe more."

I turned on Perez. "Why did you kill him?"

"No." He half closed an eye. "Me? No."

"Who did?"

"We don't know," his wife said.

I ignored her. "Look," I told him, "I don't want to turn you over unless I have to. Mr. Wolfe and I would prefer to keep you to ourselves. But if you don't open up we'll have no choice, and there may not be much time. They've got a lot of fingerprints from the tarpaulin that covered his body. I know he was killed in this house. If just one of those prints matches yours, good-by.

You're in. Since he was killed in this house, you know *something*. What?"

He said to his wife, "Felita?"

She was looking at me, her sharp black eyes into me. "You're a private detective," she said. "You told my husband that's how you make a living. So we pay you. We have some money, not much. One hundred dollars."

"What do you pay me for?"

"To be our detective."

"And detect what?"

"We'll tell you. We have the money downstairs."

"I'll earn it first. All right, I'm your detective, but I can quit any time, for instance if I decide that you or your husband killed Yeager. What do you want me to detect?"

"We want you to help us. What you said about the fingerprints. I told him he must put on gloves, but he didn't. We don't know how you know so much, but we know how it will be if you tell the police about this house. We did not kill Mr. House. Mr. Yeager. We don't know who killed him. My husband took his dead body and put it in that hole because we had to. When he came Sunday evening he told my husband to go to Mondor's at midnight and bring some things he had ordered, some caviar and roast pheasant and other things, and when my husband came up with them his dead body was here." She pointed. "There on the floor. What could we do? It was secret that he came to this house. What would happen if we called a policeman? We knew what would happen. So now we pay you to help us. Perhaps more than one hundred dollars. You will know—"

She whirled around. There had been a noise from the elevator, a click, and then a faint sound of friction, barely audible. Perez said, "It's going down. Someone down there."

"Yeah," I agreed. "Who?"

"We don't know," Mrs. Perez said.

"Then we'll see. Stay where you are, both of you." I got the Marley out.

"It's a policeman," Perez said.

"No," she said. "No key. He couldn't have Mr. House's keys because we took them."

"Shut up," I told them. "If I'm your detective, do what I say. No talking and no moving."

We stood facing the elevator. I moved to the wall and put my back to it, arm's length from the elevator door. Since it had been up when the visitor came and he had had to push the button to bring it down, he must know someone was up here and might come out with his finger on a trigger, which was where I had mine. The faint sound came again, then a click, the door opened, and out came a woman. Her back was to me as she faced Mrs. Perez.

"Thank God," she said, "it's you. I thought it would be."

"We don't know you," Mrs. Perez said.

I did. I had taken a step and got her profile. It was Meg Duncan, whom I had seen last week from a fifth-row seat on the aisle, in her star part in *The Back Door to Heaven*.

CHAPTER 4

IF YOU EVER have your pick of being jumped by a man your size or a woman who only comes to your chin, I advise you to make it the man. If he's unarmed the chances are that the very worst he'll do is floor you, but God knows what the woman will do. And you may floor him first, but you can't plug a woman. Meg Duncan came at me exactly the way a cavewoman went at her man, or some other man, ten thousand years ago, her claws reaching for me and her mouth open ready to bite. There were only two alternatives, to get too far or too close, and too close is better. I rammed into her past the claws, against her, and wrapped her, and in one second the breath was all out of her. Her mouth stayed open, but for air, not to bite. I slid around and had her arms from behind. In that position the worst you can get is a kick on a shin. She was gasping. My grip may have been really hurting her right arm because I had the gun in that hand and the butt was pressing into her. When I removed that hand to drop the Marley in my pocket she didn't move, and I turned loose and backed up a step.

"I know who you are," I said. "I caught your show last week and you were wonderful. I'm not a cop, I'm a private detective. I work for Nero Wolfe. When you get your breath you'll tell me why you're here."

She turned, slowly. It took her five seconds to make the half-turn to face me. "You hurt me," she said.

"No apology. A squeeze and a little bruise on an arm are nothing to what you had in mind."

She rubbed the arm, her head tilted back to look up at me, still breathing through her mouth. I was being surprised that I had recognized her. On the stage she was extremely easy on the eyes. Now she was just a thirty-year-old female with a good enough face, in a plain gray suit and a plain little hat, but of course she was under strain.

She spoke. "Are you Nero Wolfe's Archie Goodwin?"

"No. I'm my Archie Goodwin. I'm Nero Wolfe's confidential assistant."

"I know about you." She was getting enough air through her nose. "I know you're a gentleman." She extended a hand to touch my sleeve. "I came here to get something that belongs to me. I'll get it and go. All right?"

"What is it?"

"A—a something with my initials on it. A cigarette case."

"How did it get here?"

She tried to smile, as a lady to a gentleman, but it was a feeble effort. A famous actress should have done better, even under strain. "Does that matter, Mr. Goodwin? It's mine. I can describe it. It's dull gold, with an emerald in a corner on one side and my initials on the other."

I smiled as a gentleman to a lady. "When did you leave it here?"

"I didn't say I left it here."

"Was it Sunday evening?"

"No. I wasn't here Sunday evening."

"Did you kill Yeager?"

She slapped me. That is, she slapped at me. She was certainly impetuous. Also she was quick, but so was I. I caught her wrist and gave it a little twist, not enough to hurt much, and let go. There was a gleam in her eyes, and she looked more like Meg Duncan. "You're a man, aren't you?" she said.

"I can be. Right now I'm just a working detective. Did you kill Yeager?"

"No. Of course not." Her hand came up again, but only to touch my sleeve. "Let me get my cigarette case and go."

I shook my head. "You'll have to manage without it for a while. Do you know who killed Yeager?"

"Of course not." Her fingers curved around my arm, not a grip, just a touch. "I know I can't bribe you, Mr. Goodwin, I know enough about you to know that, but detectives do things for people, don't they? I can pay you to do something for me, can't I?

If you won't let me get my cigarette case you can get it for me, and keep it for me. You can give it to me later, you can decide when, I don't care as long as you keep it." Her fingers pressed a little. "I would pay whatever you say. A thousand dollars?"

Things were looking up, but it was getting a little complicated. At 4:30 yesterday afternoon we had had no client and no prospect of any. Then one had come but had turned out to be a phony. Then Mrs. Perez had dangled a hundred bucks and perhaps more. Now this customer was offering a grand. I was digging up clients all right, but too many clients can be worse than too few.

I regarded her. "It might work," I said. "It's like this. Actually I can't take a job; I'm employed by Nero Wolfe. He takes the jobs. I'm going to look this place over, and if I find your cigarette case, as I will if it's here, I'll take it. Give me your keys, to the door down below and the elevator."

Her fingers left my arm. "Give them to you?"

"Right. You won't need them any more." I glanced at my wrist. "It's ten-thirty-five. You have no matinee today. Come to Nero Wolfe's office at half past two. Six-eighteen West Thirty-fifth Street. Your cigarette case will be there, and you can settle it with Mr. Wolfe."

"But why can't you—"

"No. That's how it is, and I have things to do." I put a hand out. "The keys."

"Why can't I—"

"I said no. There's no argument and no time. Damn it, I'm giving you a break. The keys."

She opened her bag, fingered in it, took out a leather key fold, and handed it over. I unsnapped it, saw two Rabson keys, which are not like any others, displayed them to Perez, and asked if they were the keys to the door and the elevator. He took a look and said yes. Dropping them in a pocket, I pushed the button to open the elevator door and told Meg Duncan, "I'll see you later. Half past two."

"Why can't I stay until you find—"

"Nothing doing. I'll be too busy for company."

She stepped in, the door closed, the click came, and the faint sound. I turned to Perez.

"You've seen her before."

"No. Never."

"Phooey. When you brought things up at midnight?"

"I only saw him. She could have been in the bathroom."

"Where's the bathroom?"

He pointed. "At that end."

I went to his wife. "When she saw you she said, 'Thank God it's you.'"

She nodded. "I heard her. She must see me some time when she came in, in the hall or a door was open. We don't know her. We never saw her."

"The things you don't know. All right now, you two. It will take hours and will have to wait because I have things to do, but one question now." To him: "When you put the body in the hole why did you climb in and put the tarp over it?"

He was surprised. "But he was dead! A man dead, you cover him! I knew that thing was in there, I had seen it."

That was the moment that I decided that Cesar Perez had not killed Thomas G. Yeager. Possibly his wife had, but not him. If you had been there looking at him as he said that, you would have decided the same. When I had been trying to account for the tarp the simplest explanation had never occurred to me, that long ago people covered dead men to hide them from vultures, and it got to be a habit.

"That was decent," I said. "Too bad you didn't wear gloves. Okay, that's all for now. I have work to do. You heard me give that woman Nero Wolfe's address, Six-eighteen West Thirty-fifth Street. Be there at six o'clock this afternoon, both of you. I'm your detective temporarily, but he's the boss. You certainly need help, and after you tell him about it we'll see. Where are Yeager's keys? Don't say 'We don't know.' You said you took them. Where are they?"

"I have them safe," Mrs. Perez said.

"Where?"

"In a cake. I made a cake and put them in. There are twelve keys in a thing."

"Including the keys to the door and the elevator?"

"Yes."

I considered. I was already on thin ice, and if I took possession of something that had been taken from Yeager's body there would be no ice at all between me and suppression of evidence. No. "Don't cut the cake," I said, "and be darned sure nobody else does. Are you going anywhere today? Either of you?"

"We don't have to," she said.

"Then don't. Nero Wolfe's office at six o'clock, but I'll see you when I come down, probably in an hour or so."

"You take things?"

"I don't know. If I do I'll show them to you, including the cigarette case. If I take anything you think I shouldn't, you can call in that cop from out front."

"We couldn't," Perez said.

"He makes a joke," she told him. She pushed the button to bring the elevator up. "This is a bad day, Cesar. There will be many bad days, and he makes a joke." The elevator clicked at the top, she pushed another button, the door opened, and they entered and were gone.

I moved my eyes around. At the edge of a panel of red silk at the left was a rectangular brass plate, if it wasn't gold. I went and pushed on it, and it gave. The panel was a door. I pushed it open and stepped through, and was in the kitchen. The walls were red tile, the cupboards and shelves were yellow plastic, and the sink and appliances, including the refrigerator and electric range, were stainless steel. I opened the refrigerator door, saw a collection of various items, and closed it. I slid a cupboard door back and saw nine bottles of Dom Perignon champagne on their sides in a plastic rack. That would do for the kitchen for now. I emerged and walked the length of the yellow carpet, surrounded by silk and skin, to the other end, where there was another brass plate, or gold, at the edge of a panel. I pushed it open and was in the bathroom. I don't know what your taste is, but I liked it. It was all mirrors and marble, red marble with yellow streaks and splotches. The tub, big enough for two, was the same marble. Two of the mirrors were doors to cabinets, and they contained enough different cosmetic items to supply a harem.

I returned to the silk and skin. There were no drawers anywhere, no piece of furniture that might contain pieces of paper
on which someone had written something. There was nothing
at the telephone stand but the phone, which was yellow, and the
directory, which was in a red leather holder. But along one wall,
the one across from the bed, there was no furniture for about
thirty feet of its length, and the silk along the bottom, for three
feet up from the floor, was in little folds like a curtain, not flat
as it was everywhere else. I went and gave the silk a tug and it
parted and slid along the top, and behind it were drawer fronts,
of wood something like mahogany, but redder. I pulled one open.
Female slippers, a dozen pairs in two neat rows, various colors
and shapes and sizes. The sizes ranged from quite small to fairly
large.

I looked into only five more drawers before I went to the phone.
That was enough to make it plain that Meg Duncan wasn't the
only one who had keys to the door and elevator. There was another drawer of slippers, again assorted colors and sizes, and two
drawers of nighties, a mighty fine collection. It was after I unfolded
eight of them and spread them on the bed for comparison, and
found that they also covered a wide range in sizes, that I went
to the phone and dialed a number. There was a possibility that
it was tapped or there was an extension, but it was very slim, and
I preferred the slight risk to going out to a booth.

Saul Panzer, whose number I dialed, was the free-lance operative we called on when only the best would do. But what I got
was the answering-service girl, who said that Mr. Panzer was out
and couldn't be reached and would I leave a message. I said no
and dialed another number, Fred Durkin's, the next best, and
got him. He said he had nothing on for the day.

"You have now," I told him. "Pack a bag for a week. It will
probably be less but could be more. Come as you are, no cos-
tumes required, but have a gun. You probably won't use it, but
have it. Come to One-fifty-six West Eighty-second Street, the
basement entrance, superintendent, and push the button at the
door. It will be a man or woman, either Cuban or Puerto Rican,
I'm not sure which. They speak American. Tell him or her your

name and ask for me, and you'll have the pleasure and honor of being brought to my presence. Don't hurry. Take three minutes to pack if you want to."

"Eighty-second Street," he said. "Murder. What was his name? Yeager."

"You read too much and you're morbid and you jump to conclusions. Pack your bag and button your lip." I hung up.

Folding flimsy nighties properly is no job for a man and it takes time, but I gritted my teeth and stuck to it, because a detective is supposed to leave a place the way he found it. Them back in the drawer, I brought the elevator up, took it down, and went to an open door, the first one on the left in the hall. The Perez family was having a conference in the kitchen. Father and mother were sitting, and Maria was standing. There was more light than there had been in the front of the hall, and with that rare specimen, the more light the better. Looking at her, any man alive would have the thought, What the hell, I could wash the dishes and darn the socks myself. The beige nightie with lace around the top, medium-sized, would have fitted her fine. I made my eyes go to her parents and spoke.

"A man will come pretty soon, tall and thick in all directions. He'll give his name, Fred Durkin, and ask for me. Send him up."

I got the expected reaction from Mrs. Perez. I had no right to tell anybody about that place, they were going to pay me, and so forth. Wishing to keep on speaking terms with our clients, I took four minutes to explain why I had to leave Fred there when I went, got her calmed down, permitted my eyes to dart another glance at Maria, took the elevator back up, and resumed on the drawers where I had left off. I won't take time and space to list an inventory, but will merely say that everything that could be needed for such an establishment was there. I'll only mention two details: one, that there was only one drawer of male items, and the six suits of pajamas were all the same size; and two, the drawer in which I found Meg Duncan's cigarette case was obviously a catchall. There were three women's handkerchiefs, used, an anonymous compact, a lady's umbrella, a matchbook from Terry's Pub, and other such miscellany. I had just put it all back in and was closing the drawer when I heard the click from the elevator.

Presumably it was Fred, but possibly not, so I got the Marley out and went to the wall by the elevator door. I could hear no voices from below; the place was so thoroughly soundproofed that you could hear nothing but a faint suggestion of noise from the street traffic, and that was more felt than heard. Soon the click came again, the door opened, and Fred stepped out. He stood and swiveled his head, right and left, brought it around until he caught a glimpse of me, turned it back again, and spoke.

"Jesus Kee-rist!"

"Your new home," I told him. "I do hope you'll be happy here. The idea is, you take your pick from the pictures. Something like the Mountain Room at the Churchill with live trout and you choose the one you want for lunch. I strongly recommend the one over there sitting on a rose bush. If she can stand thorns she can stand you."

He put his bag down. "You know, Archie, I've always wondered why you didn't marry. How long have you had it?"

"Oh, ten years, I guess. I have others here and there around town. I'm turning this one over to you for a while. Kitchen, bathroom, TV, maid service. Like it?"

"Good God. I'm a married man."

"Yeah. Too bad. I'd like to stay and explain the pictures to you, but I have to go. The point is, if a visitor comes, someone should be here to receive her. It could be a him, but more likely it would be a her. Most likely there won't be any, but there might be. She might come at any hour, day or night. The less you know the better; just take my word for it that if she steps out of that elevator you are in a position to refuse to let her get back in, and there's no other way out of here. Identify yourself or not, as you prefer. Ring me, and I'll come."

He was frowning. "Alone with a woman, restraining her by force isn't so good."

"You won't have to touch her unless she starts it."

"She sticks her head out a window and yells police."

"Not a chance. There's no window, and she wouldn't want anyone to know she's here, least of all a cop. The one thing she'll want is to get out, and fast."

He was still frowning. "The hole that Yeager's body was found in is right out front. Maybe I ought to know a little more."

"Not from me. Why drag in Yeager? He's dead; I read it in the paper. If the phone rings take it and ask who it is and see what happens, but don't say who you are. That's the door to the kitchen." I pointed. "There's some fancy stuff in the refrigerator when you get hungry. The people down below are Mr. and Mrs. Cesar Perez and their daughter Maria. Did you see Maria?"

"No."

"I'm going to marry her when I find time. I'll tell Mrs. Perez to bring you up a loaf of bread, and if you have to have anything she'll get it. She and her husband are out on a limb and they're counting on me to get a ladder. Okay, enjoy the pictures. You couldn't ask for a better chance to study anatomy." I opened the elevator door.

"What if it's a man that comes?"

"It won't be. If it is, stick to the program; that's why I told you to have a gun."

"What if it's a cop?"

"One chance in a million. Not even that. Tell him you've forgotten your name and he'll have to ring me at Nero Wolfe's office. Then I'll know what happened."

"And I'll be in the coop."

"Right. But not for long. We'll have you out by Christmas easy. There's half a pound of fresh caviar in the refrigerator, twenty dollars' worth. Help yourself."

I entered the elevator. Downstairs I explained the situation to Mrs. Perez and asked her to take up a loaf of bread, and left the house. My watch said noon, on the dot, as I headed for Columbus Avenue for a taxi.

CHAPTER 5

At FIVE MINUTES past one, Wolfe, at his desk, growled at me, "Your objective was to find an acceptable client, not a pair of wretches who probably killed him and another wretch who offers a reward for a cigarette case. I concede your craft, your finesse, and your gumption, and I even felicitate you, but if you have discovered the culprits, as seems probable, where do you send a bill?"

I had reported in full, omitting only one detail, a factual description of Maria. He was quite capable of assuming, or pretending to assume, that I was prejudiced in favor of Mr. and Mrs. Perez on account of their daughter. I had described the place accurately and completely, and had even included my handling of the nightie problem. I had admitted that I had tried to get Saul Panzer (ten dollars an hour), and had got Fred Durkin instead (seven-fifty an hour) only because Saul was not available.

"I won't see them," he said.

I knew, or thought I did, where the real snag was, but I had to go easy. I nodded thoughtfully. "Of course they could have killed him," I said, "but one will get you five that they didn't. For the reasons I gave. His tone and his expression when he told me why he put the tarp over the body. The fact that she let the daughter come to the door when I rang the bell. If she had killed him she would have come herself. But chiefly, with him alive they were in clover. Of course he was paying them plenty. With him dead they're not only minus a fat income, they're in a hell of a fix, and they would have been even if I hadn't got to them. When the executor of his estate learns that he owned that house and goes to inspect it?"

I crossed my legs. "Naturally," I said, "you don't like it, I understand that. If it was just a nice place he had fixed up where he could safely spend a night now and then with his mistress, that wouldn't be so bad, but obviously it wasn't that. There are probably half a dozen women with keys to that door and elevator, and maybe twenty or more. I realize that you wouldn't like to be involved with that kind of setup, but now that I have—"

"Nonsense," he said.

I raised a brow. "Nonsense?"

"Yes. A modern satyr is part man, part pig, and part jackass. He hasn't even the charm of the roguish; he doesn't lean gracefully against a tree with a flute in his hand. The only quality he has preserved from his Attic ancestors is his lust, and he gratifies it in dark corners or other men's beds or hotel rooms, not in the shade of an olive tree on a sunny hillside. The preposterous bower of carnality you have described is a sorry makeshift, but at least Mr. Yeager tried. A pig and a jackass, yes, but the flute strain was in him too—as it once was in me, in my youth. No doubt he deserved to die, but I would welcome a sufficient inducement to expose his killer."

I suppose I was staring. "You would?"

"Certainly. But who is likely to offer it? Granting that you have shown commendable alacrity and wit, and that you are right about Mr. and Mrs. Perez, where are we? Where is a prospective client? To whom can we disclose the existence of that preposterous bower and his connection with it? Neither his family nor his business associates, surely. They would be more likely to want it concealed than disclosed, and are we blackmailers? I concede that there is one remote possibility: who is the man who came here yesterday posing as Yeager, and why did he come?"

I shook my head. "Sorry I can't oblige. Have you read my report?"

"Yes. Manifestly he is a man with a special and educated fondness for words. He said, 'Else there was no use coming.' He said, 'I can speak in assured confidence?' He said, 'That will suffice.' The last two are merely noticeable, but the first is extraordinary. 'Else' instead of 'or' or 'otherwise'? Remarkable."

"If you say so."

"I do. But also, merely talking along, he quoted from John Webster's *The Duchess of Malfi:* 'Other sins only speak; murder shrieks out.' He quoted from John Harington's *Alcilia:* 'Treason doth never prosper.' He quoted from Browning's *Paracelsus:* 'Measure your mind's height by the shade it casts.' People quote to display their erudition, but why to you? You heard him and were looking at him. Was he trying to impress you?"

"No. He was talking, that was all."

"Just so. And he had sentences at the tip of his tongue from two Elizabethans and Robert Browning. Not one man in ten thousand is familiar with both Webster and Browning. He's a pedagogue. He's a teacher of literature."

"You're not."

"I recognized only Webster. I looked up the others. I don't know Harington, and Browning repels me. So he is one in ten thousand, and there are less than a thousand of him in New York. I invite a trial of your ingenuity: if he knew Yeager was dead, either because he had killed him or otherwise, why did he come here with that tarradiddle?"

"I pass. I've already tried it, last night. If he had killed him, the only possibility was that he was cracked, and he wasn't. If he hadn't killed him but knew he was dead, the best I could do was that he wanted to call attention to that block on Eighty-second Street and that house, and to buy that I'd have to be cracked myself. An anonymous phone call to the police would have been quicker and simpler. Can you do any better?"

"No. No one can. He did not know Yeager was dead. Then, thinking Yeager alive, what did he hope to accomplish by that masquerade? He could not assume with confidence that when Yeager failed to appear you would either telephone his house or go there, but he knew that before long, either last evening or this morning, you would communicate with him, you would learn that your caller was an impostor, and you would tell Yeager about it. With what result? Merely that Yeager would know what the impostor had told you. If he identified the impostor from your description, he would know that that man knew of his visits to the Eighty-second Street address, but I reject that. If the impostor wanted Yeager to know *who* knew about that house, why all the fuss of coming to you? Why not just tell him, by phone or mail or face-to-face, or even in an anonymous note? No. He knew that Yeager would not identify him from your description. He merely wanted Yeager to know that *someone* knew of his connection with that house, and possibly also that you and I now knew about it. So I doubt if he could or would be helpful, but all the same I would like to speak with him."

"So would I. That was one reason I got Fred there. There's a bare chance that he has keys and will show up."

Wolfe grunted. "Pfui. The chance that anyone at all will come there is minute and you know it. You got Fred there because I cannot now say merely that the incident is closed. I would have to tell you to recall him, and you know that I respect your commitments as I do my own. Yes, Fritz?"

"Lunch is ready, sir. The parsley had wilted and I used chives."

"We'll see." Wolfe pushed his chair back and arose. "Pepper?"

"No, sir. I thought not, with chives."

"I agree, but we'll see."

I followed him out and across the hall to the dining room. As we finished the clam juice Fritz came with the first installment of dumplings, four apiece. Some day I would like to see how long I can keep going on Fritz's marrow dumplings, of chopped beef marrow, bread crumbs, parsley (chives today), grated lemon rind, salt, and eggs, boiled four minutes in strong meat stock. If he boiled them all at once of course they would get mushy after the first eight or ten, but he does them eight at a time, and they keep coming. They are one of the few dishes with which I stay neck and neck with Wolfe clear to the tape, and they were the reason I had let it pass when he had said he wouldn't see the clients I had got. Those marrow dumplings induce a state of mind in which anybody would see anybody. And it worked. We had finished the salad and returned to the office, and Fritz had brought coffee, when the doorbell rang. I went to the hall for a look through the one-way glass, stepped back in, and told Wolfe, "Meg Duncan. At least we might as well collect for the cigarette case. Say two bucks?"

He glared. "Confound you." He put his cup down. "What if she killed him? Does that concern us? Very well, you invited her. Five minutes."

I went to the front and opened the door. It wasn't a thirty-year-old female with a good enough face, in a plain gray suit and a plain little hat, who gave me a smile that would warm a glacier as she crossed the sill. The face had been arranged by a professional and was being handled by a professional, and while the dress and jacket were not spectacular they were by no means plain. And the voice was the voice of an angel who might consider taking a week off if she got an invitation that appealed to her. Not only did she use it on me in the hall, but also on Wolfe when I steered her to the office and he stood, inclined his head an eighth of an inch, and indicated the red leather chair.

Her smile was on full. Granting that it was professional, it was a damned good smile. "I know how busy you men are with important things," she said, "so I won't take your time." To me: "Did you find it?"

"He did," Wolfe said. He sat. "Sit down, Miss Duncan. I like eyes at my level. A brief discussion may be necessary. If you answer two or three questions satisfactorily you may have the cigarette case when you have paid me fifty thousand dollars."

The smile went. "Fifty *thousand?* That's fantastic!"

"Sit down, please."

She looked at me, saw merely a working detective, moved to the red leather chair, sat on the edge, and said, "Of course you don't mean that. You can't."

Wolfe, leaning back, regarded her. "I do and I don't. Our position—I include Mr. Goodwin—is peculiar and a little delicate. The body of a man who had died by violence was found in that hole on that street near that house. He was a man of means and standing. The police don't know of his connection with that house and his quarters there, but we do, and we intend to use that knowledge to our profit. I don't suppose you are familiar with the statutes regarding suppression of evidence of a crime. It may even—"

"My cigarette case isn't evidence of a crime!"

"I haven't said it is. It may even lead to a charge of accessory to murder. Interpretation of that statute is in some respects vague, but not in others. Knowingly concealing or disposing of a tangible object that would help to identify the criminal or convict him would of course be suppression of evidence; but words may be evidence or may not. Usually not. If you were to tell me now that you entered that room Sunday night, found Yeager's body there, and got Mr. Perez to help you take it from the house and put it in that hole, that would not be evidence. I couldn't be successfully prosecuted if I failed to tell the police what you had told me; I would merely swear that I thought you were lying."

She had slid back in the chair a little. "I wasn't in that room Sunday night."

"Not evidence. You may be lying. I'm only explaining the delicacy of our position. You told Mr. Goodwin you would pay him a thousand dollars to find your cigarette case and keep it for you, and give it to you later at his discretion. We can't accept that offer. It would engage us not to turn it over to the police even if it became apparent that it would help to identify or convict a murderer, and that's too great a risk for a thousand dollars. You may have it for fifty thousand, cash or a certified check. Do you want it?"

I *think* he meant it. I think he would have handed it over for thirty grand, or even twenty, if she had been dumb enough to pay it. He had let me go up to 82nd Street with five Cs in my pocket for one specific reason, to see if I could flush a prospect for a worthy fee, and if she was fool enough, or desperate enough, to pay twenty grand, not to mention fifty, for her cigarette case, he could call it a day and leave the murder investigation to the law. As for the risk, he had taken bigger ones. He was saying only that he would give her the case, not that he would forget about it.

She was staring at him. "I didn't think," she said, "that Nero Wolfe was a blackmailer."

"Neither does the dictionary, madam." He swiveled to the stand that had held the three Websters he had worn out and now held a new one. Opening it and finding the page, he read: " 'Payment of money exacted by means of intimidation; also, extortion of money from a person by threats of public accusation, exposure, or censure.'" He swiveled back. "I don't fit. I haven't threatened or intimidated you."

"But you . . ." She looked at me and back to him. "Where would I get fifty thousand dollars? You might as well say a million. What are you going to do? Are you going to give it to the police?"

"Not by choice. Only under the compulsion of circumstance. A factor would be your answers to my questions."

"You haven't asked me any questions."

"I do now. Were you in that room Sunday evening or night?"

"No." Her chin was up.

"When were you last there? Before today."

"I haven't said I was ever there."

"That's egregious. Your behavior this morning. Your offer to Mr. Goodwin. You had keys. When?"

She set her teeth on her lip. Five seconds. "More than a week ago. A week ago Saturday. That's when I left the cigarette case. Oh my God." She extended a hand, not a professional gesture. "Mr. Wolfe, this could ruin my career. I haven't seen him since that night. I don't know who killed him, or why, or anything. Why must you drag me into it? What good will it do?"

"I didn't drag you there this morning, madam. I don't ask how often you visited that room because your answer would be worthless, but when you did visit it were others there?"

"No."

"Was anyone ever there when you were besides Mr. Yeager?"

"No. Never."

"But other women went there. That's not surmise, it's established. Of course you knew that; Mr. Yeager was not concerned to conceal it. Who are they?"

"I don't know."

"You don't deny that you knew there were others?"

She thought she was going to, but his eyes had her pinned. She swallowed the yes and said, "No. I knew that."

"Of course. He wanted you to. His arrangement for keeping slippers and garments testifies that he derived pleasure not only from his present companion but also from her awareness that she had—uh—colleagues. Or rivals. So surely he wasn't silent about them? Surely he spoke of them, in comparison, in praise or derogation? And if he didn't name them he must have aroused conjecture. This is my most instant question, Miss Duncan: who are they?"

I had heard Wolfe ask questions of women that made them tremble, or turn pale, or yell at him, or burst into tears, or fly at him, but that was the first time I ever heard one that made a woman blush—and her a sophisticated Broadway star. I suppose it was his matter-of-fact way of putting it. I didn't blush, but I cleared my throat. She not only blushed; she lowered her head and shut her eyes.

"Naturally," Wolfe said, "you would like this episode to pass into history as quickly as possible. It might help if you will tell me something about the others."

"I can't." She raised her head. The blush was gone. "I don't know anything about them. Are you going to keep my cigarette case?"

"For the present, yes."

"You have me at your mercy." She started to rise, found that her knees were shaky, and put a hand on the chair arm to help. She got erect. "I was a fool to go there, an utter fool. I could have said—I could have said anything. I could have said I lost it. What a fool." She looked at me straight, said, "I wish I had clawed your eyes out," turned, and headed for the door. I got up and followed her, passed her in the hall, and had the front door open when she reached it. She wasn't very steady on her feet, so I watched her descend the seven steps to the sidewalk before I shut the door and returned to the office. Wolfe was in his reading position and had opened his book, *An Outline of Man's Knowledge of the Modern World,* edited by Lyman Bryson. I had spent an hour one afternoon looking it over, and had seen nothing about modern satyrs.

CHAPTER 6

Six years ago, reporting one of Wolfe's cases, one in which no fee or hope of one was involved, I tried a stunt that I got good and tired of before I was through. It took us to Montenegro, and nearly all the talk was in a language I didn't know a word of, but I got enough of it out of Wolfe later to report it verbatim. I'm not going to repeat that experience, so I'll merely give you the gist of his conversation with Mr. and Mrs. Perez when he came down from the plant rooms at six o'clock and found them there. It was in Spanish. Either he took the opportunity to speak one of his six languages, or he thought they would be freer in their native tongue, or he wanted to rile me, I don't know which. Probably all three. After they had gone he gave me the substance.

This isn't evidence; it's just what they said. They didn't know who came Sunday evening, man or woman, or how many, or when he or she or they had left. They didn't know how many different people came at different times. Sometimes they had heard footsteps in the hall, and they had always sounded like women. If a man had ever come they hadn't seen or heard him. No one had ever been in the room when they went up to clean; they didn't go up if the elevator was up there, but that had happened only five or six times in four years.

They had heard no shot Sunday evening, but even the floor of the room was soundproofed. When Perez went up at midnight there had been a smell of burnt powder, but he thought it was a weak smell and she thought it was a strong one. There had been nothing in the room that didn't belong there—no gun, no coat or hat or wrap. Yeager had been fully dressed; his hat and topcoat had been on a chair, and they had put them in the hole with the body. None of the slippers or garments or other articles were out of the drawers. The bed had not been disturbed. Everything was in place in the bathroom. They had taken nothing from Yeager's body but his keys. They had cleaned the room Monday morning, vacuumed and dusted, but had taken nothing out of it.

They had paid no rent for their basement. Yeager had paid them fifty dollars a week and had let them keep the rent they collected for the rooms on the four floors. Their total take had been around two hundred dollars a week (probably nearer three hundred and maybe more). They had no reason to suppose that Yeager had left them the house, or anything else, in his will. They were sure that none of the tenants had any connection with Yeager or knew anything about him; the renting had been completely in their hands. They had decided that one hundred dollars wasn't enough to pay Wolfe and me, and though it would take most of their savings (this isn't evidence) they thought five hundred would be better, and they had brought half of that amount along. Of course Wolfe didn't take it. He told them that while he had no present intention of passing on any of the information they had given him he had to be free to use his discretion. That started an argument. Since it was in Spanish I can't give it blow by blow, but judging from the tones and expressions, and from the fact that at one point Mrs. Perez was up and at Wolfe's desk, slapping it, it got pretty warm. She had calmed down some by the time they left.

Since they didn't leave until dinnertime and business is barred at the table, Wolfe didn't relay it to me until we were back in the office after dinner. When he had finished he said, "It's bootless. Time, effort, and money wasted. That woman killed him. Call Fred." He picked up his book.

"Sure," I said, "no question about it. It was such a nuisance, all that money rolling in, three hundred a week or more, she had to put a stop to it, and that was the easiest way, shoot him and dump him in a hole."

He shook his head. "She is a creature of passion. You saw her face when I asked if her daughter had ever gone up to that room—no, you didn't know what I had asked her. Her eyes blazed, and her voice shrilled. She discovered that Yeager had debauched her daughter and she killed him. Call Fred."

"She admitted it?"

"Certainly not. She said that her daughter had been forbidden to go up to that room and had never seen it. She resented the implication with fury. We are no longer concerned." He opened the book. "Call Fred."

"I don't believe it." My voice may have shrilled slightly. "I haven't described Maria at length and don't intend to, but when I start marrying she will be third on the list and might even be first if I didn't have prior commitments. She may be part witch but she has not been debauched. If and when she orgies with a satyr he'll be leaning gracefully against a tree with a flute in his hand. I don't believe it."

"Orgy is not a verb."

"It is now. And when I asked you this morning if there was any limit to how much I should take along and disburse if necessary, you said as dictated by my discretion and sagacity. I took five hundred, and my discretion and sagacity dictated that the best way to use it was to get Fred there and keep him there. Sixty hours at seven-fifty an hour is four hundred and fifty dollars. Add fifty for his grub and incidentals and that's the five hundred. The sixty hours will be up at eleven-thirty p.m. Thursday, day after tomorrow. Since I have met Maria and you haven't, and since you left it—"

The phone rang. I whirled my chair and got it. "Nero Wolfe's reside—"

"Archie! I've got one."

"Man or woman?"

"Woman. You coming?"

"Immediately. You'll be seeing me." I cradled the phone and stood up. "Fred has caught a fish. Female." I glanced at the wall clock: a quarter to ten. "I can have her here before eleven, maybe by ten-thirty. Instructions?"

He exploded. "What good would it do," he roared, "to give you instructions?"

I could have challenged him to name one time when I had failed to follow instructions unless forced by circumstances, but with a genius you have to be tactful. I said merely, "Then I'll use my discretion and sagacity," and went. I should have used them in the hall, to stop at the rack for my topcoat, as I discovered when I was out and headed for Tenth Avenue. A cold wind, cold for May, was coming from the river, but I didn't go back. Getting a taxi at the corner, I told the driver 82nd and Amsterdam. There might still be a cop at the hole, and even if there wasn't it would be just as well not to take a cab right to the door.

There was no cop at the hole, and no gathering of amateur criminologists, just passers-by and a bunch of teen-agers down the block. After turning in at 156, descending the three steps, and using Meg Duncan's key, I entered and proceeded down the hall; and halfway along I had a feeling. Someone had an eye on me. Of course that experience, feeling a presence you have neither seen nor heard, is as old as rocks, but it always gets you. I get it at the bottom of my spine, showing perhaps that I would be either raising or lowering my tail if I had one. At the moment I had the feeling there was a door three paces ahead of me on the right, opened to a crack, a bare inch. I kept going, and when I reached the door I shot an arm out and pushed it. It swung in a foot and was stopped, but the foot was enough. There was no light inside and the hall was dim, but I have good eyes.

She didn't move. "Why did you do that?" she asked. "This is my room." A remarkable thing; with a strong light on her, that was best, and with a dim one, *that* was best.

"I beg your pardon," I said. "As you know, I'm a detective, and detectives have bad habits. How many times have you been in the room on the top floor?"

"I'm not allowed," she said. "Would I tell you? So you could tell my mother? Excuse me, I shut the door."

She did, and I didn't block it. A nice long talk with her would be desirable, but it would have to wait. I went to the elevator and used the other key, stepped in, and was lifted.

You have expectations even when you're not aware of them. I suppose I was expecting to find a scared or indignant female sitting on a couch or chair and Fred near at hand with an eye on her. It wasn't like that. Fred was standing in the center of the room holding up his pants, with two red streaks down his cheek. For a second I thought she wasn't there; then I saw her head sticking out of the bundle on the floor. It was the yellow silk coverlet from the bed, and she was wrapped in it, with Fred's belt strapped around the middle. I went and looked down at her, and she glared up at me.

"She's not hurt any," Fred said. "I wish she was. Look at me."

The red of the streaks on his cheek was blood. He lifted a hand with a handkerchief and dabbed at it. "You said I wouldn't have to touch her unless she started it. She started it all right. Then when I went for the phone she went for the elevator, and when I went to head her off she went for the phone. So I had to wrap her up."

"Have you told her who you are?"

"No. I wouldn't do her that favor. That's her bag there." He pointed to a chair. "I haven't looked in it."

A voice came from the bundle on the floor. "Who are you?" it demanded.

I ignored her and went and got the bag and opened it. With the other usual items, it contained four that were helpful: credit cards from three stores and a driver's license. The name was Julia Mc-Gee, with an address on Arbor Street in the Village. She was twenty-nine years old, five feet five inches, white, brown hair and brown eyes. I put the stuff back in the bag and the bag on the chair, and went to her.

"I'll unwrap you in a minute, Miss McGee," I said. "His name is Fred Durkin and mine is Archie Goodwin. You may have heard of Nero Wolfe, the private detective. We work for him. Mr. Durkin is camped here because Mr. Wolfe wants to have a talk with anyone who comes to this room. I'll be glad to take you to him. I ask no questions because I'd only have to tell him what you said, and it will be simpler to let him ask them."

"Let me up!" she demanded.

"In a minute. Now that I know who you are and where to find you the situation is a little different. If you grab your bag and head for the elevator I won't try to stop you, but I advise you to count ten first. There are keys in your bag to the door downstairs and the elevator. If and when the police get to this room they will of course be interested in anyone who had keys and could have been here Sunday night. So it might be a mistake to decline my invitation. Think it over while I'm unwrapping you."

I squatted to unbuckle the belt and pull it from under her, and Fred came and took it. I couldn't stand her up to unwrap her because her feet were inside too. "The easiest way," I told her, "is to roll out while I hold the end." She rolled. That thing was ten feet square, and I never have asked Fred how he managed it. When she was out she bounced up and was on her feet. She was quite attractive, perhaps more than normally with her face flushed and her hair tousled. She shook herself, yanked her coat around into place, went and got her bag, and said, "I'm going to phone."

"Not here," I told her. "If you're leaving alone, there's a booth at the corner. If you're going with me, there's a phone in Mr. Wolfe's office."

She looked more mad than scared, but that's always a guess with a strange face. "Do you know whose room this is?" she demanded.

"I know whose it was. Thomas G. Yeager's."

"What are you doing here?"

"Skip it. I not only won't ask questions, I won't answer them."

"You have no right . . ." She let that go. "I am Mr. Yeager's secretary. I was. I came to get a notebook I left here, that's all."

"Then you have nothing to fear. If and when the police get to you, just tell them that and they'll apologize for bothering you."

"If I don't go with you, you're going to tell the police?"

"I haven't said so. Mr. Wolfe makes the decisions. I'm just the errand boy."

She moved. I thought she was bound for the phone, but she kept straight on, to the far end, to the door to the bathroom, and on through. I went and took a look at Fred's cheek. He had his belt back on. "So this was Yeager's room," he said. "Now since I know that—"

"You don't. You don't know anything. I lied to her and she fell for it. Your job is merely to be here to welcome callers. There's no harm done. Your cheek looks worse than it is, and there's stuff in the bathroom for it. You would have had to take the coverlet off anyway when you go to bed. I'll help you fold it."

I took one end and he took the other. He asked how long he

would have to hang on there, and I said until further notice, and what better could he ask? Any man with a feeling for the finer things of life would consider it a privilege to be allowed to shack up in such an art gallery as that, and he was getting paid for it, twenty-four hours a day. He said even the TV had caught it; when he turned it on what he had got was a woman in a bathtub blowing soap bubbles.

As he put the folded coverlet on a couch Julia McGee reappeared. She had adjusted the neck of her dress, put her hair in order, and repaired her face. She wasn't at all bad-looking. She came up to me and said, "All right, I'm accepting your invitation."

CHAPTER 7

WHEN YOU ENTER the hall of the old brownstone on West 35th Street, the first door on your left is to what we call the front room, and the one beyond it is to the office. Both of those rooms are soundproofed, not as perfectly as Yeager's bower of carnality, but well enough, including the doors. I took Julia McGee to the front room, had my offer to take her coat declined, and went through the connecting door to the office, closing it behind me. Wolfe was in his favorite chair with his book. He is not a fast reader, and that book has 677 pages, with about 600 words to the page. When I crossed to his desk and told him I had brought company he finished a paragraph, closed the book on a finger, and scowled at me.

I went on. "Her name is Julia McGee. She says she was Yeager's secretary, which is probably true because it can be easily checked. She says she went there tonight to get a notebook she had left there, which is a lie and not a very good one. There is no notebook in that room. When she entered and saw Fred she went for him and drew blood on his face, and he had to wrap her up in a bed cover so he could use the phone. After I got her name and address from things in her bag I told her she could either go now and explain to the police later or she could come here with me, and she came with me. I made a concession, I told her she could use the phone as soon as she got here, with us present."

He said, "Grrrrh." I gave him two seconds to add to it, but apparently that was all, so I went and opened the door to the front room and told her to come in. She came on by me, stopped to glance around, saw the phone on my desk, crossed to it, sat in my chair, and dialed. Wolfe inserted his bookmark, put the book down, leaned back, and glared at her.

She told the receiver, "I want to speak to Mr. Aiken. This is Julia McGee. . . . That's right. . . . Thank you." A one-minute wait. "Mr. Aiken? . . . Yes. . . . Yes, I know, but I had to tell you, there was a man there and he attacked me and . . . No, let me tell you, another man came and said they were working for Nero Wolfe, the detective. . . . Yes, Nero Wolfe. The second one, Archie Goodwin, said Nero Wolfe wanted to talk with anyone who came to that room and wanted me to go with him, and that's where I am now, in Nero Wolfe's office. . . . Yes. . . . No, I don't think so, they're both right here, Nero Wolfe and Archie Goodwin. . . . I don't know. . . . Yes, of course, but I don't know. . . . Wait, I'll ask."

She turned to me. "What's this address?" I told her, and she went back to the phone. "Six-eighteen West Thirty-fifth Street. . . . That's right. . . . Yes, I will." She hung up, swiveled, told Wolfe, "Mr. Aiken will be here in twenty minutes," and wriggled her coat off.

Wolfe asked, "Who is Mr. Aiken?"

Her look was what you would get from the Yankee batboy if you asked him who is Mr. Stengel. "Mr. Benedict Aiken. The president of Continental Plastic Products."

That changed my mind. Wanting my own chair, I had been about to move her to the red leather one, but she would only have to move again when the president came, so I brought one of the yellow ones for her, facing Wolfe's desk, and put her coat on the couch. As she changed to it Wolfe lifted his head to sniff. His opinion of perfume may be only a part of his opinion of women. He always thinks he smells it when there's a woman in the room. I had been closer to Julia McGee than he had, and she wasn't scented.

He eyed her. "You told Mr. Goodwin that you went to that room this evening to get a notebook you had left there. When did you leave it?"

She was meeting his eyes. "I'll wait until Mr. Aiken gets here."

Wolfe shook his head. "That won't do. I can't prevent his coming, but he'll enter only if it suits me. I want some facts before he arrives. When did you leave the notebook?"

She opened her mouth and closed it again. In a moment she spoke. "I didn't. That was a—that wasn't true. I went there this evening because Mr. Aiken asked me to."

"Indeed. To get something he had left?"

"No. I'd rather wait until he's here, but it doesn't matter. You know that place was Mr. Yeager's, so it doesn't matter. Mr. Aiken sent me there to see if there was anything there that would connect Mr. Yeager with it, that would show it was his place."

"Mr. Aiken gave you keys?"

"No, I had keys. I had been there a few times to take dictation from Mr. Yeager. I was his secretary."

Wolfe grunted. "I haven't seen that room, but Mr. Goodwin has described it. Did you think it a suitable milieu for business dictation?"

"It wasn't my place to think it was suitable or wasn't. If he thought it was—he was my boss."

Wolfe looked at me. I raised my brows. One brow up meant no, even money. Two brows up meant no, five to one. He returned to her.

"If you had found something that showed it was Mr. Yeager's place, what were you going to do with it?"

"I was going to take it. Take it away."

"As instructed by Mr. Aiken?"

"Yes."

"Why?"

"Mr. Aiken can tell you that better than I can."

"You must have a notion. You didn't think that he was merely indulging a whim."

"Of course not. The obvious reason was that he wanted to protect the reputation of Continental Plastic Products. It was bad enough, the executive vice-president being murdered. Mr. Aiken didn't want it to be known that he had been—that he had had a— a place like that."

"Do you know how Mr. Aiken found out that Mr. Yeager had that place?"

"Yes. I told him."

"When?"

"About two months ago. Mr. Yeager had had me go there twice —no, three times—to take dictation in the evening. He said he could think better, do better work, away from the office. Of course

you're right, what you said about that room. I thought it was very
—well, vulgar for him to ask me to go there. I worried about it,
and I decided my loyalty shouldn't be to Mr. Yeager, it should
be to the corporation. It paid my salary. So I told Mr. Aiken."

"What did he say?"

"He thanked me for telling him."

"What did he do?"

"I don't know. I don't know if he did anything."

"Did he speak to Mr. Yeager about it?"

"I don't know."

"Pfui. Certainly you know. If he had, Mr. Yeager would have
known you told him. Did you remark any change in Mr. Yeager's
attitude to you?"

"No."

"Did he continue to ask you to go there to take dictation?"

"Yes."

"How many times in the two months since you told Mr. Aiken?"

"Twice."

Wolfe shut his eyes and rubbed the bridge of his nose with a
fingertip. Ten seconds. His eyes opened. "When did Mr. Aiken
ask you to go there this evening?"

"This afternoon at the office. He asked if I still had the keys,
and I said yes. He asked if I had ever told anyone else about that
place, and I said no. He said it would be a great favor to the corporation if I would go there and make sure that—what I told you."

"Have you any reason to suppose that Mr. Aiken has ever been
there?"

Her eyes widened. "Of course not."

He shook his head. "No, Miss McGee. No assumption is of
course in an unsolved problem. I may if I choose assume that
you have been entirely candid with me, but I may not—"

The doorbell rang. I got up and went, and there on the stoop
was the president. The stoop light is at an angle on someone facing
the door, from the side, so features aren't distinct, but the gray
homburg and the fit of the gray topcoat were enough. I went and
opened the door and asked, "Mr. Aiken? Come in."

He stayed put. "Am I expected?"

"Yes, sir. Miss McGee is with Mr. Wolfe."

He crossed the sill, and I helped him off with his coat. With his hat off, I recognized him; he had been seated near Thomas G. Yeager in the picture I had seen in Lon Cohen's office of the banquet of the National Plastics Association. His face was well formed and well kept, and though his hair was mostly gray, he still had it. Every inch a president. He had paid at least eight times as much for his suit as the phony Yeager had paid for his. When I convoyed him to the office he stopped four steps in and said, "Good evening, Miss McGee," then turned to Wolfe and said, "Good evening, sir. I'm Benedict Aiken."

She was on her feet. I thought she had risen to show respect, but Wolfe spoke to Aiken. "I have told Miss McGee that I'll speak with you privately first. If you please, madam? The door, Archie."

"Just a minute." Aiken wasn't belligerent, just firm. "I'd like to speak with Miss McGee myself."

"No doubt." Wolfe upturned a palm. "Mr. Aiken. What Miss McGee told you on the phone was correct except for one detail, that she was attacked. I stationed a man in that room on the chance that someone would come there. Miss McGee came, and she—"

"Why are you interested in that room?"

"Because it belonged to Thomas G. Yeager and was used by him. The man didn't attack Miss McGee; she attacked him. In explaining to me why she went there she mentioned you, and I would like an explanation from you so I can compare it with hers. She may be present if you prefer, but not if she tries to interrupt. If she does, Mr. Goodwin will stop her."

Aiken looked at me, sizing me up. He went to the red leather chair and sat, in no hurry, making himself comfortable with his elbows on the arms. His eyes went to Wolfe. "Why do you think that room belonged to Thomas G. Yeager?"

"I don't think, I know."

"Why are you concerned? Whom are you acting for?"

"Myself. I have no engagement. I am in possession of a fact about a man who was murdered that is not commonly known. I am not legally obliged to communicate it to the police, and I

am exploring the possibility of using it to my profit—not by concealing it, but by exploiting it. Like doctors, lawyers, plumbers,
and many others, I get my income from the necessities, the tribu-
lations, and the misfortunes of my fellow beings. You are under
no compulsion to tell me why *you* are concerned, but I am willing
to listen. I didn't get you here."

Aiken was smiling, not with amusement. "I can't complain,"
he said, "since you have the handle. I didn't expect you to tell
me who has hired you, but it's hard to believe that no one has.
How did you find out about that room?"

Wolfe shook his head. "I owe you no light, sir. But I have not
been hired. If I had a client I would say so, of course without
naming him."

"How are you going to use the fact you possess about that
room?"

"I don't know. That will be determined by events. My man
is still there."

"When you speak of using it to your profit, of course you mean
get paid by somebody."

"Certainly."

"All right." Aiken shifted in the chair. "You want to compare
my explanation with Miss McGee's. Of course you know that
Yeager was the executive vice-president of my corporation, Continental Plastic Products. Miss McGee was his secretary. Some
two months ago she came to me and told me about that room,
that Yeager had had her go there several times in the evening
to work with him on various matters. She had no complaint of
his conduct, but she thought I should know about that room and
what it indicated of Yeager's character and habits. From her description of the room I thought she was fully justified. Obviously
it was a difficult problem. I asked her to mention it to no one, and
not to refuse to go there again; I would have to take time to consider how to deal with it."

"Did you mention it to him?"

"No. I don't know how much you know of the administrative
complexities of a large corporation, but the main question was
whether the best procedure would be to discuss it with him first

or take it up with my board of directors. I still hadn't decided yesterday when the news came that he was dead, that his body had been found in a hole in the street in front of that house. Naturally that was a shock, that he had been murdered, that was —well, very unpleasant—but it would be worse than unpleasant, it would be disastrous, if the existence of that room became known. Since his body had been found in front of that house, it would be assumed that someone involved in his activities in that room had killed him, and the investigation, the publicity, the inevitable scandal would be terrible. I was going to call an emergency meeting of my board, but decided instead to consult three of my directors in confidence. It was possible that Yeager had kept the existence of that room so secret that his connection with it would not become known. I suggested asking Miss McGee to go there and get any articles that might identify Yeager, and the suggestion was approved. And your man was there." His head turned. "Exactly what happened, Miss McGee?"

"When I got out of the elevator, there he was," she said. "I guess I lost my head. I supposed he was a detective, a police detective. I tried to get back in the elevator, and he grabbed me, and I tried to get loose but couldn't. He folded a bed cover around me and strapped it tight, and made a phone call, and after a while this man came, Archie Goodwin. He found out who I was from things in my bag and told me they were working for Nero Wolfe and they knew it was Mr. Yeager's room, and since they knew that I thought I had better come here when he asked me to. He wouldn't let me phone until I got here. I'm sorry, Mr. Aiken, but what could I do?"

"Nothing." Aiken went back to Wolfe. "So that's why *I* am concerned. You won't deny that it's a legitimate concern?"

"No indeed. Legitimate and exigent. But also desperate; you can't possibly hope that Mr. Yeager's connection with that room will never be divulged."

"I don't hope. I act. Will you tell me how you learned about it?"

"No."

"I'll pay you for it. I'll pay well."

"I don't sell information, Mr. Aiken, I sell services."

"I'm buying them. You said you weren't engaged; you are now. I'm hiring you."

"To do what?"

"Whatever may be necessary to protect the reputation and interests of my corporation, Continental Plastic Products. I am acting for the corporation."

Wolfe shook his head. "I doubt if it would work. I couldn't undertake not to disclose Mr. Yeager's connection with that room; events might take charge. The alternative would be for me to take charge of events."

"How?"

"By guiding them. It would be futile for you to pay me not to reveal what I have learned about that room, even if I were ass enough to accept it; sooner or later the police will inevitably discover it, given time. The only feasible way to protect the reputation and interests of your corporation with any hope of success would be to stop the police investigation of the murder by reaching an acceptable solution of it without involving that room."

Aiken was frowning. "But that may be impossible."

"Also it may not be. It is highly probable that whoever killed him knew of that room and its character and function; but suppose, for instance, that it was an outraged husband or father or brother or paramour. That might conceivably be established without disclosing some of the particulars, including the place where the misconduct had occurred. It would be difficult, but it might be done. It would be pointless even to conjecture until more is known."

"And if it proved to be impossible?"

Wolfe's shoulders went up an eighth of an inch and down. "You will have wasted your money. My self-esteem is not up to tackling the impossible. I remark that you are coerced not by me but by the situation. You are threatened not by me but by my possession of a fact. So you want to hire me, and I am willing to be hired, but I will perform only those services that are proper to my calling and my probity. I can't exclude any possibility, even that you killed Yeager yourself."

Aiken smiled, again not with amusement. "I can."

"Naturally." Wolfe turned. "Archie, the typewriter. Two carbons."

I whirled my chair, pulled the machine around, arranged the paper with carbons, and inserted them. "Yes, sir."

"Single-spaced, wide margins. The date. On behalf of my corporation, Continental Plastic Products, I hereby engage Nero Wolfe to investigate the circumstances of the death of Thomas G. Yeager. It is understood that Wolfe will make every effort to protect the reputation and interests of the corporation, comma, and will disclose no facts or information that will harm the corporation's repute or prestige, comma, unless he is compelled to do so by his legal obligation as a citizen and a licensed private detective, semicolon; and if he fails to observe this provision he is to receive no pay for his services or reimbursement for his expenses. The purpose of this engagement of Nero Wolfe is to prevent, comma, as far as possible, comma, any damage to the corporation as a result of the special circumstances of Yeager's death. Below a space for signature put 'President, Continental Plastic Products.' "

I had typed it as he spoke. After taking it out and running over it, I handed the original to Aiken and the carbons to Wolfe. Aiken read it twice and looked up. "Your fee isn't specified."

"No, sir. It can't be. It will depend on what and how much I do."

"Who decides if you have faithfully observed the provision?"

"Reason and good faith, applied jointly. If that failed, it would be decided by a court, but that contingency is remote."

Aiken glanced over it again, put it on the stand at his elbow, took a pen from his pocket, and signed it. I took it and gave it to Wolfe and handed one of the carbons to Aiken. He folded it and stuck it in his pocket, and spoke.

"How and when did you learn about that room?"

Wolfe shook his head. "I don't start a difficult job by babbling, even to you." He glanced at the wall clock, pushed his chair back, and arose. "It's past midnight. I'll report to you, of course, but when and what is solely in my discretion."

"That's absurd. You're working for me."

"Yes, sir. But the only test of my performance is its result. It may be that the less you know of its particulars the better." He picked up the signed original. "Do you want this back?"

"No. I want to know how you're going to proceed."

"I don't know myself."

"You know this. Did one of my directors tell you about that room?"

"No."

"Did Mrs. Yeager tell you?"

"No."

"Then who did?"

Wolfe glared at him. "Confound it, sir, shall I drop this thing in the wastebasket? Do you want this job done or not?"

"It's not what I want, it's what I'm stuck with. You have the handle." He got up. "Come, Miss McGee."

CHAPTER 8

AT HALF PAST TEN Wednesday morning I stood by the big globe in the office, twirling it, trying to find a good spot to spend my vacation in the fall. Having spent a couple of hours trying to decide what I would tell me to do if I were Wolfe, and coming to the conclusion that the most sensible would be to go out and sweep the sidewalk, it had seemed advisable to put my mind on something else for a while. When Wolfe has instructions for me in the morning he sends word by Fritz that I am to come up to his room. That morning there had been no word, and at a quarter to nine I had buzzed him on the house phone. Getting nothing but a prolonged growl, I had started to make a list of the things he might have put on my program for the day and came up with that one item: sweeping the sidewalk.

I had done fine, no question about that. I had set out at nine o'clock Tuesday morning to dig up a client, and by midnight, in only fifteen hours, we had a beaut, not only the president of a big corporation but the corporation itself. To collect a five-figure fee all we had to do was earn it. So first we . . .

We what? Our big advantage was that we knew Yeager had been killed in that room, and probably no one else knew it but the Perez family and the murderer. We also knew that Yeager had expected female company Sunday evening, since he had ordered caviar and pheasant for midnight delivery. But granting that she had come, it didn't have to be that she had killed him; she might have found him dead on arrival. Taking it from that angle, the way to start would be to get a complete list of the women who had keys. That might be done in a year or so, and the next step would be to find out which one had— Nuts.

Of the three angles to a murder problem—means, opportunity, and motive—you pick the one that seems most likely to open a crack. I crossed off opportunity. Everyone who had keys had opportunity. Then means—namely, a gun capable of sending a bullet through a skull. It had not been found, so the way to go about it was to get a complete list of the people who had keys and also had access to a gun, and then— I crossed off means. Then motive. Having no personal experience of the methods and procedures in a bower of carnality, I wasn't qualified as an expert, but surely they might have aroused strong feelings in any or all of Yeager's guests. Say there had been ten different guests in the last couple of years. Allow them three apiece of husbands, brothers, fathers, and what Wolfe called paramours, and that made forty likely prospects with first-rate motives. I crossed off motive.

With means, opportunity, and motive hopeless, all you can do is go fishing. Catch somebody in a lie. Find two pieces that are supposed to fit but don't. Find someone who saw or heard something—for example, someone in that house or that block who had noticed people entering or leaving the basement entrance of Number 156 who didn't appear to belong to the neighborhood. That program might get results if you had four or five good operatives and didn't care how long it took. But since Homicide might uncover a lead to that house any minute, and if they did they would find Fred Durkin there, and the fur would fly, and we would no longer have a client because what he wanted to buy couldn't be had, it wouldn't do. We needed either a genius or a lucky break.

Of course we had a genius, Nero Wolfe, but apparently he hadn't turned his switch on. When he came down from the plant rooms at eleven o'clock he put the day's orchid selection, Calanthe veitchi sandhurstiana, in the vase on his desk, circled to his chair and sat, glanced at his desk calendar, and looked through the morning crop of mail, which was mostly circulars and requests for contributions. He looked at me.

"What's this note on my calendar? Fourteen million, six hundred eighty-two thousand, two hundred thirty-five dollars and fifty-seven cents."

"Yes, sir. I got it from the bank. That's the cash reserve of Continental Plastic Products as shown on their statement dated January thirty-first. I thought you might like to know, and I had nothing else to do. I like to be busy at something."

"Pfui."

"Yes, sir. I agree."

"Have you considered the situation?"

"I have. It's a hell of a note. Yesterday, temporarily, we had too many clients. Two. Today we have one, and it's still too many because we can't possibly fill his order. If you're going to ask me for suggestions, don't bother. The only contribution I can make is worthless."

"What is it?"

"Julia McGee is a liar. You've heard that room described, but you haven't seen it. The man that fixed that room up, namely Yeager, did not have his secretary come there to take dictation. Any odds you want. Not even if she was a lump—he might have wanted to try an experiment—and she isn't. She has some very good points and possibilities, speaking as a satyr. So she lies, but that gets us nowhere. However she spent her evenings with him there, she could have done what she did do, squeal on him, either because the pictures bored her or because she wanted to get solid with the president. As far as the murder is concerned, it's a point in her favor. Having squealed on him, why should she shoot him? Do you want to ask her?"

"No." He took in air, all his barrel would hold, and let it out again. "I was a witling to take the job. All we can do is flounder around in the slush. As evidence of our extremity, it may be that we should find the man who got us into this pickle, despite our conclusion that he didn't know Yeager was dead. How long would it take you?"

"Something between a day and a year."

He made a face. "Or we could try a coup. We confront Mr. and Mrs. Perez with our conviction that they killed Yeager because he had defiled their daughter. We tell them that if the police learn of that room and Yeager's use of it they are probably doomed, as they are. Certainly they can't hope to stay there indefinitely. We offer them a large sum, twenty thousand, fifty thousand—no matter, it will come from that cash reserve—to go to some far corner of the earth, provided they will sign a confession that they killed Yeager because their daughter told them that he had made improper advances to her. They need not admit that the advances were successful; it can even be implied that they were never made, that their daughter had invented them. The confession will be left with us, and we'll get it to the police anonymously after they are safely out of reach. It will not mention that room. Of course the police will find it, but there will be nothing in it to connect it with Yeager. They will assume that it was his, but they can't establish it, and they do not publish assumptions that besmirch a prominent citizen."

"Wonderful," I said with enthusiasm. "It only has two minor flaws. First, since Yeager owned the house, it will be an item in his estate. Second, they didn't kill him. But what the hell, hanging a murder on—"

"That's your opinion."

"With damn good legs under it. I'll concede that you're being gallant, making Maria an inventor instead of a floozy, but it would be even better—"

I was interrupted by the doorbell. Going to the hall, I saw on the stoop what I have in mind, more or less, when I apply the word "lump" to a female. Not a hag, not a fright, just a woman, this one middle-aged or more, who would have to be completely retooled and reassembled before she could be used for show purposes. With her you would have some spare parts left when you finished, for instance the extra chin. Her well-made dark suit and her platinum mink stole were no real help. I went and opened the door and told her good morning.

"Nero Wolfe?" she asked.

I nodded. "His house."

"I want to see him. I'm Ellen Yeager. Mrs. Thomas G. Yeager."

When a caller comes without an appointment I am supposed to leave him on the stoop until I consult Wolfe, and I do, but this was a crisis. Not only were we up a stump; there was even a chance that Wolfe would be pigheaded enough to try that cockeyed stunt with the Perez family if he wasn't sidetracked. So I invited her to enter, led her to the office and on in, and said, "Mr. Wolfe, Mrs. Yeager. Mrs. Thomas G. Yeager."

He glared at me. "I wasn't informed that I had an appointment."

"No, sir. You didn't."

"I didn't stop to phone," Ellen Yeager said. "It's urgent." She went to the red leather chair and took it as if she owned it, put her bag on the stand, and aimed sharp little eyes at Wolfe. "I want to hire you to do something." She reached for the bag, opened it, and took out a checkfold. "How much do you want as a retainer?"

Client number four, not counting the phony Yeager. When I go scouting for clients I get results. She was going on. "My husband was murdered, you know about that. I want you to find out who killed him and exactly what happened, and then *I* will decide what to do about it. He was a sick man, he was oversexed, I know all about that. I've kept still about it for years, but I'm not going to let it keep me from—"

Wolfe cut in. "Shut up," he commanded.

She stopped, astonished.

"I'm blunt," he said, "because I must be. I can't let you rattle off confidential information under the illusion that you are hiring me. You aren't and you can't. I'm already engaged to investigate the murder of your husband."

"You are not," she declared.

"Indeed?"

"No. You're engaged to keep it from being investigated, to keep it from coming out, to protect that corporation, Continental Plastic Products. One of the directors has told me all about it. There was a meeting of the board this morning, and Benedict Aiken told them what he had done and they approved it. They don't care if the murderer of my husband is caught or not. They don't want him caught. All they care about is the corporation. I'll own a block of stock now, but that doesn't matter. They can't keep me from telling the District Attorney about that room if I decide to."

"What room?"

"You know perfectly well what room. In that house on Eighty-second Street where Julia McGee went last night and you got her and brought her here. Benedict Aiken told the board about it, and one of them told me." Her head jerked to me. "Are you Archie Goodwin? I want to see that room. When will you take me there?" She jerked back to Wolfe. That's a bad habit, asking a question and not waiting for an answer, but it's not always bad for the askee. She opened the checkfold. "How much do you want as a retainer?"

She was impetuous, no question about that, but she was no fool, and she didn't waste words. She didn't bother to spell it out: that if Wolfe tried to do what she thought he had been hired to do, clamp a lid on it, she could queer it with a phone call to the DA's office, and therefore he had to switch to her.

He leaned back and clasped his fingers at the center of his frontal mound. "Madam, you have been misinformed. Archie, that paper Mr. Aiken signed. Let her read it."

I went and got it from the cabinet and took it to her. To read it she got glasses from her bag. She took the glasses off. "It's what I said, isn't it?"

"No. Read it again. Archie, the typewriter. Two carbons."

I sat, pulled the machine around, arranged the paper with carbons, and inserted them. "Yes, sir."

"Single-spaced, wide margins. The date. I, comma, Mrs. Thomas G. Yeager, comma, hereby engage Nero Wolfe to investigate the circumstances of the death of my late husband. The purpose of this engagement is to make sure that my husband's murderer is identified and exposed, comma, and Wolfe is to make every effort to achieve that purpose. If in doing so a conflict arises between his obligation under this engagement and his obligation under his existing engagement with Continental Plastic Products it is understood that he will terminate his engagement with Continental Plastic Products and will adhere to this engagement with me. It is also understood that I will do nothing to interfere with Wolfe's obligation to Continental Plastic Products without giving him notice in advance."

He turned to her. "No retainer is necessary; I have none from Mr. Aiken. Whether I bill you or not, and for what amount, will depend. I wouldn't expect a substantial payment from two separate clients for the same services. And I would expect none at all from you if, for instance, I found that you killed your husband yourself."

"You wouldn't get any. There was a time when I felt like killing him, but that was long ago when the children were young." She took the original from me and put on her glasses to read it. "This isn't right. When you find out who killed him you tell me and *I* decide what to do."

"Nonsense. The People of the State of New York will decide what to do. In the process of identifying him to my satisfaction and yours I will inevitably get evidence, and I can't suppress it. Archie, give her a pen."

"I'm not going to sign it. I promised my husband I would never sign anything without showing it to him."

A corner of Wolfe's mouth went up—his version of a smile. He was always pleased to get support for his theory that no woman was capable of what he called rational sequence. "Then," he asked, "shall I rewrite it, for me to sign? Committing me to my part of the arrangement?"

"No." She handed me the papers, the one Aiken had signed and the one she hadn't. "It doesn't do any good to sign things. What counts is what you do, not what you sign. How much do you want as a retainer?"

He had just said he didn't want one. Now he said, "One dollar."

Apparently that struck her as about right. She opened her bag, put the checkfold in it, took out a purse, got a dollar bill from it, and left the chair to hand it to Wolfe. She turned to me. "Now I want to see that room."

"Not now," Wolfe said with emphasis. "Now I have some questions. Be seated."

"What kind of questions?"

"I need information, all I can get, and it will take some time. Please sit down."

"What kind of questions?"

"Many kinds. You said that you have known for years that your husband was oversexed, that he was sick, so it may be presumed that you took the trouble to inform yourself as well as you could of his efforts to allay his ailment. I want names, dates, addresses, events, particulars."

"You won't get them from me." She adjusted her stole. "I quit bothering about it long ago. Once when the children were young I asked my doctor about it, if something could be done, perhaps some kind of an operation, but the way he explained it I knew my husband wouldn't do that, and there was nothing else I could do, so what was the use? I have a friend whose husband is an alcoholic, and she has a worse—"

The doorbell rang. Dropping the papers in a drawer and stepping to the hall, I did not see another prospective client on the stoop. Inspector Cramer of Homicide West has been various things—a foe, a menace, a neutral, once or twice an ally, but never a client; and his appearance through the one-way glass, the set of his burly shoulders and the expression on his big round red face, made it plain that he hadn't come to ante a retainer. I went and slipped the chain bolt on, opened the door the two inches it permitted, and spoke through the crack.

"Greetings. I don't open up because Mr. Wolfe has company. Will I do?"

"No. I know he has company. Mrs. Thomas G. Yeager has been here nearly half an hour. Open the door."

"Make yourself at home. I'll see." I shut the door, went to the office, and told Wolfe, "The tailor. He says his man brought the suit nearly half an hour ago, and he wants to discuss it."

He tightened his lips and scowled, at me, then at her, and back at me. Whenever an officer of the law appears on the stoop and wants in, his first impulse is to tell me to tell him he's busy and can't be disturbed, and all the better if it's Inspector Cramer. But the situation was already ticklish enough. If the cops had found a trail to that house and had followed it and found Fred Durkin there, the going would be fairly tough, and making Cramer pry his way in with a warrant would only make it tougher. Also there was Mrs. Yeager. Since Cramer knew she had been here nearly half an hour, obviously they had a tail on her, and it wouldn't hurt to know why. Wolfe turned to her.

"Inspector Cramer of the police is at the door, and he knows you're here."

"He does not." She was positive. "How could he?"

"Ask him. But it may be assumed that you were followed. You are under surveillance."

"They wouldn't dare! *Me?* I don't believe it! If they—"

The doorbell rang. Wolfe turned to me. "All right, Archie."

CHAPTER 9

AT A MEETING of those two, Wolfe and Cramer, naturally I am not an impartial observer. Not only am I committed and involved; there is also the basic fact that cops and private detectives are enemies and always will be. Back of the New York cop are the power and authority of eight million people; back of the private detective is nothing but the right to life, liberty, and the pursuit of happiness, and while that's a fine thing to have it doesn't win arguments. But though I am not impartial I'm an observer, and one of the privileges of my job is to be present when Cramer walks into the office and aims his sharp gray eyes at Wolfe, and Wolfe, his head cocked a little to the side, meets them. Who will land the first blow, and will it be a jab, a hook, or a swing?

On this occasion I got cheated. That first quick impact didn't take place because Mrs. Yeager didn't let it. As Cramer crossed the sill into the office she was there confronting him, demanding, "Am I being followed around?"

Cramer looked down at her. He was polite. "Good morning, Mrs. Yeager. I hope you haven't been annoyed. When there's a murderer loose we don't like to take chances. For your protection we thought it advisable—"

"I don't need any protection and I don't want any!" With her head tilted back the crease between her chins wasn't so deep. "Did you follow me here?"

"I didn't. A man did. We—"

"Where is he? I want to see him. Bring him in here. I'm telling you and I'm going to tell him, I will *not* be followed around. Protect me?" She snorted. "You didn't protect my husband. He gets shot on the street and put in a hole and you didn't even find him. A boy had to find him. Where's this man?"

"He was merely obeying orders." Cramer's tone sharpened a

little. "And he followed you here, and maybe you *do* need protection. There are things to be protected from besides personal violence, like making mistakes. Maybe coming here was one. If you came to tell Nero Wolfe something you haven't told us, something about your husband, something that is or may be connected with his death, it *was* a mistake. So I want to know what you've said to him and what he said to you. All of it. You've been here nearly half an hour."

For half a second I thought she was going to spill it, and she did too. My guess would be that what popped into her mind was the notion that the simplest and quickest way to see that room on 82nd Street would be to tell Cramer about it, and she might actually have acted on it if Wolfe's voice hadn't come at her from behind.

"I'll return your retainer if you want it, madam."

"Oh," she said. She didn't turn. "I hired him to do something," she told Cramer.

"To do what?"

"To find out who killed my husband. You didn't even find his body, and now all you do is follow me around, and this stuff about protecting me when there's nothing to protect me from. If I had anything to tell anybody I'd tell him, not you." She took a step. "Get out of the way; I'm going to see that man."

"You're making a mistake, Mrs. Yeager. I want to know what you said to Wolfe."

"Ask him." Seeing that Cramer wasn't going to move, she circled around him, headed for the hall. I followed her out and to the front. As I reached for the knob she came close, stretched her neck to get her mouth near my ear, and whispered, "When will you take me to see that room?" I whispered back, "As soon as I get a chance." I would have liked to stay at the door to see how she went about finding her tail, but if Cramer was going to blurt at Wolfe, "When did you take over that room on Eighty-second Street?" I wanted to be present, so I closed the door and went back to the office.

Cramer wasn't blurting. He was in the red leather chair, the front half of it, with his feet planted flat. Wolfe was saying, ". . .

and that is moot. I'm not obliged to account to you for my accept-
ance of a retainer unless you charge interference with the performance of your official duty, and can support the charge."

"I wouldn't be here," Cramer said, "if I couldn't support it.
It wasn't just the report that Mrs. Yeager was here that brought
me. That would be enough, finding that you were sticking your
nose into a murder investigation, but that's not all. I'm offering
you a chance to cooperate by asking you a straight question: What
information have you got about Yeager that might help to identify
the person that killed him?"

So he knew about the room, and we were up a tree. I went to
my desk and sat. It would be hard going, and probably the best
thing for Wolfe to do would be to empty the bag and forget the
clients.

He didn't. He hung on. He shook his head. "You know better
than that. Take a hypothesis. Suppose, for instance, that I have
been informed in confidence that a certain person owed Yeager
a large sum of money and Yeager was pressing for payment. That
might help to identify the murderer, but I am not obliged to pass
the information on to you unless I am confronted with evidence
that it *would* help. Your question is straight enough, but it's impertinent, and you know it."

"You admit you have information."

"I admit nothing. If I do have information the responsibility
of deciding whether I am justified in withholding it is mine—and
the risk."

"Risk my ass. With your goddam luck, and you talk about risk.
I'll try a question that's more specific and maybe it won't be so
impertinent. Why did Goodwin phone Lon Cohen at the *Gazette*
at five o'clock Monday afternoon to ask for dope on Yeager, more
than two hours before Yeager's body was found?"

I tried to keep my face straight, and apparently succeeded,
since Cramer has good eyes with a lot of experience with faces,
and if my relief had shown he would have spotted it. Inside I
was grinning. They hadn't found the room, they had merely got
a tip from some toad at the *Gazette* and had put the screws on.

Wolfe grunted. "That is indeed specific."

"Yeah. Now you be specific. I've seen you often enough horn in on a murder case, that's nothing new, but by God this is the first time you didn't even wait until the body was found. How did you know he was dead?"

"I didn't. Neither did Mr. Goodwin." Wolfe turned a hand over. "Mr. Cramer. I don't take every job that's offered to me. When I take one I do so to earn a fee, and sometimes it's necessary to take a calculated risk. I'm taking one now. It's true that someone, call him X, said something in this room Monday afternoon that caused Mr. Goodwin to phone Mr. Cohen for information about Thomas G. Yeager. But, first, nothing that X said indicated that he knew Yeager was dead, and it is our opinion that he did not know. Second, nothing that X said indicated that Yeager was in peril, that anyone intended to kill him or had any motive for killing him. Third, nothing that X said was the truth. We have discovered that every word he uttered was a lie. And since our conclusion that he didn't know Yeager was dead, and therefore he didn't kill him, is soundly based, I am justified in keeping his lies to myself, at least for the present. I have no information for you."

"Who is X?"

"I don't know."

"Nuts. Is it Mrs. Yeager?"

"No. I probably wouldn't name him even if I could, but I can't."

Cramer leaned forward. "Calculated risk, huh? Justified. You are like hell. I remember too many—"

The phone rang, and I swiveled and got it. "Nero Wolfe's offi—"

"I've got one, Archie."

My fingers tightened around the phone, and I pressed it closer to my ear. Fred again: "That you, Archie?"

"Certainly. I'm busy." If I told him to hold the wire and went to the kitchen, Cramer would step to my desk and pick it up.

"I said I've got another one. Another woman."

"I'm not sure that was sensible, Mr. Gerson. That might get you into serious trouble."

"Oh. Somebody there?"

"Certainly." Fred had good enough connections in his skull, but the service was a little slow. "I guess I'll have to, but I don't know how soon I can make it. Hold the wire a minute." I covered the transmitter and turned to Wolfe. "That damn fool Gerson has found his bonds and has got two of his staff locked in a room. He could get hooked for more damages than the bonds are worth. He wants me to come, and of course I ought to, but."

Wolfe grunted. "You'll have to. The man's a nincompoop. You can call Mr. Parker from there if necessary."

I uncovered the transmitter and told it, "All right, Mr. Gerson, I'm on my way. Keep them locked in till I get there." I hung up and went.

At the curb in front was Cramer's car. Trading waves with the driver, Jimmy Burke, I headed east. There was no reason to suppose that Cramer had a tail posted for me, but I wasn't taking the thinnest chance of leading a city employee to 82nd Street. Getting a taxi on Ninth Avenue, I told the driver I would give directions as we went along. We turned right on 34th Street, right again on Eleventh Avenue, right again on 56th Street, and left on Tenth Avenue. By then I knew I was clear, but I kept an eye to the rear all the way to 82nd and Broadway. From there I walked.

The hole was being filled in. There was no uniform around, and no one in sight who might be representing Homicide West or the DA's bureau. Turning in at the basement entrance of 156, using Meg Duncan's key, and going down the hall, I had no feeling of eyes on me, but as I approached the end Cesar Perez appeared at the kitchen door.

"Oh, you," he said, and turned. "It's Mr. Goodwin."

His wife came from inside. "There's a woman up there," she said.

I nodded. "I came to meet her. Had you seen her before?"

"No." She looked at her husband. "Cesar, we must tell him."

"I don't know." Perez spread his hands. "You think better than I do, Felita. If you say so."

Her black eyes came at me. "If you're not an honest man, may the good God send us help. Come in here." She moved.

I didn't hesitate. Fred hadn't sounded on the phone as if he had any new scratches, and this pair might have something hot. I stepped into the kitchen. Mrs. Perez went to the table and picked up a card and handed it to me. "That man came this morning," she said.

It was the engraved card of a John Morton Seymour, with "Attorney at Law" in one corner and a midtown address in the other. "And?" I asked.

"He brought this." She picked up an envelope from the table and offered it. "Look at it."

It had been sealed and slit open. I took out a paper with the regulation blue legal backing and unfolded it. There were three typewritten sheets, very neat and professional. I didn't have to read every word to get the idea; it was a deed, signed by Thomas G. Yeager and properly witnessed, dated March 16, 1957, conveying certain property, namely the house and ground at 156 West 82nd Street, Borough of Manhattan, City of New York, to Cesar and Felita Perez. First and most interesting question, how long had they known it existed?

"He brought that and gave it to us," she said. "He said Mr. Yeager told him that if he died he must give it to us within forty-eight hours after he died. He said it was a little more than forty-eight hours but he didn't think that would matter. He said he would take care of it for us—formalities, he said—without any charge. Now we have to tell you what we were going to do. We were going away tonight. We were going somewhere and not come back. But now we argue, we fight. My husband and daughter think we can stay, but I think we must go. For the first time we fight more than just some words, so I am telling you."

Cesar had an eye half closed. "What he say yesterday," he said, "your Mr. Wolfe. He say when they find out Mr. Yeager owned this house they come here and then we have bad trouble, so we decide to go tonight. But this man today, this Mr. Seymour, he say Mr. Yeager did this paper like this so nobody could know he owned this house and we must not say he owned it. He say it is fixed so nobody will know. So I say we can stay now. It is our house now and we can take out the things we don't want up there and it can be our room. If it's too big we can put in walls. That kitchen and that bathroom are beautiful. My wife thinks better than I do nearly always, but this time I say I don't see why. Why must we run away from our own house?"

"Well." I put the deed in the envelope and tossed it on the table. "When Mr. Wolfe said yesterday that you would be in trouble when they find out that Yeager owned this house you knew they wouldn't find out, and why didn't you say so?"

"You don't listen," Mrs. Perez said. "This Mr. Seymour didn't come yesterday, he came this morning. You don't listen."

"Sure I do. But Yeager told you about that paper long ago. You knew the house would be yours if he died."

Her black eyes flashed. "If you listen do you call us liars? When we say we were going away and this Mr. Seymour comes with this paper, and now we fight?"

I nodded. "I heard you. Have you got a Bible?"

"Of course."

"Bring it here."

She left the room, not to the hall, by another door. In a moment she was back with a thick little book bound in stiff brown leather. It didn't resemble the Bibles I had seen, and I opened it for a look, but it was in Spanish. Holding it, I asked them to put their left hands on it and raise their right hands, and they obliged. "Repeat this after me: I swear on this Bible . . . that I didn't know . . . Mr. Yeager was going to give us this house . . . and I had no reason . . . to think he was going to . . . before Mr. Seymour came this morning."

I put the Bible on the table. "Okay. If Mr. Seymour says he can handle it so no one will know Yeager owned it he probably can, but there are quite a few people who already know it, including me, so I advise you not to take anything from that room, not a single thing, even if it's your property. I also advise you to stay here. I'm not saying who did the best thinking on that, but skipping out is the worst thing you could possibly do. Yeager was killed up there, and you moved the body. If you skip it could even be that Mr. Wolfe will decide he has to tell the police about you, and it wouldn't take them long to find you, and swearing on a Bible wouldn't help you then."

"They wouldn't find us," Mrs. Perez said.

"Don't kid yourself. Smarter people than you have thought they could go where they couldn't be found, and it can't be done. Forget it. I have to go upstairs and see that woman. Please accept my congratulations on having a house all your own. May a cop never enter it."

I was going, but she spoke. "If we go away, we'll tell you before we go."

"We're not going," Perez said. "We're citizens of the United States of America."

"That's the spirit," I said, and went to the elevator and pushed the button. It came, and I entered and was lifted.

That bower of carnality grew on you. Emerging from the elevator and seeing that all was serene, that Fred hadn't had to use the coverlet again, I let my eyes glance around. Unquestionably the place had a definite appeal. It would have been an interesting and instructive experiment to move in and see how long it would take to get used to it, especially a couple of pictures across from the—

But I had work to do. Fred was in a yellow silk chair, at ease, with a glass of champagne in his hand, and on a couch facing him, also with a glass of champagne, was a female who went with the surroundings much better than either Meg Duncan or Julia McGee, though of course they hadn't been relaxed on a couch. This one was rather small, all curves but not ostentatious, and the ones that caught your eye and held it were the curves of her lips—her wide, but not too wide, full mouth. As I approached she extended a hand.

"I know you," she said. "I've seen you at the Flamingo. I made a man mad once saying I wanted to dance with you. When Fred said Archie Goodwin was coming I had to sit down to keep from swooning. You dance like a dream."

I had taken the offered hand. Having shaken hands with five different murderers on previous occasions, I thought one more wouldn't hurt if it turned out that way. "I'll file that," I told her.

"If we ever team up for a turn I'll try not to trample you. Am I intruding? Are you and Fred old friends?"

"Oh no, I never saw him before. It just seems silly to call a man Mister when you're drinking champagne with him. I suggested the champagne."

"She put it in the freezer," Fred said, "and she opened it, and why waste it? I don't like it much, you know that."

"No apology needed. If she calls you Fred, what do you call her?"

"I don't call her. She said to call her Dye. I was just waiting for you."

On the couch, at arm's length from her, was a leather bag shaped like a box. I was close enough so that all I had to do to get it was bend and stretch an arm. Her hand darted out, but too late, and I had it. As I backed up a step and opened it, all she said was, "That's not nice, is it?"

"I'm only nice when I'm dancing." I went to the end of the couch and removed items one by one, putting them on the couch. There were only two things with names on them, an opened envelope addressed to Mrs. Austin Hough, 64 Eden Street, New York 14, and a driver's license, Dinah Hough, same address, thirty, five feet two inches, white, brown hair, hazel eyes. I put everything back in, closed the bag, and replaced it on the couch near her.

"I left the gun at home," she said, and took a sip of champagne.

"That was sensible. I only wanted to know how to spell Di. I may be able to save you a little trouble, Mrs. Hough. Nero Wolfe wants to see anyone who comes to this room and has keys to the door downstairs and the elevator—by the way, I left them in your bag—but if we went there now he'd be just starting lunch and you'd have to wait. We might as well discuss matters here while you finish the champagne."

"Will you have some? The bottle's in the refrigerator."

"No, thanks." I sat on the couch, four feet away, twisted around to face her. "I don't suppose the champagne's what you came here for. Is it?"

"No. I came to get my umbrella."

"Yellow with a red plastic handle?"

"No. Gray with a black handle."

"It's there in a drawer, but you'll have to manage without it for a while. If and when the police get interested in this place they won't like it if things have been taken away. How did it get here?"

"I need a refill." She was off of the couch and on her feet in one smooth movement. "Can't I bring you some?"

"No, thanks."

"You, Fred?"

"No, one's enough of this stuff."

She crossed to the kitchen door and on through. I asked Fred, "Did she try to buy you off or talk you off?"

He shook his head. "She didn't try anything. She gave me a look and saw I'm twice as big as she is, and she said, 'I don't know you, do I? What's your name?' She's a damn cool specimen if you ask me. Do you know what she asked me after we got talking? She asked me if I thought this would be a good place to have meetings of the Parent-Teachers Association. Believe me, if I was a woman and I had keys to this place and I came and found a stranger—"

Mrs. Hough had reappeared, with a full glass. She came and resumed her place on the couch without spilling a drop, lifted the glass, said, "Faith, hope, and charity," and took a sip. She adjusted her legs. "I left it here," she said. "Two weeks ago Friday, three weeks this coming Friday. It was raining. Tom Yeager had told me he knew a place that was different, worth seeing, he said, and he gave me keys and told me how to get in. When I came, this is what I found." She waved a hand. "You have to admit it's different. But there was no one here but him, and he had ideas I didn't like. He didn't actually assault me, say nothing but good of the dead, but he was pretty difficult, and I was glad to get away without my umbrella but with everything else."

She took a sip. "And when I read about his death, about his body being found in a hole in the street, this street, you can imagine. I wasn't worried about being suspected of having something to do with his death, that wasn't it, but I knew how clever they are at tracing things, and if the umbrella was traced to me, and this room described in the papers—well . . ." She gestured. "My husband, my friends, everyone who knows me—and if it got bad enough my husband might even lose his job. But this place wasn't mentioned in the papers yesterday, and when it wasn't mentioned again today I thought they probably didn't know about it, and I decided to come and see and perhaps I could get my umbrella. So here I am."

She took a sip. "And you say I can't have it and talk about going to see Nero Wolfe. It would be fun to see Nero Wolfe, I wouldn't mind that, but I want my umbrella, and I have an idea. You say it's here in a drawer?"

"Right."

"Then *you* take it, and tonight take me to the Flamingo and we'll dance. Not just a turn, we'll dance till they close, and then you might feel like letting me have the umbrella. That may sound conceited, but I don't mean it that way, I just think you *might,* and it won't hurt to find out, and anyhow you'll have the umbrella."

"Yeah." The curve of her lips really caught the eye. "And it won't be here. I appreciate the invitation, Mrs. Hough, but I'll be working tonight. Speaking of working, why would your husband lose his job? Does he work for Continental Plastic Products?"

"No. He's an assistant professor at NYU. A wife of a faculty member getting involved in a thing like this—even if I'm not really involved . . ."

There was a click in my skull. It wasn't a hunch; you never know where a hunch comes from; it was the word "professor" that flipped a switch. "What's he professor of?" I asked.

"English literature." She took a sip. "You're changing the subject. We can go to the Flamingo tomorrow night. You won't be losing anything except a few hours if you don't like me, because you'll have the umbrella." She looked at her wrist watch. "It's nearly half past one. Have you had lunch?"

"No."

"Take me to lunch and maybe you'll melt a little."

I was listening with only one ear. Teacher of literature. Measure your mind's height by the shade it casts, Robert Browning. I would have given ten to one, which would have been a sucker's bet, but a detective has as much right to look on the bright side as anyone else.

I stood up. "You're getting on my nerves, Mrs. Hough. It would be no strain at all to call you Di. I haven't seen anyone for quite a while that I would rather take to lunch or dance with, melting would be a pleasure, but I have to go. Nero Wolfe will still want to see you, but that can wait. Just one question: Where were you Sunday night from seven o'clock on?"

"No." Her eyes widened. "You *can't* mean that."

"Sorry, but I do. If you want to have another conference with yourself, I'll wait while you go to fill your glass again."

"You really mean it." She emptied the glass, taking her time. "I didn't go to the kitchen to have a conference with myself. Sunday night I was at home, at our apartment, with my husband. Seven o'clock on? We went to a restaurant in the Village a little after six for dinner, and got home after eight—around half past eight. My husband worked at some papers, and I read and watched television, and I went to bed around midnight, and stayed there, really I did. I seldom get up in the middle of the night and go and shoot a man and drop his body in a hole."

"It's a bad habit," I agreed. "Now Mr. Wolfe won't have to ask you that. I suppose you're in the phone book?" I turned to Fred. "Don't let her talk you out of the umbrella. How's the room service here? Okay?"

"No complaints. I'm beginning to feel at home. How much longer?"

"A day or a week or a year. You never had it softer."

"Hunh. You leaving her?"

"Yeah, she might as well finish the bottle. I've got an errand." As I made for the elevator Dinah Hough left the couch and headed for the kitchen. She was in there when the elevator came and I entered. Down below Mr. and Mrs. Perez were still in their kitchen, and I poked my head in and told them that their only hope of steering clear of trouble was to sit tight, and blew. At the corner of 82nd and Columbus was a drugstore where I could have treated my stomach to a glass of milk, but I didn't stop. I had a date with an assistant professor of English literature, though he didn't know it.

CHAPTER 10

IT WAS 1:40 when I left that house. It was 6:10, four and a half hours later, when I said to Austin Hough, "You know damn well you can't. Come on."

During the four and a half hours I had accomplished a good deal. I had learned that in a large university a lot of people know where an assistant professor ought to be or might be, but no one knows where he is. I had avoided getting trampled in corridors twice, once by diving into an alcove and once by fighting my way along the wall. I had sat in an anteroom and read a magazine article entitled "Experiments in Secondary Education in Japan." I had sweated for fifteen minutes in a phone booth, reporting to Wolfe on the latest developments, including the acquisition of a house by Cesar and Felita Perez. I had taken time out to find a lunch counter on University Place and take in a corned-beef sandwich, edible, a piece of cherry pie, not bad, and two glasses of milk. I had been stopped in a hall by three coeds, one of them as pretty as a picture (no reference to the pictures on the top floor of the Perez house), who asked for my autograph. They probably took me for either Sir Laurence Olivier or Nelson Rockefeller, I'm not sure which.

And I never did find Austin Hough until I finally decided it was hopeless and went for a walk in the direction of 64 Eden Street. I didn't phone because his wife might answer, and it wouldn't have been tactful to ask if her husband was in. The thing was to get a look at him. So I went there and pushed the button in the vestibule marked Hough, opened the door when the click sounded, and entered, mounted two flights, walked down the hall to a door which opened as I arrived, and there he was.

He froze, staring. His mouth opened and closed. I said, not

aggressively, just opening the conversation, "Other sins only speak; murder shrieks out."

"How in the name of God . . ." he said.

"How doesn't matter," I said. "We meet again, that's enough. Is your wife at home?"

"No. Why?"

"Why doesn't matter either if she's not here. There's nothing I'd enjoy more than chatting with you a while, but as you mentioned Monday, Mr. Wolfe comes down from the plant rooms at six o'clock, and he's in the office waiting for you. Come along."

He was deciding something. He decided it. "I don't know what you're talking about. I mentioned nothing to you Monday. I've never seen you before. Who are you?"

"I'm Thomas G. Yeager. His ghost. Don't be a sap. If you think it's just my word against yours, nuts. You can't get away with it. You know damn well you can't. Come on."

"We'll see if I can't. Take your foot away from the door. I'm shutting it."

There was no point in prolonging it. "Okay," I said, "I'll answer the question you didn't finish. This afternoon I had a talk with your wife. I got your name and address from an envelope I took from her bag."

"I don't believe it. That's a lie."

"Also in her bag was her driving license. Dinah Hough, born April third, nineteen-thirty, white, hair brown, eyes hazel. She likes champagne. She tilts her head a little to the right when she—"

"Where did you see her?"

"Where doesn't matter either. That's all you'll get from me. I told Mr. Wolfe I'd have you there at six o'clock, and it's a quarter past, and if you want—"

"Is my wife there?"

"No, not now. I'm telling you, Mr. Yeager—excuse me, Mr. Hough—if you don't want all hell to pop you'll take my hand and come along fast."

"Where's my wife?"

"Ask Mr. Wolfe."

He moved, and I sidestepped not to get bumped. He pulled

the door shut, tried it to make sure the lock had caught, and headed for the stairs. I followed. On the way down I asked which direction was the best bet for a taxi and he didn't reply. My choice would have been Christopher Street, but he turned right at the corner, towards Seventh Avenue, and won the point. We had one in three minutes, at the worst time of day. He had nothing to say en route. There was a chance, one in ten, that Cramer had a man staked to keep an eye on the old brownstone, but he wouldn't know Hough from Adam, and going in the back way through the passage from 34th Street was complicated, so we rolled to the curb in front. Mounting the stoop and finding the chain bolt was on, I had to ring for Fritz to let us in.

Wolfe was at his desk, scowling at a crossword puzzle in the *Observer*. He didn't look up as we entered. I put Hough in the red leather chair and went to mine, saying nothing. When a master brain is working on a major problem you don't butt in. In twenty seconds he muttered, "Confound it," slammed his pencil on the desk, swiveled, focused on the guest, and growled, "So Mr. Goodwin rooted you out. What have you to say for yourself?"

"Where's my wife?" Hough blurted. He had been holding it in.

"Wait a second," I put in. "I've told him I talked with his wife this afternoon and got his name and address from items in her bag. That's all."

"Where is she?" Hough demanded.

Wolfe regarded him. "Mr. Hough. When I learned Monday evening that a man named Thomas G. Yeager had been murdered, it would have been proper and natural for me to give the police a description of the man who had been here that afternoon impersonating him. For reasons of my own, I didn't. If I tell them about it now I'll give them not a description, but your name and address. Whether I do or not will depend on your explanation of that strange imposture. What is it?"

"I want to know where Goodwin saw my wife and why, and where she is. Until I know that, I'm explaining nothing."

Wolfe closed his eyes. In a moment he opened them. He nodded. "That's understandable. If your wife was a factor, you can't explain without involving her, and you won't do that unless she is already involved. Very well, she is. Monday afternoon, posing as Yeager, you told Mr. Goodwin that you expected to be followed to One-fifty-six West Eighty-second Street. When your wife entered a room in the house at that address at noon today, she found a man there who is in my employ. He notified Mr. Goodwin, and he went there and talked with her. She had keys to the house and the room. That's all I intend to tell you. Now your explanation."

I seldom feel sorry for people Wolfe has got in a corner. Usually they have asked for it one way or another, and anyhow if you can't stand the sight of a fish flopping on the gaff you shouldn't go fishing. But I had to move my eyes away from Austin Hough. His long bony face was so distorted he looked more like a gargoyle than a man. I moved my eyes away, and when I forced them back he had hunched forward and buried his face in his hands.

Wolfe spoke. "Your position is hopeless, Mr. Hough. You knew that address. You knew Yeager's unlisted telephone number. You knew that he frequented that address. You knew that your wife also went there. What did you hope to accomplish by coming here to send Mr. Goodwin on a pointless errand?"

Hough's head raised enough for his eyes to come to me. "Where is she, Goodwin?" It was an appeal, not a demand.

"I don't know. I left her in that room at that address at twenty minutes to two. She was drinking champagne but not enjoying it. The only other person there was the man in Mr. Wolfe's employ. He wasn't keeping her; she was free to go. I left because I wanted to have a look at you, but she didn't know that. I don't know when she left or where she went."

"You talked with her? She talked?"

"Right. Twenty minutes or so."

"What did she say?"

I sent a glance at Wolfe, but he didn't turn his head to meet it, so I was supposed to use my discretion and sagacity. I did so.

"She told me a lie, not a very good one. She said she had been there only once and hadn't stayed long. She had left her umbrella there and had gone today to get it. The part about the umbrella was okay; it was there in a drawer and still is. She invited me to take her to lunch. She invited me to take her to the Flamingo tonight and dance till they close."

"How do you know it was a lie, that she had been there only once?"

I shook my head. "You want too much for nothing. Just file it that I don't *think* she lied; I *know* she did. And I know you know it too."

"You do not."

"Oh, nuts. Go climb a rope."

Wolfe wiggled a finger at him. "Mr. Hough. We have humored you, but our indulgence isn't boundless. Your explanation."

"What if I don't give you one? What if I get up and walk out?"

"That would be a misfortune for both of us. Now that I know who you are I would be obliged to tell the police of your performance Monday afternoon, and I'd rather not, for reasons of my own. In that respect your interest runs with mine—and your wife's. Her umbrella is still there."

He was licked and he knew it. His face didn't go gargoyle again, but his mouth was twisted and the skin around his eyes was squeezed in as if the light was too strong.

"Circumstances," he said. "Men are the sport of circumstances. Good God, as I sat in this chair talking to Goodwin, Yeager was dead, had been dead for hours. When I read it in the paper yesterday morning I knew how it would be if you found me, and I decided what to say; I was going to deny it, but now that won't do."

He nodded, slowly. "So. Circumstances. Of course my wife shouldn't have married me. It was a circumstance that she met me at a moment when she was—but I won't go into that. I'll try to keep to the point. I was a fool to think that I might still save our marriage, but I did. She wanted things that I couldn't supply, and she wanted to do things that I am not inclined to and not equipped for. She couldn't do them with me, so she did them without me."

"The point," Wolfe said.

"Yes. This is the first time I have ever said a word about my relations with my wife to anyone. About a year ago she suddenly had a watch that must have cost a thousand dollars or more. Then other things—jewelry, clothes, a fur coat. She had frequently spent evenings out without me, but it became more than evenings; occasionally she came home after dawn. You realize that now that I've started it's difficult to confine myself to the essentials."

"Do so if possible."

"I'll try. I descended to snooping. Curiosity creeps into the homes of the unfortunate under the names of duty or pity. When my wife—"

"Is that Pascal?"

"No, Nietzsche. When my wife went out in the evening I followed her—not always, but when I could manage it. Mostly she went to a restaurant or the address of a friend I knew about, but twice she went to that address on Eighty-second Street and entered at the basement door. That was incomprehensible, in that kind of neighborhood, unless it was a dive of some sort—dope or God knows what. I went there one afternoon and pushed the button at the basement door, but learned nothing. I am not a practiced investigator like you. A man, I think a Puerto Rican, told me only that he had no vacant rooms."

He stopped to swallow. "I also snooped at home, and one day I found a phone number that my wife had scribbled on the back of an envelope. Chisholm five, three-two-three-two. I dialed it and learned that it was the residence of Thomas G. Yeager. It wasn't listed. I made inquiries and found out who he was, and I saw him, more by luck than design. Do you want to know how it happened?"

"No. You met him?"

"No. I saw him at a theater. That was two weeks ago. And three days later, Friday, a week ago last Friday, I followed her when she went out, and she went again, that was the third time, to that house on Eighty-second Street. I went and stood across the street, and very soon, not more than five minutes, Yeager came, walking. It was still daylight. He turned in, to the basement entrance, and entered. What would you have done?"

Wolfe grunted. "I wouldn't have been there."

Hough turned to me. "What would you have done, Goodwin?"

"That's irrelevant," I said. "I'm not you. You might as well ask what I would do if I were a robin and saw a boy robbing my nest. What did you do?"

"I walked up and down the block until people began to notice me, and then went home. My wife came home at six o'clock. I didn't ask her where she had been; I hadn't asked her that for a year. But I decided I must do something. I considered various things, various plans, and rejected them. I finally settled on one Sunday evening. We had had dinner—"

"Which Sunday?"

"Last Sunday. Three days ago. We had had dinner at a restaurant and returned home. My wife was watching television, and I was in my room working, only I wasn't working. I was deciding what to do, and the next day I did it. I came here and saw Archie Goodwin. You know what I said to him."

"Yes. Do you think you've accounted for it?"

"I suppose not. It was like this: I knew that when Yeager didn't turn up Goodwin would find out why, either phone him —that was why I gave him the number—or go to the house. He would want to *see* Yeager, and he would tell him about me and what I had said. So Yeager would know that someone, someone he wouldn't identify from Goodwin's description, knew about his going to that house. He would know that Archie Goodwin and Nero Wolfe also knew about it. And he would tell my wife about it and describe me to her, and she would know I knew. That was the most important. I couldn't tell her, but I wanted her to know that I knew."

His eyes came to me and returned to Wolfe. "Another thing. I knew that Archie Goodwin wouldn't just dismiss it from his mind. He would wonder why I had mentioned that particular address, and he would wonder what secret connection there might be between Yeager and that house in that neighborhood, and when Archie Goodwin wonders about anything he finds out. All of this was in my mind, but the most important was that my wife would know that I knew."

His mouth worked, and he gripped the chair arms. "And that

evening on the radio, the eleven-o'clock news, I learned that Yeager was dead, and yesterday morning in the paper I learned that he had died, had been murdered, Sunday night, and his body had been found in a hole in front of that house. Thank God my wife wasn't there Sunday night."

"You're sure of that?"

"Certainly I'm sure. We sleep in separate beds, but when she turns over I hear her. You realize—" He stopped.

"What?"

"Nothing. I was going to say you realize that I have told you things I wouldn't have thought I could possibly ever tell any-body, but you don't care about that. Perhaps I have blundered again, but I was trapped by circumstance. Is there any chance, any chance at all, that it will stay with you? I can't ask you for any consideration, I know that, after the way I imposed on Goodwin Monday afternoon. But if you could find it possible . . ."

Wolfe looked up at the clock. "It's my dinnertime. It doesn't please me to hurt a man needlessly, Mr. Hough, and your pu-erile imposition on Mr. Goodwin doesn't rankle. On the con-trary; you gave him that address and he went there, and as a result we have a client." He pushed his chair back and rose. "What you have told us will be divulged only if it becomes requisite."

"Who is your client?"

When Wolfe said that was hardly his concern, he didn't try to insist. I permitted myself to feel sorry for him again as he left the chair. He was in a hell of a spot. He wanted to see his wife, he *had* to see her, but what was he going to say? Was he going to explain that he was responsible for her finding a reception committee when she went to get her umbrella? Was he going to admit—I turned that switch off. He had married her, I hadn't. When I went to the front to let him out, I stood on the stoop for a minute to see if there was someone around who was curious enough about him to follow him. There wasn't. I shut the door and went to join Wolfe in the dining room.

The two letters in the morning mail hadn't been answered, and when we returned to the office after dinner and had finished coffee we attended to them. One was from a Putnam County farmer asking how many starlings he wanted this year, and the other was from a woman in Nebraska saying that she would be in New York for a week late in June, with her husband and two children, and could they come and look at the orchids. The reply to the first was forty; Wolfe always invites two dinner guests for the starling pie. The reply to the second was no; she shouldn't have mentioned the children. When the answers had been typed and Wolfe had signed them, he sat and watched while I folded them and put them in the envelopes, and then spoke.

"Your exclusion of Mr. and Mrs. Perez is no longer valid. They knew they would get the house."

Of course I had known that was coming. I swiveled. "It's a funny thing about the Bible. I haven't been to church for twenty years, and modern science has proved that heaven is two hundred degrees Fahrenheit hotter than hell, but if I was asked to put my hand on a Bible and swear to a lie, I'd dodge. I'd say I was a Hindu or a Buddhist—Zen, of course. And Mr. and Mrs. Perez undoubtedly go to mass once a week and probably oftener."

"Pfui. To get a house, perhaps not; but to save their skins?"

I nodded. "Thousands of murderers have lied under oath on the witness stand, but this was different. They still sort of think I'm their detective."

"You're incorrigibly mulish."

"Yes, sir. Same to you."

"Nor is that imbecile Hough excluded. I call him an imbecile, but what if he is in fact subtle, wily, and adroit? Knowing or suspecting that his wife was going to that address Sunday evening, he got her keys, went there himself, killed Yeager, and left. Monday something alarmed him, no matter what; perhaps he told his wife what he had done, or she guessed, and her attitude brought dismay. He decided he must take some action that would make it seem highly unlikely that he had been implicated, and he did. You and I concluded yesterday that the impostor had not known Yeager was dead—not an assumption, a conclusion. We now abandon it."

"It's not incredible," I conceded. "I see only three holes in it."

"I see four, but none of them is beyond patching. I'm not suggesting that we have advanced; indeed, we have taken a step backward. We had concluded that that man was eliminated, but he isn't. And now?"

We discussed it for two solid hours. By the time we went up to bed, toward midnight, it looked very much as if we had a case and a client, two clients, and we didn't hold one single card that we were in a position to play. Our big ace, that we knew about that room and that Yeager had been killed in it, was absolutely worthless. And the longer we kept it up our sleeve, the more ticklish it would be when the police found a trail to it, as they were bound to sooner or later. When Wolfe left for his elevator he was so sour that he didn't say good night. As I undressed I was actually weighing the chance, if we called Fred off, that the cops wouldn't pry it loose that we had been there. That was so ridiculous that I turned over three times before I got to sleep.

The phone rang.

I understand that some people, when the phone rings in the middle of the night, surface immediately and are almost awake by the time they get it to their ear. I don't. I am still way under. I couldn't possibly manage anything as complicated as "Nero Wolfe's residence, Archie Goodwin speaking." The best I can do is " 'Lo."

A woman said, "I want to talk to Mr. Archie Goodwin." I was still fighting my way up.

"This is Goodwin. Who is this?"

"I am Mrs. Cesar Perez. You must come. Come now. Our daughter Maria is dead. She was killed with a gun. Will you come now?"

I was out from under. "Where are you?" I reached for the switch of the bed light and glanced at the clock. Twenty-five to three.

"We are at home. They took us to look at her, and we are just come back. Will you come?"

"Is anybody there? Policemen?"

"No. One brought us home, but he is gone. Will you come?"

"Yes. Right away. As fast as I can make it. If you haven't already—"

She hung up.

I like to take my time dressing, but I am willing to make an exception when necessary. When my tie was tied and my jacket on, and my things were in my pockets, I tore a sheet from my notebook and wrote on it:

Maria Perez is dead, murdered, shot—not at home, I don't know where. Mrs. P. phoned at 2:35. I'm on my way to 82nd Street.

AG

Down one flight I went to the door of Wolfe's room and slipped the note through the crack at the bottom. Then on down, and out. At that time of night Eighth Avenue would be the best bet for a taxi, so I headed east.

CHAPTER 11

IT WAS one minute after three when I used my key at the basement door of 156 and entered. Mrs. Perez was standing there. Saying nothing, she turned and walked down the hall, and I followed. Halfway along she turned into a room on the right, the door of which I had pushed open Tuesday evening when I felt an eye on me. It was a small room; a single bed, a chest of drawers, a little table with a mirror, and a couple of chairs didn't leave much space. Perez was on the chair by the table, and on the table was a glass and a bottle of rum. As I entered he slowly lifted his head to look at me. The eye that he half closed in emergencies was nearly shut.

He spoke. "My wife told you that day we sit down with friends. Are you a friend?"

"Don't mind him," she said. "He drinks rum, half a bottle. I tell him to." She sat on the bed. "I make him come to this room, our daughter's room, and I bring him rum. I sit on our daughter's bed. That chair is for you. We thank you for coming, but now we don't know why. You can't do anything, nobody can do anything, not even the good God Himself."

Perez picked up the glass, took a swallow, put the glass down, and said something in Spanish.

I sat on the chair. "The trouble with a time like this," I said, "is that there *is* something to do, and the quicker the better. You have no room in you right now for anything except that she's dead, but I have. I want to know who killed her, and you will too when the shock eases up a little. And in order—"

"You're crazy," Perez said. "I'll kill him."

"He's a man," she told me. I thought for a second she meant that a man had killed Maria and then realized that she meant her husband.

"We'll have to find him first," I said. "Do you know who killed her?"

"You're crazy," Perez said. "Of course not."

"They took you to look at her. Where? The morgue?"

"A big building," she said. "A big room with strong light. She was on a thing with a sheet on her. There was blood on her head but not on her face."

"Did they tell you who found her and where?"

"Yes. A man found her at a dock by the river."

"What time did she leave the house and where did she go and who with?"

"She left at eight o'clock to go to a movie with friends."

"Boys or girls?"

"Girls. Two girls came for her. We saw them. We know them. We went with a policeman to see one of them, and she said Maria went with them to the movie but she left about nine o'clock. She didn't know where she went."

"Have you any idea where she went?"

"No."

"Have you any idea who killed her or why?"

"No. They asked us all these questions."

"They'll ask a lot more. All right, this is how it stands. Either there is some connection between her death and Mr. Yeager's death or there isn't. If there isn't, it's up to the police and they'll probably nail him. Or her. If there is, the police can't even get started because they don't know this was Yeager's house—unless you've told them. Have you?"

"No," she said.

"You're crazy," he said. He took a swallow of rum.

"Then it's up to you. If you tell them about Yeager and that room, they may find out who killed Maria sooner than I would. Mr. Wolfe and I. If you don't tell them, we'll find him, but I don't know how long it will take us. I want to make it clear: If her death had nothing to do with Yeager, it won't hamper the police any not to know about him and that room, so it wouldn't help to tell them. That's that. So the question is, what do you want to do if it did have something to do with Yeager? Do you want to tell the police about him and the house, and probably be charged with killing Yeager? Or do you want to leave it to Mr. Wolfe and me?"

"If we had gone away last night," Mrs. Perez said. "She didn't want to. If I had been strong enough—"

"Don't say that," he commanded her. "Don't say that!"

"It's true, Cesar." She got up and went and poured rum in his glass, and returned to the bed. She looked at me. "She never had anything with Mr. Yeager. She never spoke to him. She never was in that room. She knew nothing about all that, about him and the people that came."

"I don't believe it," I declared. "It's conceivable that an intelligent girl her age wouldn't be curious about what was going on in the house she lived in, but I don't believe it. Where was she Sunday night when you took Yeager's body out and put it in the hole?"

"She was in her bed asleep. This bed I'm sitting on."

"You thought she was. She had good ears. She heard me enter the house Tuesday evening. When I came down the hall the door to this room was open a crack and she was in here in the dark, looking at me through the crack."

"You're crazy," Perez said.

"Maria wouldn't do that," she said.

"But she did. I opened the door and we spoke, just a few words. Why shouldn't she do it? A beautiful, intelligent girl, not interested in what was happening in her own house? That's absurd. The point is this: If you're not going to tell the police about Yeager, if you're going to leave it to Mr. Wolfe and me, I've got to find out what she knew, and what she did or said, that made someone want to kill her. Unless I can do that there's no hope of getting anywhere. Obviously I won't get it from you. Have the police done any searching here?"

"Yes. In this room. The first one that came."

"Did he take anything?"

"No. He said he didn't."

"I was here," Perez said. "He didn't."

"Then if you're leaving it to us that comes first. I'll see if I can find something, first this room and then the others. Two can do it faster than one, so will you go up and tell that man to come—no. Better not. He already knows too much for his own good. What you two ought to do is go to bed, but I suppose you won't. Go to the kitchen and eat something. You don't want to be here while I'm looking. I'll have to take the bed apart. I'll have to go through all her things."

"It's no good," Mrs. Perez said. "I know everything she had. We don't want you to do that."

"Okay. Then Mr. Wolfe and I are out and the police are in. It won't be me looking, it will be a dozen of them, and they're very thorough, and you won't be here. You'll be under arrest."

"That don't matter now," Perez said. "Maybe I ought to be." He lifted the glass, and it nearly slipped from his fingers.

Mrs. Perez rose, went to the head of the bed, and pulled the coverlet back. "You'll see," she said. "Nothing."

An hour and a half later I had to admit she was right. I had inspected the mattress top and bottom, emptied the drawers, removing the items one by one, taken up the rug and examined every inch of the floor, removed everything from the closet and examined the walls with a flashlight, pulled the chest of drawers out and inspected the back, flipped through thirty books and a stack of magazines, removed the backing of four framed pictures —the complete routine. Nothing. I was much better acquainted with Maria than I had been when she was alive, but hadn't found the slightest hint that she knew or cared anything about Yeager, his guests, or the top floor.

Perez was no longer present. He had been in the way when I wanted to take up the rug, and by that time the rum had him nearly under. We had taken him to the next room and put him on the bed. Maria's bed was back in order, and her mother was sitting on it. I was standing by the door, rubbing my palms together, frowning around.

"I told you, nothing," she said.

"Yeah. I heard you." I went to the chest and pulled out the bottom drawer.

"Not again," she said. "You are like my husband. Too stubborn."

"I wasn't stubborn enough with these drawers." I put it on the bed and began removing the contents. "I just looked at the bottoms underneath. I should have turned them over and tried them."

I put the empty drawer upside down on the floor, squatted, jiggled it up and down, and tried the edges of the bottom with the screwdriver blade of my knife. Saul Panzer had once found a valuable painting under a false bottom that had been fitted on the outside instead of the inside. This drawer didn't have one. When I put it back on the bed Mrs. Perez came and started replacing the contents, and I went and got the next drawer.

That was it, and I darned near missed it again. Finding nothing on the outside of the bottom, as I put the drawer back on the bed I took another look at the inside with the flashlight, and saw a tiny hole, just a pinprick, near a corner. The drawer bottoms were lined with a plastic material with a pattern, pink with red flowers, and the hole was in the center of one of the flowers. I got a safety pin from the tray on the table and stuck the point in the hole and pried, and the corner came up, but it was stiffer than any plastic would have been. After lifting it enough to get a finger under, I brought it on up and had it. The plastic had been pasted to a piece of cardboard that precisely fitted the bottom of the drawer, and underneath was a collection of objects which had been carefully arranged so there would be no bulges. Not only had Maria been intelligent, she had also been neat-handed.

Mrs. Perez, at my elbow, said something in Spanish and moved a hand, but I blocked it. "I have a right," she said, "my daughter."

"Nobody has a right," I said. "She was hiding it from you, wasn't she? The only right was hers, and she's dead. You can watch, but keep your hands off." I carried the drawer to the table and sat in the chair Perez had vacated.

Here's the inventory of Maria's private cache:

1. Five full-page advertisements of Continental Plastic Products taken from magazines.

2. Four labels from champagne bottles, Dom Perignon.

3. Three tear sheets from the financial pages of the *Times,* the stock-exchange price list of three different dates, with a pencil

mark at the Continental Plastic Products entries. The closing prices of CPP were 62½, 61⅝, and 66¾.

4. Two newspaper reproductions of photographs of Thomas G. Yeager.

5. A newspaper reproduction of a photograph of Thomas G. Yeager, Jr., and his bride, in their wedding togs.

6. A newspaper reproduction of a photograph of Mrs. Thomas G. Yeager, Sr., with three other women.

7. A full-page reproduction from a picture magazine of the photograph of the National Plastics Association banquet in the Churchill ballroom, of which I had seen a print in Lon Cohen's office Monday evening. The caption gave the names of the others on the stage with Yeager, including one of our clients, Benedict Aiken.

8. Three reproductions of photographs of Meg Duncan, two from magazines and one from a newspaper.

9. Thirty-one pencil sketches of women's heads, faces, some with hats and some without. They were on 5-by-8 sheets of white paper, of which there was a pad on Maria's table and two pads in a drawer. In the bottom left-hand corner of each sheet was a date. I am not an art expert, but they looked pretty good. From a quick run-through I guessed that there were not thirty-one different subjects; there were second and third tries of the same face, and maybe four or five. The dates went back nearly two years, and one of them was May 8, 1960. That was last Sunday. I gave the drawing a good long look. I had in my hand a promising candidate for a people's exhibit in a murder trial. Not Meg Duncan, and not Dinah Hough. It could be Julia McGee. When I realized that I was deciding it *was* Julia McGee I quit looking at it. One of the brain's most efficient departments is the one that turns possibilities into probabilities, and probabilities into facts.

10. Nine five-dollar bills of various ages.

Mrs. Perez had moved the other chair beside me and was on it. She had seen everything, but had said nothing. I looked at my watch: twenty minutes to six. I evened the edges of the tear sheets from the *Times,* folded them double, and put the other items inside the fold. The question of obstructing justice by suppressing evidence of a crime was no longer a question. My lawyer might maintain that I had assumed that that stuff wasn't relevant to the murder of Yeager, but if he told a judge and jury that I had also assumed that it wasn't relevant to the murder of Maria Perez, he would have to concede that I was an idiot.

With the evidence in my hand, I stood up. "All this proves," I told Mrs. Perez, "is that Maria had the normal curiosity of an intelligent girl and she liked to draw pictures of faces. I'm taking it along, and Mr. Wolfe will look it over. I'll return the money to you some day, I hope soon. You've had a hard night and you've got a hard day ahead. If you have a dollar bill, please get it and give it to me. You're hiring Mr. Wolfe and me to investigate the murder of your daughter; that's why you're letting me take this stuff."

"You were right," she said.

"I've earned no medals yet. The dollar, please?"

"We can pay more. A hundred dollars. It doesn't matter."

"One will do for now."

She got up and went, and soon was back with a dollar bill in her hand. She gave it to me. "My husband is asleep," she said.

"Good. You ought to be too. We are now your detectives. A man will come sometime today, and he'll probably take you and your husband down to the District Attorney's office. They won't mention Yeager, and of course you won't. About Maria, just tell them the truth, what you've already told the policeman, about her going to the movie, and you don't know who killed her or why. Have you been getting breakfast for the man up above?"

"Yes."

"Don't bother this morning. He'll be leaving pretty soon and he won't come back." I offered a hand, and she took it. "Tell your husband we're friends," I said, and went out to the elevator.

Emerging into the bower of carnality, I switched on the light. My mind was so occupied that the pictures might as well not have been there, and anyway there was a living picture: Fred Durkin on the eight-foot-square bed, his head on a yellow pillow, and a yellow sheet up to his chin. As the light went on he stirred and blinked, then stuck his hand under the pillow and jerked it out with a gun in it.

"At ease," I told him. "I could have plugged you before you touched it. We've got all we can use, and it's time to go. There's no rush; it'll be fine if you're out of here in half an hour. Don't stop down below to find Mrs. Perez and thank her; they're in trouble. Their daughter was murdered last night—not here, not in the house. Just blow."

He was on his feet. "What the hell is this, Archie? What am I in?"

"You're in three hundred bucks. I advise you to ask me no questions; I might answer them. Go home and tell your wife you've had a rough two days and nights and need a good rest."

"I want to know one thing. Am I going to get tagged?"

"Toss a coin. I hope not. We could be lucky."

"Would it help if I wipe up here? Ten minutes would do it."

"No. If they ever get this far they won't need fingerprints. Go home and stay put. I may be ringing you around noon. Don't take any of the pictures."

I entered the elevator.

CHAPTER 12

WHEN WOLFE CAME DOWN from the plant rooms at eleven o'clock I was at my desk with the noon edition, so-called, of the *Gazette*. There was a picture of Maria Perez, dead, on the front page. She didn't really rate it, since she had had absolutely no distinction but youth and beauty, but she got a break because nobody important had been killed or robbed or arrested that night.

It was wide open. The only facts they had, leaving off the tassels, were: a) the body had been found at 12:35 a.m. by a watchman making his rounds on a North River pier in the Forties; b) she had been dead not more than three hours and probably less; c) she had been shot in the back of the head with a .32; d) she had last been seen alive by the two girl friends who had gone to the movie with her, and who said she had got up and left a little before nine o'clock and hadn't come back; she had said nothing to them; they had supposed she was going to the rest room; and e) her father and mother refused to talk to reporters. There was no hint of any suspicion that there was any connection between her death and that of Thomas G. Yeager, whose body had been found three days earlier in a hole in the street she had lived on.

I had reported briefly to Wolfe after his breakfast in his room, just the essentials. Now, as he sat at his desk, I handed him the *Gazette*. He glanced at the picture, read the story, put the paper down, and leaned back.

"Verbatim," he said.

I gave him the crop, including, of course, my call on Fred. When I had finished I handed him the evidence I had got from Maria's drawer. "One item," I said, "might mislead you—labels from four champagne bottles. I do not and will not believe that

Maria drank any of the champagne. She got the labels when her father or mother brought the bottles down to dispose of them."

"Who said so?"

"I say so."

He grunted and began his inspection. With that sort of thing he always takes his time. He looked at the back of each item as well as the front, even the advertisements, the five-dollar bills, and the tear sheets from the *Times*. Finishing with them, the labels, and the photographs, he handed them to me and tackled the drawings. After running through them, five seconds for some and up to a minute for others, he stood up and began laying them out on his desk in rows. They just about covered it. I stood and watched as he shifted them around into groups, each group being presumably different sketches of the same woman. Twice I disagreed and we discussed it. We ended up with three groups with four sketches each, five groups with three sketches each, one group with two, and two with only one. Eleven different guests in two years, and it wasn't likely that Maria had got all of them. Yeager had been a very hospitable man.

I pointed to one of the four-sketch groups. "I can name her," I said. "Ten to one. I have danced with her. Her husband owns a chain of restaurants and is twice her age."

He glared at me. "You're being frivolous."

"No, sir. The name is Delancey."

"Pfui. Name that one." He pointed to the two-sketch group. "One dated April fifteenth and the other May eighth. Last Sunday."

"I was leaving it to you. You name it."

"She has been in this room."

"Yes, sir."

"Julia McGee."

"Yes, sir. I wasn't being frivolous. I wanted to see if you would spot her. If those are the dates Maria saw the subjects in the hall, not merely the dates she made these sketches, Julia McGee was there Sunday. Either she killed him or she found him dead. If he was on his feet when she arrived she wouldn't have left before midnight, because refreshments were expected—and of course she didn't go to take dictation. And if he was alive and she was there when the murderer came she would have got it too. So if she didn't kill him she found him dead. By the way, to clear up a detail, I have entered the dollar Mrs. Perez gave me in the cash book as a retainer. I took it because I thought she would be more likely to hold on if she had us hired, and I assumed they are now eliminated. They didn't kill their daughter. I am not crowing. I would rather have been wrong than be proved right by having Maria get it, even if she asked for it."

"That she asked for it is only conjecture."

"Yeah. But our theory is that she was killed by the person who killed Yeager or we haven't got a theory, and in that case Maria must have made the contact. Suppose it was Julia McGee. She couldn't have known there was an eye on her behind that crack as she went down the hall, or if she did she couldn't have known whose eye it was. If she felt or suspected it, as I did, and pushed the door open and found Maria there, she wouldn't have gone on up and used the gun she had brought to shoot Yeager. So Maria must have made the contact yesterday, and she wouldn't do that just for the hell of it, just for the pleasure of saying, 'I saw you come in Sunday evening so I know you killed Mr. Yeager.' She wanted to make a deal. That she asked for it may be only a conjecture, but I don't make it because I like it. I would prefer to believe that she was as good inside as outside. Anyhow she didn't drink that champagne."

Wolfe said, "Mmmmh."

I pointed to one of the three-sketch groups. "That's Dinah. Mrs. Austin Hough. Maria knew how to get a likeness. She got Mrs. Delancey too."

"There is none of Meg Duncan."

"No. When she got photographs of her she didn't need a sketch."

He sat down. "Get Fred. How soon can he be here?"

"Twenty minutes."

"Get him."

I got at my phone and dialed, and Fred answered. I told him that if he could make it here in nineteen minutes two things would be waiting for him, $315 and instructions from Wolfe, and he said both would be welcome. I turned and told Wolfe, and he said, "Get Miss McGee. I'll speak to her."

That took a little longer. The trouble seemed to be, when I got the Continental Plastic Products switchboard, that Julia McGee had been Yeager's secretary, and now that he was no longer there the operator didn't know where Miss McGee was. I finally got her and signed to Wolfe, and he took his phone. I stayed on.

"Miss McGee? I must see you as soon as possible. At my office."

"Well—" She didn't sound enthusiastic. "I leave at five. Will six o'clock do?"

"No. It's urgent. As soon as you can get here."

"Can't you tell me on the phone—no, I suppose not. All right, I'll come."

"Now."

"Yes. I'll leave in a few minutes."

We hung up. Wolfe leaned back and closed his eyes. I gathered up the drawings and put them with the rest of Maria's collection. Getting a folder from the cabinet, I marked it YEAGER and put the collection in it, decided that the safe was the proper place for something that might some day be a people's exhibit, and took it there instead of the cabinet. When Wolfe's eyes opened I took him a check to sign, to Fred Durkin for three hundred fifteen & 00/100 dollars. We were now out about five Cs on the Yeager operation, and we had four clients and two bucks in retainers, plus a damn good chance of ending up in the coop for obstructing justice. As I put Fred's check on my desk the phone rang. It was Mrs. Yeager. She wanted to know when I was going to take her to see the room on 82nd Street. She also wanted to tell me that the daughter of the superintendent of that house had been mur- dered, and she thought Wolfe and I should look into it. I could do that when I took her to see the room, saving a trip. If you think I should have stopped her because phones have extensions and someone might have been on one, you are correct. I tried to. I finally managed without hanging up on her.

By then Fred was there, having been admitted by Fritz. I gave
him his check, and Wolfe gave him his instructions, which he took
without a blink. The difference in the way he takes Wolfe and
the way he takes me is not based on experience. Up in the bower,
getting it only from me, he had suspected that I was perching
him far out on a limb and he didn't like it. Now, with Wolfe,
there was no question of suspecting or not liking. He had got
the idea somehow, long ago, that there was absolutely no limit
to what Wolfe could do if he wanted to, so of course there was
no risk involved. I would like to be present to see his face if
and when Wolfe tells him to go to Moscow and tail Khrushchev.
When the doorbell rang he got up and moved to a chair over by
the bookshelves as I crossed to the hall.

And got a surprise. It was Julia McGee on the stoop, but she
wasn't alone. I stepped back in the office and told Wolfe Aiken
was with her. He scowled at me, pursed his lips, and nodded,
and I went and opened the door and they entered. For a president Aiken was polite. She was only the ex-secretary of his ex-
executive vice-president, but he let her precede him in, down the
hall, and into the office. Wolfe stood until they were seated, him
in the red leather chair and her in the one Fred had vacated.

Aiken spoke. "You sent for Miss McGee. If there has been a
development, you should have notified me. I have had no word
from you. If you have something to say to Miss McGee, I want
to hear it."

Wolfe was regarding him. "I told you Tuesday night, Mr. Aiken,
that it may be that the less you know of the particulars of my
performance the better. But it can't hurt for you to know about
this; I would almost certainly have informed you of it before the
day was out. Indeed, it is just as well to have you present." His
head turned. "Fred?"

Fred got up and came to the corner of Wolfe's desk. "Look
at Miss McGee," Wolfe told him. Fred turned for a glance at
her and turned back.

"I don't need to," he said.

"You recognize her?"

"Sure. I ought to; she gave me this." He pointed to his cheek.

"That was Tuesday evening. Had you seen her before that?"

"Yes, sir. I saw her Sunday evening when I was covering that house on Eighty-second Street. I saw her enter the house. At the basement door."

"Did you see her leave?"

"No, sir. She could have left while I was at the corner, phoning in. I phoned in every hour, as instructed. Or after I left for the night."

"Did you tell Archie, Tuesday evening, that you had seen her before?"

"No, sir. She came at me the second she saw me Tuesday evening, and it was a tangle. After Archie took her away I got to thinking. It was her I saw Sunday. I should have told you, but I knew what it would mean. It would make me a witness in a murder case, and you know how that is. But this morning I decided I'd have to. You were paying me and you were counting on me. So I came and told you."

"How sure are you that you saw Miss McGee, the woman sitting there, enter that house Sunday evening?"

"I'm dead sure. I wouldn't have come and told you if I wasn't. I know what I'm in for now."

"You deserve it. You had vital information, obtained while you were on an assignment from me, and you withheld it for thirty-six hours. I'll deal with that later. Go to the front room and stay there."

As Fred crossed to the door to the front room no eyes but Wolfe's followed him. Aiken's and mine were on Julia McGee. Hers were on a spot in the pattern of the rug, in front of her feet.

When the door had closed behind Fred, Wolfe spoke. "Miss McGee. Why did you kill him?"

"Don't answer," Aiken commanded her. He turned to Wolfe. "You're working for me. As you put it yourself, you are to make every effort to protect the reputation and interests of the corporation. What's that man's name?"

"Fred Durkin."

"Why did you have him watching that house Sunday evening?"

"On behalf of a client. In confidence."

"You have too many clients. You didn't mention it Tuesday evening. You said you had no engagement."

"We were discussing the murder of Yeager, and I had no engagement to investigate that. I'm humoring you, Mr. Aiken. My other engagements are no concern of yours if there is no conflict of interest. Why did you kill Yeager, Miss McGee?"

Aiken jerked his head to tell her not to answer, and jerked it back to Wolfe. "That's just a trick. Granting that Durkin saw her enter that house Sunday evening, that doesn't prove she killed Yeager. He may not have been there. Did Durkin see *him* enter?"

"No. But someone else did. Mr. and Mrs. Cesar Perez. The janitor and his wife. I would advise you not to approach them. They are bereaved. Their daughter died last night. Since you don't want Yeager's connection with that house disclosed, you had better leave them to Mr. Goodwin and me."

"What time did Yeager enter? Before Miss McGee or after?"

"Before. He arrived around seven o'clock. I am humoring you, sir."

"I don't appreciate it. Granting that Durkin saw Miss McGee enter, he didn't see her leave. Are you accusing her of killing Yeager there in that house and carrying his body out to the street and dumping it in that hole?"

"No. I'm not accusing her; I am confronting her with a fact." Wolfe cocked his head. "Mr. Aiken. I'm not turning our association into a conflict instead of a concert; you are. I told you Tuesday evening that the only feasible way to try to protect the reputation and interests of your corporation with any hope of success would be to stop the police investigation of the murder by reaching an acceptable solution of it without involving that room. I dare contrive such a solution and offer it only if I know what actually happened. It is established that Yeager entered that room around seven o'clock that evening, and it is a reasonable assumption that he was still there when Miss McGee arrived. You say my asking her why she killed him was a trick; certainly it was, and an ancient one; the Greeks used it two thousand years ago, and others long before. I'll withdraw that question and try another."

He turned. "Miss McGee. Was Mr. Yeager in that room when you entered it Sunday evening?"

She had finished studying the pattern of the rug some time back. Now her eyes left Wolfe to go to Aiken, and his met them. She said nothing, but he did. "All right, answer it."

She looked at Wolfe, straight. "Yes, he was there. His body was. He was dead."

"Where was the body?"

"On the floor. On the carpet."

"Did you touch it? Move it?"

"I only touched his hair, where the hole was. He was on his side with his mouth open."

"What did you do?"

"I didn't do anything. I sat on a chair a few minutes and then left."

"Exactly what time did you leave?"

"I don't know exactly. It must have been about half past nine. It was a quarter past when I got there."

"Yeager expected you at a quarter past nine?"

"No, at nine o'clock, but I was fifteen minutes late."

"You went to take dictation?"

"Yes."

"At nine o'clock Sunday evening?"

"Yes."

Wolfe grunted. "I think I'll ignore that, Miss McGee. It's a waste of time to challenge lies that are immaterial. It would be pointless to poke the fact at you that Mr. Yeager had arranged for the delivery of caviar and pheasant at midnight. Was there any indication that there had been a struggle?"

"No."

"Did you see a gun?"

"No."

"Did you take anything from the room when you left?"

"No."

"Have you ever owned a gun?"

"No."

"Or borrowed one?"

"No."

"Have you ever shot one?"

"No."

"Where did you go when you left the house?"

"I went home. My apartment. On Arbor Street."

"Did you tell anyone of your experience?"

"No. Of course not."

"You didn't tell Mr. Aiken?"

"No."

"Then he didn't know until now that you were there Sunday evening?"

"No. Nobody knew."

"Do you know what a hypothetical question is?"

"Certainly."

"I submit one. You said Tuesday evening that you decided your loyalty should be to the corporation, not to Mr. Yeager, so you betrayed him. Then if—"

"I didn't betray him. I only thought Mr. Aiken should know."

Wolfe swiveled to the Webster's Unabridged on its stand, opened it, and found the page. "Betray, verb, Definition Two: 'To prove faithless or treacherous to, as to a trust or one who trusts.'" He closed the dictionary and wheeled back. "Surely Yeager trusted you not to tell about that room, but you did. Then if—this is the hypothesis—if you went there Sunday evening, not to take dictation, but to participate in activities congenial to that décor, what am I to assume regarding your disposition at that time toward Mr. Yeager and Mr. Aiken? Had you reconsidered and decided your loyalty was to Mr. Yeager?"

It didn't faze her. She didn't chew on it. "My disposition had nothing to do with it. Mr. Yeager asked me to go there to take dictation, and I went." She was darned good. If I hadn't seen that bower I might have had a sliver of doubt myself. She went on. "That trick question you asked me, why I killed him, I want to ask you, why *would* I kill him? Would I go there to take dictation and take a gun to shoot him?"

Wolfe's shoulders went up a fraction of an inch, and down. "I said I'd ignore your purpose in going there, and I shouldn't have brought it up again. It's futile. If you had a reason for killing him, I won't learn it from you. I doubt if I'll learn anything from you. You say you went there, found him dead, and left." He leaned back, closed his eyes, and pushed his lips out. In a moment he pulled them in. Out again, in again. Out and in, out and in.

Aiken spoke. "I have things to ask Miss McGee myself, but they can wait. You have only made it worse, bringing it out that he was killed in that room. I don't think she killed him, and I don't think you do. What are you going to do now?"

No reply. Wolfe was still working his lips. "He didn't hear you," I told Aiken. "When he's doing that he doesn't hear anything or anybody. We're not here."

Aiken stared at him. He transferred the stare to Miss McGee. She didn't meet it.

Wolfe opened his eyes and straightened up. "Miss McGee. Give me the keys. To the door of that house and the elevator."

"Did you hear what I said?" Aiken demanded.

"No. The keys, Miss McGee."

"I said you've made it worse!" Aiken hit the chair arm with a fist. "Yeager dead in that room! She didn't kill him, she had no reason to, but what if she did? Do you call this protecting the interests of my corporation?"

Wolfe ignored him. "The keys, Miss McGee. You have no further use for them, and you're hardly in a position to balk. You have them?"

She opened her bag, the one I had opened Tuesday evening while she was on the floor wrapped in the coverlet, and took out the key fold. I went and got it, looked at the two keys, and handed it to Wolfe. He put it in a drawer, turned to Aiken, and inquired, "How the deuce did you get to head a large and successful corporation?"

The president goggled at him, speechless. Wolfe went on. "You spout and sputter. You say *I* have made it worse. In your business, do you blame subordinates when they expose problems not of their making which must be solved if the business is to prosper? If I hadn't resorted to humbug we wouldn't know that Yeager was killed in that room, whether by Miss McGee or another, and I might have blundered fatally. I pried it out of her by a ruse. I had cause to suspect she was there Sunday evening, but nothing that could be used as a lever on her, so I fabricated one. I had no client Sunday evening; Mr. Durkin was not posted at that house; he wasn't there to see her enter. But now that I know she did enter, and that Yeager was killed there—"

"You tricky bastard!" Aiken was on his feet. "Where's that paper I signed? I want it!"

"Nonsense." Wolfe didn't bother to tilt his head to look up at him. Conservation of energy. "Sit down. You hired me, but you can't fire me. I was already on slippery ground, withholding information; now that I know Yeager was killed in that room and his body was seen there I am not merely vulnerable, I am gravely compromised. You are in no personal jeopardy, but I am. If I had my share of prudence I would be at my telephone now, speaking to Mr. Cramer of the police. What are *you* risking? The repute of your confounded corporation. Pfui. Sit down and tell me where you were last evening from nine o'clock to midnight."

Aiken stood, glaring. His jaw was working, and a cord at the side of his neck was twitching. "It's none of your damned business where I was last evening," he said through his teeth. "I warn you, Wolfe, you're playing a dangerous game. You lie when you say Durkin wasn't at that house Sunday. How else did you know Miss McGee was there? You never have told me how you found out about that room. And you had keys. Did Durkin go up after Miss McGee left and find Yeager's body and take it out and dump it in that hole? I think he did. And now you're blackmailing me and my corporation, that's what it amounts to. All right, you had the handle Tuesday evening and you still have it, but I warn you."

"Thank you," Wolfe said politely. His head turned. "Miss McGee, where were you last evening from nine o'clock to midnight?"

"Don't answer him," Aiken commanded her. "Don't answer anything. We're going. You can answer me, but not here. Come on."

She looked at him, at Wolfe, and back at him. "But Mr. Aiken, I have to! I have to answer *that*. I told you, I thought that was what he wanted to see me about—that girl, Maria Perez." She didn't pronounce either "Maria" or "Perez" the way they did. "That's why he wants to know where I was last evening." She turned to Wolfe. "I never saw that girl. I never heard of her until I read the paper today. I didn't kill Mr. Yeager and I didn't kill her. I don't know anything about her. Last evening I had dinner with friends and I was there all evening, with them and other people, until after midnight. Their name is Quinn and they live at Ninety-eight West Eleventh Street. I had to tell him that, Mr. Aiken. It's bad enough for me without—I *had* to."

He was focused on Wolfe. "What about the girl?" he demanded. Wolfe shook his head. "Since I lie, why bother to ask?"

That was the note it ended on. Plenty of times clients have left that office boiling or sore or sulky, but I have never seen one quite as peevish as Aiken. Not, I must admit, without reason. As he said, Wolfe had the handle, and a president is used to having the handle himself. Leaving with Julia McGee, he forgot his manners, leading the way out of the office and down the hall to the door, and when I reached to get his homburg from the rack he snatched it from my hand. Miss McGee was in for a bad half-hour. I returned to the office and told Wolfe, "It's a good thing presidents don't sign corporation checks. He'd get palsy signing one made out to you. *If.*"

He grunted. "If indeed. You realize that we have never been so close to catastrophe. And ignominy."

"Yes, sir."

"It is imperative that we find the murderer before Mr. Cramer finds that room."

"Yes, sir."

"Will Mr. and Mrs. Perez hold out?"

"Yes, sir."

"Tell Fritz to set a place at lunch for Fred. Then get Saul and Orrie. Here at two-thirty. If they have other commitments I'll speak to them. I must have them this afternoon."

"Yes, sir." I moved.

"Wait. That woman, Meg Duncan—presumably she was at the theater last evening?"

"Presumably. I can find out."

"Until when?"

"The play ends about ten to eleven; then she had to change. If she had made a date with Maria Perez for eleven-thirty she could have kept it without rushing. Have I missed something?"

"No. We must cover contingencies. Instructions after you get Saul and Orrie."

I went to the kitchen to tell Fritz.

CHAPTER 13

MAY I INTRODUCE Mr. Saul Panzer and Mr. Orrie Cather? Mr. Panzer is the one in the red leather chair. Looking at him—his big nose, his little deep-set eyes, his hair that won't stay in place —you will suppose that he isn't much. Hundreds of people who have supposed that have regretted it. A good operative has to be good in a dozen different ways, and in all of them Saul is the best. Mr. Cather, in the yellow chair to Saul's left, might fool you too. He is fully as handsome as he looks, but not quite as smart as he looks, though he might be if his ego didn't get in the way. If a man is to be judged by a single act and you have a choice, the one to pick is how he looks at himself in a mirror, and I have seen Orrie do that. You have met Mr. Fred Durkin, in the chair next to Orrie's.

Wolfe and Fred and I had just come from the dining room to join Saul and Orrie in the office. During lunch I had been wondering what Wolfe had on the program for them, considering the instructions he had given me. With me it had got to the point where earning a fee was only secondary; the main question was how we were going to wriggle down off the limb we were out on; and while I fully appreciated the talents and abilities of those three men, I couldn't guess how they were going to be used to find an answer to that. So I wanted to hear that briefing, but as I went to my chair and whirled it around Wolfe spoke.

"We won't need you, Archie. You have your instructions."

I sat. "Maybe I can supply details."

"No. You had better get started."

I got up and went. There were several pointed remarks I could have made, for instance that I had a right to know what the chances were that I would sleep in my bed that night, but it might not fit his script, granting that he had one, for Saul and Fred and Orrie to know how bad it was. So I went, spry and jaunty until I was in the hall out of sight.

I had a date with an actress, made on the phone, but not for a specified minute—any time between three and four. It was five after three when I entered the lobby of the Balfour on Madison Avenue in the Sixties, gave the hallman my name, and said Miss Meg Duncan was expecting me. He gave me a knowing look and inquired, "How's the fat man?" I said, "Turn around. I'm not much good at faces, but I remember backs." He said, "You wouldn't remember mine. I used to hop at the Churchill. Has Miss Duncan lost something?"

"Questions answered while I wait," I told him. "Mr. Wolfe is just fine, thanks. Miss Duncan can't find her solid gold knuckle-duster and thinks you took it."

He grinned. "It's a treat to meet you. You can pick it up on your way out. Twelfth floor. Twelve D."

I went and entered the elevator and was lifted. Twelve D was at the end of the hall. I pushed the button, and in half a minute the door opened a crack and a voice asked who it was. I pronounced my name, the door swung wide, and a square-jawed female sergeant gave me an unfriendly look. "Miss Duncan has a bad headache," she said in a voice that went with the jaw and the look. "Can't you tell me what—"

"Mike!" A voice from inside somewhere. "Is that Mr. Goodwin?"

"Yes! He says it is!"

"Then send him in here!"

A man is bound to feel a little uneasy if he has an appointment to call on a young woman in the middle of the afternoon and is ushered into a room dimmed by venetian blinds, and she is in bed and clad accordingly, especially if as soon as the door is closed behind you she says, "I haven't got a headache, sit here," and pats the edge of the bed. Even if you are certain that you can keep control of the situation—but that's the trouble; you can't help feeling that keeping control of the situation is not what your fellow men have a right to expect of you, let alone her fellow women.

There was a chair turned to face the bed, and I took it. As I sat she asked if I had brought her cigarette case.

"No," I said, "but it's still there in the safe, and that's something. Mr. Wolfe sent me to ask you a question. Where were you yesterday evening from nine o'clock to midnight?"

If she had been on her feet, or even on a chair, I believe she would have jumped me again, from the way her eyes flashed. It was personal, not professional. "I wish I had clawed your eyes out," she said.

"I know, you said that before. But I didn't come to fire that question at you just to hear you say it again. If you have seen a newspaper you may have noticed that a girl named Maria Perez was murdered last night?"

"Yes."

"And that she lived at One-fifty-six West Eighty-second Street?"

"Yes."

"So where were you?"

"You know where I was. At the theater. Working."

"Until ten minutes to eleven. Then you changed. Then?"

She was smiling. "I don't know why I said that about clawing your eyes out. I mean I do know. Holding me so tight my ribs hurt, and then just a cold fish. Just a—a stone."

"Not a fish *and* a stone. In fact, neither. Just a detective on an errand. I still am. Where did you go when you left the theater?"

"I came home and went to bed. Here." She patted the bed. The way she used her hands had been highly praised by Brooks Atkinson in the *Times*. "I usually go somewhere and eat something, but last night I was too tired."

"Had you ever see Maria Perez? Ever run into her in that basement hall?"

"No."

"I beg your pardon; I doubled up the questions. Had you ever seen her or spoken with her?"

"No."

I nodded. "You would say that, naturally, if you thought you could make it stick. But you may have to eat it. This is how it stands. The police haven't got onto that room yet. They still haven't connected Yeager with that house. Mr. Wolfe hopes they won't, for reasons that don't matter to you. He believes that whoever killed Yeager killed Maria Perez, and so do I. He wants to find the murderer and clear it up in such a way that that house doesn't come into it. If he can do that you'll never have to go on the witness stand and identify your cigarette case. But he can do that only if he gets the facts, and gets them quick."

I left the chair and went and sat on the bed where she had patted it. "For example, you. I don't mean facts like where were you Sunday night. We haven't the time or the men to start checking alibis. I asked you about last night just to start the conversation. Your alibi for last night is no good, but it wouldn't have been even if you had said you went to Sardi's with friends and ate a steak. Friends can lie, and so can waiters."

"I was at a benefit performance at the Majestic Theater Sunday night."

"It would take a lot of proving to satisfy me that you were there without a break if I had a healthy reason to think you killed Yeager —but I'm not saying you didn't. An alibi, good or bad, isn't the kind of fact I want from you. You say you never saw or spoke with Maria Perez. Last night her mother phoned me to come, and I went, and searched her room, and hidden under a false bottom in a drawer I found a collection of items. Among them were three photographs of you. Also there was some money, five-dollar bills, that she hadn't wanted her parents to know about. I'm being frank with you, Miss Duncan; I've told you that Mr. Wolfe would prefer to close it up without the police ever learning about that room and the people who went there. But if they do learn about it, not from us, then look out. Not only that you walked in on Mr. and Mrs. Perez and me, and your cigarette case, but what if they find your fingerprints on those five-dollar bills?"

That was pure dumb luck. I would like to say that I had had a hunch and was playing it, but if I once started dolling up these reports there's no telling where I'd stop. I was merely letting my tongue go. If there was anything more in Meg Duncan than the fact (according to her) that she had gone straight home from the theater last night, I wanted to talk it out of her if possible. It was just luck that I didn't mention that the photographs were magazine and newspaper reproductions and that I tossed in the question about the bills.

Luck or not, it hit. She gripped my knee with one of the hands she used so well and said, "My God, the bills. Do they show finger-prints?"

"Certainly."

"Where are they?"

"In the safe in Mr. Wolfe's office. Also the photographs."

"I only gave her one. You said three."

"The other two are from magazines. When did you give it to her?"

"I—I don't remember. There are so many . . ."

My left hand moved to rest on the coverlet where her leg was, above her knee, the fingers bending, naturally, to the curve of the surface they were touching. Of course it would have been a mistake if I had given the hand a definite order to do that, but I hadn't. I'm not blaming the hand; it was merely taking advantage of an opportunity that no alert hand could be expected to ignore; but it got a quicker and bigger reaction than it had counted on. When that woman had an impulse she wasted no time. As she came up from the pillow I met her, I guess on the theory that she was going to claw, but her arms clamped around my neck and she took me back with her, and there I was, on top of her from the waist up, my face into the pillow. She was biting the side of my neck, not to hurt, just cordial.

The time, the place, and the girl is a splendid combination, but it takes all three. The place was okay, but the time wasn't, since I had other errands, and I doubted if the girl's motives were pure. She was more interested in a cigarette case, a photograph, and some five-dollar bills than in me. Also I don't like to be bullied. So I brought my hand up, slipped it between her face and my neck, shoved her head into the pillow while raising mine, folded the ends of the pillow over, and had her smothered. She squirmed and kicked for ten seconds and then stopped. I got my feet on the floor and my weight on them, removed my hands from the pillow, and stepped back. I spoke.

"When did you give her the photograph?"

She was panting, gasping, to catch up on oxygen. When she could she said, "Damn you, you put your hand on me."

"Yeah. Do you expect me to apologize? Patting a place on the bed for me to sit and you in that gauzy thing? You know darned well your nipples show through it. That wasn't very smart, trying to take my mind off of my work when you've got as much at stake as I have." I sat on the chair. "Look, Miss Duncan. The only way you can possibly get clear is by helping Nero Wolfe wrap it up, and we haven't got all summer. We may not even have all day. I want to know about the photograph and the five-dollar bills."

She had got her breath back and pulled the coverlet up to her chin. "You did put your hand on me," she said.

"Conditioned reflex. The wonder is it wasn't both hands. When did you give her the photograph?"

"A long time ago. Nearly a year ago. She sent a note to my dressing room at a Saturday matinee. The note said she had seen me at her house and she would like to have three tickets for next Saturday so she could bring two friends. At the bottom below her name was her address. That address . . . I had her sent in. She was incredible. I have never seen a girl as beautiful. I thought she was—that she had been . . ."

I nodded. "A guest in that room. I don't think so."

"Neither did I after I talked with her. She said she had seen me in the hall—twice, she said—and she had recognized me from pictures she had seen. She said she had never told anyone, and she wouldn't, and I gave her an autographed picture and the three tickets. That was in June, and in July we closed for a month for summer vacation, and in August she came to see me again. She was even more beautiful, she was incredible. She wanted three more tickets, and I said I'd mail them to her, and then she said she had decided she ought to have hush money. That's what she said, hush money. Five dollars a month. I was to mail it to her the first of each month, to a branch post office on Eighty-third Street, the Planetarium Station. Have you ever seen her?"

"Yes."

"Then aren't you surprised?"

"No. I quit being surprised after two years of detective work, long ago."

"I was. A girl as beautiful and proud as she was—my God, she was proud. And of course I—well, I supposed that would be only a start. Ever since then I have been expecting her to come again, to tell me she had decided five dollars a month wasn't enough, but she never did."

"You never saw her again?"

"No, but she saw me. She had told me what she did; when she heard the street door open she put out the light in her room and opened the door a crack, and after that when I went there I saw it when I went down the hall, her door open a little. It gave me a feeling—I don't know why—it made it more *exciting* that she was there looking at me." She patted the bed. "Sit here."

I stood up. "No, ma'am. It's even more of a strain when you have the cover up like that, because I know what's under it. I have chores to do. How many five-dollar bills did you send her?"

"I didn't count. It was in August, so the first one was September first, and then every month." The coverlet slipped down.

"Including May? Twelve days ago?"

"Yes."

"That makes nine. They're in Mr. Wolfe's safe. I told Mrs. Perez she'd get them back some day, but since they were hush money you have a valid claim." I took a step, stretched an arm, curved my fingers around her leg, and gave it a gentle squeeze. "See? Conditioned reflex. I'd better go." I turned and walked out. Mike, the female sergeant, appeared from somewhere as I reached the foyer, but let me open the door myself. Down in the lobby I took a moment to tell the hallman, "You can relax. We found them in her jewel box. The maid thought they were earrings." It pays to be on sociable terms with lobby sentries. As I emerged to the sidewalk my watch said 3:40, so Wolfe would be in the office, and I found a phone booth down the block and dialed.

His voice came. "Yes?" He will not answer the phone properly.

"Me. In a booth on Madison Avenue. Money paid to a blackmailer is recoverable, so those bills belong to Meg Duncan. Maria Perez spotted her in the hall a year ago and went to see her and bled her for nine months, five bucks per month. One of the biggest operations in the history of crime. Meg Duncan worked last night and went straight home from the theater and went to bed. I saw the bed and sat on it. Probably true, say twenty to one. From here it's only about eight minutes to the Yeager house. Shall I go there first?"

"No. Mrs. Yeager phoned, and I told her you would be there between five and six. She expects you to take her to see that room. Your problem."

"Don't I know it. You said when I called in you might want to send me to Saul or Fred or Orrie."

"I thought it possible, but no. Proceed."

As I went out to the curb to flag a taxi I was reflecting on Maria's practical horse sense and fine feeling. If you happen to have an autographed photograph of a person whom you are screwing for hush money, you don't keep it. The autographer had of course written something like "Best regards" or "All good wishes," and now that she was your victim it wouldn't be right to hang on to it.

CHAPTER 14

I HAD NO APPOINTMENT with Mr. or Mrs. Austin Hough, because, first, I hadn't known when I would finish with Meg Duncan, and second, I preferred to have one of them alone, it didn't matter which. So when I pushed the button in the vestibule at 64 Eden Street I didn't know if there would be anyone at home. There was. The click came; I opened the door and entered, and mounted the stairs. I wasn't awaited at the door of the apartment as before; he was standing at the top of the second flight. As I reached the landing he backed up a step. He wasn't glad to see me.

"Back again," I said politely. "Did you find your wife yesterday?"

"What do you want?" he demanded.

"Nothing startling. A couple of questions. There has been a development that complicates it a little. You probably know about it, the murder of a girl named Maria Perez."

"No. I haven't been out today. I haven't seen a paper. Who is Maria Perez?"

"Not is, was. Then the radio?"

"I haven't turned it on. Who was she?"

"The daughter of the man you saw when you went to that house on Eighty-second Street. Her body was found last night on a North River pier. She was killed, shot, between nine o'clock and midnight. Mr. Wolfe is wondering how you spent the evening. And your wife."

"Balls," he said.

My brows went up in astonishment. He certainly hadn't got that from Robert Browning, though an Elizabethan dramatist might have used it that way. I wasn't up on Elizabethan dramatists. Wherever he had got it, this was a different Austin Hough from the one I had felt sorry for yesterday afternoon—not only that word so used, but his face and bearing. This Hough wasn't asking any favors.

"So," he said, "you want to know how my wife spent last evening? You'd better ask her. Come on." He turned and headed down the hall, and I followed. The door was open. There was no foyer inside. The room, not large, had the furniture of a living room, but the walls were all books. He crossed to a door at the far end, opened it, and motioned me in. Two steps from the sill I stopped dead.

He had killed her. Granting that you shouldn't jump to conclusions, you often do, and for the second time that afternoon I saw a young woman in bed, only this one was completely covered, including her head. Not by a coverlet; a plain white sheet followed her contours, and as we entered there was no sign of movement. A corpse. I stood and stared, but Hough, passing me, spoke.

"It's Archie Goodwin, Dinah. A girl was murdered last night." He turned to me. "What was her name?"

"Maria Perez."

He turned back. "Maria Perez. She lived in that house. Goodwin wants to know what you were doing last evening between nine o'clock and midnight, and I thought you had better tell him. He saw you there in that house yesterday, so I thought he might as well see you now."

Her voice came from beneath the sheet, a mumble that I wouldn't have recognized. "No, Austin, I won't."

"But you will. Don't start it again." He was only a step from the bed. He took it, reached for the top of the sheet, and pulled it back.

I have seen better-looking corpses. The right side of her face was far from normal, but it was nothing compared to the left side. The eye was swollen shut, and the swollen cheek and jaw were the color of freshly sliced calves' liver. Her best curves, of her wide, full mouth, were puffy folds of purple. She was on her back. Her garment had just straps, no sleeves, and from the appearance of her shoulders and upper arms she couldn't have been on her side. I couldn't tell where her one eye was aimed.

Hough, one hand holding the sheet, turned to me. "I told you yesterday," he said, "that I wanted her to know I knew, but I couldn't tell her. I was afraid of what would happen if I told her. Now it has happened." He turned to her. "He wants to know where you were between nine o'clock and midnight. Tell him and he'll go."

"I was here." It was a mumble, but I got it. "Where I am now. By nine o'clock I was like this."

"Your husband left you here like this?"

"He didn't leave me. He was here with me."

"Balls," Hough said, to me. "I came here when I left you and Wolfe, and she was here, and I haven't been out of here since. Now you have seen her, and she has told you, and you can go."

"She's your wife, not mine," I said, "but has a doctor seen her?"

"No. I was filling the ice bags when you rang the bell."

I made my eyes go to her. "Shall I send a doctor, Mrs. Hough?"

"No," she said.

"Send her a bottle of champagne," he said.

And I did. That is, I sent champagne, but not to her, on impulse. When I went to Seventh Avenue to get a taxi, after I had phoned Wolfe to report on the Houghs and tell him I was on my way to Mrs. Yeager, I saw a liquor store and went in and asked if he happened to have a bottle of Dom Perignon, and he did. I told him to send it to Mr. Austin Hough, 64 Eden Street, and enclose a card on which I wrote "With the compliments of Archie Goodwin." Preferring to make it a personal matter, I didn't put it on expense. I have often wondered whether he dumped it in the garbage, or drank it himself, or shared it with her.

When I left the taxi in front of 340 East 68th Street, at two minutes past five, I stood for a glance around before going to the entrance. Here was where it had started three days ago. There was where the NYPD car had been double-parked with Purley Stebbins' driver in it. Around the corner was the lunchroom where I had phoned Lon Cohen. As I entered the vestibule to push the button I asked myself, if I had known what was ahead would I have given Mike Collins the extra forty bucks? But I didn't answer because I didn't know what was still ahead.

I didn't know how Wolfe felt about it, but I was more interested in where Mrs. Yeager had been last night than in any of the
others. Of course inheriting widows of murdered men always deserve attention, and not only that, she had known that Yeager
was not merely two-timing her, he was twenty-timing her. Her
shrugging it off was noble if true, and a good line if false. Her wanting to see that room was natural if true, and again a good line if
she had seen it before, Sunday night, when she went there to kill
him. Her alibi as published, that she had been in the country and
hadn't returned to town until Monday morning, might already have
been found leaky by the cops. I suspected that it had, since Cramer
had had a tail on her yesterday.

One point in her favor, she wasn't in bed. A uniformed maid
showed me through an arch into a living room that would have
held six of the Houghs', and in a couple of minutes our Client
Number Four appeared. I stood. She stopped just inside the arch
and said, "So you're on time. Come on." She had a hat on, and
a fur stole, not the mink.

"Are we going somewhere?" I asked, approaching.

"Certainly. You're going to show me that room. The car's
waiting."

"I'm afraid this isn't a good time, Mrs. Yeager. After what has
happened. Sit down and I'll tell you why."

"You can tell me in the car. You said yesterday you'd take me
as soon as you got a chance."

"I know. I tried to get you on the phone at ten o'clock last evening but couldn't. You weren't at home?"

"Certainly I was. My son and daughter were here, and some
friends." She moved. "Come on."

"Damn the torpedoes!" I told her back.

She whirled. For a lump she whirled well. "What did you say?"

"I said damn the torpedoes. That may be your attitude, but it's
not Mr. Wolfe's or mine. I came to tell you why we can't go there
now. Since the janitor of that house had a daughter, and last
night—"

"I know about that. I told you on the phone. She was
murdered."

"Right. And it seems likely that she was murdered by the person who murdered your husband. Incidentally, you may remember that Mr. Wolfe suggested the possibility that you killed your husband, so he thinks it's also possible that you killed Maria Perez. That's why I asked if you were at home last evening. Were you here with your son and daughter and friends all evening? Up to midnight?"

"Yes. I said yesterday, it was years ago that I felt like killing him. You're not complete fools, are you?"

"Not complete, no. All right, you didn't kill him. Or her. Some day I'll be glad to take you to see that room, but not now. It's too risky. A girl who lived there has been murdered, and at any time, day or night, a policeman or assistant district attorney may be there to ask questions of her parents or some of the tenants. There may be a man on the outside to keep an eye on the house. If either you or I was seen entering or inside that house, let alone both of us, good-by. Good-by not only to the job Aiken hired Wolfe for, but also to the one you hired him for. Another thing, you are probably still being followed around."

"They wouldn't dare."

"Wouldn't they, though. They did, didn't they? We'll have to postpone it. The room will keep."

"Are you going to take me there or not?"

"Not now. Not today."

"I thought so. There is no such room."

"Oh yes there is. I've seen it. Several times."

"I don't believe it." Her sharp little eyes were slanted up to mine. "Benedict Aiken invented it, or Nero Wolfe did, or you did. You've been making a fool of me. I suspected it yesterday, and now I know it. Get out of my house. I'm going to call the District Attorney."

I was observing an interesting fact, that two chins can look fully as determined as one. I couldn't possibly talk her out of it, and there was no use trying. I made one stab at it.

"You're looking at me, Mrs. Yeager. Our eyes are meeting. Do I look like a liar?"

"Yes."

"Okay, then you'll have to be shown. You say your car's waiting. With a chauffeur?"

"Certainly."

"Nothing doing. If this house is covered he wouldn't even have to follow to find out where we went unless the chauffeur is a hero. We'll leave together, that doesn't matter, and walk to Second Avenue. You'll wait at the corner, and when I come in a taxi you'll get in. I'll show you whether there's such a room or not."

The sharp little eyes were suspicious. "Is this another trick?"

"Why ask me, since I'm a liar? Sure, I'm kidnaping you. In my circle we call it a snatch."

It took her four seconds to decide. "All right, come on," she said, and moved.

Out on the sidewalk she stopped to speak to the chauffeur standing beside a black Lincoln, and then went with me to the corner. From there on I took the standard routine precautions, going uptown a block to get a taxi, and picking her up at the corner. I had the hackie do turns until I was sure we were unaccompanied and then drop us on Madison Avenue in the Seventies. When he was out of sight I flagged another taxi, told the driver 82nd and Amsterdam, and when we got there told him to crawl the block to Columbus. At Columbus, having seen no sign of a city employee, I told him to take 81st Street back to Amsterdam and stop at the corner. There I paid him off and took Mrs. Yeager into a drugstore and, since she suspected tricks, I had her come along to the phone booth and stand at my elbow while I dialed a number and talked. What she heard:

"Mrs. Perez? This is Archie Goodwin. I'm in a drugstore around the corner. I hope we're still friends? . . . Good. Has a policeman been there? . . . You didn't? Good. . . . No, that's all right, taking you downtown and having you sign a statement was normal, they always do. Is anyone there now? . . . Okay. I'm coming there with a woman, we'll be there in two minutes, and I'm taking her up in the elevator. We won't be there long. I may phone you this evening, or I may drop in. . . . No, but I hope there soon will be. . . . Absolutely. I'm your detective."

As I hung up Mrs. Yeager demanded, "Who was that?"

"The mother of the girl who was murdered last night. Since you didn't kill her there's no conflict of interest. Let's go."

We walked the block to 82nd, around the corner, on to Number 156, and in at the basement door. There was no one in the hall, and the door of Maria's room was shut. At the elevator I used the second key and we entered.

Not being a psychologist or a sociologist, I wouldn't know how a middle-aged widow with a double chin is supposed to react on entering a bower that her husband had used for extramarital activities, but whatever the pattern is I'll give any odds you name that Mrs. Thomas G. Yeager didn't follow it. When I switched on the lights she took a couple of steps, stopped, moved her head slowly around to the right, moved it back more slowly and to the left, and turned to face me.

"I apologize," she said.

"Accepted," I said. "Forget it."

She took a few more steps, stopped for another look around, and turned again. "No bathroom?"

I believed it only because I heard it. You haven't that privilege. "Sure," I said, "at the far end. The kitchen's at this end." I pointed. "That gold push plate is on the door." I swung my arm around. "There where the silk is tucked it's a curtain. Drawers behind it."

That ended the conversation, though her inspection took more than half an hour. First she took in the pictures, not collectively, one by one, moving along, tilting her head back for the high ones. No comment. When she slid the curtain aside and began opening drawers I went to a chair and sat. She took nothing out of the drawers and didn't poke in them. She stooped over for a close look at the carpet. She examined the upholstery on the chairs and couches. She twisted her neck up and around to survey the indirect-lighting installation. She pulled the top of the bed coverlet down to see the linen and put it neatly back again. She was in the kitchen a good five minutes, and in the bathroom longer. She did the bathroom last, and when she came out she got her stole from the couch where she had put it, and spoke.

"Do you believe that Julia McGee came here to take dictation?"

"No." I rose. "Do you?"

"Certainly not. Why do you think the person who killed my husband killed that girl?"

"It's complicated. But it's not just a guess."

"Where's her mother? I want to speak to her."

"Better not, right now." I was moving toward the elevator, and she was coming. "It hit her pretty hard. Some other day." I pushed the button, the elevator door opened, and we entered.

Just to get it straight for my own satisfaction, I have tried to figure exactly where we were when the doorbell rang in the basement. We must have been either entering the elevator or on our way down. Anyhow, I didn't hear it, so we emerged below and started up the hall. When we were about halfway to the front Mrs. Perez came out of a door ahead on the right, the one she and Maria had come out of when her husband called her my first time there, went to the street door, and opened it. As I say, I hadn't heard the doorbell, so I supposed she was going out. But she wasn't. Mrs. Yeager and I were right there when Sergeant Purley Stebbins said, "Sorry to bother you again, Mrs. Perez, but—" saw us, and stopped.

A mind can do crazy things. Mine, instead of instantly tackling the situation, took a tenth of a second to tell me how lucky I was that Stebbins hadn't been already inside and with Mrs. Perez in the hall when we stepped out of the elevator. That helped a lot, to know I was lucky.

"You?" Stebbins said. He crossed the sill. "And you, Mrs. Yeager?"

"We were just leaving," I said. "Having had a talk with Mrs. Perez."

"What about?"

"About her daughter. I suppose you know that Mrs. Yeager has hired Mr. Wolfe to find out who killed her husband. She told Cramer yesterday. She has some detective instincts herself. When she read in the paper today that a girl named Maria Perez had been murdered, shot in the head, and she had lived in this street, in the block where Yeager's body had been found, and her body had been taken somewhere and dumped just as Yeager's had been, she got the idea that there was some connection between the two murders. Mr. Wolfe thought it was possible, and so did I. Mrs. Yeager's idea was that Maria Perez might have seen the murderer dumping Yeager's body in the hole, maybe from the sidewalk as she was coming home, or maybe even from inside, from a window. Of course there were difficulties, but Mr. Wolfe thought it wouldn't hurt for me to have a talk with Maria's mother or father, and Mrs. Yeager wanted to come along. It would be a coincidence if you came with the same idea just as we were leaving. Wouldn't it?"

As I was reeling it off I knew how bad it was. First, because it was full of holes, and second, because it wasn't me. When Stebbins barked at me a question like "What about?" my natural answer would be "The weather" or something similar, and he knew it. It was against all precedent for me to oblige with a long, detailed explanation, but I had to, for Mrs. Yeager and Mrs. Perez. It was probably up the flue anyway, but there was a chance that they would catch on and help me save the pieces.

Actually it wasn't as bad as I thought. I knew so much about that house and that room that I didn't sufficiently consider that Stebbins knew nothing whatever about it, that Homicide and the DA had been assuming for three days that Yeager had been killed elsewhere and brought and dumped in that hole because it was convenient, and they had absolutely no reason to connect him with that house. And Mrs. Yeager came through like an angel. She couldn't have done better if I had spent an hour priming her. She offered a hand to Mrs. Perez and said in exactly the right tone, "Thank you, Mrs. Perez. We have both lost someone dear to us. I have to go, I'm late now. We didn't intend to keep you so long and it was very kind of you. I'll phone you later, Mr. Goodwin, or you call me." The door was standing open, and out she went. I could have kissed her on both chins.

Stebbins was eying me as if he would like to kick me on both butts, but that was only normal. "What did you ask Mrs. Perez and what did she tell you?" he demanded. He was hoarse, but that was normal too. Wolfe and I both have that effect on him, Wolfe more than me.

It was a good question. The way I had sketched it, we had come to ask Mrs. Perez about her daughter's whereabouts and movements Sunday night, and presumably she had told us; and I had no idea where Maria had been Sunday night. An excellent question. So I reverted to type. "What do you suppose I asked her? I wanted to know if it was possible that her daughter had seen someone dumping Yeager's body in that hole and climbing in to put the tarp over him. As for what she said, get the *best* evidence. She's here. Ask her."

"I'm asking you." Stebbins is not a fool.

"And I'm reserving my answer. I don't owe Mrs. Perez anything, but she has a right to decide for herself what she wants to say for the official record. Mrs. Yeager and I were merely people. You're a cop."

And by gum Mrs. Perez came through too. Not as grand a performance as Mrs. Yeager's, but plenty good enough. "What I told him was just the truth," she told Stebbins. "If my daughter saw anything like that Sunday she would tell me, so she didn't."

"Was she home all evening?"

"Yes. Two of her friends came and they watched television."

"What time did the friends come?"

"It was about eight o'clock."

"What time did they leave?"

"Right after eleven o'clock. Right after a program they like every Sunday night."

"Did your daughter go out with them?"

"No."

"Did she leave the house at all that evening?"

"No."

"Are you sure?"

She nodded. "I'm sure. We always knew where she was."

"You didn't know last night. And any time during the night, Sunday night, she could have gone to the front room and looked out through the window. Couldn't she?"

"Why would she? Why would she do that?"

"I don't know, but she could." Stebbins turned. "All right, Goodwin, I'll ride you downtown. You can tell the inspector about it."

"About what? What is there to tell?"

He stuck his chin out. "Look, you. Monday afternoon you began checking on a man that was already dead, two hours before the body was found. When the inspector goes to see Wolfe he finds the widow there, and he gets the usual crap. The widow has hired Wolfe to find out who killed her husband, which may not be against the law but it's against the policy of the New York Police Department. And I come here investigating not that murder but another one, and by God here you are, you *and* the widow, here in the house where that girl lived, talking with her mother. So you're coming downtown or you're under arrest as a material witness."

"Am I under arrest?"

"No. I said *or*."

"It's nice to have a choice." I got a quarter from my pocket, flipped it in the air, caught it, and looked at it. "I win. Let's go."

It suited me fine to get him away from Mrs. Perez and out of that house. As I mounted the three steps to the sidewalk I was thinking how different it would be if he had come thirty seconds sooner or we had left the bower thirty seconds later. As I climbed in the PD car I yawned, thoroughly. Having had less than three hours' sleep, I had been needing a good healthy yawn all day but had been too busy.

SIX HOURS LATER, at one-thirty in the morning, I was sitting in the kitchen, putting away black bread (made by Fritz), smoked sturgeon, Brie cheese, and milk, and reading the early edition of Friday's *Times,* which I had picked up on my way home from the District Attorney's office.

I was about pooped. The day had been fairly active, and the evening, an hour with Cramer and four hours with a couple of assistant DAs, had been really tough. It's a strain to answer a thousand questions put by experts when you know that: a) you have to keep a wall between two sets of facts, the ones they already know and the ones you hope to God they never will know; b) you're making a record that may hook you on a charge you can't possibly dodge; and c) one little slip could spill the soup. Of all the sessions I have had at Homicide West and the DA's office, that was the worst. There had been only two letups, when they called time out for ten minutes for me to eat an inedible ham sandwich and a pint of Grade F milk, and when I announced, around ten o'clock, that they could either let me make a phone call or lock me up for the night.

Anyone who thinks the phone booths in that building are not tapped has a right to his opinion, but so have I. Therefore when I got Wolfe and told him where I was we kept it on a high plane. I reported the encounter with Stebbins and said that as usual Cramer and the DA thought I was withholding information they had a right to, which, as he knew, was absurd. He said that he already knew of the encounter with Stebbins, that Mrs. Yeager had phoned and he had requested her to come to the office, and they had discussed the matter. He asked if it would be advisable for Fritz to keep the casseroled kidneys warm, and I said no, I was on a diet.

They finally turned me loose at a quarter to one, and when I got home the house was dark and there was no note on my desk.

When I had taken on a satisfactory amount of the bread and sturgeon and cheese, and learned from the *Times* that the District Attorney hoped he would soon be able to report progress in the Yeager murder investigation, I dragged myself up the two flights to my room. I had promised my dentist years ago that I would brush my teeth every night, but that night I skipped it.

Since I had done all my errands and there had been no note on my desk, and I was behind on sleep, I didn't turn the radio alarm on, and when I pried my eyes open enough to see the clock it said 9:38. Wolfe would have finished breakfast and gone up to the orchids. I thought another ten minutes wouldn't hurt, but I hate to dash around in the morning fog, so I turned on my will power and rolled out. At 10:17 I entered the kitchen, told Fritz good morning, and got my orange juice. At 10:56 I finished my second cup of coffee, thanked Fritz for the bacon and apricot omelet, went to the office, and started opening the mail. The sound came of the elevator and Wolfe entered, said good morning, went to his desk, and asked if there was any word from Hewitt about the Lycaste delicatissima. True to form. Granting that he knew they hadn't tossed me in the can as a material witness, since I was there, and that I had nothing urgent to report, since I wouldn't have waited until eleven o'clock, he might at least have asked how long they had kept me. Slitting envelopes, I said there was nothing from Hewitt.

"How long did they keep you?" he asked.

"Only three hours more after I phoned. I got home a little after one."

"It must have been rather difficult."

"There were spots. I refused to sign a statement."

"That was wise. Satisfactory. Mrs. Yeager told me of your impromptu explanation to Mr. Stebbins. She was impressed. Satisfactory."

Two satisfactories in one speech was a record. "Oh," I said, "just my usual discretion and sagacity. It was either that or shoot him." I took the mail to him. "Anything on the program?"

"No. We are suspended." He pushed the buzzer button, one long and one short, for beer, and got at the mail. In a moment Fritz came with a bottle and a glass. I sat and yawned, and got my notebook out. There would be letters. The phone rang. It was Lon Cohen, wanting to know if I had spent a pleasant evening at the DA's office and how had I got bail in the middle of the night. I told him bail wasn't permitted on a murder one charge; I had jumped out a window and was now a fugitive. When I hung up Wolfe was ready to dictate, but as I picked up my notebook and swiveled, the phone rang again. It was Saul Panzer. He wanted Wolfe. Wolfe didn't give me the off signal, so I stayed on.

"Good morning, Saul."

"Good morning, sir. I've got it. Tight."

"Indeed?"

"Yes, sir. A little place on Seventy-seventh Street near First Avenue. Three-sixty-two East Seventy-seventh Street. His name is Arthur Wenger." Saul spelled it. "He picked him from the photograph and he's positive. He's not sure of the day, but it was last week, either Tuesday or Wednesday, in the morning. I'm in a booth around the corner."

"Satisfactory. I want him here as soon as possible."

"He won't want to come. He's alone in the place. Ten dollars would probably do it, but you know how that is. He'll be asked if he was paid."

"He won't be asked—or if he is, I'll be foundered anyway. Ten dollars, twenty, fifty, no matter. When will you have him here?"

"Half an hour."

"Satisfactory. I'll expect you."

We hung up. Wolfe glanced up at the clock and said, "Get Mr. Aiken."

I dialed Continental Plastic Products. Mr. Aiken was in conference and couldn't be disturbed. I got that not only from a female who was polite, but also from a male who thought *he* shouldn't have been disturbed. The best I could get was that a message would be conveyed to Mr. Aiken within fifteen minutes, and I made the message brief: "Call Nero Wolfe, urgent." In nine minutes the phone rang and the polite female asked me to put Mr.

Wolfe on. I don't like that, even with a president, so I told her to put Mr. Aiken on, and she didn't make an issue of it. In a minute I had him and signed to Wolfe.

"Mr. Aiken? Nero Wolfe. I have a report to make and it's exigent. Not on the telephone. Can you be here with Miss McGee by a quarter past twelve?"

"Not conveniently, no. Can't it wait until after lunch?"

"It shouldn't. Sometimes convenience must bow to necessity. Delay would be hazardous."

"Damn it, I . . ." Pause. "You say with Miss McGee?"

"Yes. Her presence is required."

"I don't know." Pause. "All right. We'll be there."

Wolfe hung up. He cleared his throat. "Your notebook, Archie. Not a letter, a draft of a document. Not for mailing."

CHAPTER 16

ON THE WALL of the office, at the right as you enter, is a picture of a waterfall, not large, 14 by 17. Its center is one inch below my eye level, but I'm just under six feet tall. The picture was made to order. On the wall of the alcove at the end of the hall is a hinged wood panel. Swing it open, and there's the back of the picture, but your eyes go on through and you are looking into the office. At twenty minutes past twelve the eyes that were doing that belonged to Mr. Arthur Wenger of 362 East 77th Street, a skinny guy past fifty with big ears and not much hair, who had been delivered by Saul Panzer in a little less than the specified half-hour. The object in the office nearest him was the red leather chair, and its occupant, Mr. Benedict Aiken.

I wasn't in the alcove with Wenger; Saul was. Wolfe and I were at our desks in the office. Julia McGee was on a yellow chair facing Wolfe's desk. Wolfe was speaking. ". . . but before I submit my conclusion I must tell you how I came to it. When you asked me Tuesday evening who would decide if I have faithfully observed the provision of my employment, I said reason and good faith, applied jointly. You can judge fairly only if you know how I proceeded. Frankly, I am myself not entirely certain. I only know that in the circumstances— Yes, Saul?"

Saul was in the doorway. "It's a perfect fit, Mr. Wolfe."

"Very well. I'll look at it later." Wolfe went back to Aiken. "In the circumstances there was no other course open to me. As I told you, the only way to stop the police investigation of the murder was to reach an acceptable solution of it without involving that room. I have never tackled a task that looked so unpromising. Indeed, knowing as I did that Yeager had been killed in that room, it seemed all but hopeless."

"You didn't know that until you set that trap for Miss McGee yesterday." Aiken was curt.

"No. I knew it much earlier, Tuesday noon, when Mr. Goodwin reported his conversation with Mr. and Mrs. Perez, the janitor of that house and his wife. When Mr. Perez had gone up with refreshments at midnight Sunday he had found the body there, and they had taken it out and put it in that hole."

"They admitted it?"

"They had to. The alternative Mr. Goodwin offered them was worse."

"They killed him. That's obvious. They killed him."

Wolfe shook his head. "That was an acceptable conjecture until yesterday morning, but they didn't kill their daughter—and that's where my report to you begins. That conjecture was then discarded in favor of another, that that girl had been killed by the person who killed Yeager—discarded by me, not by Mr. Goodwin, who had not accepted it. Summoned to that house Wednesday night by Mrs. Perez, he searched the girl's room and found evidence that supported the second conjecture. Archie?"

I went and got Maria's collection from the safe and took it to him.

He tapped it with a fingertip. "This," he said, "is that girl's carefully hidden record of a secret venture that in the end cost her her life. It is all concerned with Thomas G. Yeager. No doubt it was initiated, as so many ventures are, by simple curiosity, stirred by the existence of the elevator and the room which she was not allowed to see. She found that by turning out the light in her room and opening her door a crack she could see visitors bound for the elevator as they came down the hall. I don't know when she first did that, but I do know that, having started, she repeated it frequently."

He picked up the tear sheets. "These are from the financial pages of the *Times,* with the entries for Continental Plastic Products marked with a pencil." He put them aside. "These are advertisements of Continental Plastic Products." He put them with the tear sheets. "Labels from champagne bottles. Mr. Goodwin is of the opinion that Miss Perez drank none of the champagne, and I concur. These items are not essentials, they are merely tassels. So are these: newspaper reproductions of photographs, two of Mr. Yeager, one of his son, and one of his wife. I mention them only to show you how diligent Miss Perez was."

He put them with the other tassels and picked up the pictures of Meg Duncan and the bills. "These two items are of more consequence: nine five-dollar bills, and three pictures of a woman who is a public figure—one from a newspaper and two from magazines. I have spoken with her, and Mr. Goodwin talked with her at length yesterday afternoon. The money was extorted from her by Miss Perez, who had seen her in that house and demanded what she called hush money. The woman sent her five dollars a month for nine months, by mail. There is no need to name her."

He opened a drawer, put the pictures and bills in it, and shut it. "But those items raise a question. Call the woman Miss X. Mr. Yeager arrived at the house Sunday evening around seven o'clock. Miss McGee arrived at a quarter past nine and found him dead. The conjecture was that Miss Perez had seen someone arrive between those hours, had recognized him or her, had concluded that he or she had killed Yeager, had undertaken a more ambitious venture in extortion, and had herself been killed. Then, since she would have recognized Miss X, why not assume that Miss X was the culprit? A reasonable assumption; but it has been established beyond question that Miss X was at a public gathering Wednesday evening until eleven o'clock, and Miss Perez left the motion-picture theater, to keep her appointment with her intended prey, before nine o'clock."

Aiken flipped an impatient hand. "You said this was urgent. What's urgent about proving that a Miss X is out of it?"

"The urgency will appear. This is a necessary prelude to it. Still another reason for excluding not only Miss X, but others: Whoever went there Sunday evening between seven and nine, with a gun and intending to use it, must have known that no other visitor would be there. What is true of Miss X is also true of every other woman who had keys to that place: First, she couldn't have gone by invitation, since Miss McGee had been invited, and Yeager entertained only one guest at a time; and second, she couldn't have expected to find him alone there on a Sunday evening—or rather, she could have expected to find him alone only if she knew that Miss McGee would arrive at nine o'clock." Wolfe's head turned. "Miss McGee. Had you told anyone that you were going there at nine o'clock?"

"No." It came out a squeak and she tried it again. "No, I hadn't."

"Then the others are excluded as well as Miss X. Now for you, madam. And the next item in Miss Perez' collection. These are pencil sketches she made of women she saw in that hall." He picked them up. "She was not without talent. There are thirty-one of them, and they are dated. Mr. Goodwin and I have studied them with care. There are four sketches each of three women, three each of five women, two of one woman, and one each of two women. The one of whom there are two sketches is you, and one of them is dated May eighth. It gave me the surmise, which I tricked you into validating, that you were there Sunday evening. Would you care to look at it?"

"No." That time it was too loud.

Wolfe put the sketches in the drawer and returned his eyes to Julia McGee. "It was the fact that those two sketches were in the collection that made it extremely doubtful that it was you who had killed Miss Perez, having been threatened with exposure by her. For there are no sketches of persons whose names she knew. There are none of Mr. Yeager or Miss X. The sketches are merely memoranda. It is highly likely that she had made one or more of Miss X, but when she had identified her from published pictures she discarded the sketches. If she had identified you, if she knew your name, she would have preserved, not the sketches, but the ground for the identification, as she did with Miss X. Surely she would not have made a second sketch of you when she saw you in the hall Sunday evening."

Aiken snorted. "You don't have to persuade us that Miss McGee didn't kill the girl. Or Yeager."

Wolfe turned to him. "I am describing my progress to my conclusion. It is apparent that Miss Perez had assembled, and was keeping hidden, a complete record of her discoveries regarding

Mr. Yeager and the visitors to that room. It is certain that she knew the name of the person whom she saw in the hall between seven and nine Sunday evening, since she was able to reach him, to confront him with her knowledge and her threat. Therefore it was a sound assumption that this collection contained an item or items on which her identification of that person was based."

He pointed to the tassels. "Two such items are there: the pictures of Mr. Yeager's wife and son, with their names. I rejected them because they did not meet the specifications. The person who went there Sunday evening with a gun and shot Yeager with it must have had keys and known how to use them, and he must have known that Miss McGee intended to arrive at nine o'clock, since otherwise he could not have expected to find Yeager alone. It was conceivable that either the wife or son met those requirements, but it was highly improbable."

He picked up the remaining item. "Adopting that reasoning, at least tentatively, I was left with this. This is a picture, reproduced in a magazine, of a gathering in the ballroom of the Churchill Hotel, a banquet of the National Plastics Association. Mr. Yeager is at the microphone. The caption gives the names of the men on the dais with him, including you. No doubt you are familiar with the picture?"

"Yes. I have it framed on the wall of my office."

"Well." Wolfe dropped it on his desk. "I asked myself, what if it was you whom Miss Perez saw in the hall on your way to the elevator Sunday evening between seven and nine? What if, having this picture in her collection, she recognized you? What if, later, having learned that Yeager had been killed up in that room—for she must have seen her father and mother transporting the body —she guessed that you had killed him, decided to make you pay for her silence, communicated with you, made an appointment to meet you, and kept it? You will concede that those were permissible questions."

"Permissible? Yes." Aiken was disdainful. "You don't need permission to ask preposterous questions."

Wolfe nodded. "Of course that was the point. Were they preposterous? To answer that, further questions had to be asked. One, could you have had keys? Two, could you have known Yeager would be there alone? Three, had you a motive?"

Wolfe stuck a finger up. "One. You could have borrowed Miss McGee's keys, but if so you would have had to return them to her before nine o'clock so she could let herself in. That did seem preposterous, that you would return the borrowed keys so she could enter, find Yeager's body, and inevitably assume that you had killed him. Not tenable."

"Do you expect me to sit here and listen to this nonsense?"

"I do. We have arrived at the urgency and you know it." Another finger up. "Two. Yes. You could have known Yeager would be there alone. Miss McGee says she told no one of her nine o'clock appointment, but that was to be expected if it was you she told." Another finger. "Three. When I first asked that question, had you a motive, I knew nothing about it, but I do now. Yesterday I made some inquiries on the telephone—I assure you they were discreet—and last evening Mrs. Yeager sat for an hour in the chair you now occupy and gave me many details. For five years, since he became executive vice-president, Yeager has been a threat to your leadership of the corporation, and in the last year the threat has become ominous and imminent. The best you could expect was that you would be made chairman of the board, removed from active control, and even that was doubtful. Since you had dominated the corporation's affairs for more than ten years, that prospect was intolerable. You can't very well challenge this, since the situation is known to many people."

Wolfe's fingers came down, and his hand dropped to the desk. "But what chiefly concerned me when you and Miss McGee left this room twenty-four hours ago was not your motive; a motive, however deeply hidden, can be exposed. The problem was the keys, and there was an obvious possibility, that you had borrowed Miss McGee's keys, not last Sunday, but at some previous date, had had duplicates made, and had returned them to her. Testing that possibility would have been hopeless if they had been ordinary keys, but Rabsons are peculiar and there aren't many of them. I decided to try. I sent for three men who help me on occasion and gave them this picture and the keys I got from Miss McGee yesterday. They had copies made of the picture and duplicates of the keys, and returned these to me. They were to start with the locksmiths nearest your home and office. Only a little more than an hour ago, just before I phoned you, one of them, Mr. Saul Panzer, turned the possibility into a fact. This is of course the crux of my report." He pushed a button on his desk. "This begot the urgency."

His eyes went to the door, and Saul appeared with Arthur Wenger. They came to the front of Wolfe's desk and turned to face Aiken. Wolfe said to Aiken, "This is Mr. Arthur Wenger. Do you recognize him?"

Aiken was staring at Wenger. He moved the stare to Wolfe. "No," he said. "I've never seen him."

"Mr. Wenger, this is Mr. Benedict Aiken. Do you recognize him?"

The locksmith nodded. "I recognized him from the picture. It's him all right."

"Where and when have you seen him before?"

"He came to my shop one day last week with a couple of Rabson keys to get duplicates made. He waited while I made them. I think it was Wednesday, but it could have been Tuesday. He's a liar when he says he's never seen me."

"How sure are you?"

"I couldn't be any surer. People are like keys; they're a lot alike but they're all different. I don't know faces as well as I know keys, but well enough. I look at keys and I look at faces."

"It's an excellent habit. That's all now, sir, but I'll appreciate it if you can spare another hour."

"I said I could."

"I know. I appreciate it."

Saul touched Wenger's arm, and they went. In the hall they turned left, toward the kitchen. Soon after Saul had phoned, Fritz had got started on a chicken pie with forcemeat and truffles for their lunch, and it would soon be ready.

Wolfe leaned back, cupped his hands over the ends of the chair arms, and spoke. "Miss McGee. Manifestly Mr. Aiken is doomed. You shifted your loyalty from Mr. Yeager to him; now you must shift it from him to yourself. You're in a pickle. If he is put on trial you'll be a witness. If you testify under oath that you did not lend him your keys and that you didn't tell him you would arrive at that house at nine o'clock Sunday evening you will be committing perjury, and it may be provable. More and worse: You may be charged as an accessory to murder. You lent him the keys, he had duplicates made, and he used the duplicates to enter a house to kill a man. You made it possible for him to enter the house without hazard, ensuring that Yeager would be alone, by arranging a nine-o'clock assignation—"

"I didn't arrange it!" Too loud again. "Nine o'clock was the usual time! And I only told Mr. Aiken because—"

"Hold your tongue!" Aiken was on his feet, confronting her. "He tricked you once and he's trying it again. We're going. I'm going, and you're going with me!"

I was up. If she had left her chair I would have moved between them and the door, but she stayed put. She tilted her head back to look up at him, and I have never seen a stonier face. "You're a fool," she said. I have never heard a harder voice. "A bungling old fool. I suspected you had killed him but I didn't want to believe it. If you had had any brains— Don't stand there glaring at me!" He was in front of her, and she moved her chair to send her eyes to Wolfe. "Yes, he borrowed my keys. He said he wanted to see the room. He had them two days. And I told him I was going there Sunday night at nine o'clock. I had promised to keep him informed. Informed! I was a fool too." Her voice stayed hard but it was also bitter. "God, what a fool."

Wolfe shook his head. " 'Fool' doesn't do you justice, Miss McGee. Say rather harpy or lamia. I'm not judging you, merely classifying you. Pfui." He turned to Aiken. "So much for what is done; now what to do."

Aiken had returned to the red leather chair. With his hands, fists, on his thighs, and his jaw clamped, he was trying to pretend he wasn't licked, but he knew he was. Knowing what was ahead after Wolfe had dictated the draft for a document, I had got the Marley from the drawer and loaded it and slipped it in my pocket, but now I knew it wouldn't be needed. I sat down.

Wolfe addressed him. "I am in a quandary. The simplest and

safest course would be to telephone Mr. Cramer of the police to
come and get you. But under the terms of your employment of me
on behalf of your corporation I am obliged to make every effort to
protect the reputation and interests of the corporation, and to
disclose no facts or information that will harm the corporation's
repute or prestige unless I am compelled to do so by my legal obligation as a citizen and a licensed private detective. That is verbatim.
Of course it isn't possible to suppress the fact that the corporation's
president murdered its executive vice-president; that isn't discus-
sible. You are doomed. With the evidence I already possess and
the further evidence the police would gather, your position is
hopeless."

He opened a drawer and took out a paper. "But it may be feasible to prevent disclosure of the existence of that room and Yeager's
connection with it, and that was your expressed primary concern
when you came here Tuesday night. I doubt if you care much now,
but I do. I want to meet the terms of my engagement as far as possible, and with that in mind I prepared a draft of a document for
you to sign. I'll read it to you." He lifted the paper and read:

"I, Benedict Aiken, make and sign this statement because it
has been made clear to me by Nero Wolfe that there is no hope
of preventing disclosure of my malefaction. But I make it of
my own free will and choice, under the coercion not of Nero
Wolfe but only of the circumstances. On the night of May 8,
1960, I killed Thomas G. Yeager by shooting him in the head.
I transported his body to West 82nd Street, Manhattan, and put
it in a hole in the street. There was a tarpaulin in the hole, and
to postpone discovery of the body I covered it with the tarpaulin.
I killed Thomas G. Yeager because he threatened to supersede
me in my office of president of Continental Plastic Products
and deprive me of effective control of the affairs of the corporation. Since I was responsible for the development and progress
of the corporation for the last ten years, that prospect was intolerable. I feel that Yeager deserved his fate, and I express no
regret or remorse for my deed."

Wolfe leaned back. "I included no mention of Maria Perez because that is not essential and it would require a lengthy explana-

tion, and there is no danger of an innocent person being held to account for her death. The police will in time file it, along with other unsolved problems. You may of course suggest changes—for example, if you do feel regret or remorse and wish to say so, I offer no objection."

He held the paper up. "Of course this, written on my typewriter, will not do. Anyhow, such a document should be a holograph to make it indubitably authentic, so I suggest that you write it by hand on a plain sheet of paper, with the date and your signature. Here and now. Also address an envelope by hand to me at this address and put a postage stamp on it. Mr. Panzer will go to a mailbox near your home and mail it. When he phones that it has been mailed you will be free to go your way." His head turned. "Is there any chance that it will be delivered here today, Archie?"

"No, sir. Tomorrow morning."

He went back to Aiken. "I shall of course communicate with the police without undue delay—say around ten o'clock." He cocked his head. "The advantage to me of this procedure is obvious; I shall be able to collect a fee from the corporation; but the advantage to you is no less clear. Surely it is to be preferred to the only alternative: immediate arrest and constraint, indictment on a murder charge, indeed two murders, disclosure of the existence of that room and of the efforts of yourself and your associates to prevent the disclosure, the ordeal of the trial, the probable conviction. Even if you are not convicted, the years ahead, at your age, are not attractive. I am merely—"

"Shut up!" Aiken barked.

Wolfe shut up. I raised my brows at Aiken. Had he actually, there under the screw, the nerve to think he might tear loose? His face answered me. The bark had come not from nerve, but from nerves, nerves that had had all they could take. I must hand it to him that he didn't wriggle or try to crawl. He didn't even stall, try to get another day or even an hour. He didn't speak; he just put out a hand, palm up. I went and got the document and gave it to him, then got a sheet of typewriter paper and a blank envelope and took them to him. He had a pen; he had taken it from his pocket. His hand was steady as he put the paper on the stand at his elbow, but it shook a little as he put pen to paper. He sat stiff and still for ten seconds, then tried again, and the hand obeyed orders.

Wolfe looked at Julia McGee and said in a voice as hard as hers had been, "You're no longer needed. Go." She started to speak, and he snapped at her, "No. My eyes are inured to ugliness, but you offend them. Get out. Go!"

She got up and went. Aiken, hunched over, writing steadily, his teeth clamped on his lip, probably hadn't heard Wolfe speak and wasn't aware that she had moved. I know I wouldn't have been, in his place.

AT 9:04 Saturday morning I buzzed the plant rooms on the house phone, and when Wolfe answered I told him, "It's here. I've opened it. Do I phone Cramer?"

"No. Any news?"

"No."

*   *   *   *

At 9:52 Saturday morning I buzzed the plant rooms again and told Wolfe, "Lon Cohen just phoned. About an hour ago a maid in Benedict Aiken's home found his body on the floor of his bedroom. Shot through the roof of the mouth. The gun was there on the floor. No further details at present. Do I phone Cramer?"

"Yes. Eleven o'clock."

"Certainly. If I also phoned Lon he would appreciate it. Is there any reason why I shouldn't?"

"No. The substance, not the text."

"Right."

*   *   *   *

At 11:08 Saturday morning Inspector Cramer, seated in the red leather chair, looked up from the paper he held in his hand and growled at Wolfe, "You wrote this."

Wolfe, at his desk, shook his head. "Not my hand."

"Nuts. You know damn well. This word 'malefaction.' Other words. It sounds like you. You did it deliberately. You let it sound like you so I would know you wrote it. Thumbing your nose at me, telling me to kiss your ass. Oh, I know it will check with his handwriting. I wouldn't be surprised if he wrote it right here, sitting in this chair."

"Mr. Cramer." Wolfe turned a hand over. "If I granted your inference I would challenge your interpretation. I would suggest that I let it sound like me out of regard for your sensibility and respect for your talents; that I wanted to make it plain that I knew you wouldn't be gulled."

"Yeah. You can have that." He looked at the paper. "It says 'it has been made clear to me by Nero Wolfe that there is no hope of preventing disclosure.' So you had evidence. You must have had damned good evidence. What?"

Wolfe nodded. "It was impossible to prevent that question. If Mr. Aiken were still alive I would of course have to answer it. You would need the evidence and I would have to surrender it. But he's dead. I'm not a lawyer, but I have consulted one. I am not obliged to reveal evidence that is not needed and could not be used in the public interest."

"It's in the public interest to know where and when the murder was committed."

"No, sir. In the police interest, not in the public interest. It's a nice point. If you want to test it you'll have to charge me, serve a warrant on me, persuade the District Attorney to prosecute, and let a judge and jury decide. With Mr. Aiken dead and his confession in hand, I doubt if you'd get a verdict."

"So do I." Cramer folded the paper and put it in the envelope, and stuck the envelope in a pocket. "Your goddam brass." He got up. "We'll see." He turned and marched out.

*   *   *   *

At 3:47 Saturday afternoon three men and a woman were in the office with Wolfe and me. The men, in yellow chairs, were members of the board of directors of Continental Plastic Products. The woman, in the red leather chair, was Mrs. Thomas G. Yeager. In their hands were sheets of paper, copies I had typed of the document we had received in the mail that morning. Wolfe was speaking.

"No. I will not. In the terms of my engagement it was neither specified nor implied that I would report the particulars of my performance. It would serve no end to display to you the evidence with which I confronted Mr. Aiken, or to tell you how I got it. As for the result, that was determined by the situation, not by me; I merely arranged the style of the denouement. If it had been left to the police, they would certainly have discovered that room, given time; once learning about the room, they would have learned everything; and Mr. Aiken, your president, would have been, instead of the object of a brief sensation, the center of a prolonged hullabaloo. As for my fee, do you question my evaluation of my services at fifty thousand dollars?"

"No," a director said, "I don't." Another said, "We haven't questioned that." The third one grunted.

"I owe you a fee too," Mrs. Yeager said.

Wolfe shook his head. "I have your dollar; I'll keep that. I told you I don't expect a payment from two different clients for the same services." He looked up at the clock; he had his date with the orchids at four. He pushed back his chair and rose. "You may keep those copies of Mr. Aiken's statement. They're cheap at the price."

*   *   *   *

At 5:14 Saturday afternoon I was sitting in the kitchen in the basement of the house at 156 West 82nd Street. Cesar Perez was slumped in a chair. His wife was sitting straight, her shoulders back. "I'm sorry," I said, "but it can't be helped. The man who killed Maria is dead, but the police don't know it. If they did they would also know about this house and about your taking Yeager's body out of it and dumping it in the hole. So they'll be bothering you some more, but probably not for long. I'd like to go to the funeral tomorrow, but I'd better not. There will probably be a policeman there. They attend the funerals of people who have been murdered when they haven't caught the murderer. I think I've told you everything you'd want to know, but do you want to ask anything?"

He shook his head. She said, "We said we would pay you one hundred dollars."

"Forget it. We had too many clients anyway. I'll keep the dollar, and I'll also keep the keys, if you don't mind, as a souvenir. You'd better have a new lock put on the door." I left the chair and stepped to the table to get a parcel wrapped in brown paper. "This is the only thing I took from the room, a woman's umbrella. I'll return it to its owner." I shook hands, with her and then with him, and blew.

I didn't go to Eden Street. I had no overwhelming desire to see the Houghs again, or Meg Duncan offstage. On Monday I sent the umbrella and the cigarette case by messenger.

*   *   *   *

I should add a note, in case anyone reading this report takes a notion to go and take a look at the bower. You won't find it on 82nd Street. Nor will you find any of the people where I have put them. The particulars of the performance were exactly as I have reported them, but for obvious reasons I have changed names and addresses and a few other details—for instance, the title of the play Meg Duncan was starring in. It's still on and she's as good as ever; I went one night last week just to see.

If Cramer reads this and drops in to inquire, I'll tell him I made it up, including this note.

Might
As Well
Be Dead

CHAPTER 1

MOST OF THE PEOPLE who come to see Nero Wolfe by appointment, especially from as far away as Nebraska, show some sign of being in trouble, but that one didn't. With his clear unwrinkled skin and alert brown eyes and thin straight mouth, he didn't even look his age. I knew his age, sixty-one. When a telegram had come from James R. Herold, Omaha, Nebraska, asking for an appointment Monday afternoon, of course I had checked on him. He was sole owner of the Herold Hardware Company, wholesale, a highly respected citizen, and rated at over half a million—a perfect prospect for a worthy fee if he had real trouble. Seeing him had been a letdown. From his looks, he might merely be after a testimonial for a gadget to trim orchid plants. He had settled back comfortably in the red leather chair.

"I guess," he said, "I'd better tell you why I picked you."

"As you please," Wolfe muttered from behind his desk. For half an hour after lunch he never gets above a mutter unless he has to.

Herold crossed his legs. "It's about my son. I want to find my son. About a month ago I put ads in the New York papers, and I contacted the New York police, and— What's the matter?"

"Nothing. Go on."

It was not nothing. Wolfe had made a face. I, at my desk, could have told Herold that unless his problem smelled like real money he might as well quit right there. One man who had made "contact" a verb in that office had paid an extra thousand bucks for the privilege, though he hadn't known it.

Herold looked doubtful; then his face cleared. "Oh. You don't like poking in a police matter, but that's all right. I've been keeping after the Missing Persons Bureau, a Lieutenant Murphy, and I've run some more newspaper ads in the Personals, but they've got no results at all, and my wife was getting impatient about it, so I phoned Lieutenant Murphy from Omaha and told him I wanted to hire a private detective agency and asked him to recommend one. He said he couldn't do that, but I can be pretty determined when I want to, and he gave me your name. He said that on a job like finding a missing person you yourself wouldn't be much because you were too fat and lazy, but that you had two men, one named Archie Goodwin and one named Saul Panzer, who were tops for that kind of work. So I wired you for an appointment."

Wolfe made the noise he uses for a chuckle, and moved a finger to indicate me. "This is Mr. Goodwin. Tell him about it."

"He's in your employ, isn't he?"

"Yes. My confidential assistant."

"Then I'll tell you. I like to deal with principals. My son Paul is my only son—I have two daughters. When he graduated from college, the University of Nebraska, I took him into my business, wholesale hardware. That was in nineteen forty-five, eleven years ago. He had been a little wild in college, but I thought he would settle into the harness, but he didn't. He stole twenty-six thousand dollars of the firm's money, and I kicked him out." His straight thin mouth tightened a little. "Out of the business and out of the house. He left Omaha and I never saw him again. I didn't want to see him, but now I do and my wife does. One month ago, on March eighth, I learned that he didn't take that money. I learned who did, and it has been proven beyond all doubt. That's being attended to, the thief is being taken care of, and now I want to find my son." He got a large envelope from his pocket, took things from it, and left his chair. "That's a picture of him, taken in June nineteen forty-five, the latest one I have." He handed me one too. "Here are six copies of it, and of course I can get more." He returned to the chair and sat. "He got a raw deal and I want to make it square with him. I have nothing to apologize for, because at the time there was good evidence that he had taken the money, but now I know he didn't and I've got to find him. My wife is very impatient about it."

The picture was of a round-cheeked kid in a mortarboard and gown, with a dimple in his chin. No visible resemblance to his father. As for the father, he certainly wasn't being maudlin. You could say he was bearing up well in the circumstances, or you could say he was plain cold fish. I preferred the latter.

Wolfe dropped the picture on the desk top. "Evidently," he muttered, "you think he's in New York. Why?"

"Because every year my wife and daughters have been getting cards from him on their birthdays—you know, those birthday cards. I suspected all along that my wife was corresponding with him, but she says not. She admits she would have, but he never gave her an address. He never wrote her except the cards, and they were all postmarked New York."

"When did the last one come?"

"November nineteenth, less than five months ago. My daughter Marjorie's birthday. Postmarked New York like the others."

"Anything else? Has anyone ever seen him here?"

"Not that I know of."

"Have the police made any progress?"

"No. None whatever. I'm not complaining; I guess they've tried; but of course in a great city like this they've got their hands full of problems and I'm only one. I'm pretty sure he came straight to New York from Omaha, by train, back eleven years ago, but I haven't been able to verify it. The police had several men on it for a week, or they said they had, but now I think they've only got one, and I agree with my wife that I've got to do something. I've been neglecting my business."

"That will never do," Wolfe said dryly. Apparently he favored the cold-fish slant too. "And no results from the newspaper advertisements?"

"No. I got letters from five detective agencies offering to help me —of course the replies were to a box number—and quite a few, at least two dozen, from crackpots and impostors. The police investigated all of them, and they were all duds."

"How were the advertisements worded?"

"I wrote them myself. They were all alike." Herold got a big leather wallet from his breast pocket, fished in it, and extracted a clipping. He twisted in his chair to get better light from a window, and read:

Paul Herold, who left Omaha, Nebraska, in 1945, will learn something to his advantage by communicating with his father immediately. It has been learned that a mistake was made. Also anyone who sees this ad and knows anything of the said Paul Herold's whereabouts, either now or at any time during the past ten years, is requested to communicate and a proper reward will be given.

X904 Times.

"I ran that in five New York papers." He returned the clipping to the wallet and the wallet to the pocket. "Thirty times altogether. Money wasted. I don't mind spending money, but I hate to waste it."

Wolfe grunted. "You might waste it on me—or on Mr. Goodwin and Mr. Panzer. Your son may have changed his name on arrival in New York—indeed, that seems likely, since neither the police nor the advertisements have found any trace of him. Do you know if he took luggage with him when he left Omaha?"

"Yes, he took all his clothes and some personal things. He had a trunk and a suitcase and a bag."

"Were his initials on any of it?"

"His initials?" Herold frowned. "Why— Oh, yes. They were on the trunk and the suitcase, presents from his mother. My wife. Why?"

"Just PH, or a middle initial?"

"He had no middle name. Just PH. Why?"

"Because if he changed his name he probably found it convenient to keep the PH. Initials on luggage have dictated ten thousand aliases. Even so, Mr. Herold, assuming the PH, it is a knotty and toilsome job, for we must also assume that your son prefers not to be found, since the advertisements failed to flush him. I suggest that you let him be."

"You mean quit looking for him?"

"Yes."

"I can't. My wife, and my daughters— Anyway, I won't. Right is right. I've got to find him."

"And you want to hire me?"

"Yes. You and Goodwin and Panzer."

"Then I must inform you that it may take months, the expenses will be considerable, the amount of my bill will not be contingent on success, and I charge big fees."

"I know you do. Lieutenant Murphy told me." Herold looked

more like a man in trouble than when he came in. "But I can call you off at any time."

"Certainly."

"All right." He took a breath. "You want a retainer."

"As an advance for expenses. More important, I want all the information you can give me." Wolfe's head turned. "Archie, your notebook."

I already had it out.

An hour later, after the client had left and Wolfe had gone up to the plant rooms for his afternoon session with Theodore and the orchids, I put the check for three thousand dollars in the safe and then got at the typewriter to transcribe my notes. When I was done I had five pages of assorted facts, one or two of which might possibly be useful. Paul Herold had a three-inch scar on his left leg, on the inside of the knee, from a boyhood accident. That might help if we found him with his pants down. It had made him 4F and kept him out of war. His mother had called him Poosie. He had liked girls, and had for a time concentrated on one at college named Arline Macy, but had not been hooked, and so far as was known had communicated with none after heading east. He had majored in Social Science, but on that his father had been a little vague. He had taken violin lessons for two years and then sold the violin for twenty bucks, and got hell for it. He had tried for football in spite of his bum knee, but didn't make the team, and in baseball had played left field for two innings against Kansas in 1944. No other sports to speak of. Smoke and drink, not to excess. Gambling, not to the client's knowledge. He had always pushed some on his allowance, but there had been nothing involving dishonesty or other moral turpitude before the blow-up.

And so on and so forth. It didn't look very promising. Evidence of some sort of dedication, such as a love for animals that hop or a determination to be President of the United States, might have helped a little, but it wasn't there. If his father had really known him, which I doubted, he had been just an ordinary kid who had had a rotten piece of luck, and now it was anybody's guess what he had turned into. I decided that I didn't appreciate the plug Lieutenant Murphy of the Missing Persons Bureau had given me,

along with Saul Panzer. Any member of the NYPD, from Com-
missioner Skinner on down, would have given a day's pay, after
taxes, to see Nero Wolfe stub his toe, and it seemed likely that
Murphy, after spending a month on it, had figured that this was a
fine prospect. I went to the kitchen and told Fritz we had taken on
a job that would last two years and would be a washout.

Fritz smiled and shook his head. "No washouts in this house,"
he said positively. "Not with Mr. Wolfe and you both here." He
got a plastic container from the refrigerator, took it to the table,
and removed the lid.

"Hey," I protested, "we had shad roe for lunch! Again for
dinner?"

"My dear Archie." He was superior, to me, only about food.
"They were merely sauté, with a simple little sauce, only chives
and chervil. These will be *en casserole,* with anchovy butter made
by me. The sheets of larding will be rubbed with five herbs. With
the cream to cover will be an onion and three other herbs, to be
removed before serving. The roe season is short, and Mr. Wolfe
could enjoy it three times a day. You can go to Al's place on Tenth
Avenue and enjoy a ham on rye with coleslaw." He shuddered.

It developed into an argument, but I avoided getting out on a
limb, not wanting to have to drop off into Al's place. We were still
at it when, at six o'clock, I heard the elevator bringing Wolfe
down from the plant rooms, and after winding it up with no hard
feelings I left Fritz to his sheets of larding and went back to the
office.

Wolfe was standing over by the bookshelves, looking at the
globe, which was even bigger around than he was, checking to
make sure that Omaha, Nebraska, was where it always had been.
That done, he crossed over to his desk, and around it, and lowered
his colossal corpus into his custom-made chair.

He cocked his head to survey the Feraghan, which covered all
the central expanse, 14 x 26. "It's April," he said, "and that rug's
dirty. I must remind Fritz to send it to be cleaned and put the
others down."

"Yeah," I agreed, looking down at him. "But for a topic for
discussion that won't last long. If you want to avoid discussing

Paul Herold start something with some body to it, like the Middle East."

He grunted. "I don't have to avoid it. According to Lieutenant Murphy, that's for you and Saul. Have you reached Saul?"

"Yes. We're going to disguise ourselves as recruiting officers for the Salvation Army. He starts at the Battery and works north, and I start at Van Cortlandt Park and work south. We'll meet at Grant's Tomb on Christmas Eve and compare notes, and then start in on Brooklyn. Have you anything better to suggest?"

"I'm afraid not." He sighed, deep. "It may be hopeless. Has that Lieutenant Murphy any special reason to bear me a grudge?"

"It doesn't have to be special. He's a cop, that's enough."

"I suppose so." He shut his eyes, and in a moment opened them again. "I should have declined the job. Almost certainly he has never been known in New York as Paul Herold. That picture is eleven years old. What does he look like now? It's highly probable that he doesn't want to be found, and, if so, he has been put on the alert by the advertisements. The police are well qualified for the task of locating a missing person, and if after a full month they— Get Lieutenant Murphy on the phone."

I went to my desk and dialed CA 6–2000, finally persuaded a sergeant that only Murphy would do, and, when I had him, signaled to Wolfe. I stayed on.

"Lieutenant Murphy? This is Nero Wolfe. A man named James R. Herold, of Omaha, Nebraska, called on me this afternoon to engage me to find his son Paul. He said you had given him my name. He also said your bureau has been conducting a search for his son for about a month. Is that correct?"

"That's correct. Did you take the job?"

"Yes."

"Fine. Good luck, Mr. Wolfe."

"Thank you. May I ask, did you make any progress?"

"None whatever. All we got was dead ends."

"Did your search go beyond your set routine?"

"That depends on what you call routine. It was a clear-cut case and the boy had had a rough deal, and you could say we made a special effort. I've still got a good man on it. If you want to send

Goodwin down with a letter from Herold we'll be glad to show him the reports."

"Thank you. You have no suggestions?"

"I'm afraid not. Good luck."

Wolfe didn't thank him again. We hung up.

"Swell," I said. "He thinks he's handed you a gazookis. The hell of it is, he's probably right. So where do we start?"

"Not at the Battery," Wolfe growled.

"Okay, but where? It may even be worse than we think. What if Paul framed himself for the theft of the twenty-six grand so as to have an excuse to get away from father? Having met father, I would buy that. And seeing the ad asking him to communicate with father—not mentioning mother or sisters, just father—and saying a mistake was made, what does he do? He either beats it to Peru or the Middle East—there's the Middle East again—or he goes and buys himself a set of whiskers. That's an idea; we can check on all sales of whiskers in the last month, and if we find—"

"Shut up. It *is* an idea."

I stared. "My God, it's not that desperate. I was merely trying to stir your blood up and get your brain started, as usual, and if you—"

"I said shut up. Is it too late to get an advertisement into to-morrow's papers?"

"The *Gazette,* no. The *Times,* maybe."

"Your notebook."

Even if he had suddenly gone batty, I was on his payroll. I went to my desk, got the notebook, turned to a fresh page, and took my pen.

"Not in the classified columns," he said. "A display two columns wide and three inches high. Headed 'To P.H.' in large boldface, with periods after the P and H. Then this text, in smaller type: 'Your innocence is known and the injustice done you is regretted.'" He paused. "Change the 'regretted' to 'deplored.' Resume: 'Do not let bitterness prevent righting of a wrong.'" Pause again. "'No unwelcome contact will be urged upon you, but your help is needed to expose the true culprit. I engage to honor your reluctance to resume any tie you have renounced.'"

He pursed his lips a moment, then nodded. "That will do. Followed by my name and address and phone number."

"Why not mention mother?" I asked.

"We don't know how he feels toward his mother."

"He sent her birthday cards."

"By what impulsion? Do you know?"

"No."

"Then it would be risky. We can safely assume only two emotions for him: resentment of the wrong done him, and a desire to avenge it. If he lacks those he is less or more than human, and we'll never find him. I am aware, of course, that this is a random shot at an invisible target and a hit would be a prodigy. Have you other suggestions?"

I said no and swiveled the typewriter to me.

CHAPTER 2

AT ANY GIVEN MOMENT there are probably 38,437 people in the metropolitan area who have been unjustly accused of something, or think they have, and 66 of them have the initials P.H. One-half of the 66, or 33, saw that ad, and one-third of the 33, or 11, answered it—three of them by writing letters, six by phoning, and two by calling in person at the old brownstone house on West 35th Street, Manhattan, which Wolfe owns, inhabits, and dominates except when I decide that he has gone too far.

The first reaction was not from a P.H. but an L.C.—Lon Cohen of the *Gazette*. He phoned Tuesday morning and asked what the line was on the Hays case. I said we had no line on any Hays case, and he said nuts.

He went on. "Wolfe runs an ad telling P.H. he knows he's innocent, but you have no line? Come on, come on. After all the favors I've done you? All I ask is—"

I cut him off. "Wrong number. But I should have known, and so should Mr. Wolfe. We do read the papers, so we know a guy named Peter Hays is on trial for murder. Not our P.H. But it could be a damn nuisance. I hope to God he doesn't see the ad."

"Okay. You're sitting on it, and when Wolfe's sitting on something it's being sat on good. But when you're ready to loosen up, think of me. My name is Damon, Pythias."

Since there was no use trying to convince him, I skipped it. I didn't buzz Wolfe, who was up in the plant rooms for his morning exercise, to ride him for not remembering there was a P.H. being tried for murder, because I should have remembered it myself.

The other P.H.'s kept me busy, off and on, most of the day. One named Phillip Horgan was no problem, because he came in person and one look was enough. He was somewhat older than our client. The other one who came in person, while we were at lunch, was tougher. His name was Perry Hettinger, and he refused to believe the ad wasn't aimed at him. By the time I got rid of him and returned to the dining room Wolfe had cleaned up the kidney pie and I got no second helping.

The phone calls were more complicated, since I couldn't see the callers. I eliminated three of them through appropriate and prolonged conversation, but the other three had to have a look, so I made appointments to see them; and since I had to stick around I phoned Saul Panzer, who came and got one of the pictures father had left and went to keep the appointments. It was an insult to Saul to give him such a kindergarten assignment, considering that he is the best operative alive and rates sixty bucks a day, but the client had asked for him and it was the client's dough.

The complication of a P.H.'s being on trial for murder was as big a nuisance as I expected, and then some. All the papers phoned, including the *Times,* and two of them sent journalists to the door, where I chatted with them on the threshold. Around noon there was a phone call from Sergeant Purley Stebbins of Homicide. He wanted to speak to Wolfe, and I said Mr. Wolfe was engaged, which he was. He was working on a crossword puzzle by Ximenes in the London *Observer.* I asked Purley if I could help him.

"You never have yet," he rumbled. "But neither has Wolfe. But when he runs a display ad telling a man on trial for murder that he knows he's innocent and he wants to expose the true culprit, we want to know what he's trying to pull and we're going to. If he won't tell me on the phone I'll be there in ten minutes."

"I'll be glad to save you the trip," I assured him. "Tell you what. You wouldn't believe me anyway, so call Lieutenant Murphy at the Missing Persons Bureau. He'll tell you all about it."

"What kind of a gag is this?"

"No gag. I wouldn't dare to trifle with an officer of the law. Call Murphy. If he doesn't satisfy you come and have lunch with us. Peruvian melon, kidney pie, endive with Martinique dressing—"

It clicked and he was gone. I turned and told Wolfe it would be nice if we could always get Stebbins off our neck as easy as that. He frowned a while at the London *Observer* and then raised his head.

"Archie."

"Yes, sir."

"That trial, that Peter Hays, started about two weeks ago."

"Right."

"The *Times* had his picture. Get it."

I grinned at him. "Wouldn't that be something? It popped into my head too, the possibility, when Lon phoned, but I remembered the pictures of him—the *Gazette* and *Daily News,* all of them, and I crossed it off. But it won't hurt to look."

One of my sixteen thousand duties is keeping a five-week file of the *Times* in a cupboard below the bookshelves. I went and slid the door open and squatted, and before long I had it, on the seventeenth page of the issue of March 27. I gave it a look and went and handed it to Wolfe, and from a drawer of my desk got the picture of Paul Herold in mortarboard and gown, and handed him that too. He held them side by side and scowled at them, and I circled around to his elbow to help. The newspaper shot wasn't any too good, but even so, if they were the same P.H. he had changed a lot in eleven years. His round cheeks had caved in, his nose had shrunk, his lips were thinner, and his chin had bulged.

"No," Wolfe said. "Well?"

"Unanimous," I agreed. "That would have been a hell of a spot to find him. Is it worth going to the courtroom for a look?"

"I doubt it. Anyway, not today. You're needed here."

But that only postponed the agony for a few hours. That afternoon, after various journalists had been dealt with, and some of the P.H.'s, and Saul had been sent to keep the appointments, we had a visitor. Just three minutes after Wolfe had left the office for his daily four-to-six conference with the orchids, the doorbell rang and I answered it. On the stoop was a middle-aged guy who would need a shave by sundown, in a sloppy charcoal topcoat and a classy new black homburg. He could have been a P.H., but not a journalist. He said he would like a word with Mr. Nero Wolfe. I said Mr. Wolfe was engaged, told him my name and station, and asked if I could be of any service. He said he didn't know.

He looked at his wristwatch. "I haven't much time," he said, looking harassed. "My name is Albert Freyer, counselor-at-law." He took a leather case from his pocket, got a card from it, and handed it to me. "I am attorney for Peter Hays, who is on trial for first-degree murder. I'm keeping my cab waiting because the jury is out and I must be at hand. Do you know anything about the advertisement Nero Wolfe put in today's papers, 'To P.H.'?"

"Yes, I know all about it."

"I didn't see it until an hour ago. I didn't want to phone about it. I want to ask Nero Wolfe a question. It is being assumed that the advertisement was addressed to my client, Peter Hays. I want to ask him straight, was it?"

"I can answer that. It wasn't. Mr. Wolfe had never heard of Peter Hays, except in the newspaper accounts of his trial."

"You will vouch for that?"

"I do vouch for it."

"Well." He looked gotten. "I was hoping— No matter. Who is the P.H. the advertisement was addressed to?"

"A man whose initials are known to us but his name is not."

"What was the injustice mentioned in the ad? The wrong to be righted?"

"A theft that took place eleven years ago."

"I see." He looked at his wrist. "I have no time. I would like to give you a message for Mr. Wolfe. I admit the possibility of coincidence, but it is not unreasonable to suspect that it may be a publicity stunt. If so, it may work damage to my client, and it may be actionable. I'll want to look into the matter further when time permits. Will you tell him that?"

"Sure. If you can spare twenty seconds more, tell me something. Where was Peter Hays born, where did he spend his boyhood, and where did he go to college?"

Having half turned, he swiveled his head to me. "Why do you want to know?"

"I can stand it not to. Call it curiosity. I read the papers. I answered six questions for you, why not answer three for me?"

"Because I can't. I don't know." He was turning to go.

I persisted. "Do you mean that? You're defending him on a murder charge, and you don't know that much about him?" He was starting down the seven steps of the stoop. I asked his back, "Where's his family?"

He turned his head to say, "He has no family," and went. He climbed into the waiting taxi and banged the door, and the taxi rolled away from the curb. I went back in, to the office, and buzzed the plant rooms on the house phone.

"Yes?" Wolfe hates to be disturbed up there.

"We had company. A lawyer named Albert Freyer. He's Peter Hays's attorney, and he doesn't know where Hays was born and brought up or what college he went to, and he says Hays has no family. I'm switching my vote. I think it's worth the trip, and the client will pay the cab fare. I'm leaving now."

"No."

"That's just a reflex. Yes."

"Very well. Tell Fritz."

The gook. I always did tell Fritz. I went to the kitchen and did so, returned to the office and put things away and locked the safe, fixed the phone to ring in the kitchen, and got my hat and coat from the rack in the hall. Fritz was there to put the chain bolt on the door.

After habits get automatic you're no longer aware of them. One day years ago a tail had picked me up when I left the house on an errand, without my knowing it, and what he learned from my movements during the next hour had cost us an extra week, and our client an extra several thousand dollars, solving a big and important case. For a couple of months after that experience I never went out on a business errand without making a point of checking my rear, and by that time it had become automatic, and I've done it ever since without thinking of it. That Tuesday afternoon, heading for Ninth Avenue, I suppose I glanced back when I had gone about fifty paces, since that's the routine, but if so I saw nothing. But in another fifty paces, when I glanced back again automatically, something clicked and shot to the upper level and I was aware of it. What had caused the click was the sight of a guy some forty yards behind, headed my way, who hadn't been there before. I stopped, turned, and stood, facing him. He hesitated, took a piece of paper from his pocket, peered at it, and started studying the fronts of houses to his right and left. Almost anything would have been better than that, even tying his shoestring, since his sudden appearance had to mean either that he had popped out of an areaway to follow me or that he had emerged from one of the houses on his own affairs; and if the latter, why stop to glom the numbers of the houses next door?

So I had a tail. But if I tackled him on the spot, with nothing but logic to go on, he would merely tell me to go soak my head. I could lead him into a situation where I would have more than logic, but that would take time, and Freyer had said the jury was out, and I was in a hurry. I decided I could spare a couple of minutes and stood and looked at him. He was middle-sized, in a tan raglan and a brown snap-brim, with a thin, narrow face and a pointed nose. At the end of the first minute he got embarrassed and mounted the stoop of the nearest house, which was the residence and office of Doc Vollmer, and pushed the button. The door was opened by Helen Grant, Doc's secretary. He exchanged a few words with her, turned away without touching his hat, descended to the sidewalk, mounted the stoop of the house next door, and pushed the button. My two minutes were up, and anyway that was enough, so I beat it to Ninth Avenue without bothering to look back, flagged a taxi, and told the driver Centre and Pearl Streets.

At that time of day the courthouse corridors were full of lawyers, clients, witnesses, jurors, friends, enemies, relatives, fixers, bloodsuckers, politicians, and citizens. Having consulted a city employee below, I left the elevator at the third floor and dodged my way down the hall and around a corner to Part XIX, expecting no difficulty about getting in, since the Hays case was no headliner, merely run-of-the-mill.

There certainly was no difficulty. The courtroom was practically empty—no judge, no jury, and even no clerk or stenographer.

And no Peter Hays. Eight or nine people altogether were scat-tered around on the benches. I went and consulted the officer at the door, and was told that the jury was still out and he had no idea when it would be in. I found a phone booth and made two calls: one to Fritz, to tell him I might be home for dinner and I might not, and one to Doc Vollmer's number. Helen Grant answered.

"Listen, little blessing," I asked her, "do you love me?"

"No. And I never will."

"Good. I'm afraid to ask favors of girls who love me, and I want one from you. Fifty minutes ago a man in a tan coat rang your bell and you opened the door. What did he want?"

"My lord!" She was indignant. "Next thing you'll be tapping our phone! If you think you're going to drag me into one of your messes!"

"No mess and no dragging. Did he try to sell you some heroin?"

"He did not. He asked if a man named Arthur Holcomb lived here, and I said no, and he asked if I knew where he lived, and I said no again. That was all. What is this, Archie?"

"Nothing. Cross it off. I'll tell you when I see you if you still want to know. As for not loving me, you're just whistling in the dark. Tell me good-by."

"Good-by forever!"

So he had been a tail. A man looking for Arthur Holcomb wouldn't need to pop or slink suddenly from an areaway. There was no profit in guessing, but as I went back down the corridor naturally I wondered whether and how and why he was connected with P.H., and if so, which one.

As I approached the door of Part XIX I saw activity. People were going in. I got to the elbow of the officer and asked him if the jury was coming, and he said, "Don't ask me, mister. Word gets around fast here, but not to me. Move along." I entered the court-room and stepped aside to be out of the traffic lane, and was sur-veying the scene when a voice at my shoulder pronounced my name. I turned, and there was Albert Freyer. His expression was not cordial.

"So you never heard of Peter Hays," he said through his teeth. "Well, you're going to hear of me."

My having no reply ready didn't matter, for he didn't wait for one. He walked down the center aisle with a companion, passed through the gate, and took a seat at the counselors' table. I followed and chose a spot in the third row on the left, the side where the defendant would enter. The clerk and stenographer were at their desks, and Assistant District Attorney Mandelbaum, who had once been given a bigger dose by Wolfe than he could swallow, was at another table in the enclosure, with his briefcase in front of him and a junior at his side. People were straggling down the aisle, and I had my neck twisted for a look at them, with a vague idea of seeing the man in the tan coat who wanted to find Arthur Holcomb, when there was a sudden murmur and faces turned left, and so did mine. The defendant was being escorted in.

I have good eyes and I used them as he crossed to a chair directly behind Albert Freyer. I only had about four seconds, for when he was seated, with his back to me, my eyes were of no use, since the picture of Paul Herold, in mortarboard and gown, had given nothing to go by but the face. So I shut my eyes to concentrate. He was and he wasn't. He could be, but. Looking at the two pictures side by side with Wolfe, I would have made it thirty to one that he wasn't. Now two to one, or maybe even money, and I would take either end. I had to press down with my fanny to keep from bobbing up and marching through the gate for a full-face close-up.

The jury was filing in, but I hardly noticed. The courtroom preliminaries leading up to the moment when a jury is going to tell a man where he stands on the big one will give any spectator either a tingle in the spine or a lump of lead in his stomach, but not that time for me. My mind was occupied, and I was staring at the back of the defendant's head, trying to make him turn around. When the officer gave the order to rise for the entrance of the judge, the others were all on their feet before I came to. The judge sat and told us to do likewise, and we obeyed. I could tell you what the clerk said, and the question the judge asked the foreman, and the questions the clerk asked the foreman, since that is court routine, but I didn't actually hear it. I was back on my target.

The first words I actually heard came from the foreman. "We

find the defendant guilty as charged, of murder in the first degree."

A noise went around, a mixture of gasps and murmurs, and a woman behind me tittered, or it sounded like it. I kept on my target, and it was well that I did. He rose and turned square around, all in one quick movement, and sent his eyes around the courtroom—searching, defiant eyes—and they flashed across me. Then the guard had his elbow and he was pulled around and down, and Albert Freyer got up to ask that the jury be polled.

At such a moment the audience is supposed to keep their seats and make no disturbance, but I had a call. Lowering my head and pressing my palm to my mouth as if I might or might not manage to hold it in, I got up and sidestepped to the aisle, and double-quicked to the rear and on out. Waiting for one of the slow-motion elevators didn't fit my mood, so I took to the stairs. Out on the sidewalk there were several citizens strung along on the look-out for taxis, so I went south a block, soon got one, climbed in, and gave the hackie the address.

The timing was close to perfect. It was 5:58 when, in response to my ring, Fritz came and released the chain bolt and let me in. In two minutes Wolfe would be down from the plant rooms. Fritz followed me to the office to report, the chief item being that Saul had phoned to say that he had seen the three P.H.'s and none of them was it. Wolfe entered, went to his desk, and sat, and Fritz left.

Wolfe looked up at me. "Well?"

"No, sir," I said emphatically. "I am not well. I am under the impression that Paul Herold, alias Peter Hays, has just been convicted of first-degree murder."

His lips tightened. He released them. "How strong an impression? Sit down. You know I don't like to stretch my neck."

I went to my chair and swiveled to face him. "I was breaking it gently. It's not an impression, it's a fact. Do you want details?"

"Relevant ones, yes."

"Then the first one first. When I left here a tail picked me up. Also a fact, not an impression. I didn't have time to tease him along and corner him, so I passed it. He didn't follow me downtown—not that that matters."

Wolfe grunted. "Next."

"When I got to the courtroom the jury was still out, but they soon came in. I was up front, in the third row. When the defendant was brought in he passed within twenty feet of me and I had a good look, but it was brief and it was mostly three-quarters and profile. I wasn't sure. I would have settled for tossing a coin. When he sat, his back was to me. But when the foreman announced the verdict he stood up and turned around to survey the audience, and what he was doing, or wanting to do, was to tell somebody to go to hell. I got his full face, and for that instant there was something in it, a kind of cocky something, that made it absolutely the face of that kid in the picture. Put a flattop and a kimono on him and take eleven years off, and he was Paul Herold. I got up and left. And by the way, another detail. That lawyer, Albert Freyer, I told him in effect that we weren't interested in Peter Hays, and he saw me in the courtroom and snarled at me and said we'd hear from him."

Wolfe sat and regarded me. He heaved a sigh. "Confound it. But our only engagement was to find him. Can we inform Mr. Herold that we have done so?"

"No. I'm sure, but not that sure. We tell him his son has been convicted of murder, and he comes from Omaha to take a look at him through the bars, and says no. That would be nice. Lieutenant Murphy expected to get a grin out of this, but that wouldn't be a grin, it would be a horse laugh. Not to mention what I would get from you. Nothing doing."

"Are you suggesting that we're stalemated?"

"Not at all. The best thing would be for you to see him and talk with him and decide it yourself, but since you refuse to run errands outside the house, and since he is in no condition to drop in for a chat, I suppose it's up to me—I mean the errand. Getting me in to him is your part."

He was frowning. "You have your gifts, Archie. I have always admired your resourcefulness when faced by barriers."

"Yeah, so have I. But I have my limitations, and this is it. I was considering it in the taxi on the way home. Cramer or Stebbins or Mandelbaum, or anyone else on the public payroll, would have to know what for, and they would tell Murphy and he would take over, and if he *is* Paul Herold, who would have found him? Murphy. It calls for better gifts than mine. Yours."

He grunted. He rang for beer. "Full report, please. All you saw and heard in the courtroom."

I obliged. That didn't take long. When I finished, with my emergency exit as the clerk was polling the jury, he asked for the *Times*'s report of the trial, and I went to the cupboard and got it —all issues from March 27 to date. He started at the beginning, and, since I thought I might as well bone up on it myself, I started at the end and went backward. He had reached April 2, and I had worked back to April 4, and there would soon have been a collision but for an interruption. The doorbell rang. I went to the hall, and seeing, through the one-way glass panel of the front door, a sloppy charcoal topcoat and a black homburg that I had already seen twice that day, I recrossed the sill to the office and told Wolfe, "He kept his word. Albert Freyer."

His brows went up. "Let him in," he growled.

CHAPTER 3

THE COUNSELOR-AT-LAW hadn't had a shave, but it must be admitted that the circumstances called for allowances. I suppose he thought he was flattening somebody when, convoyed to the office and introduced, he didn't extend a hand, but if so he was wrong. Wolfe is not a handshaker.

When Freyer had got lowered into the red leather chair Wolfe swiveled to face him and said affably, "Mr. Goodwin has told me about you, and about the adverse verdict on your client. Regrettable."

"Did he tell you you would hear from me?"

"Yes, he mentioned that."

"All right, here I am." Freyer wasn't appreciating the big, comfortable chair; he was using only the front half of it, his palms on his knees. "Goodwin told me your ad in today's papers had no connection with my client, Peter Hays. He said you had never heard of him. I didn't believe him. And less than an hour later he appears in the courtroom where my client was on trial. That certainly calls for an explanation, and I want it. I am convinced that my client is innocent. I am convinced that he is the victim of a diabolical frame-up. I don't say that your ad was a part of the plot, I admit I don't see how it could have been since it appeared on the day the case went to the jury, but I intend to—"

"Mr. Freyer." Wolfe was showing him a palm. "If you please. I can simplify this for you."

"You can't simplify it until you explain it to my satisfaction."

"I know that. That's why I am prepared to do something I have rarely done, and should never do except under compulsion. It is now compelled by extraordinary circumstances. I'm going to tell you what a client of mine has told me. Of course you're a member of the New York bar?"

"Certainly."

"And you are attorney-of-record for Peter Hays?"

"Yes."

"Then I'm going to tell you something in confidence."

Freyer's eyes narrowed. "I will not be bound in confidence in any matter affecting my client's interests."

"I wouldn't expect you to. The only bond will be your respect for another man's privacy. The interests of your client and my client may or may not intersect. If they do we'll consider the matter; if they don't, I shall rely on your discretion. This is the genesis of that advertisement."

He told him. He didn't report our long session with James R. Herold verbatim, but neither did he skimp it. When he was through, Freyer had a clear and complete picture of where we stood up to four o'clock that afternoon, when Freyer had rung our doorbell. The lawyer was a good listener and had interrupted only a couple of times, once to get a point straight and once to ask to see the picture of Paul Herold.

"Before I go on," Wolfe said, "I invite verification. Of course Mr. Goodwin's corroboration would have no validity for you, but you may inspect his transcription of the notes he made, five typewritten pages. Or you can phone Lieutenant Murphy, provided you don't tell him who you are. On that, of course, I am at your mercy. At this juncture I don't want him to start investigating a possible connection between your P.H. and my P.H."

"Verification can wait," Freyer conceded. "You would be a fool to invent such a tale, and I'm quite aware that you're not a fool." He had backed up in the chair and got more comfortable. "Finish it up."

"There's not much more. When you told Mr. Goodwin that your client's background was unknown to you and that he had no family, he decided he had better have a look at Peter Hays, and he went to the courtroom for that purpose. His first glimpse of him, when he was brought into court, left him uncertain; but when, upon hearing the verdict, your client rose and turned to face the crowd, his face had a quite different expression. It had, or Mr. Goodwin thought it had, an almost conclusive resemblance to the picture of the youthful Paul Herold. When you asked to see the picture, I asked you to wait. Now I ask you to look at it. Archie?"

I got one from the drawer and went and handed it to Freyer. He studied it a while, shut his eyes, opened them again, and studied it some more. "It could be," he conceded. "It could easily be." He looked at it some more. "Or it couldn't." He looked at me. "What was it about his face when he turned to look at the crowd?"

"There was life in it. There was—uh—spirit. As I told Mr. Wolfe, he was telling someone to go to hell, or ready to."

Freyer shook his head. "I've never seen him like that, with any life in him. The first time I saw him he said he might as well be dead. He had nothing but despair, and he never has had."

"I take it," Wolfe said, "that as far as you know he *could* be Paul Herold. You know nothing of his background or connections that precludes it?"

"No." The lawyer considered it. "No, I don't. He has refused to disclose his background, and he says he has no living relatives. That was one of the things against him with the District Attorney —not evidential, of course, but you know how that is."

Wolfe nodded. "Now, do you wish to verify my account?"

"No. I accept it. As I said, you're not a fool."

"Then let's consider the situation. I would like to ask two questions."

"Go ahead."

"Is your client in a position to pay adequately for your services?"

"No, he isn't. Adequately, no. That is no secret. I took the case at the request of a friend—the head of the advertising agency he works for—or worked for. All his associates at the agency like him and speak well of him, and so do others—all his friends and acquaintances I have had contact with. I could have had dozens of character witnesses if that would have helped any. But in addition to the prison bars he has erected his own barrier to shut the world out—even his best friends."

"Then if he is Paul Herold it seems desirable to establish that fact. My client is a man of substantial means. I am not trying to stir your cupidity, but the laborer is worthy of his hire. If you're convinced of your client's innocence you will want to appeal, and

that's expensive. My second question: will you undertake to resolve our doubt? Will you find out, the sooner the better, whether
your P.H. is my P.H.?"

"Well." Freyer put his elbows on the chair arms and flattened
his palms together. "I don't know. He's a very difficult man. He
wouldn't take the stand. I wanted him to, but he wouldn't. I don't
know how I'd go about this. He would resent it, I'm sure of that,
after the attitude he has taken to my questions about his background, and it might become impossible for me to continue to represent him." Abruptly he leaned forward and his eyes gleamed.
"And I want to represent him! I'm convinced he was framed, and
there's still a chance of proving it!"

"Then if you will permit a suggestion"—Wolfe was practically
purring—"do you agree that it's desirable to learn if he is Paul
Herold?"

"Certainly. You say your client is in Omaha?"

"Yes. He returned last night."

"Wire him to come back. When he comes tell him how it stands,
and I'll arrange somehow for him to see my client."

Wolfe shook his head. "That won't do. If I find that it is his son
who has been convicted of murder of course I'll have to tell him,
but I will not tell him that it *may* be his son who has been convicted
of murder and ask him to resolve the matter. If it is not his son,
what am I? A bungler. But for my suggestion: if you'll arrange for
Mr. Goodwin to see him and speak with him, that will do it."

"How?" The lawyer frowned. "Goodwin has already seen him."

"I said 'and speak with him.'" Wolfe turned. "Archie. How long
would you need with him to give us a firm conclusion?"

"Alone?"

"Yes. I suppose a guard would be present."

"I don't mind guards. Five minutes might do it. Make it ten."

Wolfe went back to Freyer. "You don't know Mr. Goodwin, but
I do. And he will manage it so that no resentment will bounce to
you. He is remarkably adroit at drawing resentment to himself
to divert it from me or one of my clients. You can tell the District
Attorney that he is investigating some aspect of the case for you;
and as for your client, you can safely leave that to Mr. Goodwin."

He glanced up at the wall clock. "It could be done this evening. Now. I invite you to dine with me here. The sooner it's settled the better, both for you and for me."

But Freyer wouldn't buy that. His main objection was that it would be difficult to get access to his convicted client at that time of day even for himself, but also he wanted to think it over. It would have to wait until morning. When Wolfe sees that a point has to be conceded he manages not to be grumpy about it, and the conference ended much more sociably than it had begun. I went to the hall with Freyer and got his coat from the rack and helped him on with it, and let him out.

Back in the office, Wolfe was trying not to look smug. As I took the picture of Paul Herold from his desk to return it to the drawer, he remarked, "I confess his coming was opportune, but after your encounter with him in the courtroom it was to be expected."

"Uh-huh." I closed the drawer. "You planned it that way. Your gifts. It might backfire on you if his thinking it over includes a phone call to Omaha or even one to the Missing Persons Bureau. However, I admit you did the best you could, even inviting him to dinner. As you know, I have a date this evening, and now I can keep it."

So he dined alone, and I was only half an hour late joining the gathering at Lily Rowan's table at the Flamingo Club. We followed the usual routine, deciding after a couple of hours that the dance floor was too crowded and moving to Lily's penthouse, where we could do our own crowding. Getting home around three o'clock, I went to the office and switched a light on for a glance at my desk, where Wolfe leaves a note if there is something that needs early-morning attention, found it bare, and mounted the two flights to my room.

For me par in bed is eight full hours, but of course I have to make exceptions, and Wednesday morning I entered the kitchen at nine-thirty, only half awake but with my hair brushed and my clothes on, greeted Fritz with forced cheerfulness, got my orange juice, which I take at room temperature, from the table, and had just swallowed a gulp when the phone rang. I answered it there, and had Albert Freyer's voice in my ear. He said he had arranged it and I was to meet him in the City Prison visitors' room at ten-thirty. I said I wanted to be alone with his client, and he said he understood that but he had to be there to identify me and vouch for me.

I hung up and turned to Fritz. "I'm being pushed, damn it. Can I have two cakes in a hurry? Forget the sausage, just the cakes and honey and coffee."

He protested, but he moved. "It's a bad way to start a day, Archie, cramming your breakfast down."

I told him I was well aware of it and buzzed the plant rooms on the house phone to tell Wolfe.

CHAPTER 4

I wasn't exactly alone. Ten feet to my right a woman sat on a wooden chair just like mine, staring through the holes of the steel lattice at a man on the other side. By bending an ear I could have caught what the man was saying, but I didn't try because I assumed she was as much in favor of privacy as I was. Ten feet to my left a man on another chair like mine was also staring through the lattice, at a lad who wasn't as old as Paul Herold had been when the picture was taken. I couldn't help hearing what he was saying, and apparently he didn't give a damn. The boy across the lattice from him was looking bored. There were three or four cops around, and the one who had brought me in was standing back near the wall, also looking bored.

During the formalities of getting passed in, which had been handled by Freyer, I had been told that I would be allowed fifteen minutes, and I was about to leave my chair to tell the cop that I hoped he wouldn't start timing me until the prisoner arrived, when a door opened in the wall on the other side of the lattice and there he was, with a guard behind his elbow. The guard steered him across to a chair opposite me and then backed up to the wall, some five paces. The convict sat on the edge of the chair and blinked through the holes at me.

"I don't know you," he said. "Who are you?"

At that moment, with his pale hollow cheeks and his dead eyes and his lips so thin he almost didn't have any, he looked a lot more than eleven years away from the kid in the flattop.

I hadn't decided how to open up because I do better if I wait until I have a man's face to choose words. I had a captive audience, of course, but that wouldn't help if he clammed up on me. I tried to get his eyes, but the damn lattice was in the way.

"My name is Goodwin," I told him. "Archie Goodwin. Have you ever heard of a private detective named Nero Wolfe?"

"Yes, I've heard of him. What do you want?" His voice was hollower than his cheeks and deader than his eyes.

"I work for Mr. Wolfe. Day before yesterday your father, James R. Herold, came to his office and hired him to find you. He said he had learned that you didn't steal that money eleven years ago, and he wanted to make it square with you. The way things stand that may not mean much to you, but there it is."

Considering the circumstances, he did pretty well. His jaw sagged for a second, but he jerked it up, and his voice was just the same when he said, "I don't know what you're talking about. My name is Peter Hays."

I nodded at him. "I knew you'd say that, of course. I'm sorry, Mr. Herold, but it won't work. The trouble is that Mr. Wolfe needs money, and he uses part of it to pay my salary. So we're going to inform your father that we have found you, and of course he'll be coming to see you. The reason I'm here, we thought it was only fair to let you know about it before he comes."

"I haven't got any father." His jaw was stiff now, and it affected his voice. "You're wrong. You've made a mistake. If he comes I won't see him!"

I shook my head. "Let's keep our voices down. What about the scar on your left leg on the inside of the knee? It's no go, Mr. Herold. Perhaps you can refuse to see your father—I don't know how much say they give a man in your situation—but he'll certainly come when we notify him. By the way, if we had had any doubt at all of your identity you have just settled it, the way you said if he comes you won't see him. Why should you get excited about it if he's not your father? If we've made a mistake the easiest way to prove it is to let him come and take a look at you. We didn't engage to persuade you to see him; our job was just to find you, and we've done that, and if—"

I stopped because he started to shake. I could have got up and left, since my mission was accomplished, but Freyer wouldn't like it if I put his client in a state of collapse and just walked out on him, and after all Freyer had got me in. So I stuck. There was a counter on both sides to keep us away from the lattice, and he had his fists on his, rubbing it with little jerks.

"Hang on," I told him. "I'm going. We thought you ought to know."

"Wait." He stopped shaking. "Will you wait?"

"Sure."

He took his fists off the counter, and his head thrust forward. "I can't see you very well. Listen to me, for God's sake. For God's sake don't tell him. You don't know what he's like."

"Well, I've met him."

"And my mother and sisters, they'll know. I think they believed I was framed on stealing that money, I think they believed me, but he didn't, and now I've been framed again. For God's sake don't tell him. This time it's all over, I'm going to die, and I might as well be dead now, and it's not fair for me to have this too. I don't want them to know. My God, don't you see how it is?"

"Yeah, I see how it is." I was wishing I had gone.

"Then promise me you won't tell him. You look like a decent guy. If I've got to die for something I didn't do, all right, I can't do anything about that, but not this too. I know I'm not saying this right, I know I'm not myself, but if you only—"

I didn't know why he stopped, because, listening to him, I didn't hear the cop approaching from behind. There was a tap on my shoulder, and the cop's voice.

"Time's up."

I arose.

"Promise me!" Paul Herold demanded.

"I can't," I told him, and turned and walked out.

Freyer was waiting for me in the visitors' room. I don't carry a mirror, so I don't know how my face looked when I joined him, but when we had left the building and were on the sidewalk, he asked, "It didn't work?"

"You can't always tell by my expression," I said. "Ask the people I play poker with. But if you don't mind I'll save it for Mr. Wolfe, since he pays my salary. Coming along?"

Evidently he was. I'll hand it to him that he could take a hint. In the taxi, when I turned my head to the window to study the scenery as we rolled along, he made no attempt to start a conversation. But he overdid it a little. When we stopped at the curb in front of the old brownstone, he spoke.

"If you want a word with Wolfe first I'll wait out here."

I laughed. "No, come on in and I'll find you some earmuffs."

I preceded him up the stoop and pushed the button, and Fritz let us in, and we put our hats and coats on the rack and went down the hall to the office. Wolfe, at his desk pouring beer, shot me a glance, greeted Freyer, and asked if he would like some beer. The lawyer declined and took the red leather chair without waiting for an invitation.

I stood and told Wolfe, "I saw him and talked with him. Instead of a yes or no, I'd like to give you a verbatim report. Do you want Mr. Freyer to hear it?"

Wolfe lifted his glass from the tray. "Is there any reason why he shouldn't?"

"No, sir."

"Then go ahead."

I didn't ham it, but I gave them all the words, which was no strain, since the only difference between me and a tape recorder is that a tape recorder can't lie. I lie to Wolfe only on matters that are none of his business, and this was his business. As I say, I didn't ham it, but I thought they ought to have a clear picture, so I described Paul Herold's condition—his stiff jaw, his shaking, his trying to shove his fists through the counter, and the look in his eyes when he said it wasn't fair for him to have this too. I admit one thing: I made the report standing up so I could put my fists on Wolfe's desk to show how Paul Herold's had looked on the counter. When I was through I slid the chair out from my desk and sat.

"If you still want a firm conclusion," I said, "it is yes."

Wolfe put his glass down, took in air clear to his belly button, and shut his eyes.

Freyer was shaking his head with his jaw set. "I've never had a case like it," he said, apparently to himself, "and I never want another one." He looked at Wolfe. "What are you going to do? You can't just shut your eyes on it."

"They're my eyes," Wolfe muttered, keeping them closed. In a moment he opened them. "Archie. That's why you wanted Mr. Freyer to hear your report, to make it even more difficult."

I lifted my shoulders and dropped them. "No argument."

"Then send Mr. Herold a telegram, saying merely that we have found his son, alive and well, here in New York. That was our job. Presumably he will come."

Freyer made a noise and came forward in his chair. I looked at Wolfe, swallowed, and spoke.

"You do it. I've got a sore finger. Just dial Western Union, WO two-seven-one-one-one."

He laughed. A stranger would have called it a snort, but I know his different snorts. He laughed some more.

"It's fairly funny," I said, "but have you heard the one about the centipede in the shoe store?"

Freyer said positively, "I think we should discuss it."

Wolfe nodded. "I agree. I was merely forcing Mr. Goodwin to reveal his position." He looked at me. "You prefer to wire Mr. Herold that I have decided I don't like the job?"

"If those are the only alternatives, yes. As he said, he might as well be dead. He's practically a corpse, and I don't have to rob corpses to eat and neither do you."

"Your presentment is faulty," Wolfe objected. "No robbery is contemplated. However, I am quite willing to consider other alternatives. The decision, of course, is mine. Mr. Herold gave me the job of finding his son, and it is wholly in my discretion whether to inform him that the job is done."

He stopped to drink some beer. Freyer said, "As the son's attorney, I have some voice in the matter."

Wolfe put the glass down and passed his tongue over his lips. "No, sir. Not on this specific question. However, though you have no voice you certainly have an interest, and it deserves to be weighed. We'll look at it first. Those two alternatives, telling my client that his son is found, or telling him that I withdraw from my job, call them *A* and *B*. If *A*, my surmise is that you would be through. He would come to see his son, and survey the situation, and decide whether to finance an appeal. If he decided no, that would end it. If he decided yes, he would probably also decide that you had mishandled the case and he would hire another lawyer. I base that on the impression I got of him. Archie?"

"Right." I was emphatic.

Wolfe returned to Freyer. "And if *B,* you'd be left where you are now. How much would an appeal cost?"

"That depends. A lot of investigation would be required. As a minimum, twenty thousand dollars. To fight it through to the end, using every expedient, a lot more."

"Your client can't furnish it?"

"No."

"Can you?"

"No."

"Then *B* is no better for you than *A.* Now what about me? *A* should be quite simple and satisfactory. I've done a job and I collect my fee. But not only must I pay my bills, I must also sustain my self-esteem. That man, your client, has been wounded in his very bowels, and to add insult to his injury as a mere mercenary would be a wanton act. I can't afford it. Even if I must gainsay Rochefoucauld, who wrote that we should only affect compassion, and carefully avoid having any."

He picked up his glass, emptied it, and put it down. "Won't you have some beer? Or something else?"

"No, thank you. I never drink before cocktail time."

"Coffee? Milk? Water?"

"No, thanks."

"Very well. As for *B,* I can't afford that either. I've done what I was hired to do, and I intend to be paid. And I have another reason for rejecting *B.* It would preclude my taking any further interest in this affair, and I don't like that. You said yesterday that you are convinced that your client is innocent. I can't say that I am likewise convinced, but I strongly suspect that you're right. With reason."

He paused because we were both staring and he loves to make people stare.

"With reason?" Freyer demanded. "What reason?"

Satisfied with the stares, he resumed. "When Mr. Goodwin left here yesterday afternoon to go to look at your client, a man followed him. Why? It's barely possible that it was someone bearing a grudge on account of some former activity of ours, but highly unlikely. It would be puerile for such a person merely to follow Mr. Goodwin when he left the house. He must be somehow connected with a present activity, and we are engaged in none at the moment except Mr. Herold's job. Was Mr. Herold checking on us? Absurd. The obvious probability is that my advertisement was responsible. Many people—newspapers, the police, you yourself—had assumed that it was directed at Peter Hays, and others might well have done so. One, let us say, named X. X wants to know why I declare Peter Hays to be innocent, but does not come, or phone, to ask me; and he wants to know what I am doing about it. What other devices he may have resorted to, I don't know; but one of them was to come, or send someone, to stand post near my house."

Wolfe turned a hand over. "How account for so intense and furtive a curiosity? If the murder for which Peter Hays was on trial was what it appeared to be—a simple and commonplace act of passion—who could be so inquisitive and also so stealthy? Then it wasn't so simple. You said yesterday that you were convinced that your client was the victim of a diabolical frame-up. If you're correct, no wonder a man was sent to watch my house when I announced, on the last day of his trial, that he was known to be innocent—as was assumed. And it is with reason that I suspect that there is someone, somewhere, who felt himself threatened by my announcement. That doesn't convince me that your client is innocent, but it poses a question that needs an answer."

Freyer turned to me. "Who followed you?"

I told him I didn't know, and told him why, and described the tail.

He said the description suggested no one to him and went back to Wolfe. "Then you reject *A* and *B* for both of us. Is there a *C*?"

"I think there is," Wolfe declared. "You want to appeal. Can you take preliminary steps for an appeal without committing yourself to any substantial outlay for thirty days?"

"Yes. Easily."

"Very well. You want to appeal and I want to collect my fee. I warned my client that the search might take months. I shall tell him merely that I am working on his problem, as I shall be. You will give me all the information you have, all of it, and I'll investigate. In thirty days—much less, I hope—I'll know where we stand. If it is hopeless there will be nothing for it but *A* or *B*, and that decision can wait. If it is promising we'll proceed. If and when we get evidence that will clear your client, my client will be informed and he will foot the bill. Your client may not like it but he'll have to lump it; and anyway, I doubt if he would really rather die in the electric chair than face his father again, especially since he will be under no burden of guilt, either of theft or of murder. I make this proposal not as a paragon, but only as a procedure less repugnant than either *A* or *B*. Well, sir?"

The lawyer was squinting at him. "You say you'll investigate. Who will pay for that?"

"I will. That's the rub. I'll hope to get it back."

"But if you don't?"

"Then I don't."

"There should be a written agreement."

"There won't be. I take the risk of failure; you'll have to take the risk of my depravity." Wolfe's voice suddenly became a bellow. "Confound it, it is your client who has been convicted of murder, not mine!"

Freyer was startled, as well he might be. Wolfe can bellow. "I meant no offense," he said mildly. "I had no thought of depravity. As you say, the risk is yours. I accept your proposal. Now what?"

Wolfe glanced up at the wall clock and settled back in his chair. A full hour till lunchtime. "Now," he said, "I want all the facts. I've read the newspaper accounts, but I want them from you."

CHAPTER 5

PETER HAYS had been convicted of killing the husband of the woman he loved, on the evening of January 3, by shooting him in the side of the head, above the left ear, with a Marley .38. I might as well account for things as I go along, but I can't account for the Marley because it had been taken by a burglar from a house in Poughkeepsie in 1947 and hadn't been seen in public since. The prosecution hadn't explained how Peter Hays had got hold of it, so you can't expect me to.

The victim, Michael M. Molloy, forty-three, a real-estate broker, had lived with his wife, no children, in a four-room apartment on the top floor, the fifth, of a remodeled tenement on East 52nd Street. There was no other apartment on the floor. At 9:18 p.m. on January 3 a man had phoned police headquarters and said he had just heard a shot fired on one of the upper floors of the house next door. He gave the address of the house next door, 171 East 52nd Street, but hung up without giving his name, and he had never been located, though of course the adjoining houses had been canvassed. At 9:23 a cop from a prowl car had entered the building. When he got to the top floor, after trying two floors below and drawing blanks, he found the door standing open and entered. Two men were inside, one alive and one dead. The dead one, Molloy, was on the living-room floor. The live one, Peter Hays, with his hat and topcoat on, had apparently been about to leave, and when the cop had stopped him he had tried to tear away and had to be subdued. When he was under control the cop had frisked him and found the Marley .38 in his topcoat pocket.

All that had been in the papers. Also:

Peter Hays was a copywriter. He had been with the same advertising agency, one of the big ones, for eight years, and that was as far back as he went. His record and reputation were clean, with no high or low spots. Unmarried, he had lived for the past three years in an RBK—room, bath and kitchenette—on West 63rd Street. He played tennis, went to shows and movies, got along all right with people, had a canary in his room, owned five suits of clothes, four pairs of shoes, and three hats, and had no car. A key to the street door of 171 East 52nd Street had been found on his key ring. The remodeled building had a do-it-yourself elevator, and there was no doorman.

The District Attorney's office, the personnel of Homicide West, all the newspapers, and millions of citizens, were good and sore at Peter Hays because he wasn't playing the game. The DA and cops couldn't check his version of what had happened, and the papers couldn't have it analyzed by experts, and the citizens couldn't get into arguments about it, because he supplied no version. From the time he had been arrested until the verdict came, he had refused to supply anything at all. He had finally, urged by his lawyer, answered one question put by the DA in a private interview: had he shot Molloy? No. But why and when had he gone to the apartment? What were his relations with Molloy and with his wife? Why was a key to that building on his key ring? Why did he have the Marley .38 in his pocket? No reply. Nor to a thousand other questions.

Other people had been more chatty, some of them on the witness stand. The Molloys' daily maid had seen Mrs. Molloy and the defendant in close embrace on three different occasions during the past six months, but she had not told Mr. Molloy because she liked Mrs. Molloy and it was none of her business. Even so, Mr. Molloy must have been told something by somebody, or seen or heard something, because the maid had heard him telling her off and had seen him twisting her arm until she collapsed. A private detective, hired by Molloy late in November, had seen Mrs. Molloy and Peter Hays meet at a restaurant for lunch four times, but nothing juicier. There were others, but those were the outstanding items.

The prosecution's main attraction, though not its mainstay, had been the widow, Selma Molloy. She was twenty-nine, fourteen years younger than her husband, and was photogenic, judg-

ing from the pictures the papers had run. Her turn on the witness
stand had sparked a debate. The Assistant DA had claimed the
right to ask her certain questions because she was a hostile witness, and the judge had refused to allow the claim. For example,
the ADA had tried to ask her, "Was Peter Hays your lover?" but
he had to settle for "What were the relations between you and
Peter Hays?"

She said she liked Peter Hays very much. She said she regarded
him as a good friend, and she had affection for him, and believed
he had affection for her. The relations between them could not
properly be called misconduct. As for the relations between her
and her husband, she had begun to feel less than a year after their
marriage, which had taken place three years ago, that the marriage
had been a mistake. She should have known it would be, since for
a year before their marriage she had worked for Molloy as his
secretary, and she should have known what kind of man he was.
The prosecutor had fired at her, "Do you think he was the kind
of man who should be murdered?" and Freyer had objected
and been sustained, and the prosecutor had asked, "What kind
of man was he?" Freyer had objected to that too as calling for an
opinion on the part of the witness, and that had started another
debate. It was brought out, specifically, that he had falsely accused her of infidelity, had physically mistreated her, had abused
her in the presence of others, and had refused to let her get a di-
vorce.

She had seen Peter Hays at a New Year's Eve party three days
before the murder, and had not seen him since until she entered
the courtroom that day. She had spoken with him on the telephone
on January 1 and again on January 2, but she couldn't remember
the details of the conversations, only that nothing noteworthy had
been said. The evening of January 3 a woman friend had phoned
around seven-thirty to say that she had an extra ticket for a show
and invited her to come, and she had accepted. When she got
home, around midnight, there were policemen in her apartment and
she was told the news.

Freyer had not cross-examined her. One of the hundred or so
details of privileged communications between a lawyer and a client

furnished us by Freyer explained that. He had promised Peter
Hays he wouldn't.

Wolfe snorted, not his laughing snort. "Isn't it," he inquired,
"a function of counsel to determine the strategy and tactics of
defense?"

"When he can, yes." Freyer, who had spent three-quarters of
an hour reviewing the testimony and answering questions about
it, had lubricated himself with a glass of water. "Not with this client. I've said he is difficult. Mrs. Molloy was the prosecution's last
witness. I had five, and none of them helped any. Do you want to
discuss them?"

"No." Wolfe looked at the wall clock. Twenty minutes to lunch.
"I've read the newspaper accounts. I would like to know why
you're convinced of his innocence."

"Well—it's a combination of things. His expressions, his tones
of voice, his reactions to my questions and suggestions, some questions he has asked me—many things. But there was one specific
thing. During my first talk with him, the day after he was arrested,
I got the idea that he had refused to answer any of their questions
because he wanted to protect Mrs. Molloy—either from being
accused of the murder, or of complicity, or merely from harassment. At our second talk I got a little further with him. I told him
that exchanges between a lawyer and his client were privileged
and their disclosure could not be compelled, and that if he continued to withhold vital information from me I would have to retire from the case. He asked what would happen if I did retire
and he engaged no other counsel, and I said the court would ap-
point counsel to defend him; that on a capital charge he would
have to be represented by counsel. He asked if anything he told
me would have to come out at the trial, and I said not without his
consent."

The water glass had been refilled and he took a sip. "Then he
told me some things, and more later. He said that on the evening
of January third he had been in his apartment, alone, and had
just turned on the radio for the nine-o'clock news when the
phone rang. He answered it, and a man's voice said, 'Pete Hays?
This is a friend. I just left the Molloys, and Mike was starting to

beat her up. Do you hear me?' He said yes and started to ask a
question, but the man hung up. He grabbed his hat and coat and
ran, took a taxi across the park, used his key on the street door,
took the elevator to the fifth floor, found the door of the Molloy
apartment ajar, and went in. Molloy was lying there. He looked
through the apartment and found no one. He went back to Molloy and decided he was dead. A gun was on a chair against the
wall, fifteen feet from the body. He picked it up and put it in his
pocket, and was looking around to see if there was anything else
when he heard footsteps in the hall. He thought he would hide,
then thought he wouldn't, and as he started for the door the policeman entered. That was his story. This is the first time anyone
has heard it but me. I could have traced the cab, but why spend
money on it? It could have happened just as he said, with only one
difference, that Molloy was alive when he arrived."

Wolfe grunted. "Then I don't suppose that convinced you of
his innocence."

"Certainly not. I'll come to that. To clean up as I go along:
when I had him talking I asked why he had the key, and he said
that on taking Mrs. Molloy home from the New Year's Eve party
he had taken her key to open the door for her and had carelessly
neglected to return it to her. Probably not true."

"Nor material. The problem is murder, not the devices of gal-
lantry. What else?"

"I told him that it was obvious that he was deeply attached to
Mrs. Molloy and was trying to protect her. His rushing to her on
getting the anonymous phone call, his putting the gun in his pocket,
his refusal to talk to the police, not only made that conclusive but
also strongly indicated that he believed, or suspected, that she had
killed her husband. He didn't admit it, but he didn't deny it, and
for myself I was sure of it—provided he hadn't killed him himself.
I told him that his refusal to divulge matters even to his attorney
was understandable as long as he held that suspicion, but that now
that Mrs. Molloy was definitely out of it I expected of him full and
candid cooperation. She was completely in the clear, I said, because the woman and two men with whom she had attended the
theater had stated that she had been with them constantly

throughout the evening. I had a newspaper with me containing that news, and had him read it. He started to tremble, and the newspaper shook in his hands, and he called on God to bless me. I told him he needed God's blessing more than I did."

Freyer cleared his throat and took a gulp of water. "Then he read it again, more slowly, and his expression changed. He said that the woman and the men were old and close friends of Mrs. Molloy and would do anything for her. That if she had left the theater for part of the time they wouldn't hesitate to lie for her and say she hadn't. That there was no point in his spilling his guts— his phrase—unless it cleared him of the murder charge, and it probably wouldn't, and even if it did, then she would certainly be suspected and her alibi would be checked, and if it proved to be false she would be where he was then. I couldn't very well impeach his logic."

"No," Wolfe agreed.

"But I was convinced of his innocence. His almost hysterical relief on learning of her alibi, then the doubt creeping in, then his changing expression as he read the paper again and grasped the possibilities—if that was all counterfeit I should be disbarred for incompetence."

"Certainly I'm not competent to judge," Wolfe stated, "since I didn't see him. But since I have my own reason for not thinking it as simple as it seems I won't challenge yours. What else?"

"Nothing positive. Only negatives. I had to promise him I wouldn't cross-examine Mrs. Molloy, or quit the case, and I didn't want to quit. I had to accept his refusal to take the witness stand. If he had been framed the key question was the identity of the man who had made the phone call that made him dash to the Molloy apartment, but he said he had spent hours trying to connect the voice with someone he knew, and couldn't. The voice had been hoarse and guttural and presumably disguised, and he couldn't even guess.

"Two other negatives. He knew of no one who bore him enough ill will to frame him for murder, and he knew of no one who might have wanted Molloy out of the way. In fact he knows very little about Molloy—if he is to be believed, and I think he is. Of course the ideal suspect would be a man who coveted Mrs. Molloy and schemed to remove both her husband and Peter Hays at one stroke, but he is sure there is no such man. On those matters, and others, I have had no better luck with Mrs. Molloy."

"You have talked with her?"

"Three times. Once briefly and twice at length. She wanted me to arrange for her to see Peter, but he refused to permit it. She wouldn't tell me much about her relations with Peter, and there was no point in pressing her; I knew all I needed to know about that. I spent most of my time with her asking about her husband's activities and associates—everything about him. It had become apparent that I couldn't possibly get my client acquitted unless I found a likely candidate to replace him. She told me all she could, in fact she told me a lot, but there was a drag on her, and it wasn't hard to guess what the drag was. She thought Peter had killed her husband. The poor woman was pathetic; she kept asking me questions about the gun. It was obvious how her mind was working. She was willing to accept it that Peter had acted in a fit of passion, but if it had happened that way, how account for his having the gun with him? I asked her if there was any chance that the gun had been her husband's, there in the apartment, and she was sure there wasn't. When I told her that Peter had denied his guilt, and that I believed him, and why, she just stared at me. I asked her if she had in fact been continuously with her companions at the theater that evening, and she said yes, but her mind wasn't on that, it was on Peter. I honestly think she was trying to decide whether I really believed him or was only pretending to. As for what she told me about her husband, I didn't have the funds for a proper investigation—"

He stopped because Fritz had entered and was standing there. Fritz spoke. "Luncheon is ready, sir."

Wolfe got up. "If you'll join us, Mr. Freyer? There'll be enough to go around. Chicken livers and mushrooms in white wine. Rice cakes. Another place, Fritz."

CHAPTER 6

AT FOUR O'CLOCK that afternoon I left the house, bound for 171 East 52nd Street, to keep an appointment, made for me by Freyer, with Mrs. Michael M. Molloy.

After lunch we had returned to the office and taken up where we had left off. Freyer had phoned his office to send us the complete file on the case, and it had arrived and been pawed over. I had summoned Saul Panzer, Fred Durkin, Orrie Cather, and Johnny Keems to report to the office at six o'clock. They were our four main standbys, and they would call for a daily outlay of $160, not counting expenses. If it lasted a month, 30 times 160 equals 4800, so Wolfe's self-esteem might come high if he found he couldn't deliver.

Nothing had come of any of the leads suggested by what Mrs. Molloy had told Freyer about her deceased husband, and no wonder, since they had been investigated only by a clerk in Freyer's office and a sawbuck squirt supplied by the Harland Ide Detective Agency. I will concede that they had dug up some relevant facts: Molloy had had a two-room office in a twenty-story hive on 46th Street near Madison Avenue, and it said on the door MICHAEL M. MOLLOY, REAL ESTATE. His staff had consisted of a secretary and an errand boy. His rent had been paid for January, which was commendable, since January 1 had been a holiday and he had died on the third. If he had left a will, it had not turned up. He had been a fight fan and an ice-hockey fan. During the last six months of his life he had taken his current secretary, whose name was Delia Brandt, to dinner at a restaurant two or three times a week, but the clerk and the squirt hadn't got any deeper into that.

Mrs. Molloy hadn't been very helpful about his business affairs. She said that during her tenure as his secretary he had apparently transacted most of his business outside the office, and she had never known much about it. He had opened his own mail, which hadn't been heavy, and she had written only ten or twelve letters a week for him, and less than half of them had been on business matters. Her chief function had been to answer the phone and take messages when he was absent, and he had been absent most of the time. Apparently he had been interested almost exclusively in rural properties; as far as she knew, he had never had a hand in any New York City real-estate transactions. She had no idea what his income was, or his assets.

As for people who might have had a motive for killing him, she had supplied the names of four men with whom he had been on bad terms, and they had been looked into, but none of them seemed very promising. One of them had merely got sore because Molloy had refused to pay on a bet the terms of which had been disputed, and the others weren't much better. It had to be a guy who had not only croaked Molloy but had also gone to a lot of trouble to see that someone else got hooked for it, specifically Peter Hays, and that called for a real character.

In the taxi on my way uptown, if someone had hopped in and offered me ten to one that we had grabbed the short end of the stick, I would have passed. I will ride my luck on occasion, but I like to pick the occasion.

Number 171 East 52nd Street was an old walk-up which had had a thorough job of upgrading, inside and out, along with the houses on either side. They had all been painted an elegant gray, one with yellow trim, one with blue, and one with green. In the vestibule I pushed the button at the top of the row, marked MOLLOY, took the receiver from the hook and put it to my ear, and in a moment was asked who it was. I gave my name, and, when the latch clicked, pushed the door open, entered, and took the do-it-yourself elevator to the fifth floor. Emerging, I took a look around, noting where the stairs were. After all, this was the scene of the crime, and I was a detective. Hearing my name called, I turned. She was standing in the doorway.

She was only eight steps away, and by the time I reached her I had made a decision which sometimes, with one female or another, may take me hours or even days. I wanted no part of her. The reason I wanted no part was that just one look had made it plain that if I permitted myself to want a part it would be extremely difficult to keep from going on and wanting the whole; and that was highly inadvisable in the circumstances. For one thing, it wouldn't have been fair to P.H., handicapped as he was. This would have to be strictly business, not only outwardly but inwardly. I admit I smiled at her as she moved aside to let me enter, but it was merely a professional smile.

The room she led me into, after I put my coat and hat on a chair in the foyer, was a large and attractive living room with three windows. It was the room that P.H. had entered to find a corpse—if you're on our side. The rugs and furniture had been selected by her. Don't ask me how I know that; I was there and saw them, and saw her with them. She went to a chair over near a window, and, invited, I moved one around to face her. She said that Mr. Freyer had told her on the phone that he was consulting with Nero Wolfe, and that Mr. Wolfe wanted to send his assistant, Mr. Goodwin, to have a talk with her, and that was all she knew. She did not add, "What do you want?"

"I don't know exactly how to begin," I told her, "because we have different opinions on a very important point. Mr. Freyer and Mr. Wolfe and I all think Peter Hays didn't kill your husband, and you think he did."

She jerked her chin up. "Why do you say that?"

"Because there's no use beating around the bush. You think it because there's nothing else for you to think, and anyhow you're not really thinking. You've been hit so hard that you're too numb to think. We're not. Our minds are free and we're trying to use them. But we'd like to be sure on one point: if we prove we're right, if we get him cleared—I don't say it looks very hopeful, but if we do—would you like that or wouldn't you?"

"Oh!" she cried. Her jaw loosened. She said, "Oh," again, but it was only a whisper.

"I'll call that a yes," I said. "Then just forget our difference of opinion, because opinions don't count anyway. Mr. Freyer spent five hours with Nero Wolfe today, and Mr. Wolfe is going to try to find evidence that will clear Peter Hays. He has seen reports of your conversations with Freyer, but they didn't help any. Since you were Molloy's secretary for a year and his wife for three years, Mr. Wolfe thinks it likely—or, say, possible—that at some time you saw or heard something that would help. Remember he is assuming that someone else killed Molloy. He thinks it's very improbable that a situation existed which resulted in Molloy's murder, and that he never said or did anything in your presence that had a bearing on it."

She shook her head, not at me but at fate. "If he did," she said, "I didn't know it."

"Of course you didn't. If you had you would have told Freyer. Mr. Wolfe wants to try to dig it up. He couldn't ask you to come to his office so he could start the digging himself, because he has to spend two hours every afternoon playing with orchids, and at six o'clock he has a conference scheduled with four of his men who are going to be given other assignments—on this case. So he sent me to start in with you. I'll tell you how it works by giving you an example. Once I saw him spend eight hours questioning a young woman about everything and nothing. She wasn't suspected of anything; he was merely hoping to get some little fact that would give him a start. At the end of eight hours he got it: she had once seen a newspaper with a piece cut out of the front page. With that fact for a start, he got proof that a man had committed a murder. That's how it works. We'll start at the beginning, when you were Molloy's secretary, and I'll ask questions. We'll keep at it as long as you can stand it."

"It seems—" Her hand fluttered. I caught myself noticing how nice her hands were, and had to remind myself that that had all been decided. She said, "It seems so empty. I mean I'm empty."

"You're not really empty, you're full. When and where did you first meet Molloy?"

"That was four years ago," she said. "The way you—what you want to try—wouldn't it be better to start later? If there was a situation, the way you say, it would have been more recent, wouldn't it?"

"You never know, Mrs. Molloy." It seemed stiff to be calling her Mrs. Molloy. She fully deserved to be called Selma. "Anyhow, I have my instructions from Mr. Wolfe—and by the way, I skipped something. I was to tell you how simple it could have been. Say I decided to kill Molloy and frame Peter Hays for it. The drugstore on the corner is perfectly placed for me. Having learned that you are out for the evening and Molloy is alone in the apartment, at nine o'clock I phone Peter Hays from the booth in the drugstore and tell him—Freyer has told you what Peter says I told him. Then I cross the street to this house, am admitted by Molloy, shoot him, leave the gun here on a chair, knowing it can't be traced, go back down to the street, watch the entrance from a nearby spot until I see Hays arrive in a taxi and enter the building, return to the drugstore, and phone the police that a shot has just been fired on the top floor of One-seventy-one East Fifty-second Street. You couldn't ask for anything simpler than that."

She was squinting at me, concentrating. It gave the corners of her eyes a little upturn. "I see," she said. "Then you're not just—" She stopped.

"Just playing games? No. We really mean it. Settle back and relax a little. When and where did you first meet Molloy?"

She interlaced her fingers. No relaxing. "I wanted another job. I was modeling and didn't like it, and I knew shorthand. An agency sent me to his office, and he hired me."

"Had you ever heard of him before?"

"No."

"What did he pay you?"

"I started at sixty, and in about two months he raised it to seventy."

"When did he begin to show a personal interest in you?"

"Why—almost right away. The second week he asked me to have dinner with him. I didn't accept, and I liked the way he took it. He knew how to be nice when he wanted to. He always was nice to me until after we were married."

"Exactly what were your duties? I know what you told Freyer, but we're going to fill in."

"There weren't many duties, really—I mean there wasn't much work. I opened the office in the morning—usually he didn't come until around eleven o'clock. I wrote his letters, but that didn't amount to much, and answered the phone, and did the filing, what there was of it. He opened the mail himself."

"Did you keep his books?"

"I don't think he had any books. I never saw any."

"Did you draw his checks?"

"I didn't at first, but later he asked me to sometimes."

"Where did he keep his checkbook?"

"In a drawer of his desk that he kept locked. There wasn't any safe in the office."

"Did you do any personal chores for him? Like getting prize-fight tickets or buying neckties?"

"No. Or very seldom. He did things like that himself."

"Had he ever been married before?"

"No. He said he hadn't."

"Did you go to prizefights with him?"

"Sometimes I did, not often. I didn't like them. And later, the last two years, we didn't go places together much."

"Let's stick to the first year, while you were working for him. Were there many callers at the office?"

"Not many, no. Many days there weren't any."

"How many in an average week, would you say?"

"Perhaps—" She thought. "I don't know, perhaps eight or nine. Maybe a dozen."

"Take the first week you were there. You were new then and noticing things. How many callers were there the first week, and who were they?"

She opened her eyes at me. Wide open, they were quite different from when they were squinting. I merely noted that fact professionally. "But Mr. Goodwin," she said, "that's impossible. It was four years ago!"

I nodded. "That's just a warm-up. Before we're through you'll be remembering lots of things you would have thought impossible, and most of them will be irrelevant and immaterial. I hope not all of them. Try it. Callers the first week."

We kept at it for nearly two hours, and she did her best. She enjoyed none of it, and some of it was really painful, when we were on the latter part of the year, the period when she was cottoning to Molloy, or thought she was, and was making up her mind to marry him. She would have preferred to let the incidents of that period stay where they were, down in the cellar. I won't say it hurt me as much as it did her, since with me it was strictly business, but it was no picnic. Finally she said she didn't think she could go on, and I said we had barely started.

"Then tomorrow?" she asked. "I don't know why, but this seems to be tougher than it was with the police and the District Attorney. That seems strange, since they were enemies and you're a friend—you are a friend, aren't you?"

It was a trap, and I dodged it. "I want what you want," I told her.

"I know you do, but I just can't go on. Tomorrow?"

"Sure. Tomorrow morning. But I'll have some other errands, so it will have to be with Mr. Wolfe. Could you be at his office at eleven o'clock?"

"I suppose I could, but I'd rather go on with you."

"He's not so bad. If he growls just ignore it. He'll dig up something quicker than I would, in order to get rid of you. He doesn't appreciate women, and I do." I got out a card and handed it to her. "There's the address. Tomorrow at eleven?"

She said yes, and got up to see me to the door, but I told her that with a friend it wasn't necessary.

CHAPTER 7

WHEN I GOT BACK to 35th Street it was half-past six and the conference was in full swing.

I was pleased to see that Saul Panzer was in the red leather chair. Unquestionably Johnny Keems had made a go for it, and Wolfe himself must have shooed him off. Johnny, who at one time, under delusions of grandeur, had decided my job would look better on him or he would look better on it, no matter which, but had found it necessary to abandon the idea, was a pretty good operative but had to be handled. Fred Durkin, big and burly and bald, knows exactly what he can expect of his brains and what he can't, which is more than you can say for a lot of people with a bigger supply. Orrie Cather is smart, both in action and in appearance. As for Saul Panzer, I thoroughly approve of his preference for free-lancing, since if he decided he wanted my job he would get it—or anybody else's.

Saul, as I say, was in the red leather chair, and the others had three of the yellow ones in a row facing Wolfe's desk. I got greetings and returned them, and circled around to my place. Wolfe remarked that he hadn't expected me so early.

"I tired her out," I told him. "Her heart was willing but her mind was weak. She'll be here at eleven in the morning. Do you want it now?"

"If you got anything promising."

"I don't know whether I did or not. We were at it nearly two hours, and mostly it was just stirring up the dust, but there were a couple of things, maybe three, that you might want to hear. One day in the fall of nineteen fifty-two, she thinks it was October, a man called at the office, and there was a row that developed into combat. She heard a crash and went in, and the caller was flat on the floor. Molloy told her he would handle it, and she returned to the other room, and pretty soon the caller came out on his feet and left. She doesn't know his name, and she didn't hear what the row was about because the door between the rooms was shut."

Wolfe grunted. "I hope we're not reduced to that. And?"

"This one was earlier. In the early summer. For a period of about two weeks a woman phoned the office nearly every day. If Molloy was out she left word for him to call Janet. If Molloy was in and took the call he told her he couldn't discuss the matter on the phone and rang off. Then the calls stopped and Janet was never heard from again."

"Does Mrs. Molloy know what she wanted to discuss?"

"No. She never listened in. She wouldn't."

He sent me a sharp glance. "Are you bewitched again?"

"Yes, sir. It took four seconds, even before she spoke. From now on you'll pay me but I'll really be working for her. I want her to be happy. When that's attended to I'll go off to some island and mope." Orrie Cather laughed, and Johnny Keems tittered. I ignored them and went on. "The third thing was in February or March nineteen fifty-three, not long before they were married. Molloy phoned around noon and said he had expected to come to the office but couldn't make it. His ticket for a hockey game that night was in a drawer of his desk, and he asked her to get it and send it to him by messenger at a downtown restaurant. He said it was in a small blue envelope in the drawer. She went to the drawer and found the envelope, and noticed that it had been through the mail and slit open. Inside there were two things: the hockey ticket and a blue slip of paper, which she glanced at. It was a bill from the Metropolitan Safe Deposit Company for rent of a safe-deposit box, made out to Richard Randall. It caught her eye because she had once thought she might marry a man named Randall but had decided not to. She put it back in the envelope, which was addressed to Richard Randall, but if she noticed the address she has forgotten it. She had forgotten the whole incident until we dug it up."

"At least," Wolfe said, "if it's worth a question we know where to ask it. Anything else?"

"I don't think so. Unless you want the works."

"Not now." He turned to the others. "Now that you've heard Archie, you gentlemen are up to date. Have you any more questions?"

Johnny Keems cleared his throat. "One thing. I don't get the idea of Hays being innocent. I only know what I read in the papers, but it certainly didn't take the jury very long."

"You'll have to take that from me." Wolfe was brusque. You have to be brusque with Johnny. He turned to me. "I've explained the situation to them in some detail, but I have not mentioned our client's name or the nature of his interest. We'll keep that to ourselves. Any more questions?"

There were none.

"Then we'll proceed to assignments. Archie, what about phone booths in the neighborhood?"

"The drugstore that Freyer mentioned is the nearest place with a booth. I didn't look around much."

He went to Durkin. "Fred, you will try that. The phone call to Peter Hays, at nine o'clock, was probably made from nearby, and the one to the police, at nine-eighteen, had to be made as quickly as possible after Peter Hays was seen entering the building. The hope is of course forlorn, since more than three months have passed, but you can try it. The drugstore seems the likeliest, but cover the neighborhood. If both phone calls were made from the same place, it's possible you can jog someone's memory. Start this evening, at once. The calls were made in the evening. Any questions?"

"No, sir. I've got it." Fred never takes his eyes off of Wolfe. I think he's expecting him to sprout either a horn or a halo, I'm not sure which, and doesn't want to miss it. "Shall I go now?"

"No, you might as well stay till we're through." Wolfe went to Cather. "Orrie, you will look into Molloy's business operations and associates and his financial standing. Mr. Freyer will see you at his office at ten in the morning. He'll give you whatever information he has, and you will start with that. Getting access to Molloy's records and papers will be rather complicated."

"If he kept books," I said, "they weren't in his office. At least Mrs. Molloy never saw them, and there was no safe."

"Indeed." Wolfe's brows went up. "A real-estate brokerage business and no books? I think, Archie, I'd better have a full report on the dust you stirred up." He returned to Orrie. "Since Molloy died intestate, as far as is known, his widow's rights are paramount in such matters as access to his records and papers, but they should be exercised as legal procedure provides. Mr. Freyer says that Mrs. Molloy has no attorney, and I'm going to suggest to her that she retain Mr. Parker. Mr. Freyer thinks it inadvisable to suggest him, and I agree. If Molloy kept no records in his office you will first have to find them. Any questions?"

Orrie shook his head. "Not now. I may have after I've talked with Freyer. If I do I'll phone you."

Wolfe made a face. Except in emergencies the boys never call between nine and eleven in the morning or four and six in the afternoon, when he is up in the plant rooms, but even so the damn phone rings when he's deep in a book or working a cross-word or busy in the kitchen with Fritz, and he hates it. He went to Keems.

"Johnny, Archie will give you names and addresses. Mr. Thomas L. Irwin and Mr. and Mrs. Jerome Arkoff. They were Mrs. Molloy's companions at the theater; it was Mrs. Arkoff who phoned Mrs. Molloy that she had an extra ticket and invited her to join them. That may have no significance; X may merely have been awaiting an opportunity and grasped it; but he must have known that Mrs. Molloy would be out for the evening, and it is worth inquiry. Two investigators looked into it for Mr. Freyer, but they were extraordinarily clumsy, judging by their reports. If you get any hint that the invitation to Mrs. Molloy was designed, confer with me at once. I have known you to overstrain your talents."

"When?" Johnny demanded.

Wolfe shook his head. "Some other time. Will you communicate with me if you find cause for suspicion?"

"Sure. If you say so."

"I do say so." Wolfe turned to Saul Panzer. "For you, Saul, I had something in mind, but it can wait. It may be worth the trouble to learn why Molloy had in his possession an envelope addressed to Richard Randall, containing a bill for rental of a safe-deposit box, even though it was more than three years ago. If it were a simple matter to get information from the staff of a safe-deposit company about a customer I wouldn't waste you on it, but I know it isn't. Any questions?"

"Maybe a suggestion," Saul offered. "Archie might phone Lon Cohen at the *Gazette* and ask him to give me a good print of a picture of Molloy. That would be better than a newspaper reproduction."

The other three exchanged glances. They were all good operatives, and it would have been interesting to know, as a check on their talents, whether they had all caught the possibility as quickly as Saul had that Molloy had himself been Richard Randall. There was no point in asking them, since they would all have said yes.

"That will be done," Wolfe told him. "Anything else?"

"No, sir."

Wolfe came to me. "Archie. You've gone through Mr. Freyer's file and seen the report on Miss Delia Brandt, Molloy's secretary at the time of his death. You know where to find her."

"Right."

"Please do so. If she has anything we can use, get it. Since you are working for Mrs. Molloy you may need her approval. If so, get that."

Saul smiled. Orrie laughed. Johnny tittered. Fred grinned.

CHAPTER 8

I JOINED Wolfe in the dining room at seven-fifteen as usual, and sat at table, but I didn't really dine because I had an eight-thirty date down in the Village and had to rush it some. Par for Wolfe from clams to cheese is an hour and a half.

Dating Delia Brandt hadn't been any strain on my talents. I had got her on the phone at the first try, given her my own name and occupation, and told her I had been asked by a client to see her and find out if she could supply enough material on Michael M. Molloy, her late employer, for a magazine article under her by-line, to be ghosted by the client. The proceeds would be split. After a few questions she said she would be willing to consider it and would be at home to me at eight-thirty. So I hurried a little with the roast duckling and left Wolfe alone with the salad.

It wouldn't have hurt the house at 43 Arbor Street any to get the same treatment as the one at 171 East 52nd. The outside could have used some paint, and a do-it-yourself elevator would have been a big improvement on the narrow, dingy wooden stairs. Three flights up, she was not waiting on the threshold to greet me, and, finding no button to push, I tapped on the door. From the time it took her you might have thought she had to traverse a spacious reception hall, but when the door opened the room was right there. I spoke.

"My name's Goodwin. I phoned."

"Oh," she said, "of course. I had forgotten. Come in."

It was one of those rooms that call for expert dodging to get anywhere. God knows why the piano bench was smack in the main traffic lane, and He also knows why there was a piano bench at all, since there was no piano. Anyway it was handy for my hat and coat. She crossed to a couch and invited me to sit, and since there was no chair nearby I perched on the couch too, twisting around to face her.

"I really had forgotten," she said apologetically. "My mind must have been soaring around." She waved a hand to show how a mind soars.

She was young, well shaped and well kept, well dressed and well shod, with a soft, clear skin and bright brown eyes, and well-cut fine brown hair, but a mind that soared. . . .

"Didn't you say you were a detective?" she asked. "Something about a magazine?"

"That's right," I told her. "This editor thinks he'd like to try a new slant on a murder. There have been thousands of pieces about murderers. He thinks he might use one called 'The Last Month of a Murdered Man' or 'The Last Year of a Murdered Man.' By his secretary."

"Oh, not my name?"

"Sure, your name too. And, now that I've seen you, a good big picture of you. I wouldn't mind having one myself."

"Now don't get personal."

It was hard to believe, the contrast between what my eyes saw and my ears heard. Any man would have been glad to walk down a theater aisle with her, but there would have to be an understanding that she would keep her mouth shut.

"I'll try not to," I assured her. "I can always turn my back. The idea is this: you'll tell me things about Mr. Molloy, what he said and did and how he acted, and I'll report to the editor, and if he thinks there's an article in it he'll come and talk with you. How's that?"

"Well, it couldn't be called 'The Last Year of a Murdered Man.' It would have to be called 'The Last Ten Months of a Murdered Man' because I only worked for him ten months."

"Okay, that's even better. Now. I understand—"

"How many days are there in ten months?"

"It depends on the months. Roughly three hundred."

"We could call it 'The Last Three Hundred Days of a Murdered Man.'"

"A good idea. I understand that occasionally you had dinner with Molloy at a restaurant. Was it—"

"Who told you that?"

I had three choices: get up and go, strangle her, or sit on her. "Look, Miss Brandt. I'm being paid by the hour and I've got to earn it. Was it to discuss business matters or was it social?"

She smiled, which made her even prettier. "Oh, that was just social. He never talked about business to me. It had got so he didn't want to have dinner with his wife, and he hated to eat alone. I'd love to put that in. I know some people think I allowed him liberties, but I never did."

"Did he try to take liberties?"

"Oh, of course. Married men always do. That's because with their wives it's not a liberty any more."

"Yeah, that's why I've never married. Did he—"

"Oh, aren't you married?"

But you've had enough of her. So had I, but I was on duty, and I stuck with it for three solid hours. I had to go through another ordeal, about halfway through. We were thirsty, and she went to the kitchenette for liquid, and came back with a bottle of ginger ale, a bottle of gin, and two glasses with one cube of ice in each. I apologized, said I had ulcers, and asked for milk. She said she didn't have any, and I asked for water. I will go beyond the call of duty in a pinch, but I wouldn't drink gin and ginger ale to get the lowdown on Lizzie Borden. It was bad enough to sit there and watch her sipping away at it.

In the taxi on my way downtown to keep the date, I had felt some slight compunction at imposing on a poor working girl with a phony approach. In the taxi on my way home, having told her I would let her know if the editor still liked the idea, my conscience was sound asleep. If a conscience could snore, it probably would have.

Wolfe, who rarely turns in before midnight, was at his desk, reading *A Secret Understanding* by Merle Miller. He didn't look up when I entered, so I went to the safe for the expense book and entered the amounts I had given the hired help for expenses, a hundred bucks for each, put the book back and closed the safe and locked it, and cleared up my desk. I refuse to meet a cluttered desk in the morning.

Then I stood and looked down at him. "Excuse me. Anything from Fred or Johnny that needs attention?"

He finished a paragraph and looked up. "No. Fred called at eleven and reported no progress. Johnny didn't call."

"Shall I save mine for morning?"

"No. That woman will be here. Did you get anything?"

"I don't know." I sat. "She's either a featherbrain or a damn good imitation. She starts every other sentence with 'Oh.' You'd walk out on her in three minutes. She drinks four parts ginger ale and one part gin."

"No."

"Yes."

"Good heavens. Did you?"

"No. But I had to watch her. Two items. One day last October a button on his coat was loose and she offered to sew it on for him. While she was doing so some papers fell out of the pocket and when she picked them up she glanced at them. So she says; papers can fall out of pockets or they can be taken out. Anyhow, she was looking at one of the papers which was a list of names and figures when he suddenly entered from his room, snatched the paper from her, and gave her hell. He slapped her, but that's off the record because she doesn't want it to be in the article, and besides he apologized and bought her champagne at dinner that evening. She says he was so mad he turned white."

"And the names and figures?"

"I hoped you would ask that. She can't remember. She thinks the figures were amounts of money, but she's not sure."

"Hardly a bonanza."

"No, sir. Neither is the other item, but it's more recent. One day between Christmas and New Year's he asked her how she would like to take a trip to South America with him. He had to go on business and would need a secretary. I should mention that he had been trying to take liberties and she hadn't allowed it. She liked the idea of a trip to South America, but, knowing that what are liberties up here are just a matter of course down there, she told him she'd think it over. He said there wouldn't be much time for thinking it over because the business matters wouldn't wait. He also said they were confidential matters and made her promise she wouldn't mention the proposed trip to anyone. She put him off and hadn't said yes or no by January third, the day he died. So she says. I think she said yes. She is not a good liar. I didn't mention that her mind soars."

"Soars where?"

I waved a hand. "Just soars. You would enjoy her."

"No doubt." He looked up at the clock. Past midnight. "Has she a job?"

"Oh, yes. With an import firm downtown. Apparently no connection."

"Very well." He pushed his chair back, yawned, and got up. "Johnny should have reported. Confound him, he's too set on a master stroke."

"Instructions for morning?"

"No. I'll need you here for developments. If any. Good night."

He went, to the elevator, and I went, to the stairs. Up in my room, undressing, I decided to dream of Selma Molloy—something like her being trapped in a blazing building, at an upper window, afraid to jump for the firemen's net. I would march up, wave the firemen aside, stretch my arms, and down she would come, light as a feather, into my embrace. The light as a feather part was important, since otherwise there might have been some bones broken. I didn't consider this reneging on my decision, because you can't hold a man responsible for his dreams. But I didn't follow through on it. No dreams at all. In the morning I didn't even remember that I had been going to dream, but I never do remember anything in the morning until I have washed and showered and shaved and dressed and made my way down to the kitchen. With the orange juice the fog begins to lift, and with the coffee it's all clear. It's a good thing Wolfe breakfasts in his room, on a tray taken up by Fritz, and then goes up to the plant rooms. If we met before breakfast he would have fired me or I would have quit long ago.

Thursday started busy and kept it up. There were three letters from P.H.s, answers to the ad, in the morning mail, and I had to answer them. There was a phone call from Omaha, from James R. Herold. His wife was impatient. I told him we had five men working on the case, including Saul Panzer and me, and we would report as soon as there was anything worth reporting. Fred Durkin came in person to confer. He had visited five establishments with phone booths within two blocks of the 52nd Street house, and had found no one who remembered anything about any user of the phone around nine o'clock on January 3. The soda jerk who had been on duty at the drugstore that evening had left and gone somewhere in Jersey. Should Fred find him? I told him yes and wished him luck.

Orrie Cather phoned from Freyer's office to ask if we had arranged with Mrs. Molloy to hire a lawyer to establish her position legally, and I told him no, that would be done when she came to see Wolfe.

Lon Cohen of the *Gazette* phoned and said he had a riddle for me. It goes like this, he said. "Archie Goodwin tells me on Tuesday that he and Nero Wolfe aren't interested in the Hays murder trial. The P.H. in Wolfe's ad is a different person, no connection. But Wednesday evening I get a note from Goodwin asking me to give the bearer, Saul Panzer, a good clear print of a picture of Michael M. Molloy. Here's the riddle: what's the difference between Archie Goodwin and a double-breasted liar?"

I couldn't blame him, but neither could I straighten him out. I told him the note Saul had brought him must have been a forgery, and promised to give him a front-page spread as soon as we had one.

Selma Molloy came on the dot at eleven. I let her in and took her coat, a quiet gray plaid, in the hall, and was putting it on a hanger when the elevator bumped to a stop and Wolfe emerged. He stopped, facing her, inclined his head nearly an inch when I pronounced her name, turned, and made for the office, and I convoyed her in and to the red leather chair. He sat and leveled his eyes at her, trying not to scowl. He hates to work, and this would probably be not only an all-day session, but all day with a woman. Then he had an idea. His head turned and he spoke.

"Archie. Since I'm a stranger to Mrs. Molloy, and you are not, it might be better for you to tell her about the legal situation regarding her husband's estate."

She looked at me. In her apartment she had sat with her back to a window, and here she was facing one, but the stronger light gave me no reason to lower my guard.

She squinted at me. "His estate? I thought you wanted to go on from yesterday."

"We do," I assured her. "By the way, I told you I wouldn't be here, but my program was changed. The estate thing is a part of the investigation. We want access to Molloy's records and papers, and since no will has been found the widow has a right to them, and you're the widow. Of course you can let us look at anything that's in the apartment, but there should be some legal steps—for instance, you should be named as administrator."

"But I don't want to be administrator. I don't want anything to do with his estate. I might have wanted some of the furniture, if—" She let it hang. She shook her head. "I don't want anything."

"What about cash for your current expenses?"

"I wondered about that yesterday, after you had gone." Her eyes were meeting mine, straight. "Whether Nero Wolfe was expecting me to pay him."

"He isn't." I looked at Wolfe, and his head moved left, just perceptibly, and back. So we were still keeping our client under our hat. I met her eyes again. "Our interest in the case developed through a conversation with Mr. Freyer, and all we expect from you is information. I asked about cash only because there must be some in your husband's estate."

"If there is I don't want it. I have some savings of my own, enough to go along on a while. I just don't know what I'm going to do." She pinned her lower lip with her teeth, and after a moment released it. "I don't know what I'm going to do, but I don't want to be his administrator or have anything to do with it. I should have left him long ago, but I had married him with my eyes open and my silly pride—"

"Okay, but it might help if we could take a look at his papers. For instance, his checkbook. Miss Brandt tells me that the furniture in the office was sold, and that before it was taken away some man went through the desks and removed the contents. Do you know about that?"

"Yes, that was a friend of mine—and he had been a friend of my husband's—Tom Irwin. He said the office should be closed up and I asked him to attend to it."

"What happened to the stuff he took?"

"He brought it to the apartment. It's there now, in three cartons. I've never looked at it."

"I would like to. You'll be here with Mr. Wolfe for quite a while. I could go up to the apartment and do it now if you're willing to let me have the key."

Without the slightest hesitation she said, "Of course," and opened her handbag. It didn't put her down a notch in my book —her being so trustful with a comparative stranger. All it meant was that with her P.H. convicted of murder she didn't give a damn about anything at all, and besides, I was the comparative stranger. Glancing at Wolfe and getting a nod, I went to her and took the keys, told her I would let her know if I found anything helpful and would give her a receipt for anything I brought away, and headed for the hall. I had just taken my topcoat from the rack when the doorbell rang, and a look through the one-way glass panel showed me Saul Panzer out on the stoop. Putting the coat back, I opened up.

There are things about Saul I don't understand and never will. For instance, the old cap he always wears. If I wore that cap while tailing a subject I'd be spotted in the first block. If I wore it while calling on people for information they would suspect I was cuckoo or quaint and draw the curtains. But Saul never gets spotted unless he wants to, and for extracting material from people's insides nothing can equal him except a stomach pump. While he was hanging up his coat and sticking the cap in its pocket I stepped to the office door to tell Wolfe, and Wolfe said to bring him in. He came, and I followed him.

"Yes?" Wolfe inquired.

Saul, standing, shot a glance at the red leather chair and said, "A report."

"Go ahead. Mrs. Molloy's interest runs with ours. Mrs. Molloy, this is Mr. Panzer."

She asked him how he did and he bowed. That's another thing about him, his bow; it's as bad as his cap. He sat down on the nearest yellow chair, knowing that Wolfe wants people at eye level, and reported.

"Two employees of the Metropolitan Safe Deposit Company identified a picture of Michael M. Molloy. They say it's a picture of Richard Randall, a renter of a box there. I didn't tell them it was Molloy, but I think one of them suspects it. I didn't try to find out what size the box is or when he first rented it or any other details, because I thought I'd better get instructions. If they get stirred up enough to look into it and decide that one of their boxes was probably rented under another name by a man who has been murdered, they'll notify the District Attorney. I don't know the law, I don't know what rights the DA has after he has got a conviction, since he couldn't be looking for evidence, but I thought you might want to get to the box first."

"I do," Wolfe declared. "How good is the identification?"

"I'd bank on it. I'm satisfied. Do you want to know just how it went?"

"No. Not if you're satisfied. How much are they already stirred up?"

"I think not much. I was pretty careful. I doubt if either of them will go upstairs with it, but they might, and I thought you might want to move."

"I do." Wolfe turned. "Mrs. Molloy. Do you know what this is about?"

"Yes, I think so." She looked at me. "Isn't it what I told you yesterday, the envelope and slip of paper when I was looking for the hockey ticket?"

"That's it," I told her.

"And you've found out already that my husband was Richard Randall?"

"We have," Wolfe said, "and that changes the situation. We must find out what is in that box as soon as possible, and to do so we must, first, demonstrate that Randall was Molloy, and, second, establish your right to access. Since in handling his safe-deposit box a man certainly makes fingerprints, the first presents no technical problem, but it must wait upon the second. When you said, madam, that you would have nothing to do with your husband's estate, I understood and respected your attitude. Rationally it could not be defended, but emotionally it was formidable; and when feeling takes over sense is impotent. Now it's different. We must see the contents of that box, and we can get to it only through you. You will have to assert your rights as the widow and take control of the estate. The law can crawl and usually does, but in an emergency it can— What are you shaking your head for?"

"I've told you. I won't do that."

Hearing her tone, and seeing her eyes and her jaw, he started to glare but decided it wouldn't work. So he turned to me. "Archie."

I did the glaring, at him, and then toned the glare down as I transferred it to her. "Mrs. Molloy," I said, "Mr. Wolfe is a genius, but geniuses have their weak spots, and one of his is that he pretends to believe that attractive young women can refuse me nothing. It comes in handy when an attractive young woman says no to something he wants, because it's an excuse for passing the buck to me, which he just did. I don't know what to do with it and he can't expect me to—he just said himself that when feeling takes over sense is impotent, so what good will it do to try to reason with you? But may I ask you a question?"

She said yes.

"Suppose no good grounds for a retrial or an appeal are found, and the sentence is carried out, and Peter Hays dies in the electric chair, and some time later, when a court gets around to it, that safe-deposit box is opened and it contains something that starts an investigation and leads to evidence that someone else committed the murder. What would your feeling be then?"

She had her lip pinned again, and had to release it to say, "I don't think that's a fair question."

"Why not? All I did was suppose, and it wasn't inconceivable. That box may be empty, but it *could* contain what I said. I think the trouble is that you don't believe there is any evidence, in that safe-deposit box or anywhere else, that will clear Peter Hays, because he's guilty, so why should you do something you don't want to do?"

"That's not true! It's not true!"

"You know damn well it's true."

Her head went down, forward, and her hands came up to cover her face. Wolfe glowered at me. From that room he has walked out on a lot of different people, but when a woman goes to pieces he doesn't walk out, he runs. I shook my head at him. I didn't think Selma Molloy was going to slip the bit.

She didn't. When she finally raised her head her eyes met mine and she said calmly, "Listen, Mr. Goodwin. Didn't I help all I could yesterday and didn't I come today? You know I did. But how can I claim any rights as Mike Molloy's widow when for two years I bitterly regretted I was his wife? Don't you see it's impossible? Isn't there some other way? Can't I ask for someone else to be administrator and he can have rights?"

"I don't know," I told her. "That's a legal question."

"Get Mr. Parker," Wolfe snapped.

I turned and pulled the phone to me and dialed. Since Nathaniel Parker had answered some ten thousand legal questions for us over the years I didn't have to look up the number. While I was getting him Saul Panzer asked Wolfe if he should leave, and was told to wait until there was some place for him to leave for. When I had Parker, Wolfe took his phone.

I had to admire his performance. He would have liked to tell Parker that we were being obstructed by a perverse and capricious female, but with her sitting there that would have been inadvisable, so he merely said that for reasons of her own the widow refused to assert her claims, and put the legal problem. From there on his part was mostly grunts.

When he hung up he turned to the female. "Mr. Parker says it's complicated, and since it's urgent he wants to ask you some questions. He will be here in twenty minutes. He says it will expedite matters if you will decide whom you would like to suggest as administrator. Have you anyone in mind?"

"Why—no." She frowned. She looked at me, and back at him. "Could it be Mr. Goodwin?"

"My dear madam." Wolfe was exasperated. "Use your faculties. You met Mr. Goodwin yesterday for the first time, in his capacity as a private investigator. It would be highly inappropriate, and the court would find it so. It should be someone you know well, and trust. What about the man who closed the office and took the cartons to your apartment? Thomas Irwin."

"I don't think—" She considered it. "I don't think I'd want to ask him to do this. His wife wouldn't like it. But I wouldn't mind asking Pat Degan. He might say no, but I could ask him."

"Who is he?"

"Patrick A. Degan. He's the head of the Mechanics Alliance Welfare Association. His office isn't far from here, on Thirty-ninth Street. I could call him now."

"How long have you known him?"

"Three years, since I was married. He was a friend of my husband's, but he always— I mean, he really is my friend, I'm sure he is. Shall I call him? What will I say?"

"Tell him you wish to request a favor of him, and ask him to come here. Now, if possible. If he asks questions tell him you would rather not discuss it on the phone. And I venture a suggestion, in case he comes and consents to act. Legal services will be required, and he may want to name the lawyer to be engaged to perform them. I urge you not to agree. From a legal standpoint it will be your interests the lawyer will represent, whether you wish to renounce them or not, and it will be proper and desirable for you to choose him."

"Why can't I choose the lawyer he names?"

"Because I wouldn't trust him. Because I suspect Mr. Degan of having killed your husband."

She goggled at him. "You suspect Pat Degan? You never heard of him until just now!"

Wolfe nodded. "I made it sensational. Purposely. I suspect each and all of your husband's associates, as I must until I have reason to discriminate, and Mr. Degan is one of them. I advise you not to let him name the lawyer. If you are at a loss to choose one, I suggest Nathaniel Parker, who will be here shortly. I have dealt with him many years, and I recommend him without reservation. As for trusting me, either you believe that I am earnestly seeking an end you desire or it is folly for you to be here at all."

It was a good pitch, but it didn't do the job—not completely. She looked at me, looking the question instead of asking it.

I gave her a strictly professional smile. "Parker is as good as they come, Mrs. Molloy."

"All right, then." She arose. "May I use the phone?"

CHAPTER 9

SINCE PATRICK A. DEGAN was the first suspect we had laid eyes on, unless you want to count Albert Freyer or Delia Brandt, naturally I gave him some attention, and I had plenty of opportunity during the hour that the conference lasted. In appearance I wouldn't have called him sinister—a medium-sized specimen in his early forties with a fair start on a paunch, round face, wide nose, and dark brown eyes that moved quickly and often. He greeted Selma Molloy as a friend, taking her hand in both of his, but not as one who had been bewitched by her into shooting her husband and framing her P.H. for it. I had him mostly in profile during the conference, since he was on a yellow chair facing Wolfe, with Nathaniel Parker on another one between Degan and me. After making the phone call, Mrs. Molloy had returned to the red leather chair. Saul Panzer had retired to one in the rear, over by the bookshelves.

When the situation had been explained to Degan by Mrs. Molloy and she had asked the favor, he wasted five minutes trying to get her to change her mind. When he saw that was no go, he said he would be willing to do what she wanted provided it was legally feasible, and on that point he would have to consult his lawyer. She said of course he would want to ask his lawyer about it, but her lawyer, Mr. Parker, was right there and would explain how it could be done. Not bad for a girl who wasn't using her faculties. Degan turned his quick brown eyes on Parker, polite but not enthusiastic. Parker cleared his throat and started in. That was the first he had heard that he was Mrs. Molloy's counsel, since he had had only a minute or two with us before Degan arrived, but he didn't raise the point.

From there on it got highly technical, and I had a notion, rejected as unprofessional, to give Mrs. Molloy's faculties a recess by taking her up to the plant rooms and showing her the orchids. Anyone sufficiently interested can call Parker at his office, Phoenix 5–2382, and get the details. What it boiled down to was that there were three different ways of handling it, but one would be much too slow, and which of the other two was preferable? Degan made two phone calls to his lawyer, and finally they got it settled. Parker would start the ball rolling immediately, and Degan agreed to be available for an appearance before a judge on short notice. Parker thought we might get a look at the inside of the safe-deposit box by Monday, and possibly sooner. He was just getting up to go when the phone rang and I answered it.

It was Sergeant Purley Stebbins of Homicide West. He told me some news, and I asked a few questions, and when he asked me a question I decided I didn't know the answer and asked him to hold the wire. Covering the transmitter, I turned to Wolfe.

"Stebbins. At eleven-forty-eight last night a man was hit by a car on Riverside Drive in the Nineties, and killed. The body has been identified as that of John Joseph Keems. About an hour ago the car that hit him was found parked on upper Broadway, and it's hot. It was stolen last night from where it was parked on Ninety-second Street. The fact that it was a stolen car makes Purley think it may have been premeditated murder, possibly in connection with a case Keems was working on, and, knowing that Johnny Keems often does jobs for you, he asks if he was working for you last night. I told him you sometimes hire an operative without telling me, and I'd ask you. I'm asking you."

"Tell him I'm engaged and you'll call him back."

I did so, hung up, and swiveled. Wolfe's lips were tight, his eyes were half closed, and his temple was twitching. He met my eyes and demanded, "You knew him. How much chance is there that he would have let a car kill him by inadvertence?"

"Practically none. Not Johnny Keems."

Wolfe's head turned. "Saul?"

"No, sir." Saul had got to his feet while I was reporting to Wolfe. "Of course it could happen, but I agree with Archie."

Wolfe's head turned more, to the left. "Mrs. Molloy, if Mr. Goodwin was correct when he said that you believe there can be no evidence that will clear Peter Hays, this bitter pill for me is not so bitter for you. Not only can there be such evidence, there will be. Johnny Keems was working for me last night, on this case, and he was murdered. That settles it. You have been told that I thought it likely that Peter Hays is innocent; now I know he is."

His head jerked right. "Mr. Parker, the urgency is now pressing. I beg you to move with all possible speed. Well?"

I wouldn't say that Parker moved with all possible speed, but he moved. He made for the hall and was gone.

Degan, lifted from his chair by Wolfe's tone and manner, had a question. "Do you realize what you're saying?"

"Yes, sir, I do. Why? Do you challenge it?"

"No, I don't challenge it, but you're worked up and I wondered if you realized that you were practically promising Mrs. Molloy that Peter Hays will be cleared. What if you're giving her false hopes? What if you can't make good on it? I think I have the right to ask, as an old friend of hers."

"Perhaps you have." Wolfe nodded at him. "I concede it. It's a stratagem, Mr. Degan, directed at myself. By committing myself to Mrs. Molloy, before witnesses, I add to other incentives that of preserving my self-conceit. If the risk of failure is grave for her it is also grave for me."

"You didn't have to make it so damned positive." Degan went to Mrs. Molloy and put a hand on her shoulder. "I hope to God he's right, Selma. It's certainly rough on you. Anything more I can do?"

She said no and thanked him, and I went to the hall to let him out. Back in the office, Saul had moved back to a seat up front, presumably by invitation, and Wolfe was lecturing Mrs. Molloy.

". . . and I'll answer your question, but only on condition that henceforth you confide in no one. You are to tell no one anything you may learn of my surmises or plans. If I suspected Mr. Degan, as I did and do, I now have better reason to suspect other friends of yours. Do you accept the condition?"

"I'll accept anything that will help," she declared. "All I asked was what he was doing—the man that was killed."

"And I want to tell you because you may be of help, but first I must be assured that you will trust no one. You will repeat nothing and reveal nothing."

"All right. I promise."

Regarding her, he rubbed the end of his nose with a finger tip. It was a dilemma that had confronted him many times over the years. There were very few men whose tongues he had ever been willing to rely on, and no women at all, but she might have facts he needed and he had to risk it. So he did.

"Mr. Keems left here shortly after seven o'clock last evening with specific instructions, to see the three people who were with you at the theater the evening of January third. He was to learn— What's the matter?"

Her chin had jerked up and her lips had parted. "You might have told me that you suspect me too. I suppose you did, when you said you suspect all of my husband's associates."

"Nonsense. His target was not your alibi. He was to learn all the circumstances of the invitation you got to use an extra theater ticket. That was what got you away from your apartment for the evening. Whoever went there to kill your husband certainly knew you were safely out of the way; and not only that, he may have arranged for your absence. That was what Mr. Keems was after. He had the names and addresses of Mr. Irwin and Mr. and Mrs. Arkoff, and he was to report to me at once if he got any hint that the invitation to you was designed. He didn't report, but he must have got a hint, or someone thought he did; and it must have been a betraying hint, since to suppress it someone stole an automobile and killed him with it. That is not palpable, but it's highly probable, and it's my assumption until it's discredited."

"But then—" She shook her head. "I just don't believe— Did he see them? Who did he see?"

"I don't know. As I say, he didn't report. We'll find out. I want all you can tell me about that invitation. It came from Mrs. Arkoff?"

"Yes. She phoned me."

"When?"

"At half-past seven. I told all about it on the—at the trial."

"I know you did, but I want it first-hand. What did she say?"

"She said that she and Jerry—her husband—had asked Tom and Fanny Irwin to dinner and a show, and she and Jerry were at the restaurant, and Tom had just phoned that Fanny had a headache and couldn't come and he would meet them in the theater lobby, and Rita—that's Mrs. Arkoff—she asked me to come, and I said I would."

"Did you go to the restaurant?"

"No, there wasn't time, and I had to dress. I met them at the theater."

"At what time?"

"Half-past eight."

"They were there?"

"Rita and Jerry were. We waited a few minutes for Tom, and then Rita and I went on in and Jerry waited in the lobby for Tom. Rita told him to leave the ticket at the box office, but he said no, he had told him they'd meet him in the lobby. Rita and I went on in because we didn't want to miss the curtain. It was Julie Harris in *The Lark*."

"How soon did the men join you?"

"It was quite a while. Almost the end of the first act."

"When does the first act end?"

"I don't know. It's rather long."

Wolfe's head moved. "You've seen that play, Archie?"

"Yes, sir. I would say a quarter to ten, maybe twenty to."

"Have you seen it, Saul?"

"Yes, sir. Twenty to ten."

"You know that?"

"Yes, sir. Just my habit of noticing things."

"Don't disparage it. The more you put in a brain, the more it will hold—if you have one. How long would it take to get from One-seventy-one East Fifty-second Street to that theater?"

"After nine o'clock?"

"Yes."

"With luck, if you were in a hurry, eight minutes. That would be a minimum. From that up to fifteen."

Wolfe turned. "Mrs. Molloy, I wonder that you haven't considered the possible significance of this. The anonymous call to the police, saying that a shot had been heard, was at nine-eighteen. The police arrived at nine-twenty-three. Even if he waited to see them arrive, and he probably didn't, he could have reached the theater before the first act ended. Didn't that occur to you?"

She was squinting at him. "If I understand you—you mean didn't it occur to me that Jerry or Tom might have killed Mike?"

"Obviously. Didn't it?"

"No!" She made it a little louder than it had to be, and I hoped Wolfe understood that she was raising her voice not at him, but at herself. It hadn't occurred to her because the minute she had learned, on getting home that January night, that her husband had been found with a bullet in his head, and that P.H., with a gun in his pocket, had tried to force his way out, she thought she knew what had happened, and it had settled in her like a lump of lead. But she wasn't going to tell Wolfe that. She told him instead. "There was no reason for Jerry to kill him. Or Tom. Why? And they had been in the bar across the street. Tom came not long after Rita and I went in, and said he needed a drink, and they went and had one."

"Which one of them told you that?"

"Both of them. They told Rita and me, and we said they must have had more than one."

Wolfe grunted. "Go back a little. Wouldn't it have been the natural thing for Mr. Arkoff to leave the ticket at the box office instead of waiting in the lobby?"

"Not the way it was. Rita didn't ask him to leave it at the box office, she told him to, and he doesn't like to have her tell him to do things. So she does." She came forward in the chair. "Listen, Mr. Wolfe," she said earnestly. "If that man getting killed, if that means what you think it does, I don't care what happens to anybody. I haven't been caring what happened to me, I've just been feeling I might as well be dead, and I'm certainly not going to start worrying about other people, not even my best friends. But I think this is no use. Even if they lied about being in the bar, neither of them had any *reason!*"

"We'll see about that," he told her. "Someone had reason to

fear Johnny Keems enough to kill him." He glanced up at the clock. "Luncheon will be ready in seven minutes. You'll join us? You too, Saul. Afterward you'll stay here to be on hand if Mr. Parker needs you. And Mrs. Molloy, you'll stay too and tell me everything you know about your friends, and you'll invite them to join us here at six o'clock."

"But I can't!" she protested. "How can I? Now?"

"You said you weren't going to worry about them. Yesterday morning Peter Hays, talking with Mr. Goodwin, used the same words you have just used. He said he might as well be dead. I intend that both of you—"

"Oh!" she cried, to me. "You saw him? What did he say?"

"I was only with him a few minutes," I told her. "Except that he might as well be dead, not much. He can tell you himself when we finish this job." I went to Wolfe. "I've got to call Purley. What do I tell him?"

He pinched his nose. He has an idea that pinching his nose makes his sense of smell keener, and a faint aroma of cheese dumplings was coming to us from the kitchen. "Tell him that Mr. Keems was working for me last evening, investigating a confidential matter, but I don't know whom he had seen just prior to his death; and that we'll inform him if and when we get information that might be useful. I want to speak with those people before he does."

As I turned to dial, Fritz entered to announce lunch.

CHAPTER 10

NOT LONG AGO I got a letter from a woman who had read some of my accounts of Nero Wolfe's activities, asking me why I was down on marriage. She said she was twenty-three years old and was thinking of having a go at it herself. I wrote her that as far as I knew there was absolutely nothing wrong with marriage; the trouble was the way people handled it, and I gave her a couple of examples. The examples I used were Mr. and Mrs. Jerome Arkoff and Mr. and Mrs. Thomas L. Irwin, though I didn't mention their names, and I had got my material from what I saw and heard in the first five minutes after they arrived at Wolfe's place that Thursday at six o'clock.

They all arrived together, and there was a little bustle in the hall, getting their things off and disposed of. That was finished and I was ready to herd them down the hall and into the office when Rita Arkoff touched her husband's elbow, pointed to a chair against the wall, and told him, "Your hat, Jerry. Hang it up."

No wonder he hadn't left the ticket at the box office. Before he could react normally, like making a face at her or telling her to go to hell, I got the hat myself and put it on the rack, and we proceeded to the office, where the Irwins immediately contributed their share. I had the chairs spaced comfortably to give everyone elbow room, but Tom Irwin pushed his close to his wife's, sat, and took her hand in his and held onto it. I am not by any means against holding hands, in wedded bliss or unwedded, but only if both hands want to, and Fanny Irwin's didn't. She didn't actually try to pull it away, but she sure would have liked to. I hope the examples I gave her will keep my twenty-three-year-old correspondent from developing into an order-giver or a one-way hand-holder, but leave it to her, she'll find some kind of monkey wrench to toss into the machinery, and if she doesn't her husband will.

However, I'm getting ahead of myself. Before six o'clock came, and brought the two couples, there were other happenings. My lunch was interrupted twice. Fred Durkin phoned to say that he had seen the soda jerk who had moved to Jersey, and got nothing, and had worn out his welcome at all places with phone booths within two blocks of 171 East 52nd Street. I told him to come in. Orrie Cather phoned to ask if we had an administrator yet, and I told him also to come in. They arrived before we finished lunch, and, back in the office, Wolfe told them about Johnny Keems.

They agreed with Saul and me that the odds were big that the car that had hit enough of him to kill him had been not careless but careful. They hadn't had much love for him, but they had worked a lot with him. As Fred Durkin said, "Lots of worse guys are still walking around." Orrie Cather said, "Yes, and one of them has got something coming." No one mentioned that until he got it they had better keep an eye out when crossing a street, but they were all thinking it.

They were given errands. Saul was to go to Parker's office to be at hand. Orrie, armed with Selma Molloy's keys, was to go to her apartment and inspect the contents of the three cartons. Fred, supplied by Mrs. Molloy with descriptions of Jerome Arkoff and Tom Irwin, was to go to the Longacre Theatre and the bar across the street and see if he could find someone who could remember as far back as January 3. Fred was getting the scraps.

When they had gone Wolfe tackled Mrs. Molloy again, to get the lowdown on her friends. Using the phone in the kitchen while he was busy with the staff, she had asked them to come to Wolfe's office at six o'clock. I don't know what she had told them, since she couldn't very well say that Wolfe wanted to find out which one of them had killed Mike Molloy, but anyhow they had said they would come. I had suggested that she could tell them that Wolfe was working with Freyer and was trying to find some grounds for an appeal, and probably she did.

Of course Wolfe had her cornered. If there was any chance of springing her P.H. she was all for it, but friends are friends, for people who are entitled to have any, until shown to be otherwise. If you want to take the word of one bewitched, she handled it very nicely. She stuck strictly to facts. For instance, she did not say that Fanny Irwin and Pat Degan were snatching a snuggle; she merely said that Rita Arkoff thought they were.

Jerome Arkoff, thirty-eight, a husky six-footer with a long solemn face, gray-blue eyes, a long nose, and big ears, according to the description she had given Fred Durkin, was a television producer, successful enough to have ulcers. She had met him through Rita, who had been a model when Selma was, and who had married Arkoff about the time Selma had quit modeling and gone to work for Molloy. Arkoff and Molloy had met through their wives' friendship, and there had been nothing special in their relations, either of harmony or of hostility. If there had been anything between them that could possibly have led to murder, Selma knew nothing of it. She conceded it was conceivable that Molloy and Rita had put horns on Arkoff without her ever suspecting it, and Arkoff had removed the blot by blotting out Molloy, but not that he had also framed Peter Hays. Arkoff had liked Peter Hays.

Thomas L. Irwin, forty, was slender, handsome, and dark-skinned, with a skimpy black mustache. He was an executive in a big printing company, in charge of sales. Selma had met him shortly after her marriage, about the same time she had met Patrick Degan. His company did printing for Degan's organization, the Mechanics Alliance Welfare Association, MAWA for short. Fanny Irwin called Degan "Mawa." Irwin and Molloy had got on each other's nerves and had had some fairly hot exchanges, but Selma had never seen any indication of serious enmity.

It was a thin crop. Wolfe poked all around, but the only real dirt he found was Rita Arkoff's suspicion about Fanny Irwin and Pat Degan, and that wasn't very promising. Even if it was true, and even if Irwin had been aware of it or suspected it, he could hardly have expected to relieve his feelings by killing Molloy. Wolfe abandoned it as fruitless and had gone back to the relationships among the men when a phone call came from Saul Panzer, from Parker's office. Some papers were ready for Mrs. Molloy to sign before a notary and would she please come at once. She left, and five minutes later it was four o'clock and Wolfe went up to the plant rooms.

With a couple of hours to go before company was expected, I would have liked to take a trip up to 52nd Street and help Orrie paw through the cartons, but I had been instructed to stay put, and it was just as well. There were phone calls—one from Lon Cohen, one from our client in Omaha, and one from Purley Stebbins, wanting to know if we had got a line on Johnny Keems's movements and contacts Wednesday evening. I told him no and he was skeptical. When the doorbell rang a little after five o'clock I expected to find Purley on the stoop, come to do a little snarling, but it was a stranger—a tall, slim, narrow-shouldered young man, looking very grim. When I opened the door he was going to push right in, but I was wider and heavier than he was. He announced aggressively, "I want to see Archie Goodwin."

"You are."

"I are what?"

"Seeing Archie Goodwin. Who am I seeing?"

"Oh, a wise guy."

We were off to a bad start, but we got it straightened out that he meant that I was a wise guy, not that I was seeing one; and after I had been informed that his name was William Lesser and he was a friend of Delia Brandt I let him in and took him to the office. When I offered him a chair he ignored it.

"You saw Miss Brandt last night," he said, daring me to try to crawl out of it.

"Right," I confessed.

"About a piece about Molloy for some magazine."

"Right."

"I want to know what she told you about her and Molloy."

I swiveled the chair at my desk and sat. "Not standing up," I told him. "It would take too long. And besides, I'd want—"

"Did she mention me?"

"Not that I remember. I'd want some kind of a reason. You don't look like a city detective. Are you her brother or uncle or lawyer or what?"

He had his fists on his hips. "If I was her brother my name

wouldn't be Lesser, would it? I'm a friend of hers. I'm going to marry her."

I raised the brows. "Then you're off on the wrong foot, brother. A happy marriage must be based on mutual trust and understanding, so they say. Don't ask me what she told me about her and Molloy, ask her."

"I don't have to ask her. She told me."

"I see. If that's how it is you'd better sit down. When are you going to be married?"

The chair I had offered was right beside him. He looked at the seat of it as if he suspected tacks, looked back at me, and sat. "Listen," he said, "it's not the way you make it sound. I told her I was coming to see you. It's not that I don't trust her, it's having it come out in a magazine. Haven't I got a right to find out what's going to be printed about my wife and a man she used to work for?"

"You certainly have, but she's not your wife yet. When is the wedding?"

"Right away. We got the license today. Next week."

"Congratulations. You're a lucky man, Mr. Lesser. How long have you known her?"

"About a year. A little over. Now are you going to tell me what I asked?"

"I have no objection." I crossed my legs and leaned back. "This may ease your mind a little, the fact that the magazine wouldn't dream of printing anything Miss Brandt disapproved of, or anything her husband disapproved of. Invasion of privacy. And you've given me an idea. The article would be a lot better with some real love interest. You know what the slant is, the last ten months of a murder victim as seen by his secretary. Well, all the time she is working for him, and letting him take her out to dinner because she feels sorry for him, her heart is already in bond to another. She is deeply in love with a young man she intends to marry. That would make it a masterpiece—the contrast between the tragedy of the man who is going to die but doesn't know it, and the blush and promise of young love. Huh?"

"I guess so. What did she tell you?"

"Don't worry about that." I waved it away. "When it's written you and she can change anything you don't like, or take it out. When were you engaged?"

"Well—it was understood quite a while ago."

"Before the murder?"

"Formally engaged, no. Does that matter?"

"Maybe not. While she's being sorry for Molloy she can either be promised to another or just hoping she soon will be. It would be swell if we could work in some reference, a sort of minor key, to the murderer. We could call him that, since he's been convicted. Only I don't suppose you knew Peter Hays."

"No."

"Did you know about him? Did you know he was in love with Mrs. Molloy?"

"No. I never heard of him until he was arrested."

"It doesn't really matter. I thought perhaps Miss Brandt had mentioned him to you. Of course Molloy told her about him."

"How do you know he did? Did she say so?"

"I don't remember." I considered. "I'd have to look at my notes, and they're not here. Did she tell you about Molloy asking her to go to South America with him?"

"No, she didn't." Lesser was looking aggressive again. "I didn't come to tell you what she told me, I came to ask you what she told you."

"I know you did." I was sympathetic. "But you have my word that nothing will be printed that you don't like, and that's what you were concerned about. I can't tell you about my talk with Miss Brandt because I was working for a client and my report of that talk is his property. But I think—"

"Then you're not going to tell me."

"I'd like to, but I can't. But I think—"

He got up and walked out. From the back he looked even thinner than from the front. I went to the hall to be polite, but he already had his coat off the rack and was reaching for the doorknob. He banged the door shut behind him, and I returned to the office. The wall clock said twenty-five to six. Delia Brandt might have got home from work, or, since she had gone with Lesser to get their marriage license, she might have taken the day off. I got at the phone and dialed the number of her apartment. No answer.

I thought him over. There was one nice thing about him, he had had the makings of a motive, which was more than I could say for anyone else on the list. And he might easily have known enough about Peter Hays to get the idea of framing him for it. But how could he have arranged for Fanny Irwin to have a headache and stay home, and for Rita Arkoff to invite Selma Molloy to use the ticket? Even if that wasn't essential, if he was merely waiting for an opportunity to knock, how did he know it was knocking? How did he know Mrs. Molloy was away from the apartment and would stay away? It was worth looking for answers to those questions, because there was another nice thing about him: a wife cannot be summoned to testify against her husband.

I dialed Delia Brandt's number again, and got her.

"I've just heard a piece of news," I told her. "That you're going to be married. I'm calling to wish you luck, and happiness, and everything that goes with it."

"Oh, thank you! Thank you very much. Is Bill there with you?"

"No, he left a few minutes ago. A fine young man. It was a pleasure to meet him. Apparently he was a little worried about the magazine article, but I promised him he would have a chance to veto anything he didn't like. So you knew he was coming to see me?"

"Oh, sure. He said he wanted to, and I thought since he was going to be my husband it was only natural. Did you tell him everything—what did you tell him?"

It didn't look like paradise to me, him wanting to know what she had told me, and her wanting to know what I had told him, and they weren't even married yet. "Nothing much," I assured her. "Really nothing. After the promise I gave him it wasn't necessary. Oh, by the way, now that I have you on the phone, I missed one bet entirely last night. At the end of the article, a sort of a climax, you ought to tell where you were and what you were doing the evening of January third. At the very minute Molloy was murdered, just after nine o'clock, if you remember. Do you?"

"Certainly I do. I was with Bill. We were dining and dancing at the Dixie Bower. We didn't leave until after midnight."

"That's wonderful. That will fit right in with an idea I had and told Bill about, how all the time you were trying to be nice to Molloy because you were sorry for him you were deeply in love with a young man who—"

She cut me off. "Oh, the bell's ringing! It must be Bill."

A little click and she was gone. It didn't matter much, since there was soon an interruption at my end. I had just hung up when the sound came of Wolfe's elevator descending, and he had just entered and was crossing to his desk when the doorbell rang and I had to go to the hall to receive the company. I have already told about that, about Rita Arkoff ordering her mate to hang up his hat, and about Tom Irwin moving his chair next to his wife's and holding her hand. But, looking back, I see that I haven't mentioned Selma Molloy. I could go back and insert her, but I don't care to cover up. I am not responsible for my subconscious, and if it arranged, without my knowing it, to leave Selma out because it didn't want you to know how it felt about her, that's its lookout. I now put her back in. Around five o'clock she had returned from her errand at Parker's office, and, at Wolfe's suggestion, had gone up to the plant rooms to look at the orchids. He had brought her down with him, and she was sitting in the red leather chair, after greeting her friends. Try again, subconscious.

CHAPTER 11

THE EXCHANGE of greetings between Selma and the quartet had seemed a little cramped for old friends, but that might have been expected. After all, she was aiding and abetting a program that might lead to one of them getting charged with murder, and they had been invited by her to the office of a well-known private detective. When they had got seated she sent her eyes to Wolfe and kept them there. Their eyes were more interested in her than in Wolfe. I concentrated on them.

Selma's descriptions of Tom and Jerry had been adequate and accurate. Jerome Arkoff was big and broad, taller than me, and so solemn it must have hurt, but it could have been the ulcers that hurt. Tom Irwin, with his dark skin and thin little clipped mustache, looked more like a saxophone artist than a printing executive, even while holding his wife's hand. His wife, Fanny, was obviously not at her best, with her face giving the impression that she was trying not to give in to a raging headache, but even so she was no eyesore. Under favorable conditions she would have been very decorative. She was a blonde, and a headache is much harder on a blonde than on a brunette; some brunettes are actually improved by a mild one. This brunette, Rita Arkoff, didn't need one. There was a faint touch of snake hips in her walk, a faint suggestion of slant at the corners of her eyes, and a faint hint of a pout in the set of her well-tinted lips. But an order-giver . . .

Wolfe's eyes went from the Arkoffs on his left to the Irwins on his right. "I don't presume," he said, "to thank you for coming, since it was at Mrs. Molloy's request. She has told you what I'm after. Mr. Albert Freyer, counsel for Peter Hays, wishes to establish a basis for a retrial or an appeal, and I'm trying to help him. I assume you are all in sympathy with that?"

They exchanged glances. "Sure we are," Jerome Arkoff declared. "If you can find one. Is there any chance?"

"I think so." Wolfe was easy and relaxed. "Certain aspects have not been thoroughly investigated—not by the police because of the overwhelming evidence against Peter Hays, and not by Mr. Freyer because he lacked funds and facilities. They deserve—"

"Does he have funds now?" Tom Irwin asked. His voice didn't fit his physique. You would have expected a squeak, but it was a deep baritone.

"No. My interest has been engaged, no matter how, and I am indulging it. Those aspects deserve inquiry, and last evening I sent a man to look into one of them—a man named Johnny Keems, who worked for me intermittently. He was to learn if there was any possibility that on the evening the murder was committed, January third, the invitation to Mrs. Molloy to join a theater party had been designed with the purpose of getting her out of the way. Of course it didn't—"

"You sent that man?" Arkoff demanded.

His wife looked reproachfully at her friend. "Selma darling, really! You know perfectly well—"

"If you please!" Wolfe showed her a palm, and his tone sharpened. "Save your resentment for a need; I'm imputing no malignity to any of you. I was about to say, it didn't have to be designed, since the murderer may have merely seized an opportunity; and if it was designed, it didn't have to be one of you who designed it. You might have been quite unaware of it. That was what I sent Mr. Keems to find out, and he was to begin by seeing you, all four of you. First on his list was Mrs. Arkoff, since she had phoned the invitation to Mrs. Molloy." His eyes leveled at Rita. "Did he see you, madam?"

She started to answer, but her husband cut in. "Hold it, Rita." Apparently he could give orders too. He looked at Wolfe. "What's the big idea? If you sent him why don't you ask him? Why drag us down here? Did someone else send him?"

Wolfe nodded. He closed his eyes for a moment, and opened them, and nodded again. "A logical inference, Mr. Arkoff, but wrong. I sent him, but I can't ask him, because he's dead. On Riverside Drive in the Nineties, shortly before midnight last night, an automobile hit him and killed him. It's possible that it was an accident, but I don't think so. I think he was murdered. I think that, working on the assignment I had given him, he had uncovered something that was a mortal threat to someone. Therefore I must see the people he saw and find out what was said. Did he see you, Mrs. Arkoff?"

Her husband stopped her again. "This is different," he told Wolfe, and he looked and sounded different. "*If* he was murdered. What makes you think it wasn't an accident?"

Wolfe shook his head. "We won't go into that, Mr. Arkoff, and we don't have to because the police also suspect that it wasn't. A sergeant at the Homicide Bureau phoned me today to ask if Mr. Keems was working for me last night, and if so, what his assignment was and whom he had seen. Mr. Goodwin put him off—"

"He phoned again later," I put in.

"Yes? What did you tell him?"

"That we were trying to check and would let him know as soon as we had anything useful."

Wolfe went back to them. "I wanted to talk with you people myself first. I wanted to learn what you had told Mr. Keems, and whether he had uncovered anything that might have threatened one of you or someone else. I'll have—"

Fanny Irwin blurted, "He didn't uncover anything with me!" She had got her hand back from her husband's hold.

"Then that's what I'll learn, madam. I'll have to tell the police what he was to do and whom he was to see; that can't be postponed much longer; but it may make things easier for you if I can also tell them that I have talked with you—depending, of course, on what you tell me. Or would you prefer to save it for the police?"

"My God." Tom Irwin groaned. "This is a nice mess."

"And we can thank you for it," Arkoff told Wolfe. "Sicking your damn snoop on us." His head turned. "And you, Selma. You started it."

"Let Selma alone," Rita ordered him. "She's had a rough time and you can't blame her." She looked at Wolfe, and she wasn't pouting. "Let's go ahead and get it over with. Yes, your man saw me, at my apartment. He came when I was about ready to leave, to meet my husband for dinner. He said he was investigating the possibility of a new trial for Peter Hays. I thought he was after Selma's alibi and I told him he might as well save his breath because she was with me every minute, but it was the invitation he wanted to ask about. He asked when I first thought of asking Selma, and I said at the restaurant when Tom phoned and told me Fanny couldn't make it. He asked why I asked Selma instead of someone else, and I said because I liked her and enjoyed her company, and also because when Tom phoned I asked him if he wanted to suggest anyone and he suggested Selma. He asked if Tom gave any special reason for having Selma, and I said he didn't have to because I wanted her anyway. He was going to ask more, but I was late and I said that was all I knew anyhow. So that was all—no, he asked when he could see my husband, and I told him we'd be home around ten o'clock and he might see him then."

"Did he?"

"Yes. We got home a little after ten and he was waiting down in the lobby."

Wolfe's eyes moved. "Mr. Arkoff?"

Jerry hesitated, then shrugged. "I talked with him there in the lobby. I didn't take him upstairs because I had some scripts to go over. He asked me the same things he had asked my wife, but I couldn't tell him as much as she had because she had talked with Tom on the phone. I really couldn't tell him anything. He tried to be clever, asking trick questions about how it was decided to invite Mrs. Molloy, and finally I got fed up and told him to go peddle his papers."

"Did he say anything about having seen Mr. or Mrs. Irwin?"

"No. I don't think so. No."

"Then he left?"

"I suppose so. We left him in the lobby when we went to the elevator."

"You and your wife went up to your apartment?"

"Yes."

"What did you do the rest of the evening?"

Arkoff took a breath. "By God," he said, "if anyone had told me an hour ago that I was going to be asked where I was at the time of the murder I would have thought he was crazy."

"No doubt. It does often seem an impertinence. Where were you?"

"I was in my apartment, working with scripts until after midnight. My wife was in another room, and neither of us could have gone out without the other one knowing it. No one else was there."

"That seems conclusive. Certainly either conclusive or collusive." Wolfe's eyes went right. "Mr. Irwin, since Mr. Keems had been told that you had suggested Mrs. Molloy, I presume he sought you. Did he find you?"

From the expression on Tom Irwin's face, he needed a hand to hold. He opened his mouth and closed it again. "I'm not sure I like this," he said. "If I'm going to be questioned about a murder I think I'd rather be questioned by the police."

"Oh, for heaven's sake," his wife protested. "He won't bite you! Do what Rita did, get it over with!" She went to Wolfe. "Do you want me to tell it?"

"If you were present, madam."

"I was. That man—what was his name?"

"John Joseph Keems."

"It was nearly nine o'clock when he came, and we were just going out. We had promised to drop in at a party some friends were giving for somebody, and we would have been gone if my maid hadn't had to fix the lining of my wrap. He said the same thing he told Rita, about the possibility of a new trial for Peter Hays, and he asked my husband about the phone call to the restaurant. Rita has told you about that. Actually—"

"Did your husband's account of it agree with Mrs. Arkoff's?"

"Of course. Why wouldn't it? Actually, though, it was I who suggested asking Selma Molloy. While Tom was at the phone I told him to tell her to ask Selma because I could trust him with her. It was partly a joke, but I'm one of those jealous wives. Then he wanted to ask some more questions, I mean that man Keems, but by that time my wrap was ready and we had told him all we knew. That was all there was to it."

"Did your husband tell him that you had suggested asking Mrs. Molloy?"

"Yes, I'm pretty sure— Didn't you, Tom?"

"Yes."

"And you went to the party? How late did you stay?"

"Not late at all. It was a bore, and my husband was tired. We got home around eleven and went to bed. We sleep in the same room."

Wolfe started to make a face, realized he was doing it, and called it off. The idea of sleeping in the same room with anybody on earth, man or woman, was too much. "Then," he asked, "you had only that one brief talk with Mr. Keems? You didn't see him again?"

"No. How could we?"

"Did you see him again, Mr. Irwin?"

"No."

"Can you add anything to your wife's account of your talk with him?"

"No. That was all there was to it. I might add that our maid sleeps in, and she was there that night."

"Thank you. That should be helpful. I'll include it in my report to the police." Wolfe went back to the wife. "One little point, Mrs. Irwin. If you decided earlier in the day that you wouldn't be able to go to the theater that evening, you might have mentioned it to someone, for instance to some friend on the phone, and you might also have mentioned, partly as a joke, that you would suggest that Mrs. Molloy be asked in your place. Did anything like that happen?"

She shook her head. "No, it couldn't have, because I didn't decide not to go until just before my husband came home."

"Then your headache was a sudden attack?"

"I don't know what you would call sudden. I was lying down with it most of the afternoon, and taking emagrin, and I was hoping it would go away. But I had to give up."

"Do you have frequent headaches?"

Irwin burst out, "What the hell has that got to do with it?"

"Probably nothing," Wolfe conceded. "I'm fishing white water, Mr. Irwin, and am casting at random."

"It seems to me," Arkoff put in, "that you're fishing in dead water. Asking Mrs. Molloy didn't have to be designed at all. If Peter Hays didn't kill Molloy, if someone else did, of course it was somebody who knew him. He could have phoned Molloy and said he wanted to see him alone, and Molloy told him to come to the apartment, they would be alone there because Mrs. Molloy had gone to the theater. Why couldn't it have happened like that?"

"It could," Wolfe agreed. "Quite possible. The invitation to Mrs. Molloy was merely one of the aspects that deserved inquiry, and it might have been quickly eliminated. But not now. Now there is a question that must be answered: who killed Johnny Keems, and why?"

"Some damned fool. Some hit-and-run maniac."

"Possibly, but I don't believe it. I must be satisfied now, and so must the police, and even if you people are innocent of any complicity you can't escape harassment. I'll want to know more than I do now about the evening of January third, about what happened at the theater. I understand— Yes, Archie?"

"Before you leave last night," I said, "I have a question to ask them."

"Go ahead."

I leaned forward to have all their faces as they turned to me. "About Johnny Keems," I said. "Did he ask any of you anything about Bill Lesser?"

They had never heard the name before. You can't always go by the reaction to a sudden unexpected question, since some people are extremely good at handling their faces, but if that name meant anything to one or more of them they were better than good. They all looked blank and wanted to know who Bill Lesser was. Of course Wolfe would also have liked to know who he was but didn't say so. I told him that was all, and he resumed.

"I understand that Mrs. Molloy and Mrs. Arkoff went in to their seats before curtain time, and that Mr. Arkoff and Mr. Irwin joined them about an hour later, saying they had been in a bar across the street. Is that correct, Mr. Arkoff?"

Arkoff didn't care for that at all, and neither did Irwin. Their position was that their movements on the evening of January 3 had no significance unless it was assumed that one or both of them might have killed Molloy and framed Peter Hays, and that was absurd. Wolfe's position was that the police would ask him if he had questioned them about January 3, and if he said he had and they had balked, the police would want to know why.

Rita told her husband to quit arguing and get it over with, and that only made it worse, until she snapped at him, "What's so touchy about it? Weren't you just dosing up?"

He gave her a dirty look and then transferred it to Wolfe. "My wife and I," he said, "met Mrs. Molloy in the theater lobby at half-past eight. The ladies went on in and I waited in the lobby for Irwin. He came a few minutes later and said he wanted a drink, and he also said he didn't care much for plays about Joan of Arc. We went across the street and had a couple of drinks, and by the time we got in to our seats the first act was about over."

Wolfe's head turned. "You corroborate that, Mr. Irwin?"

"I do."

Wolfe turned a hand over. "So simple, gentlemen. Why all the pother? And with a new and quite persuasive detail, that Mr. Irwin doesn't care for plays about Joan of Arc—an inspired hoyden. To show you to what lengths an investigation can be carried, and sometimes has to be, a dozen men could make a tour of Mr. Irwin's friends and acquaintances and ask if they have ever heard him express an attitude toward Joan of Arc and plays about her. I doubt if I'll be driven to that extremity. Have you any questions?"

They hadn't, for him. Rita Arkoff got up and went to Selma, and Fanny Irwin joined them. The men did too, for a moment, and then headed for the hall, and I followed them. They got their coats on and stood and waited, and finally their women came, and I opened the door. As they moved out Rita was telling the men that she had asked Selma to come and eat with them, but she had said she wasn't up to it. "And no wonder," Rita was saying as I swung the door to.

When I re-entered the office Selma didn't look as if she were up to anything whatever, sitting with her shoulders slumped and her head sagging and her eyes closed. Wolfe was speaking, inviting her to stay for not only dinner but also the night. He said he wanted her at hand for consultation if occasion arose, but that wasn't it. She had brought word from Parker that the court formalities might be completed in the morning, and if so we might get to the safe-deposit box by noon. For that Mrs. Molloy would be needed, and Wolfe would never trust a woman to be where she was supposed to be when you wanted her. Therefore he was telling her how pleasant our south room was, directly under his, with a good bed and morning sunshine, but no sale, not even for dinner. She got to her feet, and I went to the hall with her.

"It's hopeless, isn't it," she said, not a question. I patted her shoulder professionally and told her we had barely started.

In the office again, Wolfe demanded, "Who is Bill Lesser?"

I told him, reporting it verbatim, including my phone call to Delia Brandt, and explaining I had hoped to get a glimmer from one or more of the quartet at sound of the name. He wasn't very enthusiastic but admitted it was worth a look and said we would put Fred Durkin on it. I asked if I should phone Purley Stebbins, and he said no, it was too close to dinnertime and he wanted first to think over his talk with Mrs. Molloy's friends.

He heaved a sigh. "Confound it," he complained, "no gleam anywhere, no little fact that stings, no word that trips. I have no appetite!"

I snorted. "That's the least of my worries," I declared.

CHAPTER 12

I NEVER DID PHONE Purley because I didn't have to.

Fred Durkin called during dinner and said he had had no better luck at the theater and the bar than at the phone-booth places, and I told him to come in, and he was there by the time we returned to the office with coffee. He had drawn nothing but blanks and I was glad we had a bone for him with a little meat on it. He was to do a take on William Lesser—address, occupation, and the trimmings—and specifically, had he been loose at 11:48 Wednesday night? That last seemed a waste of time and energy, since I had it entered that the Arkoffs and Irwins had never heard of him, but Wolfe wanted a little fact that stung and you never can tell. Just before Fred left Orrie Cather came.

Orrie brought a little package of items he had selected from the cartons in the Molloy apartment, and if they were the cream the milk must have been dishwater. He opened the package on my desk and we went through the treasure together, while Wolfe sat and read a book. There was a desk calendar with an entry on the leaf for January 2, *Call B,* and nothing else; a batch of South American travel folders; half a dozen books of matches from restaurants; a stack of carbon copies of letters, of which the most exciting was one to the Pearson Appliance Corporation telling them what he thought of their electric shaver; and more of the same.

"I don't believe it," I told Orrie. "You must have brought the wrong package."

"Honest to God," he swore. "Talk about drek, I never saw anything to equal it."

"Not even check stubs?"

"Not a stub."

I turned to Wolfe. "Mike Molloy was one of a kind. Meeting sudden death by violence in the prime of his manhood, as you

would put it, he left in his office not a single item that would interest a crow, let alone a detective. Not even the phone number of
his barber. No gleam anywhere."

"I wouldn't put it that way. Not 'prime of manhood.' "

"Okay. But unless he expected to get killed—"

The door bell rang. I stepped to the door to the hall, switched
on the stoop light, took a look, and turned.

"Cramer. Alone."

"Ah." Wolfe lifted his eyes from the book. "In the front room,
Orrie, if you please? Take that stuff with you. When Mr. Cramer
has passed through you might as well leave, and report in the
morning."

I stood a moment until Orrie had gathered up the treasure and
started for the door to the front room, and then went to the hall
and opened up. Many a time, seeing the burly breadth and round
red face of Inspector Cramer of Homicide there on the stoop, I
had left the chain bolt on and spoken with him through the crack,
but I now swung the door wide.

"Good evening," I said courteously.

"Hello, Goodwin. Wolfe in?"

That was a form of wit. He knew damn well Wolfe was in,
since he was never out. If I had been feeling sociable I would have
reciprocated by telling him no, Wolfe had gone skating at Rockefeller Center, but the haul Orrie had brought had been hard on my
sense of humor, so I merely admitted him and took his coat. He
didn't wait for escort to the office. By the time I got there he was
already in the red leather chair and he and Wolfe were glaring at
each other. They do that from force of habit. Which way they go
from the glare, toward a friendly exchange of information or toward a savage exchange of insults, depends on the circumstances.
That time Cramer's opening pass was mild enough. He merely remarked that Goodwin had told Sergeant Stebbins he would call
him back and hadn't done so. Wolfe grunted and merely remarked
that he didn't suppose Cramer had come in person for information
which Mr. Goodwin could have given Mr. Stebbins on the phone.

"But he didn't," Cramer growled.

"He will now," Wolfe growled back. "Do you want him to?"

"No." Cramer got more comfortable. "I'm here now. There's more to it than Johnny Keems, but I'll take that first. What was he doing for you last night?"

"He was investigating a certain aspect of the murder of Michael M. Molloy on January third."

"The hell he was. I thought a murder investigation was finished when the murderer was tried and convicted."

Wolfe nodded. "It is. But not when an innocent man is tried and convicted."

It looked very much as if they were headed for insults. But before Cramer had one ready Wolfe went on. "You would ask, of course, if I have evidence to establish Peter Hays's innocence. No, I haven't. My reasons for thinking him innocent would not be admissible as evidence, and would have no weight for you. I intend to find the evidence if it exists, and Johnny Keems was looking for it last night."

Cramer's sharp gray eyes, surrounded by crinkles, were leveled at Wolfe's brown ones. He was not amused. On previous occasions, during a murder investigation, he had found Wolfe a thorn in his hide and a pain in his neck, but this was the first time it had ever happened after it had been wrapped up by a jury.

"I am familiar," he said, "with the evidence that convicted Hays. I collected it, or my men did."

"Pfui. It didn't have to be collected. It was there."

"Well, we picked it up. What aspect was Keems working on?"

"The invitation to Mrs. Molloy to go to the theater. On the chance that it was designed, to get her away from the apartment. His instructions were to see Mr. and Mrs. Arkoff and Mr. and Mrs. Irwin, and to report to me if he got any hint of suspicion. He didn't report, which was typical of him, and he paid for his disdain. However, I know that he saw those four, all of them. They were here this afternoon for more than an hour. He saw Mrs. Arkoff at her apartment shortly after eight o'clock, and returned two hours later and saw her and her husband. In between those two visits he saw Mr. and Mrs. Irwin at their apartment. Do you want to know what they say they told him?"

Cramer said he did, and Wolfe obliged. He gave him a full and

fair report, including all essentials, unless you count as an essential
his telling them that he wanted to talk with them before he told
the police what Johnny Keems had been doing—and anyway
Cramer could guess that for himself.

At the end he added a comment. "The inference is patent. Either
one or more of them were lying, or Johnny saw someone besides
them, or his death had no connection with his evening's work. I
will accept the last only when I must, and apparently you will too
or you wouldn't be here. Did the circumstances eliminate fortuity?"

"If you mean could it have been an accident, it's barely possible.
It wasn't on the Drive proper, it was on one of those narrow side
approaches to apartment houses. A man and woman were in a
parked car a hundred feet away, waiting for someone. The car was
going slow when it passed them, going up the lane. They saw Keems
step into the lane from between two parked cars, and they think
the driver of the car blinked his lights, but they're not sure. As the
car approached Keems it slowed nearly to a stop, and then it took
a sudden spurt and swerved straight at Keems, and that was it. It
kept going and had turned a corner before the man and woman were
out of their car. You know we found the car this morning parked
on upper Broadway, and it was stolen?"

"Yes."

"So it doesn't look like fortuity. I must remember to use that
in a report. You said it could be that one of them was lying, or
more than one. What do you think?"

Wolfe puckered his lips. "It's hard to say. It can't very well be
just one of them, since their alibis are all in pairs—the two men in
the bar the evening of January third, and for last night man and
wife at home together in both cases. Of course you know their
addresses, since you collected the evidence against Peter Hays."

"They're in the file." Cramer's eyes came to me. "In the neighborhood, Goodwin?"

"Near enough," I told him. "The Arkoffs in the Eighties on Central Park West, and the Irwins in the Nineties on West End
Avenue."

"Not that that's important. You understand, Wolfe, as far as
I'm concerned the Hays case is closed. He's guilty as hell. You ad-

mit you have no evidence. It's Keems I'm interested in. If it was homicide, homicide is my business. That's what I'm after."

Wolfe's brows went up. "Do you want a suggestion?"

"I can always use a suggestion."

"Drop it. Charge Johnny Keems's death to accident and close the file. I suppose a routine search for the hit-and-run driver must be made, but confine it to that. Otherwise you'll find that the Hays case is open again, and that would be embarrassing. For all I know you may have already been faced with that difficulty and that's why you're here—for instance, through something found in Johnny Keems's pockets. Was there something?"

"No."

Wolfe's eyes were narrowed at him. "I am being completely candid with you, Mr. Cramer."

"So am I. Nothing was found on Keems but the usual items—keys, cigarettes, driving license, handkerchief, a little cash, pen and pencil. After what you tell me I'm surprised he didn't have a memo of those people's names and addresses. Didn't you give him one, Goodwin?"

"No. Johnny didn't believe in memos. He didn't even carry a notebook. He thought his memory was as good as mine, but it wasn't. Now it's no good at all."

He went back to Wolfe. "About your being completely candid, I didn't think I'd go into this, but I will. Tuesday's papers had an ad headed 'To P.H.' and signed by you. Tuesday noon Sergeant Stebbins phoned to ask Goodwin about it, and Goodwin told him to ask Lieutenant Murphy of the Missing Persons Bureau. What he learned from Murphy satisfied him, and me too, that your ad hadn't been directed at Peter Hays but at a man named Paul Herold, and we crossed it off as coincidence. But Wednesday morning, yesterday, Goodwin goes to the City Prison and has a talk with Peter Hays. News of that gets to Murphy, and he sees Hays and asks him if he is Paul Herold, and Hays says no. But here you are saying you think Hays is innocent and up to your neck in it hell for breakfast. If you had Keems investigating one aspect, how many men have you got on other aspects? You don't toss money around just to see it flutter in the breeze. So if you're being so god-dam candid, who's your client?"

Wolfe nodded. "That would interest you, naturally. I'm sorry, Mr. Cramer, I can't tell you. You can ask Mr. Albert Freyer, counsel for Peter Hays, and see if you have better luck."

"Nuts. Is Peter Hays Paul Herold?"

"He told Mr. Goodwin he is not. You say he told Lieutenant Murphy he is not. He should know."

"Then why are you on the warpath?"

"Because both my curiosity and cupidity have been aroused, and together they are potent. Believe me, Mr. Cramer, I have been candid to the limit of my discretion. Will you have some beer?"

"No. I'm going. I have to start somebody on these Arkoffs and Irwins."

"Then the Hays case is open again. That is not a gibe, merely a fact. Can you spare me another minute? I would like to know exactly what was found in Johnny Keems's pockets."

"I've told you." Cramer got up. "The usual items."

"Yes, but I'd like a complete list. I would appreciate it, if you'll indulge me."

Cramer eyed him. He could never make up his mind whether Wolfe was really after something or was merely putting on an act. Thinking he might find out, he turned to me. "Get my office, Goodwin."

I swiveled and dialed, and when I had the number Cramer came to my desk and took it. I was supposing he would tell someone to get the list from the file and read it off to me, but no sir. That way I could have faked something, and who would trust Goodwin? He stayed at the phone, and when the list had been dug out and was called off to him he relayed it to me, item by item, and I wrote it down. As follows:

Motor operator's license
Social Security card
Eastern Insurance Co. Identification card
2 tickets to baseball game for May 11th
3 letters in envelopes (personal matters)

Newspaper clipping about fluorine in drinking water
$22.16 in bills and coins
Pack of cigarettes
2 books of matches
4 keys on a ring
1 handkerchief
Ballpoint pen
Pencil
Pocket knife

I started to hand it to Wolfe, but Cramer reached and grabbed it. When he had finished studying it he returned it to me and I passed it to Wolfe, and Cramer asked him, "Well?"

"Thank you very much." Wolfe sounded as if he meant it. "One question: is it possible that something, some small article, was taken from his clothing before this list was made?"

"Possible, yes. Not very likely. The man and woman who saw it from the parked car are respectable and responsible citizens. The man went to where the body was lying, and the woman blew the horn, and an officer came in a couple of minutes. The officer was the first one to touch the body. Why? What's missing?"

"Money. Archie, how much did you give Johnny for expenses?"

"One hundred dollars."

"And presumably he had a little of his own. Of course, Mr. Cramer, I am not ass enough to suggest that you have a thief on your force, but that hundred dollars belonged to me, since Johnny Keems had possession of it as my agent. If by any chance it should turn up—"

"Goddam you, I ought to knock you through that wall," Cramer said through his teeth, and whirled and tramped out.

I waited until I heard the front door slam, then went to the hall and on to the one-way glass panel to see him cross the sidewalk and climb into his car. When I returned to the office Wolfe was sitting with his fingers interlaced at the apex of his central mound, trying not to look smug.

I stood and looked down at him. "I'll be damned," I said. "So you've got your little fact that stings. Next, who did he grease with it?"

He nodded. "Not too difficult, I should think. Apparently you share my assumption that he bribed somebody?"

"No question about it. Johnny wasn't perfect, but he came close to it about money. That hundred bucks was yours, and for him that was that." I sat down. "I'm glad to hear that it won't be difficult to find out who got it. I was afraid it might be."

"I think not—at least not to reach an assumption worth testing. Let us suppose it was you instead of Johnny. Having seen Mrs. Arkoff, you arrive at the Irwins' apartment and find them about ready to leave, being detained by a necessary repair to Mrs. Irwin's garment which is being made by the maid. Mostly they merely confirm what Mrs. Arkoff has already told you, but contribute one new detail: that the suggestion to invite Mrs. Molloy came originally from Mrs. Irwin. That is interesting, even provocative, and you want to pursue it, and try to, but by then the maid has the garment repaired and Mrs. Irwin puts it on, and they leave. You leave with them, of course, going down in the elevator with them, and they go off. There you are. You have seen three of them and have only one more on your list, it's a little after nine o'clock, and there is an hour to pass before you can see Mr. Arkoff. What do you do?"

"Nothing to it. As soon as the Irwins are out of sight I go back upstairs and see the maid."

"Would Johnny?"

"Absolutely."

"Then he did. Worth testing, surely."

"Yeah, it stings, all right. If that maid took your hundred bucks she'll take more." I looked at my wrist. "Ten minutes to eleven. Shall I give her a whirl now?"

"I think not. Mr. and Mrs. Irwin might be there."

"I can phone and find out."

"Do so."

I got the number from the book and dialed it, and after four whirrs a female voice told me hello.

I sent my voice through my nose. "May I speak to Mrs. Irwin, please?"

"This is Mrs. Irwin. Who is this?"

I cradled it, gently, not to be rude, and turned. "Mrs. Irwin answered. I guess it will have to wait until morning. I'll call Mrs. Molloy first and get the maid's name. She probably knows it."

Wolfe nodded. "It will be ticklish, and it must not be botched."

"Right. I'll bring her here and take her to the basement and hold matches to her toes. I have a remark. Your asking Cramer for a list of the contents of Johnny's pockets, that was only par for a genius, but your bumping him off the trail by pretending you wanted your money back—I couldn't have done it better myself. Satisfactory. I hope I'm not flattering you."

"Not likely," he grumbled, and picked up his book.

CHAPTER 13

THE MAID'S NAME was Ella Reyes. I got that from Selma Molloy on the phone at eight o'clock Friday morning, and also that she was around thirty years old, small and neat, the color of coffee with cream, and had been with the Irwins for about a year.

But I didn't get to tackle her. Relieving Fritz of the chore of taking Wolfe's breakfast tray up to his room, where, a mountain of yellow silk pajamas, he stood barefoot in the flood of sunshine near a window, I learned that he had shifted the line-up. Orrie Cather was to call on the man and woman who, sitting in a parked car, had seen the end of Johnny Keems. Their name and address was in the papers, as well as the fact that they agreed that the driver of the hit-and-run car had been a man, and that was about all. They had of course been questioned by old hands at it, but Wolfe wanted Orrie to get it direct.

Saul Panzer was to take the maid, write his own opening, and ad lib it from there. He was to be equipped with five hundred bucks from the safe, which, added to the C he already had, would make six hundred. A rosy prospect for Ella Reyes, since it would be tax-free. I was to be on call for the ceremony of opening the safe-deposit box, if and when it was scheduled. Wolfe was good enough to supply a reason for giving Saul the maid and me the ceremony. He said that if difficulties arose Mrs. Molloy would be more tractable with me present. Wit.

I was fiddling around the office when Wolfe came down from the plant rooms at eleven o'clock. Saul had arrived at nine and got a thorough briefing and five Cs, and departed, and Orrie had come and gone, to see the eyewitnesses. Parker phoned a little after ten, said he would probably get the court order before noon, and told me to stand by. I asked if I should alert Mrs. Molloy, and he said she wouldn't be needed, so I phoned her that she could relax.

Feeling that the situation called for a really cutting remark to the wit, I concocted a few, but none of them was sharp enough, so when he entered and crossed to his desk I merely said, "Mrs. Molloy isn't coming to the party. You have bewitched her. She admits she wouldn't stay last night because she was afraid to trust herself so close to you. She never wants to go anywhere any more unless you are there."

He grunted and picked up a catalogue that had come in the morning mail, and the phone rang. It was Parker. I was to meet him and Patrick Degan at the Metropolitan Safe Deposit Company at noon.

When I got there, on Madison Avenue in the Forties, five minutes early, I discovered that I hadn't exaggerated when I called it a party, and nobody was late. There were ten of us gathered down in the anteroom of the vaults: Parker; Degan; two officers of the safe deposit company; an attendant of the same; an Assistant District Attorney with a city dick, known to me, apparently as his bodyguard; a fingerprint scientist from the police laboratory, also known to me; a stranger in rimless cheaters whose identity I learned later; and me. Evidently opening a safe-deposit box outside of routine can be quite an affair. I wondered where the mayor was.

After the two MSDC officers had thoroughly studied a document Parker had handed them we were all escorted through the steel barrier and into a room, not any too big, with three chairs and a narrow table in its center. One of the MSDC officers went out and in a couple of minutes came back, carrying a metal box about twenty-four by eight by six, not normally, but with his fingertips hooked under the bottom edges at front and back. Before an appreciative audience he put it down, tenderly, on the table, and the fingerprint man took the stage, putting his case also on the table and opening it.

I wouldn't say that he stretched it purposely, playing to the gallery, but he sure did an all-out job. He was at it a good half-hour, covering top, sides, ends, and bottom, with dusters, brushes, flippers, magnifying glasses, camera, and print records which came from a brief case carried by the Assistant DA. They should have furnished more chairs.

He handled his climax fine, putting all his paraphernalia back in his case and shutting it before he told us, "I identify six separate prints on the box as the same as those on the records marked Michael M. Molloy. Five other prints are probably the same but I wouldn't certify them. Some other prints may be."

Nobody applauded. Someone sighed, tired of standing up. Parker addressed the stranger with the rimless cheaters. "That meets the provisions of the order, doesn't it?"

"Yes," the stranger conceded, "but I think the expert should certify it in writing."

That started an argument. The expert was allergic to writing. He would maintain his conclusion orally, without reservation, before nine witnesses, but he wouldn't sign a statement until he had made a prolonged study in the laboratory of his photographs and Molloy's recorded prints, and had his findings verified by a colleague. That wasn't very logical, but they couldn't budge him. Finally the stranger said he would stand by his concession that the oral conclusion satisfied the order, and told the MSDC officer to give Parker the box and the key—the duplicate key which had been provided by the MSDC to open the compartment the box had been in. Parker said no, give them to Mr. Degan. But before Degan got them he had to sign a receipt for them.

"All right, open it," the Assistant DA told him.

Degan stood with a hand resting on the box and sent his quick brown eyes around the arc. "Not in public," he said, politely but firmly. "This was Mr. Molloy's box, and I represent his estate by a court order. If you will leave, please? Or if you prefer, I'll take it to another room."

Another argument, a free-for-all. They wanted to see the box opened, but in the end had to give up, when the Assistant DA reluctantly agreed with Parker that Degan's position was legally sound. He left the room, with his bodyguard, and the fingerprint scientist followed them. The two MSDC officers didn't like it at all, but with the law gone they had no choice, so out they went.

Degan looked at the stranger in rimless cheaters and demanded, "Well, sir?"

"I stay," the stranger declared. "I represent the New York State Tax Commission." He was close enough to the table to reach the box by stretching an arm.

"Death and taxes," Parker told Degan. "The laws of nature and the laws of man. You can't budge him. Close the door, Archie."

"Behind you," Degan said. He was looking at Parker. "As you go out."

Parker smiled at him. "Oh, come. Mr. Goodwin and I are not the public. We have a status and a legitimate interest. It was through us that you got that box."

"I know it." Degan kept his hand on it. "But I am now legally in charge of Molloy's estate, temporarily at least, and my only proper obligation is to the estate. You're a lawyer, Mr. Parker, you know that. Be reasonable! What do I actually know about what Nero Wolfe is after or what you're after? Only what you've told me. I don't say that I think you already know about something that's in this box, and that I'm afraid Goodwin will grab it and run, but I do say that it's my responsibility to run no risk of any kind in guarding the estate, and the fact that I got the responsibility through you has nothing to do with it. Isn't that reasonable?" It was an appeal.

"Yes," Parker said, "it's eminently reasonable. I can't challenge it, and I don't. But we're not going to leave. We're not going to grab anything, or even touch anything unless invited, but we're going to see what you find in that box. If you summon help and demand that we be put out I doubt if you'll be obeyed, under the circumstances. If we leave we all leave, and I shall go to Judge Rucker at once and complain that you refuse to open the box in the presence of the widow's counsel. I believe he would enjoin you from opening it at all, pending a hearing."

Degan picked up the box.

"Hold it," I told him. I stepped and closed the door and stepped back. "Mr. Parker has covered most of the ground, but he didn't mention what we'll do if you try moving to another room. That's my department. I'll stand with my back against the door." I moved. "Like this. I'm three inches taller than you and fifteen pounds heavier in spite of your belly, and with the box you'll only have one hand. Of course you can try, and I promise not to hurt you. Much."

He regarded me, not cordially, and breathed.

"This is a farce," Parker declared. He came and joined me with his back against the door. "Now. Now or never. Go ahead and open it. If Goodwin leaps for you I'll trip him. After all, I'm a member of the bar and an officer of the law."

Degan was a stubborn devil. Even then he took another twenty seconds to consider the situation, after which he moved to the far end of the table, facing us at a distance of twelve feet, put the box down, and lifted the lid. The tax man moved with him and was at his elbow. The raised lid obstructed our view, and the inside was not visible, except to him and the New York State Tax Commission. They stared at it a moment, then Degan put a hand in. When he withdrew it, it held a bundle of lettuce three inches thick, fastened with rubber bands. He inspected it all over, put it on the table beside the box, inserted his hand again, and took out another bundle. And others. Eight of them altogether.

He looked at us. "By God," he said, with a little shake in his voice, "I'm glad you fellows stayed. Come and look."

We accepted the invitation. The box was empty. The top bills on five of the bundles were Cs, on two of them fifties, and on the other one a twenty. They were used bills, held tight and compact by the rubber bands. They wouldn't run as healthy as new stuff, around 250 to the inch, but they were not hay.

"Quite a hoard," Parker said. "No wonder you're glad we stayed. If I had been here alone I would have been tempted myself."

Degan nodded, looking dazed. "I'll be damned. We'll have to count it. Will you help me count it?"

We obliged him. I moved the chairs up and we sat, Degan at the table end and Parker and I at either elbow, and started in. The tax man was right behind Degan's shoulder, bending over to breathe down the back of his neck. It took a long while because

Degan wanted each bundle counted by all of us, which seemed reasonable, and one of the bundles of fifties had to be gone over six times to reach agreement. When we finished each bundle was topped with a slip of paper with the amount and our initials on it. On another slip Degan listed the amounts and got a total. $327,640.00.

If you don't believe it I'll spell it out. Three hundred and twenty-seven thousand, six hundred and forty berries.

Degan looked at Parker. "You expected this?"

"No. I had no expectations whatever."

He looked at me. "Did you?"

I shook my head. "Same here."

"I wonder. I wonder what Wolfe expected."

"You'd have to ask him."

"I would like to. Is he in his office?"

I looked at my wrist. "He will be for another fifteen minutes. Lunch at one-thirty on Friday."

"We might make it." He returned the bundles to the box, locked it, picked it up, and headed for the door, with the New York State Tax Commission practically stepping on his heels. Parker and I followed, and waited outside while he went with an attendant and the tax man to have the box slid into its niche and locked in, and when he rejoined us we mounted together to the street floor. There the tax man parted from us. Except for interested glances from a couple of guards we drew no attention inside, but the press was on the job. As we emerged to the sidewalk a journalist blocked our path and said the public wanted to know what had been found in Molloy's box, and when we refused to spill it he stayed right with us until we were in the taxi with the door shut.

The midtown traffic kept us from getting to the old brownstone before one-thirty, but since as far as I knew Patrick A. Degan was still a suspect I took him in along with Parker. Herding them into the office, I crossed the hall to the dining room and shut the door. Wolfe, in the big chair with arms, at the far end of the table, had just started operating on an eight-inch ring of ham and sweetbreads mousse.

"You brought visitors," he accused me.

"Yes, sir. Parker and Degan. I know you won't work with the feedbag on, but we found a third of a million dollars in used currency in the safe-deposit box, and Degan wants to ask you if you knew it was there. Shall they wait?"

"Have they eaten?"

"No."

Of course that wouldn't do. The thought of a hungry human, even a hungry murder suspect, even a hungry woman, in his house, is intolerable. So we had luncheon guests. They and I split the mousse that was waiting for me, and while we finished it Fritz manufactured a celery and mushroom omelet. Wolfe tells me there was a man in Marseilles who made a better omelet than Fritz, but I don't believe it. The guests protested that the mousse was all they wanted, but I noticed that the omelet was cleaned up, though I admit Wolfe took a portion just to taste.

Leaving the dining room, I gave Wolfe a sign, and, letting Parker conduct Degan to the office, he and I went to the kitchen, and I reported on the ceremony of opening the box. He listened with a scowl, but not for me. He hates to stand up right after a meal, and he hates to sit down in the kitchen because the stools and chairs aren't fit to sit on—for him.

When I was through he demanded, "How sure are you that the box contained nothing but the money?"

"Dead sure. My eyes were glued to him, and they're good eyes. Not a chance."

"Confound it," he muttered.

"My God," I complained, "you're hard to satisfy. Three hundred and twenty-seven thou—"

"But only that. It's suggestive, of course, but that's all. When a man is involved in a circumstance pressing enough to cause his murder he must leave a relic of it somewhere, and I had hoped it was in that box. Very well. I want to sit down."

He marched to the office, and I followed.

Parker had let Degan have the red leather chair, and Degan had lit a cigar, so Wolfe's nose twitched as he got his bulk adjusted in his chair.

"You gentlemen doubtless have your engagements," he said, "so I apologize for keeping you so long, but I never discuss business at the table. Mr. Goodwin has told me what you found in that box. A substantial nest egg. You have a question for me, Mr. Degan?"

"A couple," Degan said, "but first I must thank you for the lunch. The best omelet I ever ate!"

"I'll tell Mr. Brenner. It will please him. And the question?"

"Well." He blew smoke, straight at his host. "Partly it's just plain curiosity. Were you expecting to find a large sum of money in the box?"

"No. I had no specific expectation. I was hoping to find something that would forward the job I'm on, as I told you yesterday, but I had no idea what it might be."

"Okay." Degan gestured with the cigar. "I'm not a suspicious man, Mr. Wolfe, anyone who knows me will tell you that, but now I've got this responsibility. The thought would have occurred to anybody, finding that fortune in that box, what if you knew it was there or thought it was? And now that it's been found, what if you are figuring that a sizable share of it will be used to pay you for this job you're doing?"

Wolfe grunted. "Surely that's a question for me to ask, not answer. What if I am?"

"Then you are."

"I haven't said so. But what if I am?"

"I don't know. I don't know what to say." Degan took a puff, and this time blew it at Parker. "Frankly, I'm sorry I agreed to this. I did it for a friend who has had a tough break, Selma Molloy, and I wish I hadn't. I'm on a spot. I know she's all for the job you're doing, trying to find grounds for a new trial for Peter Hays, and I am too, personally, so you might think I'd be willing to commit the estate to pay for your services and expenses, but the hell of it is that she says she won't take the estate or any part of it. That didn't matter when there were no visible assets to speak of, but now it does. It will go to someone eventually, relatives always turn up when there's a pile in it, and what will they say if I've paid you some of it? You see my problem." He took a puff.

"I do indeed." Wolfe's lips were slightly twisted—one of his smiles. "But you asked the wrong question. Instead of asking *what* if I am you should have asked *if* I am. The answer is no. I shall not demand, or accept if offered, anything from that trove."

"You won't? You mean that?"

"I do."

"Then why didn't you say so?"

"I have said so." Wolfe's lips straightened. "And now that I have answered your questions, I beg you to reciprocate. You knew Mr. Molloy for some years. Have you any knowledge of the source of that money?"

"No. I was absolutely amazed when I saw it."

"Please bear with me. I don't challenge you, I'm merely trying to stimulate you. You were intimate with him?"

"Intimate? I wouldn't say intimate. He was one of my friends, and I did a little business with him from time to time."

"What kind of business?"

"I bought advice from him now and then." Degan reached to break cigar ash into the tray. "In connection with investments of my organization. He was an expert on certain areas of the real-estate market."

"But you didn't pay him enough to supply an appreciable fraction of that fortune in the box."

"My God, no. On an average, maybe two or three thousand a year."

"Was that the main source of Molloy's income, supplying investment advice regarding real estate?"

"I couldn't say. It may have been, but he did some brokerage and I think he did a little operating on his own. I never heard him say much about his affairs. He had a close mouth."

Wolfe cocked his head. "I appeal to you, Mr. Degan. You had a problem and I relieved you of it. Now I have one. I want to know where that money came from. Surely, in your long association with Mr. Molloy, both business and social, he must have said or done something that would furnish a hint of activities which netted him a third of a million dollars. Surely he did, and if it meant nothing to you at the time, it might now if you recall it. I ask you to make the effort. If, as you said, you wish me success in my efforts on behalf of Mrs. Molloy, I think my request is justified. Don't you agree?"

"Yes, I do." Degan looked at his watch and arose. "I'm late for an appointment. I'll put my mind on it and let you know if I remember anything." He turned, and turned back. "I know a few people who had dealings with Molloy. Do you want me to ask them?"

"Yes indeed. I would appreciate it."

"I suppose you'll ask Mrs. Molloy yourself."

Wolfe said he would, and Degan went. Returning to the office after seeing him out, I stopped at the sill because Parker was on his feet, set to go. He told me not to bother, but I like to be there when the gate of Wolfe's castle opens to the world, so I got his coat from the rack and held it for him.

In the office, Wolfe was having a burst of energy. He had left his chair to get the ashtray Degan had used and was on his way to the door of the bathroom in the corner, to dump it. When he reappeared I asked him, "Nothing from Saul or Fred or Orrie?"

He returned the tray to its place, sat, rang for beer, two short and one long, and roared at me, "No!"

When a hippopotamus is peevish it's a lot of peeve. I should have brought a bundle of Cs for him to play with, and told him so.

CHAPTER 14

How MUCH Wolfe likes to show the orchids to people depends on who it is. Gushers he can stand, and even jostlers. The only ones he can't bear are those who pretend they can tell a P. stuartiana from a P. schilleriana but can't. And there is an ironclad rule that except for Fritz and me, and of course Theodore, who is there all the time, no one goes to the plant rooms for any other purpose than to look at orchids.

Since he refuses to interrupt his two daily turns up there for a trip down to the office, no matter who or what, there have been some predicaments over the years. Once I chased a woman who was part gazelle clear to the top of the second flight before I caught her. The rule hasn't been broken more than half a dozen times altogether, and that afternoon was one of them.

He was in no better mood at four o'clock than an hour earlier. Fred Durkin had come with a report on William Lesser. He was twenty-five years old, lived with his parents on Washington Heights, had been to Korea, was a salesman for a soft-drink distributor, and had never been in jail. No discoverable connection with the Arkoffs or Irwins. No one who had heard him announce that a man named Molloy was going to cart his girl off to South America and he intended to prevent it. No one who knew he had a gun. And more negatives. Wolfe asked Fred if he wanted to try Delia Brandt, disguised as the editor who wanted the magazine article, and Fred said no. As I said before, Fred knows what he can expect of his brains and what he can't. He was told to go and dig some more at Lesser, and went.

Orrie Cather, who came while Fred was there, also drew a blank. The man and woman who had seen the car hit Johnny Keems were no help at all. They were sure the driver had been a man, but whether he was broad or narrow, light or dark, big or little, or with or without a clipped mustache, they couldn't say. Wolfe phoned Patrick Degan at his office and got eight names and addresses from him, friends and associates of Molloy who might furnish some hint of where the pile had come from, and told Orrie to make the rounds.

No word from Saul Panzer.

At half-past four I went to answer the doorbell, and there was the predicament on the stoop. I didn't know it was the predicament; I thought it was just our client, James R. Herold of Omaha, coming for a progress report; so I swung the door wide and welcomed him and took his things and ushered him to the office and moved a chair so he would be facing me. I told him on the way that Wolfe wouldn't be available until six o'clock but I was at his service. I admit that with the light from the window on his face I should have guessed he hadn't come merely for a report. He looked, as he hadn't before, like a man in trouble. His thin straight mouth was now tight and drawn, and his eyes were more dead than alive. He spoke. "I'd rather see Wolfe but I guess you'll do. I want to pay him to date, the expenses. I'd like to have an itemized account. Lieutenant Murphy has found my son, and I've seen him. I won't object if you want to add a small fee to the expenses."

At least I know a predicament when it pushes my nose in. When a man as pigheaded as Wolfe has ironclad rules he's stuck with them. If I went upstairs to him and broke the news there wasn't a chance. He would tell me to tell Herold that he would like to discuss the matter and would be down at six o'clock; and it was ten to one, from the look on Herold's face and the tone of his voice, that he wouldn't wait. He would say we could mail him a bill and get up and go.

So I stood up. "About the fee," I said, "I wouldn't want to decide that. That's up to Mr. Wolfe. Come along and we'll see what he says. This way."

I used the elevator instead of the stairs because the noise it made would notify Wolfe that something drastic was happening. Pushing the button to bring it down, entering with the ex-client, and pushing the button marked R for roof, my mind wasn't on the predicament at all, it was on Murphy. If I had had him there I wouldn't have said a word. I wouldn't have bothered with words. As we stopped at the top and the door slid open I told Herold, "I'll lead the way, if you don't mind."

It's hard to believe anyone could go along those aisles without seeing the array of color at all, but my mind was on Murphy. I don't know where Herold's was. Wolfe wasn't in the first room, the cool one, nor in the second, the medium, nor in the third, the tropical, and I went on through to the potting room. He was with Theodore at the bench, and turned to glare at us with a pot in one hand and a bunch of sphagnum in the other. With no greeting for the man who, in his ignorance, he thought was still his client, he barked at me, "Why this intrusion?"

"To report," I said. "Mr. Herold just came, and I told him you were engaged and took him to the office, and this is what he said. Quote." I recited Herold's little speech verbatim, and ended, "Unquote."

He had several choices. The rule that nobody came to the roof except to look at orchids had already been broken, by me. He could break the other one by going down to the office with us, or he could tell Herold that he would join him in the office at six o'clock, or he could throw the pot at me. He chose none of them. He turned his back on us, put the pot on the bench, tossed the sphagnum aside, got a trowelful of the charcoal and osmundine mixture from the tub, and dumped it into the pot. He reached for another pot and repeated the operation. And another. When six pots had been prepared he turned around and spoke.

"You have a record of the expenses, Archie."

"Yes, sir."

"Invoice them, including the commitments for today, and add the fee. The fee is fifty thousand dollars."

He turned to the bench and picked up a pot. I said, "Yes, sir," turned to go, and told Herold, "Okay, he's the boss."

"He's not my boss." He was staring at Wolfe's back, which is an eyeful. "You don't mean that. That's ridiculous!" No reaction. He took a step and raised his voice. "You haven't earned any fee at all! Lieutenant Murphy phoned me last night, and I took a plane, and he arranged for me to see my son. Do you even know where he is? If you do, why didn't you tell me?"

Wolfe turned and said quietly, "Yes, I know where he is. I suspect you, Mr. Herold."

"*You* suspect *me*? Of what?"

"Of chicanery. Mr. Murphy has his own credit and glory to consider, and so couldn't be expected to toot my horn, but I do not believe he made no mention of the part I've played. He's not an utter fool. I think you came here aware that I have earned a fee and conceived a shoddy stratagem to minimize it. The fee is fifty thousand dollars."

"I won't pay it!"

"Yes, you will." Wolfe made a face. "I don't run from contention, sir, but this sort of squabble is extremely distasteful. I'll tell you briefly how it will go. I'll render my bill, you'll refuse to pay it, and I'll sue you. By the time the action goes to trial I shall be armed with evidence that I not only found your son, which is what you hired me to do, but that I also freed him from a charge of murder by proving his innocence. Actually I doubt if you'll let it go to trial. You'll settle."

Herold looked around, saw a big comfortable chair, moved to it, and sat. Presumably he had had a tough day.

"That's my chair," Wolfe snapped. He can snap. "There are stools."

Three sound reasons: one, he didn't like Mr. Herold; two, he wanted to squash him; and three, if it went on he might want the chair himself. If Herold got to his feet and stayed on them he was still a contender; if he stayed in the chair he was cornered; if he took to a stool he was licked. He went to a stool and got on it. He spoke, not squabbling.

"Did you say you can prove his innocence?"

"No. Not now. But I expect to." Wolfe propped the back of his lap against the bench. "Mr. Goodwin saw him and talked with him Wednesday morning, day before yesterday, and established that he is your son. He didn't want you to be notified. That's an understatement. Did you speak with him today?"

"I saw him. He wouldn't speak to me. He denied me. His mother is coming."

That was some improvement. Before it had been only "my wife." Now it was "his mother." One big unhappy family.

He went on. "I didn't want her to, but she's coming. I don't know whether he'll speak to her or not. He hasn't just been arrested, he's been convicted, and the District Attorney says there can't be any question about it. What makes you think he's innocent?"

"I don't think it, I know it. One of my men has been killed —and I haven't earned a fee? Pfui. You'll know about it when the time comes."

"I want to know about it now."

"My dear sir." Wolfe was scornful. "You have fired me. We are adversaries in a lawsuit, or soon will be. Mr. Goodwin will conduct you downstairs." He turned, picked up a pot, and got a trowelful of the charcoal-osmundine mixture. That, by the way, was fake. You don't put that mixture in a pot until you have covered the bottom with crock.

From his perch on the stool Herold had him more in profile than full-face. He watched for four pots and then spoke. "I haven't fired you. I didn't know what the situation was. I don't now, and I want to."

Wolfe asked, not turning, "You want me to go on?"

"Yes. His mother is coming."

"Very well. Archie, take Mr. Herold to the office and tell him about it. Omit our inference from the contents of Johnny's pockets. We can't risk Mr. Cramer's meddling in that for the present."

I asked, "Give him everything else?"

"You might as well."

Getting down off the stool, Herold tripped on his own toe and nearly fell. To give him footwork practice I took him back down by way of the stairs.

He wasn't much impressed by my outline of the situation, but he had probably had all the impressions he had room for in one day. The guy was in shock. However, when he left we were still hired. He gave me the name of his hotel, and I said we would report any developments. At the door I told him it wouldn't be a good idea for his wife to come to see Wolfe, because when Wolfe was deep in a case he was apt to forget his manners. I didn't add that he was also apt to forget his manners when he wasn't deep in a case.

Alone again, I had a notion to try a few phone calls. In discussing an assignment for Orrie we had considered my tail—the party in a tan raglan and a brown snap-brim who had started to stalk me Tuesday afternoon when I left the house to go to the courtroom for a look at Peter Hays. Since there had been no sign of him since, the assumption was that somebody's curiosity had been aroused by the newspaper ad and he had lost interest after the jury had settled Hays's hash. We had decided it would be useless to put Orrie on it, since there was nowhere to start, but it wouldn't do any harm for me to phone a few of the agencies I was acquainted with and chat a little. The chance was slim that one of them had been hired to put a man on me, and slimmer still that they would spill it to me, but things do sometimes slip out in a friendly conversation, and I might as well be trying it as merely sitting on my fanny. I considered it, and decided to hit Del Bascom first, and was just starting to dial when two interruptions came at once. Wolfe came down from the plant rooms and Saul Panzer arrived.

Saul's face will never tell you a damn thing when he's playing poker with you, or playing anything else that calls for cover, but he's not so careful with it when he doesn't have to be, and at sight of it as I let him in I knew he had something hot.

Wolfe knew it too, and he was on edge. As Saul was turning a chair around he demanded, "Well?"

Saul sat. "From the beginning?"

"Yes."

"I phoned the apartment at nine-thirty-two and a woman answered and I asked to speak to Ella Reyes. She asked who I was and I said a Social Security investigator. She asked what I wanted with Ella Reyes and I said there was apparently a mix-up in names and I wanted to check. She said she wasn't there, and she wasn't sure when she would be, and I thanked her. So already it had a twist. A maid who sleeps in wasn't there and it wasn't known when she would be. I went to the apartment house and identified myself to the doorman."

You should hear Saul identifying himself. What he meant was that after three minutes with the doorman they were on such good terms that he was allowed to take the elevator without a phone call to announce him. It's no good trying to imitate him; I've tried it.

"I went up to Apartment Twelve-B, and Mrs. Irwin came to the door. I told her I had another errand in the neighborhood and dropped in to see Ella Reyes. She said she wasn't there and still didn't know when she would be. I pressed a little, but of course I couldn't overdo it. I said the mix-up had to do with addresses, and maybe she could straighten it out, and asked if her Ella Reyes had another address, perhaps her family's address, at Two-nineteen East One-hundred-and-twelfth Street. She said not that she knew of, that her Ella Reyes' family lived on East One-hundred-and-thirty-seventh Street. I asked if she could give me the number, and she went to another room and came back and said it was Three-oh-six East One-hundred-and-thirty-seventh Street."

Saul looked at me. "Do you want to note that, Archie?" I did so and he resumed. "I went down and asked the doorman if he had noticed Mrs. Irwin's maid going out this morning, and he said no, and he hadn't noticed her coming in either. He said Thursday was her night out and she always came in at eight o'clock Friday morning and he hadn't seen her. He asked the elevator man, and he hadn't seen her either. So I went to Three-oh-six East One-hundred-and-thirty-seventh Street. It's a dump, a cold-water walk-up. I saw Ella Reyes' mother. I was as careful as possible, but it's hard to be careful enough with those people. Anyway, I got it that Ella always came home Thursday nights and she hadn't showed up. Mrs. Reyes had been wanting to go to a phone and call Mrs. Irwin, but she was afraid Ella might be doing something she wouldn't want her employer to know about. She didn't say that, but that's what it was.

"I spent the rest of the day floundering around. Back at the Irwins' address the doorman told me that Ella Reyes had left as usual at six o'clock yesterday, alone. Mrs. Reyes had given me the names of a couple of Ella's friends, and I saw them, and they gave me more names. Nobody had seen her or heard from her. I phoned Mrs. Irwin twice during the afternoon, and I phoned headquarters once an hour to ask about accidents, of course not mentioning Ella Reyes. My last call to headquarters, at five o'clock, I was told that the body of a woman had been found behind a pile of lumber on the Harlem River bank near One-hundred-and-fortieth Street, with nothing on it to identify it. The body was on its way to the morgue. I went there, but the body hadn't arrived yet. When it came I looked at it, and it fits Mrs. Molloy's description of Ella Reyes—around thirty, small and neat, coffee with cream. Only the head wasn't neat. The back of the skull was smashed. I just came from there."

I stood up, realized that that didn't help matters any, and sat down. Wolfe took a long deep breath through his nose, and let it out through his mouth.

"I needn't ask," he said, "if you communicated your surmise."

"No, sir. Of course not. A surmise isn't enough."

"No. What time does the morgue close?"

That's one way I know he's a genius. Only a genius would dare to ask such a question after functioning as a private detective for more than twenty years right there in Manhattan, and specializing in murder. The hell of it was, he really didn't know.

"It doesn't close," Saul said.

"Then we can proceed. Archie. Call Mrs. Molloy and ask her to meet you there."

"Nothing doing," I said firmly. "There are very few women I would ask to meet me at the morgue, and Mrs. Molloy is not one of them. Anyway, her phone may be tapped. This sonofabitch probably taps lines in between murders to pass the time. I'll go and get her."

"Then go."

I went.

I SAT ON A CHAIR facing her. I had accepted the offer of a chair because on the way uptown in the taxi I had made a decision which would prolong my stay a little. She was wearing a lightweight woolen dress, lemon-colored, which could have been Dacron or something, but I prefer wool.

"When I first saw you," I told her, "fifty hours ago, I might have bet you one to twenty that Peter Hays would get clear. Now it's the other way around. I'll bet you twenty to one."

She squinted at me, giving the corners of her eyes the little upturn, and her mouth worked. "You're just bucking me up," she said.

"No, I'm not, but I admit it's a lead. We need your help. You remember I phoned you this morning to get the name of Mrs. Irwin's maid and a description of her. A body of a woman with a battered skull was found today behind a lumber pile on One-hundred-and-fortieth Street, and it is now in the morgue. We think it's Ella Reyes but we're not sure, and we need to know. I'm going to take you down there to look. It's your turn."

She sat and regarded me without blinking. I sat and waited. Finally she blinked.

"All right," she said, "I'll go. Now?"

No shivers or shudders, no squeals or screams, no string of questions. I admit the circumstances were very favorable, since one thing was so heavy on her mind that there was no room for anything else.

"Now it is," I told her. "But you'll pack a bag for a night or two and we'll take it along. You'll stay at Wolfe's house until this thing is over."

She shook her head. "I won't do that. I told you yesterday. I have to be alone. I can't be with people and eat with people."

"You don't have to. You can have your meals in your room, and it's a nice room. I'm not asking you, lady, I'm telling you. Fifty hours ago I had to swallow hard to keep from having personal feelings about you, and I don't want to do it again, as I would have to if *you* were found with your skull battered. I'm perfectly willing to help get your guy out to you alive, but not to your corpse. This specimen has killed Molloy, and Johnny Keems, and now Ella Reyes. I don't know his reason for killing her, but he might have as good a one for killing you, or think he had, and he's not going to. Go pack a bag, and step on it. We're in a hurry."

I'll be damned if she didn't start to reach out a hand to me and then jerk it back. The instinct of a woman never to pass up an advantage probably goes back to when we had tails. But she jerked it back.

She stood up. "I think this is foolish," she said, "but I don't want to die now." She left me.

Another improvement. It hadn't been long since she had said she might as well be dead. She reappeared shortly with a hat and jacket on and carrying a brown leather suitcase. I took the case, and we were off.

To save time I intended to explain the program en route in the taxi, but I didn't get to. After I had told the hackie, "City Mortuary, Four hundred East Twenty-ninth," and he had given us a second look, and we had started to roll, she said she wanted to ask me a question and I told her to shoot.

She moved closer to me to get her mouth six inches from my ear, and asked, "Why did Peter try to get away with the gun in his pocket?"

"You really don't know," I said.

"No, I— How could I know?"

"You might have figured it out. He thought your fingerprints were on the gun and he wanted to ditch it."

She stared. Her face was so close I couldn't see it. "But how could— Oh, no! He couldn't think that! He couldn't!"

"If you want to keep this private, tone it down. Why couldn't he? You could. Sauce for the goose and sauce for the gander.

You are now inclined to change your mind, but you have been worked on. He hasn't been in touch as you have, so I suppose he still thinks it. Why shouldn't he?"

"Peter thinks I killed Mike?"

"Of course. Since he knows he didn't. Goose is right."

She gripped my arm with both hands. "Mr. Goodwin, I want to see him. I've *got* to see him *now!*"

"You will, but not where we're going and not now. And for God's sake don't crumple on me at this point. Steady the nerves and stiffen the spine. You've got a job to do. I should have stalled and saved it for later, but you asked me."

So when the cab stopped at the curb in front of the morgue I hadn't briefed her, and, not caring to share it with the hackie, I told him to wait, with the suitcase as collateral, helped her out, and walked her down to the corner and back. Uncertain of the condition of her wits after the jolt I had given her, I made darned sure she had the idea before going inside.

Since I was known there, I had considered sending her in alone, but decided not to risk it. In the outer room I told the sergeant at the desk, whose name was Donovan, that my companion wanted to view the body of the woman which had been found behind a lumber pile. He put an eye on Mrs. Molloy.

"What's her name?"

"Skip it. She's a citizen and pays her taxes."

He shook his head. "It's a rule, Goodwin, and you know it. Give me a name."

"Mrs. Alice Bolt, Churchill Hotel."

"Okay. Who does she think it is?"

But that, as I knew, was not a rule, so I didn't oblige. After a brief wait an attendant who was new to me took us through the gate and along the corridor to the same room where Wolfe had once placed two old dinars on the eyes of Marko Vukcic's corpse. Another corpse was now stretched out on the long table under the strong light, with its lower two-thirds covered with a sheet. At the head an assistant medical examiner whom I had met before was busy with tools. As we approached he told me hello, suspended operations, and backed up a step. Selma had her fingers around my arm, not for support, but as part of the program. The head of the object was on its side, and Selma stooped for a good view at a distance of twenty inches. In four seconds she straightened up and squeezed my arm, two little squeezes.

"No," she said.

It wasn't in the script that she was to hang onto my arm during our exit, but she did, out to the corridor and all the way to the gate and on through. In the outer corridor I broke contact to cross to the desk and tell Donovan that Mrs. Bolt had made no identification, and he said that was too bad.

On the sidewalk I stopped her before we got in earshot of the hackie and asked, "How sure are you?"

"I'm positive," she said. "It's her."

Crossing town on 34th Street can be a crawl, but not at that time of day. Selma leaned back with her eyes closed all the way. She had had three severe bumps within the hour: learning that her P.H. thought she had killed her husband, taking it that he hadn't, and viewing a corpse. She could use a recess.

So when we arrived at the old brownstone I took her up the stoop and in, told her to follow me, and, with the suitcase, mounted one flight to the South Room. It was too late for sunshine, but it's a nice room even without it. I turned on the lights, put the suitcase on the rack, and went to the bathroom to check towels and soap and glasses. She sank into a chair. I told her about the two phones, house and outside, said Fritz would be up with a tray, and left her.

Wolfe was in the dining room, staving off starvation, with Saul Panzer doing likewise, and Fritz was standing there.

"We have a house guest," I told them. "Mrs. Molloy. With luggage. I showed her how to bolt the door. She doesn't feel like eating with people, so I suppose she'll have to get a tray."

They discussed it. The dinner dish was braised pork filets with spiced wine, and they hoped she would like it. If she didn't, what? It was eight o'clock, and I was hungry, so I left it to them and went to the kitchen and dished up a plate for myself. By the time I returned the tray problem had been solved, and I took my place, picked up my knife and fork, and cut into a filet.

I spoke. "I was just thinking, as I dished this pork, about the best diet for a ballplayer. I suppose it depends on the player. Take a guy like Campanella, who probably has to regulate his intake—"

"Confound you, Archie."

"What?" I raised my brows. "No business talk at the table is your rule, not mine. But to change the subject, just for conversation, the study of the human face under stress is absolutely fascinating. Take, for instance, a woman's face I was studying just half an hour ago. She was looking at a corpse and recognizing it as having belonged to a person she knew, but she didn't want two bystanders to know that she recognized it. She wanted to keep her face deadpan, but under the circumstances it was difficult."

"That must have been interesting," Saul said. "You say she recognized it?"

"Oh, sure, no question about it. But you gentlemen continue the conversation. I'm hungry." I forked a bite of filet to my mouth.

It was a tough day for rules. Still another one got a dent when, the dessert having been disposed of, we went to the office for coffee, but that happened fairly often.

I reported, in detail as usual, but not in full. Certain passages of my talk with Mrs. Molloy were not material, and neither was the fact that she had started to put out a hand to me and jerked it back. We discussed the situation and the outlook. The obvious point of attack was Mr. and Mrs. Thomas L. Irwin, but the question was how to attack. If they denied any knowledge of the reason for their maid's absence, and if, told that she had been murdered, they denied knowledge of that too, what then? Saul and I did most of the talking. Wolfe sat and listened, or maybe he didn't listen.

But the only point in keeping the identity of the corpse to ourselves was to have first call on the Irwins and Arkoffs, and if we weren't going to call we might as well let the cops take over. Of course they were already giving the lumber pile and surroundings the full routine, and putting them on to the Irwins and Arkoffs wouldn't help that any, but someone who knew what the medical examiner gave as the time of death should at least ask them where they were between this hour and that hour Thursday night. That was only common politeness.

When Fritz came to bring beer and reported that Mrs. Molloy had said she liked the pork very much but had eaten only one small piece of it, Wolfe told me to go and see if she was comfortable. When I went up I found that she hadn't bolted the door. I knocked and got a call to enter, and did so. She was on her feet, apparently doing nothing. I told her that if she didn't care for the books on the shelf there were a lot more downstairs, and asked if she wanted some magazines or anything else. While I was speaking the doorbell rang downstairs, but with Saul there I skipped it. She said she didn't want anything; she was going to bed and try to sleep.

"I hope you know," she added, "that I realize how wonderful you are. And how much I appreciate all you're doing. And I hope you won't think I'm just a silly goose when I ask if I can see Peter tomorrow. I want to."

"I suppose you could," I said. "Freyer might manage it. But you shouldn't."

"Why not?"

"Because you're the widow of the man he's still convicted of murdering. Because there would be a steel lattice between you with guards present. Because he would hate it. He still thinks you killed Molloy, and that would be a hell of a place to try to talk him out of it. Go to bed and sleep on it."

She was looking at me. She certainly could look straight at you. "All right," she said. She extended a hand. "Good night."

I took the hand in a professional clasp, left the room, pulling the door shut as I went, and went back down to the office to find Inspector Cramer sitting in the red leather chair and Purley Stebbins on one of the yellow ones, beside Saul Panzer.

CHAPTER 16

As I CIRCLED AROUND Saul and Purley to get to my desk Cramer was speaking.

". . . and I'm fed up! At one o'clock yesterday afternoon Stebbins phoned and told Goodwin about Johnny Keems and asked him if Keems was working for you, and Goodwin said he would have to ask you and would call back. He didn't. At four-thirty Stebbins phoned again, and Goodwin stalled him again. At nine-thirty last evening I came to see you, and you know what you told me. Among other things—"

"Please, Mr. Cramer." Wolfe might have been gently but firmly stopping a talky brat. "You don't need to recapitulate. I know what has happened and what was said."

"Yeah, I don't doubt it. All right, I'll move to today. At five-forty-two this afternoon Saul Panzer is waiting at the morgue to view a body when it arrives, and he views it, and beats it. At seven-twenty Goodwin shows up at the morgue to view the same body, and has a woman with him, and he says they can't identify it and goes off with the woman. He gives her name as Mrs. Alice Bolt— Mrs. Ben Bolt, I suppose—and her address as the Churchill Hotel. There is no Mrs. Bolt registered at the Churchill. So you're up to your goddam tricks again. You not only held out on us about Keems for eight hours yesterday, you held out on me last night, and I'm fed up. Facts connected with a homicide in my jurisdiction belong to me, and I want them."

Wolfe shook his head. "I didn't hold out on you last night, Mr. Cramer."

"Like hell you didn't!"

"No, sir. I was at pains to give you all the facts I had, except one, perhaps—that despite Peter Hays's denial we had concluded he is Paul Herold. But you took care of that, characteristically.

Knowing, as you did, that James R. Herold was my client, you notified him that you thought you had found his son and asked him to come and verify it, omitting the courtesy of even telling me you had done so, let alone consulting me in advance. Considering how you handle facts I give you, it's a wonder I ever give you any at all."

"Nuts. I didn't notify James R. Herold. Lieutenant Murphy did."

"After you had told him of your talk with me." Wolfe flipped a hand to push it aside. "However, as I say, I gave you all the facts I had relevant to your concern. I reported what had been told me by Mr. and Mrs. Arkoff and Mr. and Mrs. Irwin. And I made a point of calling to your attention a most significant fact—more than significant, provocative—the contents of Johnny Keems's pockets. You knew, because I told you, these things: that Keems left here at seven-thirty Wednesday evening to see the Arkoffs and Irwins, with a hundred dollars in his pocket for expenses; that during his questioning of the Irwins their maid had been present, and the questioning had been cut short by the Irwins' departure; and that only twenty-two dollars and sixteen cents had been found on his body. I gave you the facts, as of course I should, but it was not incumbent on me to give you my inference."

"What inference?"

"That Keems had spent the hundred dollars in pursuance of his mission, that the most likely form of expenditure had been a bribe, and that a probable recipient of the bribe was the Irwins' maid. Mr. Goodwin got the maid's name, and a description of her, from Mrs. Molloy, and Mr. Panzer went to see her and couldn't find her. He spent the day at it and was finally successful. He found her at the morgue, though the identification was only tentative until Mrs. Molloy verified it."

"That's not what Goodwin told Donovan. He said she couldn't make an identification."

"Certainly. She was in no condition to be pestered. Your colleagues would have kept at her all night. I might as well save you the trouble of a foray on her apartment. She is in this house, upstairs asleep, and is not to be disturbed."

"But she identified that body?"

"Yes. Positively. As Miss Ella Reyes, the Irwins' maid."

Cramer looked at Stebbins, and Stebbins returned it. Cramer took a cigar from his pocket, rolled it between his palms, and stuck it in his mouth, setting his teeth in it. I have never seen him light one. He looked at Stebbins again, but the sergeant had his eyes at Wolfe.

"I realize," Wolfe said, "that this is a blow for you and you'll have to absorb it. It is now next to certain that an innocent man stands convicted of murder on evidence picked up by your staff, and that's not a pleasant dose—"

"It's far from certain."

"Oh, come, Mr. Cramer. You're not an ass, so don't talk like one. Keems was working on the Molloy murder, and he was killed. He made a contact with Ella Reyes, and she was killed—and by the way, what money was found on her, if any?"

Cramer took a moment to answer, because he would have preferred not to. But the newspaper boys probably already had it. Even so, he didn't answer, he asked, and not Wolfe, but me.

"Goodwin, the hundred you gave Keems. What was it?"

"Five used tens and ten used fives. Some people don't like new ones."

His sharp gray eyes moved. "Was that it, Purley?"

"Yes, sir. No purse or handbag was found. There was a wad in her stocking, ten fives and five tens."

Wolfe grunted. "They belong to me. And speaking of money, here's another point. I suppose you know that I learned that Molloy had rented a safe-deposit box under an alias, and a man named Patrick A. Degan was appointed administrator of the estate, and in that capacity was given access to the box. The safe-deposit company had to have a key made. When Mr. Degan opened the box, with Mr. Goodwin and Mr. Parker present, it was found to contain three hundred and twenty-seven thousand, six hundred and forty dollars in currency. But—"

"I didn't know *that*."

"Mr. Degan will doubtless confirm it for you. But the point is, where is Molloy's key to that box? Almost certainly he carried it on his person. Was it found on his corpse?"

"Not that I remember." Cramer looked at Stebbins. "Purley?" Stebbins shook his head.

"And Peter Hays, caught, as you thought, red-handed. Did he have it?"

"I don't think so. Purley?"

"No, sir. He had keys, but none for a safe-deposit box."

Wolfe snorted. "Then consider the high degree of probability that Molloy was carrying the key and the certainty that it was not found on him or on Peter Hays. Where was it? Who took it? Is it still far from certain, Mr. Cramer?"

Cramer put the cigar in his mouth, chewed on it, and took it out again. "I don't know," he rasped, "and neither do you, but you sure have stirred up one hell of a mess. I'm surprised I didn't find those people here—the Arkoffs and Irwins. That must be why you were saving the identification, to have a crack at them before I did. I'm surprised I didn't find you staging one of your goddam inquests. Are they on the way?"

"No. Mr. Goodwin and Mr. Panzer and I were discussing the situation. I don't stage an inquest, as you call it, until I am properly equipped. Obviously the question is, where did Keems go and whom did he see after he talked with the maid? The easiest assumption is that he stayed at the Irwins' apartment until they came home, but there is nothing to support it, and that sort of inquiry is not my métier. It is too laborious and too inconclusive, as you well know. Of course your men will now question the doorman and elevator man, but even if they say that Keems went up again shortly after he left Wednesday night with the Irwins, and didn't come down until after the Irwins returned, what if the Irwins simply deny that he was there when they came home—deny that they ever saw or heard of him again after they left?"

Wolfe gestured. "However, I am not deprecating such inquiry—checking of alibis and all the long and intricate routine—only I have neither the men nor the temper for it, and you have. For it you need no suggestions from me. If, for example, there is discoverable evidence that Keems returned to the Arkoffs' apartment after talking with Ella Reyes, you'll discover it, and you're welcome to. I'm quite willing for you to finish the job. Since you don't want two unsolved homicides on your record you'll use all your skills and resources to solve them, and when you do you will inevitably clear Peter Hays. I've done my share."

"Yeah. By getting two people murdered."

"Nonsense. That's childish, Mr. Cramer, and you know it."

Stebbins made a noise, and Cramer asked him, "You got a question, Purley?"

"Not exactly a question," Purley rumbled. He was always a little hoarser than normal in Wolfe's presence, from the strain of controlling his impulses. Or rather, one impulse, the one to find out how many clips it would take to make Wolfe incapable of speech. He continued. "Only I don't believe it, that Wolfe's laying off. I never saw him lay off yet. He's got something he's holding onto, and when we've got the edges trimmed by doing all the work that he's too good for he'll spring it. Why has he got that Molloy woman here? You remember the time we got a warrant and searched the whole damn house, and up in the plant rooms he had a woman stretched out in a box covered with moss or something and he was spraying it with water, which we found out later. I can go up and bring her down, or we can both go up. Goodwin won't try stopping an officer of the law, and if he—"

He stopped and was on his feet, but I had already buzzed the South Room on the house phone and in a second was speaking.

"Archie Goodwin, Mrs. Molloy. Bolt your door, quick. Step on it. I'll hold on."

"It's already bolted. What—"

"Fine. Sorry to bother you, but a character named Stebbins, a sort of a cop, is having trouble with his brain, and I thought he might go up and try to annoy you. Forget it, but don't unbolt the door for anybody but me until further notice."

I hung up and swiveled. "Sit down, Sergeant. Would you like a glass of water?"

The cord at the side of his big neck was tight. "We're in the house," he told Cramer, hoarser than ever, "and they're obstructing justice. She recognized a corpse and denied it. She's a fugitive. To hell with the bolt."

He knew better, but he was upset. Cramer ignored him and demanded of Wolfe, "What does Mrs. Molloy know that you don't want me to know?"

"Nothing whatever, to my knowledge." Wolfe was unruffled. "Nor do I. She is my guest. It would be vain to submit her to your importunity even if you requested it civilly, and Mr. Stebbins should by now know the folly of trying to bully me. If you wish the identification confirmed, why not Mr. or Mrs. Irwin or a member of Ella Reyes' family? The address is— Saul?"

"Three-oh-six East One-hundred-and-thirty-seventh Street."

Purley got out his notebook and wrote. Cramer threw the chewed cigar at my wastebasket, missing as usual, and stood up. "This may be the time," he said darkly, "or it may not. The time will come." He marched out, and Purley followed. I left it to Saul to see them out, thinking that as Purley passed by at the door he might accidentally get his fist in my eye and I might accidentally get my toe on his rump, and that would only complicate matters.

When Saul came back in, Wolfe was leaning back with his eyes closed and I was picking up Cramer's cigar. He asked me if there was a program for him, and I said no.

"Sit down," I told him. "There soon will be. As you know, Mr. Wolfe thinks better with his eyes shut."

The eyes opened. "I'm not thinking. There's nothing to think about. There is no program."

That's what I was afraid of. "That's too bad," I said sympathetically. "Of course if Johnny was still around it would be worse because you would have five of us to think up errands for instead of only four."

He snorted. "That's bootless, Archie. I'm quite aware that Johnny was in my service when he died, and his disregard of instructions didn't lift my onus. By no means. But Mr. Cramer and his army are at it now, and you would be lost in the stampede. The conviction of Peter Hays is going to be undone, and he knows it. He picked up the evidence that doomed him; now let him pick up the evidence that clears him."

"If he does. What if he doesn't?"

"Then we'll see. Don't badger me. Go up and let Mrs. Molloy thank you properly for your intrepidity in saving her from annoyance. First rumple your hair as evidence of the fracas." Suddenly he roared, "Do you think I enjoy sitting here while that bull smashes through to the wretch I have goaded into two murders?"

I said distinctly, "I think you enjoy sitting here."

Saul asked sociably, "How about some pinochle, Archie?"

WE DIDN'T PLAY pinochle for three nights and two days, but we might as well have. Friday night, Saturday, Saturday night, Sunday, and Sunday night.

It was not a vacuum. Things happened. Albert Freyer spent an hour with Wolfe Saturday morning, got a full report on the situation, and walked out on air. He even approved of letting the cops take it from there, since it was a cinch they couldn't nail the killer of Johnny Keems and Ella Reyes without unnailing Peter Hays. James R. Herold phoned twice a day, and Sunday afternoon came in person and brought his wife along. She taught me once more that you should never seal your verdict until the facts are in. I was sure she would be a little rooster-pecked specimen, and she was little, but in the first three minutes it became clear that at pecking time she went on the theory that it was more blessed to give than to receive. I won't say that I reversed the field on him entirely, but I understood him better. If and when he mentioned again that his wife was getting impatient I would know where my sympathy belonged if I had any to spare. Also he brought her after four o'clock, when he knew Wolfe would be up in the plant rooms, which was both intelligent and prudent. I made out fairly well with her, and when they left we still had a client.

Patrick A. Degan phoned Saturday morning and came for a talk at six o'clock. Apparently his main concern was to find out from Selma Molloy what her attitude was toward the $327,640.00, and he tried to persuade her that she would be a sap to pass it up, but he took the opportunity to discuss other developments with Wolfe and me. It had got in the paper, the *Gazette,* that Nero Wolfe's assistant, Archie Goodwin, had been at the morgue to look at the body of Ella Reyes, and that therefore there was probably some connection between her and Johnny Keems, though the police

refused to say so, and Degan wanted to know. The interview ended
on a sour note when Wolfe commented that it was natural for Degan to show an interest in that detail, since Ella Reyes had been
Mrs. Irwin's maid and Degan was on familiar terms with Mrs.
Irwin. When that warmed Degan up under the collar, Wolfe tried
to explain that the word "familiar" implied undue intimacy only
when it was intended to, and that he had given no reason for in-
ferring such an intention, but Degan hadn't cooled off much when
he left.

Since we wanted to keep informed fully and promptly on the
progress of Cramer and his army, and therefore had to be on speaking terms, we graciously permitted Sergeant Stebbins an audience
with Mrs. Molloy Saturday afternoon, and he was with her three
hours, and Fritz served refreshments. We were pleased to hear
later, from her, that Purley had spent a good third of the time on
various aspects of the death of her husband, such as possible motives for Arkoff or Irwin to want him removed. The Molloy case
had definitely been taken off the shelf. From the questions Purley
asked it was evident that no one had been eliminated and no one
had been treed. When I asked him, as he departed, if they were
getting warm, he was so impolite that I knew the temperature had
gone down rather than up.

Saturday evening Selma ate with us in the dining room, and Sunday at one she joined us again for chicken fricassee with dumplings,
Methodist style. Fritz is not a Methodist, but his dumplings are
plenty good enough for angels.

Saul Panzer and Orrie Cather spent the two days visiting with
former friends of Molloy's, spreading out from the list Patrick
Degan had supplied, and concentrating on digging up a hint of the
source of the third of a million in the safe-deposit box. Saul thought
he might have found one Sunday morning, but it petered out. Fred
Durkin plugged away at William Lesser and got enough material
to fill three magazines, but none of it showed a remote connection
with either the Arkoffs or Irwins, and that was essential. However,
Fred got results, of a kind. Sunday afternoon, while I was down in
the basement with Selma, teaching her how to handle a billiard cue,
the doorbell rang, and I went up to find Fritz conversing through

the crack permitted by the chain bolt, with Delia's Bill. It was my first contact with a suspect for many hours, and I felt like greeting him with a cordial handshake, but he wasn't having any. He was twice as grim as he had been before. In the office he stood with his fists on his hips and read the riot act. He had found out who the guy was going around asking about him, and that he worked for Nero Wolfe, and so did I, and the guff about the magazine article had been a blind, and he damn well wanted to know. It was rather confused the way he put it, and not clear at all exactly what he wanted to know, but I got the general idea. He was sore.

Neither of us got any satisfaction out of it. For him, I wouldn't apologize or promise to lock Wolfe and myself up for kidding Delia Brandt and damaging his reputation; and for me, he wasn't answering questions. He wasn't even hearing questions. He wouldn't even tell me when they were going to be married. I finally eased him to the hall and along to the door and on out, and went back to the basement to resume the billiard lesson.

Late that evening, Sunday, Inspector Cramer turned up, and when, after he got his big broad behind deposited in the red leather chair, Wolfe invited him to have some beer and he accepted, I knew he didn't have to be asked how they were making out. They weren't. He takes Wolfe's beer only when he wants it understood that he's only human and should be treated accordingly. He tried to be tactful because he had no club to use, but what it amounted to was that he had got nowhere at all after two nights and two days, and he wanted the fact or facts that Wolfe was reserving for future use.

Wolfe didn't have any, and said so. But that didn't satisfy Cramer, and never will, on account of certain past occasions, so it ended with him bouncing up, his glass still half full of beer, and tramping out.

When I returned from closing the door after him I told Wolfe cheerfully, "Forget it, he's just tired. In the morning he'll be back on the job, full of whatever he's full of. In a month or so he'll pick up a trail, and by August he'll have it wrapped up. Of course by that time Peter Hays will be electrocuted, but what the hell, they can apologize to his father and mother and two sis—"

"Shut up, Archie."

"Yes, sir. If I wasn't afraid to leave Mrs. Molloy alone here with you I'd resign. This job is too dull. In fact, it doesn't seem to be a job."

"It will be." He took in air down to his waist, or where it would have been if he had one. When it was out he muttered, "It will have to be. When you become insufferable something has to be done. Have Saul and Fred and Orrie here at eight in the morning."

I locked the safe, made my desk neat, and went up to my room to call the boys from there, leaving him sitting behind his desk, an ideal model for an oversized martyr.

In a way he has spoiled me. Some of the spectacular charades he has thought up have led me to expect too much, and it was something of a letdown Monday morning when I learned what the program was. Nothing but another treasure hunt, and not even a safe-deposit box. I admit that it did the trick, but at the time it struck me as a damned small mouse to come out of so big a mountain.

I had made sacrifices, having rolled out early enough to finish my breakfast by the time Saul and Fred and Orrie arrived at eight, only to find that it hadn't been necessary when Wolfe told me on the house phone to bring them up at a quarter to nine. When the time came I led the way up the two flights and found his door standing open, and we entered. He was seated at the table near a window, his breakfast gone, but still with coffee, with the morning *Times* propped on the reading rack. He greeted the staff and asked me if there was any news, and I said no. I had phoned Stebbins and he had not bitten my ear off only because you can't bite over the wire.

He took a sip of coffee and put the cup down. "Then we'll have to try. You will go, all four, to Mrs. Molloy's apartment, and search it, covering every inch. Take probes for the upholstery and whatever tools may be required. The devil of it is you won't know what you're looking for."

"Then how will we know when we find it?"

"You won't, with any certainty. But we know that a situation existed which led to Molloy's murder; that he had cached a large sum of money in a safe-deposit box under an alias; that he was contemplating departure from the country; and that exhaustive inquiry among his friends and associates has disclosed no hint of where the money came from or when or how he got it. Further, there was no such hint found on his person, or among the papers taken from his office, or in his apartment, or in the safe-deposit box. I don't believe it. I do not believe that no such hint exists. As I said to Archie on Friday, when a man is involved in a circumstance pressing enough to cause his murder he must leave a relic of it somewhere, and I had hoped it was in that box. When it wasn't I should have persisted, but other matters intervened—for one thing, a woman got killed."

He took a sip of coffee. "We want that relic. It could be a portfolio, a notebook, a single slip of paper. It could be some object other than a record on paper, though I have no idea what. There are of course numberless places he could have left it—with some friend, checked at a hotel or other public place—but first we'll try his apartment, since it is as likely as any and is accessible. Regarding each article you see and touch you must ask yourselves, 'Could this possibly be it?' Archie, you will explain the matter to Mrs. Molloy, ask if she wishes to accompany you, and if not get her permission and the key. That's all, gentlemen. I don't ask if you have any questions, since I wouldn't know the answers to them. Archie, leave the phone number on my desk, in case I need to get you."

We went. I turned off one flight down. I knew she was up, since Fritz had delivered her breakfast tray. By then I was on sufficiently familiar terms with her—the word "familiar" implying no undue intimacy—to have a private knock, 2-1-2, and I used it and was told to enter. She was in a dressing gown or house gown or negligee or dishabille—anyway, it was soft and long and loose and lemon-colored—and without make-up. Without lipstick her mouth was even better than with. A habit of observation of minor details is an absolute must for a detective. We exchanged good mornings and I told her there had been no developments worth mentioning, but there was a program. When I explained it she said she didn't believe there could be anything in the apartment she didn't know about, but I reminded her that she hadn't even bothered to open the cartons that had come from the office, and asked if she had got rid of Molloy's clothing and other effects. She said no, she hadn't felt like touching them, and nothing had been taken away. I told her the search would be extremely thorough, and she said she didn't mind. I asked if she wanted to go along, and she said no.

"You'll think I'm crazy," she said, "after my not wanting to come here, but now I never want to enter that door again. I guess that was one thing that was wrong with me—I should have got out of there."

I told her that the only thing that had been wrong with her was that she thought Peter Hays had killed Molloy, whereas now she didn't, got the keys from her, went downstairs, where the hired help was waiting for me in the hall, put the phone number on Wolfe's desk, told Fritz where we were going, and left. Saul and Fred had assembled a kit of tools from the cupboard in the office where we kept an assortment of everything from keys to jimmies.

If I described every detail of our performance in the Molloy apartment that day between 9:35 a.m. and 3:10 p.m. you might get some useful pointers on how to look for a lost diamond or postage stamp, but if you haven't lost a diamond or a postage stamp it wouldn't interest you. When we got through we knew a lot of things: that Molloy had hoarded old razor blades in a cardboard box in his dresser; that someone had once upon a time burned a little hole in the under side of a chair cushion, probably with a cigarette, and at a later time someone had stuffed a piece of lemon peel in the hole, God knew why; that there were three loose tiles in the bathroom wall and a loose board in the living-room floor; that Mrs. Molloy had three girdles, liked pale yellow underwear and white nighties, used four different shades of nylons, and kept no letters except those from a sister who lived in Arkansas; that apparently there were no unpaid bills other than one for $3.84 from a laundry; that none of the pieces of furniture had hollow legs; that if a jar of granulated sugar slips from your hand and spills you have a problem; and a thousand others. Saul and I together went over every scrap of the contents of the three cartons, already inspected by Orrie.

It would be misleading to say we found nothing whatever. We

found two empty drawers. They were the two top drawers, one on each side, of a desk against the wall of what Molloy might have called his den. None of the six keys Selma had given me fitted their locks, which were good ones, Wetherbys, and Saul had to work on them with the assortment in the kit. The drawers were as empty as the day they were built, and had presumably been locked from force of habit.

At 3:10 p.m. I used the phone there in the apartment and told Wolfe the bad news, including the empty drawers. Orrie said to tell him that never had so many searched so long for so little, but it didn't appeal to me. Wolfe told me to tell Fred and Orrie that was all for the day and to bring Saul in with me. After making a tour to verify that we were leaving things as we had found them, we moved out. Down on the sidewalk we parted, Fred and Orrie heading for the corner to get a drink to drown the disappointment, and Saul and I, with the kit of tools, flagging a taxi. It wasn't a cheerful ride. If the best the genius could do was start us combing the metropolitan area, including Jersey and Long Island, for a relic that might not exist, the future wasn't very bright.

But he had something a little more specific. We had barely crossed the sill to the office when he blurted at me, "About that Delia Brandt. About Molloy's proposal to her of a trip to South America. You said last Wednesday that she told you she had put him off, but you thought she lied. Why did you think she lied?"

I stood. "The way she said it, the way she looked, the way she answered questions about it. And just her. I had formed an opinion of her."

"Have you changed your opinion? Since she is going to marry William Lesser?"

"Hell no. She couldn't go to South America with a dead man, and evidently, from Fred's reports, she was playing Lesser all the time on an option. If Lesser found out what the score was and decided to take—"

"That's not my target. If Molloy was preparing to decamp and take that girl with him, and if she had agreed to go, he might have entrusted certain objects to her care—for example, some of the objects he removed from the empty drawers you found. Is it fantastic

to assume that he left them in her apartment for safekeeping pending departure?"

"No, not fantastic. I wouldn't trust her with a subway token,
but apparently his opinion of her wasn't the same flavor as mine.
It's quite possible."

"Then you and Saul will go and search her apartment. Now."

When Wolfe gets desperate he is absolutely fearless. He will
expose me to the risk of a five-year stretch up the river without
batting an eye. That's okay, since I am old enough to vote and can
always say no, but that time he was inviting another party too, so
I turned to look at Saul. He merely asked, "Will she be there?"

"If she's working, probably not until around five-thirty, maybe
later. If she's there I might be able to take her out to buy champagne, but then you'd have to do the work. Shall I phone?"

"You might as well."

I went to my desk and dialed the number, waited through fifteen
whirrs, hung up, and swiveled. "No answer. If you like the idea,
we won't want the kit, just some of the keys. The door downstairs
has a Manson lock, old style. The one to her apartment is a Wyatt.
You know more about them than I do."

Saul brought the kit to my desk and opened it, selected four
strings of keys and dropped them in his pocket, and closed the kit.
While he was doing that I went to the cupboard and got two pairs
of rubber gloves.

"I must remind you," Wolfe said as we started out, "that prudence is no shame to valor. I shall not evade my responsibility as
accessory."

"Much obliged," I thanked him. "If we're caught we'll say you
begged us not to."

We went to Ninth Avenue for a taxi, and on the way downtown
discussed modus operandi. Not that it needed much discussion.
Dismissing the cab on Christopher Street, we walked on to Arbor
Street, rounded the corner, and continued to Number 43. Nobody
had painted it in the five days since I had seen it. We entered the
vestibule, and I pushed the button marked Brandt. Getting no
click, I pushed it again, and, after another wait, a third time.

"Okay," I told Saul, and stepped to the outer door, which was standing open, for an outlook. Arbor Street is not Fifth Avenue, and only two boys and a woman with a dog had passed by when Saul told my back, "Come on in." It had taken him about a minute and a half. We entered.

He preceded me up the narrow dingy stairs, the idea being that we would do a quick once-over and then I would stand guard outside, at the head of the stairs, while he dug deeper. As we reached the top of the third flight he had a string of keys in his hand, ready to tackle the Wyatt, but I remembered that prudence is no shame to valor and went to the door first and knocked. I waited, knocked louder, got no response, and stepped aside for Saul. The Wyatt took longer than the one downstairs, perhaps three minutes. When he got it he pushed the door open. Since I was supposed to be in command, the proper thing would have been for him to let me go in first, but he crossed the threshold, saying, "Jumping Jesus."

I was at his elbow, staring with him. At my former visit it had been one of those rooms that call for expert dodging to get anywhere. Now it would have taken more than dodging. The piano bench was still where it belonged, in the center of the main traffic lane, and the other pieces of furniture were more or less in place, but otherwise it was a first-rate mess. Cushions had been ripped open and the stuffing pulled out and scattered around; books and magazines were off their shelves and helter-skelter on the floor; flowerpots had been dumped and dropped; and the general effect was about what you would get if you turned a room over to a dozen orangoutangs and told them to enjoy themselves.

"He didn't leave it as neat as we—" I started to comment, and stopped. Saul had spotted it too, and we moved together, on past the piano bench. It was Delia Brandt, on the floor near the couch where I had sat with her. She was on her face, her legs stretched out. I squatted on one side and Saul on the other, but one feel of her bare forearm was enough to show that no tests were necessary. She had been dead at least twelve hours and probably longer. We didn't look for a wound because that wasn't necessary either. A cord as thick as a clothesline was tight around her neck.

We got erect and I stepped through the clutter to a doorway, the door standing open, for a look at the bedroom, while Saul went

and closed the door to the hall. The bedroom was even worse, with
the bed torn apart, the innards of the mattress all over, and clothing and other objects sprayed around. A glance in the bathroom
showed that it had not been neglected. Back in the living room,
Saul was standing looking down at her.

"He killed her," he said, "before he started looking. Stuff from
cushions on top of her."

"Yeah, so I noticed. He worked the bedroom and closets too,
so there's nothing left for us except one thing. She's got her clothes
on. Either he found it or something scared him out or what he was
after was too bulky to be on her."

"The clothes women wear nowadays he wouldn't have to take
them off. Why the gloves? Going to rake through the leavings?"

"No. Put them on." I handed him a pair, and started pulling
mine on. "We'll try the one thing he left. Unless you've got a date."

"You don't make prints on clothes."

"You don't make prints on anything with gloves on." I got my
knife from my pocket, opened it, squatted, slipped two fingers
under the neck of the blouse, and slit it down to the waist. Saul,
squatting on the other side, unzipped the skirt and moved to the
feet to take the hem and pull the skirt off. I told him to look at the
shoes, which were house sandals, tied on, and he did so, removing
them and tossing them aside. The slip was as simple as the blouse.
I cut the straps and slit it down the back from top to bottom and
pushed it to either side. The pants were simple too; I got my fingers
inside under the hips, and Saul worked them down and off. The
girdle was slower, since I didn't care to scratch the skin. Saul
squatted on the other side again and helped me keep it lifted enough
to slit it and leave her intact.

"She's good and cold," he said.

"Yeah. Stuff the edges under and we'll roll her over to you."

He did so, and with one hand under a hip and the other under a
shoulder I rolled her, and Saul eased her as she came, and she was
on her back. That way, face up, it was something else. The face of
a girl who was strangled to death twelve or fourteen hours ago is
not a girl's face. Saul covered it with what was left of a cushion and
then helped me finish the operation. There was nothing between

the blouse and the slip, and nothing between the slip and the girdle, and nothing between the girdle and the skin, but when I lifted the brassiere and she was naked, there it was, fastened between the breasts with tape. A key. I pulled it loose, pulled the tape off, gave it a look, said, "Grand Central locker, out quick," went to the bedroom for a blanket, and came back and covered her. Saul was at the door, peeling his gloves off, and I had mine off by the time I joined him. He used one of his to turn the doorknob, and, in the hall, to pull the door shut. The spring lock clicked and we made for the stairs.

We saw no one on the way down, but as we stepped out to the sidewalk a man turned in, evidently a tenant, as he gave us a glance. However, he was two seconds too late to be able to swear that we had been inside the house. When we had turned the corner and were on Christopher Street, Saul asked, "Walking for our health?"

"I could use some health after that," I told him. "I suppose it doesn't matter how you do it if you do it, but some ways seem worse than others. At Seventh Avenue we'll split. One of us will take the subway and shuttle to Grand Central, and the other will phone Centre Street and go and report to Wolfe. Which do you prefer?"

"I'll take Grand Central."

"Okay." I handed him the locker key. "But it's possible there's an eye on it, no telling whose. You'd better give me the keys and gloves."

He transferred them to my pocket as we walked. At Seventh Avenue he went for the subway stairs and I entered the cigar store at the corner, found the phone booth, dialed SP 7–3100, and, when I got a voice, whined into the transmitter, high and thin, "Name and address, Delia Brandt, B-R-A-N-D-T, Forty-three Arbor Street, Manhattan. Got it?"

"Yes. What—"

"I'm telling you. I think she's dead. In her apartment. You'd better hurry." I hung up, heard the rattle, felt in the coin-return cup to see if the machine had swallowed the wrong way because you never know, departed, and got a taxi.

When I got out in front of the old brownstone it was a quarter to five, precisely one hour since Wolfe had told us he wouldn't evade his responsibility as accessory. With the chain bolt on as usual during my absence, Fritz had to come to let me in, and after one glance at my face he said, "Ah."

"Right," I told him. "Ah it is. But I don't want you to be an accessory too, so if they ask you how I looked say just like always, debonair."

In the office I put the gloves and strings of keys away and then went to my desk and buzzed the plant rooms. He must have been hard at work, for it took him a while to answer.

"Yes?"

"Sorry to disturb you, but I thought you ought to know that it's more serious than breaking and entering. It's also disturbing a body in a death by violence. Her apartment looked as if a hurricane had hit it, and she was on the floor, dead and cold. Strangled. We took her clothes off and found a key to a Grand Central checking locker taped to her skin, and took it and left. I phoned the police from a booth, and Saul has gone to Grand Central to see what's in the locker. He should be here in about twenty minutes."

"When did she die?"

"More than twelve hours ago. That's the best I can do."

"What time was William Lesser here yesterday?"

"Four-forty."

Silence. Then: "There is nothing to say or do until we learn what is in the locker. If it is merely another fortune in currency— But speculation is idle. Whatever it is, you and Saul will examine it."

I choked the temptation to ask if he wanted us to bring it up to the plant rooms. He would have had to say no, and to pile that on top of the news of another corpse would have been hitting him when he was down. But I had no ironclad rules between me and normal conduct, so when he hung up I went out to the stoop to wait for Saul. I even went down the seven steps to the sidewalk. Two neighborhood kids who were playing catch on the pavement stopped, stepped onto the opposite curb, and stood watching me. That house and its occupants had been centers of attraction, either sinister or merely mysterious, I wasn't sure which, ever since a boy named Pete Drossos had been let in by me for a conference with Wolfe and had got murdered the next day. By the time I looked at my wristwatch the tenth time the situation was a little strained, with them standing there staring at me, and I was about ready to retreat to an inside post behind the glass panel when a taxi came rolling up and stopped at the curb, and Saul climbed out, after paying the driver, with a medium-sized black leather suitcase dangling in his hand. Letting him have the honor of delivering the bacon, I followed him up the steps and on in. He took it to the office and put it on a chair.

At a glance it had been manhandled. The lock had been pried open, not by an expert, and it was held shut only by the catches at the ends. I asked Saul, "Do you want to tell me or shall I tell you?"

"You tell me."

"Glad to. Wolfe guessed right. Molloy had it stowed in her apartment, and after his death, maybe right away or maybe only yesterday, she busted it open and took a look." I hefted it. "Another deduction: she didn't clean it out. Because if she had why should she stash it in a locker and tape the key to her hide, and also because it's not empty. Wolfe says we're to examine it, but first, I think, for prints."

I went to the cupboard and got things and we set to work. We weren't as expert as the scientist had been with the safe-deposit box, but when we got through we had an assortment of photographs marked with locations that were nothing to be ashamed of. Of course they were only for future reference, since we had no samples of anybody for comparison. After putting them in envelopes and putting things away, we placed the suitcase on my desk and opened it.

It was about two-thirds full of a mixed collection. There were shirts and ties, probably his favorites that he couldn't bear to leave, a pair of slippers, six tubes of Cremasine for shaving, two suits of pajamas, socks and handkerchiefs, and other miscellaneous personal items. Stacking them on the desk, we came to a bulging leather briefcase. It should have been dusted for prints too, but we were too warm to wait, and I lifted it out, opened it, and extracted the contents.

It wasn't a relic, it was a whole museum. Saul pulled a chair up beside mine, and we went through it together. I won't describe the items, or even list them, because it would take too long and also because it was Wolfe who had guessed where they were and he should have the pleasure of showing them. We had just reached the bottom of the pile when six o'clock brought Wolfe down from the plant rooms. He started for his desk, veered to come to mine, and glared down at the haberdashery.

"That's just packing," I told him. I tapped the pile of papers. "Here it is. Enough relics to choke a camel."

He picked it up and circled around his desk to his chair and started in. Saul and I put the rest of the stuff back in the suitcase and closed it, and then sat and watched. For ten minutes the only sounds were rustlings of the papers and Wolfe's occasional grunts. He had nearly reached the bottom of the stack when the phone rang and I answered it.

"Nero Wolfe's office, Archie Good—"

"This is Stebbins. About a woman named Brandt, Delia Brandt. When did you see her last?"

"Hold it a second while I sneeze." I covered the transmitter and turned. "Stebbins asking about Delia Brandt, if you're interested." Wolfe frowned, hesitated, took his phone, and put it to his ear. I uncovered the transmitter and sneezed at it and then spoke.

"I hope I'm not going to have a cold. The last one I had—"

"Quit stalling," he snarled. "I asked you a question."

"I know you did, and you ought to know better by this time. If there's any good reason, or even a poor one, why I should answer questions about a woman named Delia Brandt, what is it?"

"Her body has been found in her apartment. Murdered. Your name and address are on the memo page in her phone book, the last entry. When did you see her last?"

"My God. She's dead?"

"Yeah. When you're murdered you're dead. Quit stalling."

"I'm not stalling. If I didn't react you might think I killed her myself. The first and last time I saw her was last Wednesday evening around nine-thirty, at her apartment. We were collecting background on Molloy, and she was his secretary for ten months, up to the time he died. I had a brief talk with her on the phone late Thursday afternoon. That's all."

"You were just collecting background?"

"Right."

"We'd like to have you come and tell us what you collected. Now."

"Where are you?"

"At Homicide West. I just got here with a man named William Lesser. When did you see him last?"

"Give me a reason. I always need a reason."

"Yeah, I know. He came to Delia Brandt's apartment twenty minutes ago and found us there. He says he had a date with her. He also says he thinks you killed her. Is that a good enough reason? When did you see him last?"

I never got to answer that. Wolfe's voice broke in.

"Mr. Stebbins, this is Nero Wolfe. I would like to speak with Mr. Cramer."

"He's busy." I swear Purley got hoarser the instant he heard Wolfe. "We want Goodwin down here."

"Not until I have spoken with Mr. Cramer."

Silence; then: "Hold it. I'll see."

We waited. I looked at Wolfe, but it was one-way because his eyes were closed. He opened them only when Cramer's voice came.

"You there, Wolfe? Cramer. What do you want?"

"I want to expose a murderer, and I'm ready to. If you wish to be present, bring Mr. and—"

"I'm coming there right now!"

"No. I have to study some documents. You wouldn't get in. Come at nine o'clock, and bring Mr. and Mrs. Irwin and Mr. and Mrs. Arkoff—and you may as well bring Mr. Lesser. He deserves to be in the audience. The others must be. Nine o'clock."

"Goddam it, I want to know—"

"You will, but not now. I have work to do."

He cradled his phone, and I followed suit. He spoke. "Archie, phone Mr. Freyer, Mr. Degan, and Mr. Herold. If he wishes to bring his wife he may. For this sort of thing the bigger the audience the better. And inform Mrs. Molloy."

"Mrs. Molloy won't be here."

"She is here."

"I mean she won't be in the audience, not if Herold is. She doesn't know Peter Hays is Paul Herold, and let him tell her if and when he wants to. Anyway she doesn't want to be with people, and you don't need her."

"Very well." He leered at me. He may have thought it was a tender glance of sympathy, but I call it a leer. "It is understood, of course, that you were not there today. If an explanation of how I got this material is required I'll supply it."

"Then that's all for me?" Saul asked.

"No. You'll be at his elbow. He has degenerated into a maniac. If you'll dine with us? Now I must digest this stuff."

He went back to the pile of papers.

CHAPTER 18

THE HOST was late to the party, but it wasn't his fault. I wasn't present at the private argument Cramer insisted on having with Wolfe in the dining room, being busy elsewhere, but as I passed in the hall, admitting guests as they arrived, I could hear their voices through the closed door. Since the door to the office was soundproofed and I kept it shut, they weren't audible in there.

The red leather chair was of course reserved for Inspector Cramer, and Purley Stebbins was on one nearby against the wall, facing the gathering. Jerome and Rita Arkoff and Tom and Fanny Irwin were in the front row, where Saul and I had spaced the chairs, but Irwin had moved his close to his wife's—not, however, taking her hand to hold. Mr. and Mrs. Herold and Albert Freyer were grouped over by the globe, off apart. Back of the Arkoffs and Irwins were William Lesser and Patrick Degan, and between them and slightly to the rear was Saul Panzer. That way the path from me to Degan was unobstructed and Saul was only an arm's length from him.

It was a quarter past nine, and the silence, broken only by a mutter here and there, was getting pretty heavy when the door opened and Wolfe and Cramer entered. Wolfe crossed to his desk and sat, but Cramer stood to make a speech.

"I want you to understand," he told them, "that this is not an official inquiry. Five of you came here at my request, but that's all it was, a request. Sergeant Stebbins and I are here as observers, and we take no responsibility for anything Nero Wolfe says or does. As it stands now, you can walk out whenever you feel like it."

"This is a little irregular, isn't it, Inspector?" Arkoff asked.

"I said you can walk out," Cramer told him. He stood a moment, turned and sat, and scowled at Wolfe.

Wolfe was taking them in. "I'm going to begin," he said con-
versationally, "by reporting a coincidence, though it is unessential. It is unessential, but not irrelevant. Reading the *Times* at
breakfast this morning, I noticed a Washington dispatch on page
one." He picked up a newspaper from his desk. "If you'll indulge
me I'll read some of it:

> "A total disclosure law requiring all private welfare and pen-
> sion plans to open books to governmental inspection was rec-
> ommended today by a Senate subcommittee. The proposal was
> based on a two-year study that disclosed practices ranging from
> sloppy bookkeeping to a $900,000 embezzlement.
> "The funds have grown to the point, the committee said, that
> they now provide benefits to 29,000,000 workers and to 46,000,-
> 000 dependents of these workers. Assets of the pension funds
> alone now total about 25 billion dollars, it was said.
> "The Senate group, headed by Senator Paul H. Douglas,
> Democrat of Illinois, said: 'While the great majority of welfare
> and pension programs are being responsibly and honestly ad-
> ministered, the rights and equities of the beneficiaries in many
> instances are being dangerously ignored. In other cases, the
> funds of the programs are being dissipated and at times become
> the hunting ground of the unscrupulous.'"

Wolfe put the paper down. "It goes on, but that will do. I read
it for the record and because it juxtaposed two things: the word
'welfare' and large sums of money. For a solid week I had been
trying to find a hint to start me on the trail of the man who killed
Michael Molloy—and subsequently Johnny Keems and Ella Reyes
—enough of one at least to stir my pulse, to no avail. This, if not
a flare, was at least a spark. Patrick Degan was the head of an
organization called the Mechanics Alliance Welfare Association,
and a large sum of money had been found in a safe-deposit box
Molloy had rented under an assumed name."

He pushed the newspaper aside. "That faint hint, patiently and
persistently pursued, might eventually have led me to the truth,
but luckily it wasn't needed. I have here in my drawer a sheaf of
papers which contain evidence of these facts: that from nineteen-
fifty-one to nineteen-fifty-five Molloy made purchases of small

pieces of land in various parts of the country; that their value, and the amounts of money he had to put up, were negligible; that in each case the purchaser of record was some 'camp'—examples are the Wide World Children's Camp and the Blue Sky Children's Camp; that these camps, twenty-eight in all, borrowed a total of nearly two million dollars from Mr. Degan's organization on mortgages; that Molloy's share of the loot was one-fourth and Degan's share three-fourths, from which each had presumably to meet certain expenses; and that the date of the last such loan on mortgage was October seventeenth, nineteen-fifty-five. I can supply many details, but those are the essentials. Do you wish to comment, Mr. Degan?"

Of course all eyes were on him, but his were only for Wolfe. "No," he said, "except that it's outrageous and libelous and I'll get your hide. Produce your sheaf of papers."

Wolfe shook his head. "The District Attorney will produce them when the time comes. But I'll humor your curiosity. When Molloy decided to leave the country with his loot, alarmed by the Senate investigation, and to take his secretary, Delia Brandt, with him, he stowed his records in a suitcase and left it in Delia Brandt's apartment. That is suggestive, since prudence would have dictated their destruction. It suggests that he foresaw some future function for them, and the most likely one would have been to escape penalty for himself by supplying evidence against you. No doubt you foresaw that too, and that's why you killed him. Do you wish to comment?"

"No. Go ahead and hang yourself."

"Wait a minute," Cramer snapped. "I want to see those papers."

"Not now. By agreement I have an hour without interruption."

"Where did you get them?"

"Listen and you'll know." Wolfe returned to Degan. "The best conjecture is that you knew Molloy had those records, some in your writing, and you knew or suspected he was preparing to decamp. If you demanded that he give them to you or destroy them in your presence, he refused. After you killed him you had no time to search the apartment, but enough to go through his clothing, and it must have been a relief to find the key to the safe-deposit box, since that was the most likely repository of the records—but it was a qualified relief, since you didn't dare to use the key. If you still have it, and almost certainly you have, it can be found and will be a damaging bit of evidence. You now have another, as the administrator of Molloy's estate, but surely the safe-deposit company can distinguish between the original and the duplicate they had to have made—and by the way, what would you have done if, opening the box in the presence of Mr. Goodwin and Mr. Parker, you had found the records in it? Had you decided on a course?"

Degan didn't reply. "Get on," Cramer rasped. "Where did you get them?"

Wolfe ignored him. "However, they weren't there. Another question: how did you dare to kill him when you didn't know where they were? But I'll venture to answer that myself. By getting Peter Hays there and giving the police an obvious culprit, you insured plenty of time and opportunity for searching the apartment as an old friend of Mrs. Molloy's. She is not present to inform us, but that can wait."

"Where is she?" Cramer demanded.

Ignored again. "You must admit, Mr. Degan, that luck was with you. For instance, the safe-deposit box. You had the key, but even if you had known the name Molloy had used in renting it, and you probably didn't, you wouldn't have dared to try to get at it. Then fortune intervened, represented by me. I got you access to the box. But in spite of that good fortune you weren't much better off, for the records weren't there, and until you found them you were in great jeopardy. What did you do? I wouldn't mind paying you the compliment of supposing that you conceived the notion that Molloy had cached the records in Delia Brandt's apartment, and you approached her, but I doubt if you deserve it. It is far more likely that she approached you; that, having decided to marry William Lesser, she wanted to get rid of Molloy's suitcase, still in her apartment; that before doing so she forced it open and inspected its contents; that if items such as passports and steamship or airplane tickets were there she destroyed them; that she examined the sheaf of papers and from them learned that there was a large sum of money somewhere and that you had been involved with Molloy in extensive and lucrative transactions and probably knew where the money was. She was not without cunning. Before approaching you she took the suitcase, with the records in it, to Grand Central Terminal and put it in a checking locker. Then she saw you, told you what she knew and what she had, and demanded the money."

"That's a lie!" William Lesser blurted.

Wolfe's eyes darted to him. "Then what did she do? Since you know?"

"I don't know, but I know she wouldn't do that! It's a lie!"

"Then let me finish it. A lie, like a truth, should reach its destination. And that, Mr. Degan, was where luck caught up with you. You couldn't give her the money from the safe-deposit box, but even if you gave her a part of your share of the loot and she surrendered the records to you, you couldn't empty her brain of what she knew, and as long as she lived she would be a threat. So last night you went to her apartment, ostensibly, I presume, to give her the money and get the records, but actually to kill her, and you did so. I don't know— *Saul!*"

I wouldn't say that Saul slipped up. Sitting between Lesser and Degan, naturally he was concentrating on Degan, and Lesser gave no warning. He just lunged, right across Saul's knees, either to grab Degan or hit him, or maybe both. By the time I got there Saul had his coattail, jerking him off, Degan was sitting on the floor, and Purley Stebbins was on the way. But Purley, who has his points, wasn't interested in Lesser, leaving him to Saul. He got his big paws on Degan's arm, helped him up, and helped him down again onto the chair, while Saul and I bulldozed Lesser to the couch. When we were placed again it was an improvement: Stebbins on one side of Degan and Saul on the other, and Lesser on the sidelines. Cramer, who had stood to watch the operation, sat down.

Wolfe resumed. "I was saying, Mr. Degan, that I don't know whether you searched her apartment for the records, but naturally— Did he, Mr. Cramer?"

"Someone did," Cramer growled. "Good. I'm stopping this

right here. I want to see those records and I want to know how
you got them."

Wolfe looked at the wall clock. "I still have thirty-eight minutes
of my hour. If you interpose authority of course you have it.
But I have your word. Is it garbage?"

Cramer's face got redder, and his jaw worked. "Go ahead."

"I should think so." Wolfe returned to Degan. "You did search,
naturally, without success. You weren't looking for something as
small as a key, but even if you had been you still wouldn't have
found it, for it was destined for me. How it reached me is a detail
Mr. Cramer may discuss with me later if he still thinks it worth
while; all that concerns you is that I received it, and sent Mr.
Panzer with it to Grand Central, and he returned with the suitcase. From it I got the sheaf of papers now in my drawer. I was
inspecting them when Mr. Cramer phoned me shortly after six
o'clock, and I arranged with him for this meeting. That's all, Mr.
Degan."

Wolfe's eyes went left, and his voice lifted and sharpened. "Now
for you, Mrs. Irwin. I wonder if you know how deep your hole
is?"

"Don't say anything, Fanny." Irwin stood up. "We're going.
Come on, Fanny." He took her shoulder and she came up to her
feet.

"I think not," Wolfe said. "I quote Mr. Cramer: 'As it stands
now, you can walk out whenever you feel like it.' But the standing
has been altered. Archie, to the door. Mr. Cramer, I'll use re-
straint if necessary."

Cramer didn't hesitate. He was gruff. "I think you'd better stay
and hear it out, Mr. Irwin."

"I refuse to, Inspector. I'm not going to sit here while he insults and bullies my wife."

"Then you can stand. Stay at the door, Goodwin. No one leaves
this room until I say so. That's official. All right, Wolfe. God help
you if you haven't got it."

Wolfe looked at her. "You might as well sit down, Mrs. Irwin.
That's better. You already know most of what I'm going to tell
you, perhaps all. Last Wednesday evening a man named Keems,

in my employ, called at your apartment and spoke with you and your husband. You were leaving for a party and cut the interview short. Keems left the building with you, but soon he went back to your apartment and talked with your maid, Ella Reyes, and gave her a hundred dollars in cash. In return she gave him information. She told him that on January third you complained of no headache until late in the afternoon, immediately after you received a phone call from Patrick Degan. She may even—"

"That isn't true." Fanny Irwin had to squeeze it out.

"If you mean she didn't tell him that, I admit I can't prove it, since Johnny Keems and Ella Reyes are both dead. If you mean that didn't happen, I don't believe you. She may even have also told him that she heard the phone conversation on an extension, and that Mr. Degan told you to withdraw from the theater party that evening, giving a headache as an excuse, and to suggest that Mrs. Molloy be invited in your stead."

"You know what you're saying," Jerome Arkoff said darkly.

"I do," Wolfe told Mrs. Irwin, not him. "I am charging you with complicity in the murder of Michael Molloy, and, by extension, of Johnny Keems and Ella Reyes and Delia Brandt. With that information from your maid, Keems, ignoring the instructions I had given him, sought out Degan. Degan, seeing that he was in great and imminent peril, acted promptly and effectively. On some pretext, probably of taking Keems to interview some other person, he had Keems wait for him at a place not frequented at that time of night while he went for his car; and instead of going for his car he stole one, drove it to the appointed place, and killed Keems with it."

Wolfe's head moved. "Do you wish to challenge that detail, Mr. Degan? Have you an alibi for that night?"

"I'm listening," Degan said, louder than necessary. "And don't forget others are listening too."

"I won't." Wolfe returned to Fanny Irwin. "But Degan had learned from Keems the source of his information, and Ella Reyes was almost as great a menace as Keems had been. Whether he communicated with her directly or through you, I don't know. He arranged to meet her, and killed her, and put the body where it was not found until somewhat later, taking her handbag to delay identification. By then he was no better than a maniac, and when, two or three days afterward, he was confronted with still another threat, this time from Delia Brandt, qualms, either of conscience or of trepidation, bothered him not at all. But I wonder about you. You felt no qualms? You feel none?"

"Don't say anything," her husband told her. He had her hand.

"I'm not sure that's good advice," Wolfe said. "There are certainly people present who would question it. If you'll turn your head, madam, to your right and rear, there by the big globe—the man on the left and the woman beside him—they are the parents of Peter Hays, who has been convicted of a murder you helped to commit. The other man is also deeply interested; he is Peter Hays's counsel. Now if you'll turn your head the other way. The man on the couch, who lost control of himself a few minutes ago, is—or was—the fiancé of Delia Brandt. They were to be married—tomorrow, Mr. Lesser?"

No reply.

Wolfe didn't press him. "And standing at the door is Archie Goodwin, and on Mr. Degan's left is Saul Panzer. They were friends and colleagues of Johnny Keems—and I myself knew Keems for some years and had esteem for him. I'm sorry I can't present to you any of the friends or family of Ella Reyes; you knew her better than anyone else here."

"What the hell good does this do?" Jerome Arkoff demanded.

Wolfe ignored it. "The point is this, Mrs. Irwin. Mr. Degan is done for. I have this sheaf of papers in my drawer. The key for the safe-deposit box which he took from Molloy's body will almost certainly be found in Degan's possession. There are other items —for example, when Mr. Goodwin left this house last Tuesday a man followed him, and that man will be found and will tell who engaged him. I'll stake my reputation that it was Degan. Now that we know that Degan killed those four people, the evidence will pile up. Fingerprints in Delia Brandt's apartment, his movements Wednesday night and Thursday night and Sunday night, an examination of the books of his organization; it will be overwhelming."

"What do you want of me?" she asked. They were her first words since he had called her a murderer.

"I want you to consider your position. Your husband advises you to say nothing, but he should consider it too. You are clearly open to a charge as accessory to murder. If you think you must not admit that Degan phoned you on January third, and suggested that you withdraw from the theater party and that Mrs. Molloy be asked in your stead, you are wrong. Such an admission would injure you only if it carried the implication that you knew why Degan wanted Mrs. Molloy away from her apartment—knew it either when he made the suggestion or afterward. And such an implication is not inherent. It is even implausible, since Degan wouldn't want to disclose his intention to commit murder. He could have told you merely that he wanted a private conversation with you and asked you to make an opportunity for that evening, and his suggestion of Mrs. Molloy could have been off-hand. If so, it is unwise and dangerous for you to keep silent, for silence can carry implications too. If Degan merely wanted an opportunity to discuss some private matter—"

"That was it!" she said, for all to hear.

Her husband let go of her hand.

Jerome Arkoff croaked, "Don't be a goddam fool, Tom! This is for keeps!"

Rita sang out, "Go on, Fanny! Spit it out!"

Fanny offered both hands to her husband, and he took them. She gave him her eyes too. "You know me, Tom. You know I'm yours. He just said he had to see me, he had to tell me something. He came to the apartment, but now I see, because he didn't come until nearly ten—"

Degan went for her. Of course it was a convulsion rather than a calculated movement. It couldn't very well have been calculated, since Saul and Purley were right there beside him, and since, even if he got his hands on her and somehow managed to finish her, it wouldn't have helped his prospects any. It was as Wolfe had said, after killing four people he was no better than a maniac, and, hearing her blurting out her contribution to his doom, he acted like one. He never touched her. Saul and Purley had him and jerked him back, and those two together are enough for any maniac.

Irwin was on his feet. So were the Arkoffs, and so was Cramer. Albert Freyer went loping over to my desk and reached for the phone.

Wolfe was speaking. "I'm through, Mr. Cramer. Twelve minutes short of my hour."

They didn't need me for a minute or two. I opened the door to the hall and went upstairs to report to Mrs. Molloy. She had it coming to her if anyone did. And from her room I could chase Freyer off the phone and call Lon Cohen at the *Gazette* and give him some news.

CHAPTER 19

A FEW DAYS LATER Cramer dropped in at six o'clock and called me Archie when I let him in. After getting settled in the red leather chair, accepting beer, and exchanging some news and views with Wolfe, he stated, not aggressively, "The District Attorney wants to know where and how you got the key to the locker. I wouldn't mind knowing myself."

"I think you would," Wolfe declared.

"Would what?"

"Would mind. It would only ruffle you to no purpose. If the District Attorney persists, and I tell him it came to me in the mail and the envelope has been destroyed, or that Archie found it on the sidewalk, what then? He has the murderer, and you delivered him. I doubt if you will persist."

He didn't.

The problem of the fee, which had to be settled as soon as Peter Hays had been turned loose, was a little more complicated. Having mentioned to James R. Herold, while under a strain, the sum of fifty thousand dollars, Wolfe wanted to stick to it, but fifty grand and expenses seemed pretty steep for a week's work, and besides, he was already in the 80% bracket. He solved it very neatly, arranging for Herold to donate a check for $16,666.67 to Johnny Keems's widow and one for the same amount to Ella Reyes' mother. That left $16,666.66, plus expenses, for Wolfe, and makes a monkey out of people who call him greedy, since he got only $16,666.66 instead of $16,666.67. And P.H., after he got from under, finally conceded that his father and mother were his parents, though the announcement of the wedding in the *Times* had it Peter Hays, and the *Times* is always right.

They were married a month or so after Patrick A. Degan had been convicted of first-degree murder, and a couple of weeks later they called at the office. I wouldn't have recognized P.H. as the guy I had seen that April day through the steel lattice. He looked comparatively human and even acted human. I want to be fair, but I also want to report accurately, and the fact is that he didn't impress me as any particular treat. When they got up to go Selma Hays moved to the corner of Wolfe's desk and said she had to kiss him. She said she doubted if he wanted to be kissed, but she simply had to.

Wolfe shook his head. "Let us forgo it. You wouldn't enjoy it and neither would I. Kiss Mr. Goodwin instead; that will be more to the point."

I was right there. She turned to me, and for a second she thought she was going to, and so did I. But as pink started to show in her cheeks she drew back, and I said something, I forget what. That girl has sense. Some risks are just too big to take.

The Final Deduction

CHAPTER 1

"Your name, please?"

I asked her only as a matter of form. Having seen her picture in newspapers and magazines at least a dozen times, and having seen her in person at the Flamingo and other spots around town, I had of course recognized her through the one-way glass in the door as I went down the hall to answer the doorbell, though she wasn't prinked up for show. There was nothing dowdy about her brown tailored suit or fur stole or the hundred-dollar pancake on her head, but her round white face, too white there in daylight, which could be quite passable in a restaurant or theater lobby, could have stood some attention. It was actually flabby, and the rims of her eyes were red and swollen. She spoke.

"I don't think . . ." She let it hang a moment, then said, "But you're Archie Goodwin."

I nodded. "And you're Althea Vail. Since you have no appointment, I'll have to tell Mr. Wolfe what you want to see him about."

"I'd rather tell him myself. It's very confidential and very urgent."

I didn't insist. Getting around as I do, and hearing a lot of this and that, both true and false, I had a guess on what was probably biting her, and if that was it I would enjoy watching Wolfe's face as she spilled it, and hearing him turn her down. So I admitted her. The usual routine with a stranger who has no appointment is to leave him or her on the stoop while I go and tell Wolfe, but I can make exceptions, and it was a raw windy day for late April, so I took her to the front room, the first door on your left when you are inside, returned to the hall, and went to the second door on the left, to the office.

Wolfe was on his feet over by the big globe, glaring at a spot on it. When I had gone to answer the bell he had been glaring at Cuba, but he had shifted to Laos.

"A woman," I said.

He stuck with Laos. "No," he said.

"Probably," I conceded. "But she says it's urgent and confidential, and she could pay a six-figure fee without batting an eye. Her name is Althea Vail. Mrs. Jimmy Vail. You read newspapers thoroughly, so you must know that even the *Times* calls him Jimmy. Her eyes are red, presumably from crying, but she is now under control. I don't think she'll blubber."

"No!"

"I didn't leave her on the stoop because of the weather. She's in the front room. I have heard talk of her, and I understand that she is prompt pay."

He turned. "Confound it," he growled. He took in a bushel of air through his nose, let it out through his mouth, and moved. Behind his desk he stood, a living mountain, beside his oversized chair. He seldom rises to receive a caller, woman or man, but since he was already on his feet it would take no energy to be polite, so why not? I went and opened the connecting door to the front room, told Mrs. Vail to come, presented her, and convoyed her to the red leather chair near the end of Wolfe's desk. Sitting, she gave the stole a backward toss, and it would have slid to the floor if I hadn't caught it. Wolfe had lowered his 285 pounds into his chair and was scowling at her, his normal attitude to anyone, especially a woman, who had the gall to come uninvited to the old brownstone on West 35th Street, his house, expecting him to go to work.

Althea Vail put her brown leather bag on the stand at her elbow. "First," she said, "I'd better tell you how I got here."

"Not material," Wolfe muttered.

"Yes it is," she declared. It came out hoarse, and she cleared her throat. "You'll see why. But first of all it has to be understood that what I'm going to tell you is absolutely in confidence. I know about you, I know your reputation, or I wouldn't be here, but it has to be definite that this is in *complete confidence*. Of course I'm going to give you a check as a retainer, and perhaps I should do that before . . ." She reached to the stand for her bag. "Ten thousand dollars?"

Wolfe grunted. "If you know about me, madam, you should know that that's fatuous. If you want to hire me to do a job, what is it? If I take it, a retainer may or may not be required. As for confidence, nothing that you tell me will be revealed unless it involves a crime which I am obliged, as a citizen and a licensed private detective, to report to authority. I speak also for Mr. Goodwin, who is in my employ and who—"

"It does involve a crime. Kidnaping is a crime."

"It is indeed."

"But it must *not* be reported to authority."

My brows were up. Seated at my desk, my chair swiveled to face her, I crossed off the guess I had made. Apparently I wouldn't get to watch Wolfe's face while a woman asked him to tail her husband, or to hear him turn her down. He was speaking.

"Certainly kidnaping is unique. The obligation not to withhold knowledge of a major crime must sometimes bow to other considerations, for instance saving a life. Is that your concern?"

"Yes."

"Then you may trust our discretion. We make no firm commitment, but we are not fools. I suppose you have been warned to tell no one of your predicament?"

"Yes."

"Then I was wrong. How you got here is material. How did you?"

"I phoned a friend of mine, Helen Blount, who lives in an apartment on Seventy-fifth Street, and arranged it with her. The main entrance to the apartment house is on Seventy-fifth Street, but the service entrance is on Seventy-fourth Street. I phoned her at half past ten. I told my chauffeur to have my car out front at half past eleven. At half past eleven I went out and got in my car and was driven to my friend's address. I didn't look behind to see if I was being followed because I was afraid the chauffeur would notice. I got out and went into the apartment house—the men there know me—and I went to the basement and through to the service entrance on Seventy-fourth Street, and Helen Blount was there in her car, and I got in, and she drove me here. So I don't think there's the slightest chance that they know I'm seeing Nero Wolfe. Do you?"

Wolfe turned to me. "Archie?"

I nodded. "Good enough. Hundred to one. But if someone's waiting in Seventy-fifth Street to see her home and she never shows, he'll wonder. It would be a good idea to go back before too long and enter on Seventy-fourth and leave on Seventy-fifth. I would advise it."

Her red-rimmed eyes were at me. "Of course. What would be too long?"

"That depends on how patient and careful he is, and I don't know him." I glanced at my wrist. "It's twenty-five after twelve. You got there a little more than half an hour ago. You could reasonably be expected to stay with your friend quite a while, hours maybe. But if he knows you well enough to know that your friend Helen Blount lives there he might call her number and ask for you and be told that you're not there and you haven't been there. I have never known a kidnaper personally, but from what I've read and heard I've got the impression that they're very sensitive."

She shook her head. "He won't be told that. Helen told her maid what to say. If anyone asks for me, or her either, he'll be told that we're busy and can't come to the phone."

"Good for you. But there's Helen Blount. She knows you came to see Nero Wolfe."

"She doesn't know what for. That's all right, I can trust her, I *know* I can." Her eyes went back to Wolfe. "So that's how I got here. When I leave I have to go to my bank, and then I'll go back to Seventy-fourth Street." It was coming out hoarse again, and she cleared her throat and coughed. "It's my husband," she said. She got her bag and opened it and took out an envelope. "He didn't come home Sunday night, and yesterday this came in the mail."

Her chair was too far away for her to hand it to Wolfe without getting up, and of course he wouldn't, so I did. It was an ordinary off-white envelope with a typewritten address to Mrs. Jimmy Vail, 994 Fifth Avenue, New York City, no zone number, and was postmarked BRYANT STA APR 23 1961 11:30 PM. Sunday, day before yesterday. The flap had been cut clean with a knife or opener, no jagged edges. I handed it to Wolfe, and after a glance at the address and postmark he removed the contents, a folded sheet of cheap bond paper, also off-white, five by eight unfolded, the kind you get in scratch pads. He held it to his left, so I could read it too. We no longer have it, but from some shots I took of it the next day I can have it reproduced for you to look at. It may tell you what it told Wolfe about the person who typed it. Here it is:

```
    We have got your Jimmy safe and
sound.  We haven't hurt him any and
you can have him back all in one piece
for $500,000 if you play it right and
keep it strictly between you and us.
We mean strictly.  If you try any
tricks you'll never see him again.
You'll get a phone call from Mr. Knapp
and don't miss it.
```

Wolfe dropped it on the desk pad and turned to Althea Vail. "I can't forgo," he said, "an obvious comment. Surely this is humbug. Kidnaping is a desperate and dangerous operation. It's hard to believe that a man committed to it, a man who has incurred its mortal risks, could be in a mood to make a pun—that in chosing an alias to use on the phone, for himself in his role as kidnaper, he would select 'Knapp.' It must be flummery. If not, if this thing is straightforward"—he tapped the paper with a finger— "the man who wrote it is most extraordinary. Is your husband a practical joker?"

"No." Her chin had jerked up. "Are you saying it's a joke?"

"I suggested the possibility, but I also suggested an alternative, that you have a remarkable man to deal with. Have you heard from Mr. Knapp?"

"Yes. He phoned yesterday afternoon, my listed number. I had told my secretary that I expected the call, and she listened on an extension. I thought she might as well because she opens my mail and she had read that thing."

"What did he say?"

"He told me what to do. I'm not going to tell you. I'm going to do exactly what he said. I don't need you for that. What I need you for, I want my husband back. Alive. I know they may have killed him already, I know that, but—" Her chin had started to work, and she pressed her lips together to stop it. She went on, "If they have, then I'll want you to find them if the police and the FBI don't. But on the phone yesterday that man said he was all right, and I believe him. I *must* believe him!"

She was on the edge of the chair. "But don't kidnapers often kill after they get the money? So they can't be traced or recognized? Don't they?"

"That has happened."

"Yes. That's what I need you for. Doing what he said, getting the money to them, I'll do that myself, there's nothing you can do about that. I've told my banker I'm coming to get the money this afternoon, and I'll do—"

"Half a million dollars?"

"Yes. And I'll do exactly what that man said, but that's all I can do, and I want him back. I want to be sure I'll get him back. That's what I need you for."

Wolfe grunted. "Madam. You can't possibly mean that. You are not a nincompoop. How could I conceivably proceed? The only contact with that punster or an accomplice will be your delivery of the money, and you refuse to tell me anything about it. Pfui. You can't possibly mean it."

"But I do. I do! That's why I came to *you!* Is there anything you can't do? Aren't you a genius? How did you get your reputation?" She took a checkfold from her bag and slipped a pen from a loop. "Will ten thousand do for a retainer?"

She had a touch of genius herself, or it was her lucky day, asking him if there was anything he couldn't do and waving a check at him. He leaned back, closed his eyes, and cupped the ends of the chair arms with his hands. I expected to see his lips start moving in and out, but they didn't; evidently this one was too tough for any help from the lip routine. Mrs. Vail opened the checkfold on the stand at her elbow, wrote, tore the check from the fold, got up and put it on Wolfe's desk, and returned to the chair. She started to say something, and I pushed a palm at her. A minute passed, another, and two or three more, before Wolfe opened his eyes, said, "Your notebook, Archie," and straightened up.

I got my notebook and pen. But instead of starting to dictate he closed his eyes again. In a minute he opened them and turned to Mrs. Vail.

"The wording is important," he said. "It would help to know how *he* uses words. You will tell me exactly what he said on the phone."

"No, I won't." She was emphatic. "You would try to do something, some kind of trick. You'd have Archie Goodwin do something. I know he's clever and you may be a genius, but I'm not going to risk that. I told that man I would do exactly what he told me to, and do it alone, and I'm not going to tell you. What wording is important? Wording of what?"

Wolfe's shoulders went up an eighth of an inch and down again. "Very well. His voice. Did you recognize it?"

She stared. "Recognize it? Of course not!"

"Had you any thought, any suspicion, that you had ever heard it before?"

"No."

"Was he verbose, or concise?"

"Concise. He just told me what to do."

"Rough or smooth?"

She considered. "Neither one. He was just—matter-of-fact."

"No bluster, no bullying?"

"No. He said this would be my one chance and my husband's one chance, but he wasn't bullying. He just said it."

"His grammar? Did he make sentences?"

She flared. "I wasn't thinking of grammar! Of course he made sentences!"

"Few people do. I'll rephrase it: Is he an educated man? 'Educated' in the vulgar sense, as it is commonly used."

She considered again. "I said he wasn't rough. He wasn't vulgar. Yes, I suppose he is educated." She gestured impatiently. "Isn't this wasting time? You're not enough of a genius to guess who he is or where he is from how he talked. Are you?"

Wolfe shook his head. "That would be thaumaturgy, not genius. When and where did you last see your husband?"

"Saturday morning, at our house. He left to drive to the country, to our place near Katonah, to see about things. I didn't go along because I wasn't feeling well. He phoned Sunday morning and said he might not be back until late evening. When he hadn't come at midnight I phoned, and the caretaker told me he had left a little after eight o'clock. I wasn't really worried, not really, because sometimes he takes a notion to drive around at night, just anywhere, but yesterday morning I *was* worried, but I didn't want to start calling people, and then the mail came with that thing."

"Was he alone when he left your place in the country?"

"Yes. I asked the caretaker."

"What is your secretary's name?"

"My secretary? You jump around. Her name is Dinah Utley."

"How long has she been with you?"

"Seven years. Why?"

"I must speak with her. You will please phone and tell her to come here at once."

Her mouth opened in astonishment. It snapped shut. "I will not," she said. "What can she tell you? She doesn't know I've come to you, and I don't want her to. Not even her. I trust her absolutely, but I'm not going to take *any* chances."

"Then there's your check." Wolfe pointed to it, there on his desk. "Take it and go." He made a face. "I must have some evidence of your bona fides, however slight. I do know you are Mrs. Jimmy Vail, since Mr. Goodwin identifies you, but that's all I know. Did that thing come in the mail and did you get a phone call from Mr. Knapp? I have only your unsupported word. I will not be made a party to some shifty hocus-pocus. Archie. Give Mrs. Vail her check."

I got up, but she spoke. "It's no hocus-pocus. My God, hocus-pocus? My husband—they'll kill him! My not wanting anyone to know I've come to you, not even my secretary—isn't that right? If you expect her to tell you what he said on the phone, she won't. I'll tell her not to."

"I won't ask her." Wolfe was curt. "I'll merely ask her how he said it. If you have been candid, and I have no reason to think you haven't, you have no valid objection to my speaking with her. As for her knowing that you have come to me, Mr. Knapp will soon know that himself—or I hope he will."

She gawked. "*He* will know? How?"

"I'll tell him." He turned. "Archie. Can we get an advertisement in the evening papers?"

"Probably, the late editions," I told him. "The *Post* and *World-Telegram,* we can try. The *Gazette,* yes, with Lon Cohen's help." I was back in my chair with notebook and pen. "Classified?"

"No. It must be conspicuous. Two columns wide, or three. Headed in thirty-six-point, boldface, extended, 'To Mr. Knapp.' Then in twelve-point: 'The woman whose property is in your possession has engaged my services (period). She is now in my office (period). She has not told me what you said to her on the phone Monday afternoon (comma), and she will not tell me (period). I know nothing of the instructions you gave her (comma), and I do not expect or care to know (period). She has hired me for a specific job (comma), to make sure that her property is returned to her in good condition (comma), and that is the purpose of this notice (paragraph).

"'For she has hired me for another job should it become necessary (period). If her property is not returned to her (comma), or if it is damaged beyond repair (comma), I have engaged to devote my time (comma), energy (comma), and talent (comma), for as long as may be required (comma), to ensure just and fitting requital (semicolon); and she has determined to support me to the full extent of her resources (period). If you do not know enough of me to be aware of the significance of this engagement to your future (comma), I advise you to inform yourself regarding my competence and my tenacity (period).' Beneath, in fourteen-point boldface, 'Nero Wolfe.' To be billed to me. Can you do it by phone?"

"To Lon Cohen at the *Gazette,* yes. The others, maybe." I swiveled and reached for the phone, but he stopped me.

"Just a moment." He turned to Mrs. Vail. "You heard that. As you said, your husband may already be dead. If so, I am irrevocably committed by the publication of that notice. Are you? No matter what it costs in time and money?"

"Certainly. If they kill him—certainly. But I don't— Is that *all* you're going to do, just that?"

"I may not do it, madam, and if I don't I shall do nothing. There's nothing else I *could* do. I'll proceed if, and after, you give me another check for fifty thousand dollars and phone your secretary to come here at once." He slapped the chair arm. "Do you realize that I will be staking my repute, whatever credit I have established in all my years? That's what you must pay for; and the commitment. If your husband is already dead, or if Mr. Knapp, not seeing my notice or ignoring it, kills him after he gets the money, I shall have no alternative; and what if you default? I might have to spend much more than sixty thousand dollars. Of course if your husband returns safely there will be no commitment and I'll return some of it to you. How much will be in my discretion. Less if I learn that my notice was a factor; more if it wasn't. I value my reputation, which I am risking in your interest, but I am not rapacious." He looked up at the wall clock. "If what Mr. Knapp told you to do is to be done tonight, the notice must appear today to have any effect. It's nearly one o'clock."

The poor woman—or rather, the rich woman—had her teeth clamped on her lip. She looked at me. People often do that when they are being bumped around by Wolfe, apparently hoping I will come and pat them. Sometimes I wouldn't mind obliging them, but not Althea Vail, Mrs. Jimmy Vail. She just didn't warm me. Meeting her eyes, I let mine be interested but strictly professional, and when she saw that was all I had to offer she left me.

She got out her checkfold, put it on the stand, and wrote, her teeth still clamping her lip. When she tore it out I was there to take it and hand it to Wolfe. Fifty grand. Wolfe gave it a glance, dropped it on his desk, and spoke.

"I hope you'll get a large part of it back, madam. I do indeed. You may use Mr. Goodwin's phone to call your secretary. When that's done he'll use it to place that notice, in all three papers if possible."

She fluttered a hand. "Is it really necessary, Mr. Wolfe? My secretary?"

"Yes, if you want me to proceed. You're going to your bank, and it will soon be lunchtime. Tell her to be here at three o'clock."

She got up and went to my chair, sat, and dialed.

CHAPTER 2

When Dinah Utley arrived at 3:05, five minutes late, Wolfe was at his desk with a book, *The Lotus and the Robot,* by Arthur Koestler. We had started lunch later than usual because Wolfe had told Fritz not to put the shad roe in the skillet until he was notified, and it was close to half past one when I finally quit trying to persuade the *Post* and *World-Telegram* to get the ad in. Nothing doing. It was all set for the *Gazette,* thanks to Lon Cohen, who knew from experience that he would get a tit for his tat if and when. It was also set for all editions of the morning papers. The bulldogs would be out around eleven, and if Mr. Knapp saw one after he got the money and before he erased Jimmy Vail, he might change the script.

Our client had left, headed for her bank, as soon as it was definite from Lon Cohen that the ad would be in the last two editions. Part of the time while I was phoning, for some minutes at the end, Wolfe was standing at my elbow, but not to listen to me. He had the note Mrs. Vail had got from Mr. Knapp in his hand, and he pulled my typewriter around and studied the keyboard, then looked at the note, then back at the keyboard; and he kept that up, back and forth, until Fritz came to announce lunch. That was no time for me to comment or ask a question, with sautéed shad roe fresh and hot from the skillet, and the sauce, with chives and chervil and shallots, ready to be poured on, and of course nothing relating to business is ever mentioned at the table, so I waited until we had left the dining room and crossed the hall back to the office to say, "That note was typed on an Underwood, but not mine, if that's what you were checking. The 'a' is a little off-line. Also it wasn't written by me. Whoever typed it has a very uneven touch."

Sitting, he picked up *The Lotus and the Robot.* His current

book is always on his desk, at the right edge of the pad, in front
of the vase of orchids. That day's orchids were a raceme of Miltonia vexillaria, brought by him as usual when he had come down
from the plant rooms at eleven o'clock. "Ummmp," he said. "I
was merely testing a conjecture."

"Any good?"

"Yes." He opened the book to his place and swiveled, giving
me his acre or so of back. If I wanted to test a conjecture I would
have to use one of my own. A visitor was due in ten minutes,
and since according to him the best digestive is a book because
it occupies the mind and leaves the stomach in privacy, he darned
well was going to get a few pages in. And when, a quarter of an
hour later, I having spent most of it inspecting the note from Mr.
Knapp with occasional glances at my typewriter keyboard, the
doorbell rang, and I went to the hall and returned with the visitor,
and pronounced her name, and put her in the red leather chair,
Wolfe stuck with his book until I had gone to my desk and sat.
Then he marked his place and put it down, looked at her, and
said, "Are you an efficient secretary, Miss Utley?"

Her eyes widened a little, and she smiled. If she had been doing any crying along with her employer it had certainly left no
traces. At sight I had guessed her age at thirty, but that might have
been a couple of years short.

"I earn my salary, Mr. Wolfe," she said.

She was cool—cool eyes, cool smile, cool voice. With some cool
ones the reaction is that it would be interesting to apply a little
heat and see what happens, and you wouldn't mind trying, but
with others you feel that they are cool clear through, and she was
one of them, though there was nothing wrong with her features
or figure. You could even call her a looker.

Wolfe was taking her in. "No doubt," he said. "As you know,
Mrs. Vail phoned you from here. I heard her tell you not to tell
me what Mr. Knapp said to her on the phone yesterday, but you
may feel that she is under great strain and your judgment on that
point is better than hers. Do you?"

"No." Very cool. "I'm in her employ."

"Then I won't try to cajole you. Do you always open Mrs. Vail's mail?"

"Yes."

"Everything that comes?"

"Yes."

"How many items were there in yesterday morning's mail?"

"I didn't count them. Perhaps twenty."

"The envelope with that note in it, did you open it first or further along in the process?"

Of course that tactic is three thousand years old, maybe more, asking for a detail of a reported action, looking for hesitation or confusion. Dinah Utley smiled. "I always sort it out first, leaving circulars and other obvious stuff until later. Yesterday there were four—no, five—that I opened at once. The envelope with that note was the third one I opened."

"Did you show it to Mrs. Vail at once?"

"Certainly. I took it to her room."

"Were you present Sunday night when she phoned to the country to ask about her husband?"

"No. I was in the house, but I was in bed."

"What time yesterday did the call come from Mr. Knapp?"

"Eight minutes after four. I knew that might be important somehow, and I made a note of it."

"You listened to that conversation?"

"Yes. Mrs. Vail had told me to take it down, and I did."

"Then you know shorthand?"

"Of course."

"Are you a college graduate?"

"Yes."

"Do you type with two fingers, or four?"

She smiled. "All of them. By touch." She turned a hand over. "Really, Mr. Wolfe. Isn't this rather silly? Is it going to get Mr. Vail back alive?"

"No. But it may conceivably serve a purpose. Naturally you want to be with Mrs. Vail, and she wants you; I won't keep you much longer. There's no point now in asking you about that man's voice and diction; even if I got a hint that suggested another wording for the notice it's too late. But you will please let Mr. Goodwin take samples of your fingerprints. Archie?"

That roused her a little. "*My* fingerprints? Why?"

"Not to get Mr. Vail back alive. But they may be useful later on. It's barely possible that Mr. Knapp or an accomplice inadvertently left a print on that note. To your knowledge, has anyone handled it besides Mrs. Vail and you?"

"No."

"And Mr. Goodwin and me. We shall get Mrs. Vail's. Mr. Goodwin is an expert on prints, and even if Mr. Vail returns safely, as I hope he will, we'll want to know if there are any unidentifiable prints on that note. Do you object to having your prints taken?"

"Of course not. Why should I?"

"Then Archie?"

I had opened a desk drawer and was getting out the equipment —ink with dauber and surfaced paper. I prefer a dauber to a pad. Knowing now, as I did, what the conjecture was that Wolfe had been testing when he inspected my typewriter keyboard with the note from Mr. Knapp in his hand, and therefore also knowing why I was to take Dinah Utley's prints, it wasn't necessary to write her name on the paper, but I did anyway. She got up and came to my desk and I did her right hand first. She had good hands, firm, smooth, well kept, with long slender fingers. No rings. With her left hand, when I had done the thumb, index, and middle, and started to daub the ring finger, I asked casually, "What's this? Scald it?"

"No. Shut a drawer on it."

"The pinkie too. I'll go easy."

"It's not very tender now. I did it several days ago."

But I went easy, there being no point in making her suffer, since we had no use for the prints. As she cleaned her fingers with solvent and tissues she asked Wolfe, "You don't really think a kidnaper would be fool enough to leave his fingerprint on that note, do you?"

"No," Wolfe said, "not fool enough. But possibly distraught enough. One thing more, Miss Utley. I would like you to know that

I'm aware that the primary concern is the safety of Mr. Vail. I have done all I can. Archie, show her a copy of the notice."

I got it from my desk and handed it to her. Wolfe waited until she had finished reading it to say, "That will appear, prominently, in today's *Gazette* and the morning papers. If the kidnaper sees it, it may have an effect; it certainly will if he has some knowledge of me. For I will have publicly committed myself, and if he kills Mr. Vail he will be doomed inevitably. A month, a year, ten years; no matter. It's regrettable that you or I can't reach him, to make that clear to him."

"Yes, it is." Still perfectly cool. She handed me the notice. "Of course he may not have as high an opinion of your abilities as you have." She turned to go, after three steps stopped and turned her head to say, "He might even think the police are more dangerous than you are," and went. There ahead of her, and preceding her to the hall and the front door. I let her out; and, expecting no thanks or good day, got none.

Returning to the office, I stopped in front of Wolfe's desk, stood looking down at him, and said, "So she typed it."

He nodded. "Of course I didn't—"

"Excuse me. I'll do the spiel. When you first looked at it you noticed, as I did, that whoever typed it had an uneven touch. Later, while I was phoning, you looked at it again, got an idea, and came and compared it with the keyboard, and you saw that all the letters that were faint were on the left—not just left of center, but at the left end. W, E, A, S, and D. So you conjectured that the typist had been someone who used all his fingers, not just two or four, and that for some—"

"And probably typed by touch, because—"

"Excuse me, I'm doing the spiel. The touch was merely a probable. And for some reason the ring and little finger of his left hand had not hit the keys as hard as the other fingers, not nearly as hard. Okay. I caught up with you after lunch, while you were reading, just before she came. You saw me comparing the note with the keyboard."

"No. I was reading."

"Let me not believe that. You miss nothing, though you often pretend to. You saw me all right. Then she came, and you went on ahead of me again, and I admit I ought to be docked. My eyes are as good as yours, and I had been closer to her than you were, but you noticed that the tips of those two fingers on her left hand were discolored and slightly swollen, and I didn't. Of course when you told her we wanted her prints I saw it, and you will ignore what I said about being docked because I found out how and when the fingers got hurt. Any corrections?"

"No. It is still a conjecture, not a conclusion."

"Damn close to it. One will get you fifty. That it is just a coincidence that she, a touch typist, living in that house, hurt just those two fingers, just at that time, just enough to make her go easy with them but not enough to stop using them—nuts. One will get you a hundred. So you had her read that notice and rubbed it in, thinking she'll get in touch with Mr. Knapp. Why did you let her walk out?"

Wolfe nodded. "The alternative was obvious. Go at her. Would she have yielded?"

"No. She's tough."

"And if Mr. Vail is already dead, as he well may be, it would be folly to let her know what we suspect. If he is alive, no better. She would have flouted me. Detain her forcibly, as a hostage, on a mere suspicion, however well grounded, and notify Mr. Knapp that we would exchange her for Mr. Vail? That would have been a coup, but how to reach Mr. Knapp? It's too late to get another notice in the paper. Have you a suggestion?"

"Yes. I go to see Mrs. Vail to ask her something, no matter what, and I manage somehow to get something written on the type-writer Dinah Utley uses. Of course she could have used another machine for the note, but if what I got matched the note, that would settle that."

He shook his head. "No. You have ingenuity and can even be delicate, but Miss Utley would almost certainly get a hint. Besides, to ask a question she asked, would it help to get Mr. Vail back alive? No." He glanced at the clock. In ten minutes he would leave for his four-to-six afternoon session in the plant rooms. Time enough for a few pages. He reached and got his book and opened to his place.

CHAPTER 3

It's POSSIBLE that I have given a wrong impression of Jimmy Vail, and if so I should correct it.

Age, thirty-four; height, five feet ten; weight, 150. Dark eyes, sometimes lazy and dull, sometimes bright and very quick. Smooth dark hair, nearly black, and a neat white face with a wide mouth. I had seen him about as often as I had seen his wife, since they were nearly always together at a restaurant or theater. In 1956 he had made a big splash at the Glory Hole in the Village with a thirty-minute turn of personal chatter, pointed comments on everyone and everything. Althea Tedder, widow of Harold F. Tedder, had seen him there, and in 1957 she had married him, or he had married her, depending on who is talking.

I suppose any woman who marries a man a dozen years younger is sure to get the short end of the stick when her name comes up among friends, let alone enemies, no matter what the facts are. The talk may have been just talk. Women of any age liked Jimmy Vail and liked to be with him, there was no question about that, and undoubtedly he could have two-timed his middle-aged wife any day in the week if he felt like it, but I had never with my own eyes seen him in the act. I'm merely saying that as far as I know, disregarding talk, he was a model husband. I had expected her to ask Wolfe to put a tail on him because I assumed that her friends had seen to it that she knew about the talk.

She also had made a public splash, twenty-five years back—Althea Purcell as the milkmaid in *Meadow Lark*—and she had quit to marry a man somewhat older and a lot richer. They had produced two children, a son and a daughter; I had seen them a couple of times at the Flamingo. Tedder had died in 1954, so Althea had waited a decent interval to get a replacement.

Actually, neither Jimmy nor Althea had done anything notorious, or even conspicuous, during the four years of their marriage. They were mentioned frequently in print only because they were expected to do something any minute. She had left Broadway in the middle of a smash hit to marry a middle-aged rich man with a prominent name, and he had left the mike in the middle of *his* smash hit to marry a middle-aged rich woman. With the Tedder house and the Tedder dough taken over by a pair like that, anything might happen and probably would. That was the idea.

Now something *had* happened, something sensational, two days ago, and not a word about it in print. There was nothing in Nero Wolfe's notice to Mr. Knapp to connect it with the Vails. If Helen Blount, Mrs. Vail's friend, saw it, she might make a guess, but not for publication. I saw it not long after Wolfe went up to the plant rooms. Not waiting until five-thirty, when a late edition of the *Gazette* is delivered to the old brownstone, I took a walk to the newsstand at 34th and Eighth Avenue. It was on page five, with plenty of margin. No one named Knapp could possibly miss it, but of course that wasn't his name.

I had a date for that evening, dinner with a friend, and a show, and it was just as well. Most of the chores of a working detective, even Nero Wolfe's right hand, not to mention his legs, are routine and pretty damn dull, and the idea of tailing a woman taking half a million bucks to a kidnaper was very tempting. Not only would it have been an interesting way to spend an evening, but there were a dozen possibilities. But since it was Wolfe's case and I was working for him, I couldn't do it without his knowledge and consent, and it would have been a waste of breath to mention it. He would have said pfui and picked up his book. So at six o'clock I went up to my room and changed and went to my date. But off and on that evening I wondered where our client was and how she was making out, and when I got home around one o'clock I had a job keeping myself from dialing her number before I turned in.

The phone rang. Of all the things that I don't want to be wakened by, the one I resent most is the phone. I turned over, forced my eyes open enough to see that it was light and the clock said 7:52, reached for the receiver and got it to my ear, and managed to get it out: "Nero Wolfe's residence, Archie Goodwin speaking."

"Mr. Goodwin?"

"I thought I said so."

"This is Althea Vail. I want to speak to Mr. Wolfe."

"Impossible, Mrs. Vail. Not before breakfast. If it's urgent, tell me. Have you—"

"My husband is back! Safe and sound!"

"Good. Wonderful. Is he there with you?"

"No, he's at our country place. He just phoned, ten minutes ago. He's going to bathe and change and eat and then come to town. He's all right, perfectly all right. Why I'm phoning, he promised them he would say nothing, absolutely nothing, for forty-eight hours, and I'm not to say anything either. I didn't tell him I had gone to Nero Wolfe; I'll wait till he gets here. Of course I don't want Mr. Wolfe to say anything. Or you. That's why I'm phoning. You'll tell him?"

"Yes. With pleasure. You're sure it was your husband on the phone?"

"Certainly I'm sure!"

"Fine. Whether the notice helped or not. Will you give us a ring when your husband arrives?"

She said she would, and we hung up. The radio clicked on, and a voice came: ". . . has five convenient offices in New York, one at the—" I reached and turned it off. When I get to bed after midnight I set it for eight o'clock, the news bulletins on WQXR, but I didn't need any more news at the moment. I had a satisfactory stretch and yawn, said aloud, "What the hell, no matter what Jimmy Vail says we can say Mr. Knapp *must* have seen it," yawned again, and faced the fact that it takes will power to get on your feet.

With nothing pending I took my time, and it was after eight-thirty when I descended the two flights to the ground floor, entered the kitchen, told Fritz good morning, picked up my glass of orange juice, took a healthy sip, and felt my stomach saying thanks. I had considered stopping at Wolfe's room on the way down but had vetoed it. He would have been in the middle of breakfast, since Fritz takes his tray up at eight-fifteen.

"No allspice in the sausage," Fritz said. "It would be an insult. The best Mr. Howie has ever sent us."

"Then double my order." I swallowed juice. "You give me good news, so I'll give you some. The woman that came yesterday gave us a job, and it's already done. All over. Enough to pay your salary and mine for months."

"*Fort bien.*" He spooned batter on the griddle. "You did it last night?"

"No. He did it sitting down."

"Yes? But he would do nothing without you to *piquer.*"

"How do you spell that?"

He spelled it. I said, "I'll look it up," put my empty glass down, went to the table against the wall where my copy of the *Times* was on the rack, and sat. I kept an eye on my watch, and at 8:57, when I had downed the last bite of my first griddle cake and my second sausage, I reached for the house phone and buzzed Wolfe's room.

His growl came. "Yes?"

"Good morning. Mrs. Vail called an hour ago. Her husband had just phoned from their house in the country. He's at large and intact and will come to town as soon as he cleans up and feeds. He promised someone, presumably Mr. Knapp, that neither he nor his wife will make a peep for forty-eight hours, and she wants us to keep the lid on."

"Satisfactory."

"Yeah. Nice and neat. But I'll be taking a walk, to the bank to deposit her checks, and it's only five more blocks to the *Gazette.* It's bound to break soon, and I could give it to Lon Cohen to hold until we give the word. He'd hold it, you know that, and he would deeply appreciate it."

"No."

"You mean he wouldn't hold it?"

"No. He has shown that he can be trusted. But I haven't seen Mr. Vail, nor have you. It's useful to have Mr. Cohen in our debt, but no. Perhaps later in the day." He hung up. He would be two minutes late getting to the plant rooms on the roof. As Fritz brought my second cake and pair of sausages I said, "For a bent nickel I'd go up and peekay him."

He patted my shoulder and said, "Now, Archie. If you should, you will. If you shouldn't, you won't."

I buttered the cake. "I *think* that's a compliment. It's tricky. I'll study it."

For the next couple of hours, finishing breakfast and the *Times* (the notice was on page twenty-six), opening the mail, dusting our desks, removing yesterday's orchids and putting fresh water in the vase, walking to the bank and back, and doing little miscellaneous office chores, I considered the situation off and on. It seemed pretty damn silly, being hired in connection with something as gaudy as the kidnaping of Jimmy Vail, merely to put an ad in the paper and collect a fee and then call it a day. But what else? I'm more than willing to peekay Wolfe when there's any point or profit to it, but with Jimmy Vail back in one piece the job Wolfe had been hired for was done, so what? As soon as it broke, an army of cops and FBI scientists would be after Mr. Knapp, and they'd probably get him sooner or later. We were done, except for one little detail, to see Jimmy Vail whole. Mrs. Vail had said she would give us a ring when he arrived, and I would go up and ask him if Mr. Knapp had shown him the *Gazette* with the notice in it.

I didn't have to. At 11:25 the doorbell rang. Wolfe had come down from the plant rooms and gone to his desk, put a spray of Oncidium marshallianum in the vase, torn yesterday from his desk calendar, and gone through the mail, and was dictating a long letter to an orchid collector in Guatemala. He hates to be interrupted when he's doing something really important, but Fritz was upstairs, so I went, and there he was on the stoop. I told Wolfe, "Jimmy Vail in person," and went and opened the door, and he said, "Maybe you know me? I know you." He stepped in. "You're a hell of a good dancer."

I told him he was too, which was true, took his coat and hat and put them on the rack, and took him to the office, and he crossed to Wolfe's desk, stood, and said, "I know you don't shake hands. I once offered to fight a man because he called you a panjandrum; of course I knew he was yellow. I'm Jimmy Vail. May I sit down? Preferably in the red leather chair. There it is." He went and sat, rested his elbows on the chair arms, crossed his legs, and said, "If I belch you'll have to pardon me. I had nothing but cold canned beans for two days and three nights, and I overdid it on the bacon and eggs. My wife has told me about hiring you. Never has so much been spent on so little. Naturally I don't like being called my wife's property—who would?—but I realize you had to. I only saw it when my wife showed it to me, and I don't know whether they saw it or not. Is that important?"

You wouldn't have thought, looking at him and listening to him, that he had just spent sixty hours in the clutches of kidnapers, living on cold beans, and maybe not long to live even on beans, but of course he had cleaned up and had a meal, and the talk I had heard had never included any suggestion that he was a softy. His face was dead white, but it always was, and smooth and neat as it always was, and his dark eyes were bright and clear.

"It would be helpful to know," Wolfe said, "but it isn't vital. You came to tell me that? That you don't know?"

"Not actually." Vail lifted a hand to the neighborhood of his right temple and flipped his middle finger off the tip of his thumb. He had made that gesture famous during his career at the Glory Hole. "I just mentioned it because it may be important to us, my wife and me. If one of them saw that thing in the paper they know my wife has told you about it, and that may not be too good. That's why I came and came quick. They told me to keep my trap shut for forty-eight hours, until Friday morning, and to see that my wife did too, or we would regret it. I think they meant it. I got a strong impression that they mean what they say. So my wife and I are going to keep it to ourselves until Friday morning, but what about you? You could put another notice in the paper to Mr. Knapp, saying that since the property has been returned the case is closed as far as you're concerned. That you're no longer interested. What do you think?"

Wolfe had cocked his head and was eying him. "You're making an unwarranted assumption, Mr. Vail—that I too will keep silent until Friday morning. I told your wife that the obligation not to withhold knowledge of a major crime must sometimes bow to other considerations, for instance saving a life, but you are no longer in jeopardy. Now that I've seen you alive and at freedom, I cannot further postpone reporting to authority. A licensed private detective is under constraints that do not apply to the ordinary citizen. I don't want to subject you or your wife—"

The phone rang, and I swiveled to get it. "Nero Wolfe's office, Archie Good—"

"This is Althea Vail. Is my husband there?"

"Yes, he—"

"I want to speak to him."

She sounded urgent. I proceeded as I did not merely out of curiosity. There was obviously going to be a collision between Wolfe and Jimmy Vail about saving it until Friday, and if that was what she was urgent about I wanted to hear it firsthand. So I told her to hold the wire, told him his wife wanted to speak to him, and beat it, to the kitchen and the extension there. As I got the receiver to my ear Mrs. Vail was talking.

". . . terrible has happened. A man just phoned from White Plains, Captain Saunders of the State Police, he said, and he said they found a dead body, a woman, and it's Dinah Utley, they think it is, and they want me to come to White Plains to identify it or send someone. My God, Jimmy, *could* it be Dinah? How could it be Dinah?"

JIMMY: I don't know. Maybe Archie Goodwin will know; he's listening in on an extension. Did he say how she was killed?

ALTHEA: No. He—

JIMMY: Or where the body was found?

ALTHEA: No. He—

JIMMY: Or why they think it's Dinah Utley?

ALTHEA: Yes, things in her bag and in the car. Her car was there. I don't think—I don't want to—can't I send Emil?

JIMMY: Why not? How about it, Goodwin? Emil is the chauffeur. He can certainly tell them whether it's Dinah Utley or not. Must my wife go? Or must I go?

It was no use pretending I wasn't there. "No," I said, "not just for identification. Of course if it's Dinah Utley they'll want to ask both of you some questions, if there's any doubt about how she died, but for that they can come to you. For identification only, even I would do. If you want to ask Mr. Wolfe to send me."

ALTHEA: Yes! Do that, Jimmy!

JIMMY: Well . . . maybe . . . where did he say to come in White Plains?

ME: I know where to go.

ALTHEA: It must be Dinah! She didn't come home last night and now—this is terrible—

JIMMY: Take it easy, Al. I'll be there soon. Just take it easy and . . .

I cradled the phone and went back to the office. Vail was hanging up as I entered. I said to him, "Naturally I want to hear what a client of Mr. Wolfe's has to say on his phone. And naturally you knew I would." I turned to Wolfe. "A state cop called Mrs. Vail from White Plains. They have found a woman's body, he didn't say where, and from articles in her bag and her car they think it's Dinah Utley. Also there must have been something that connected her with Mrs. Vail, maybe just the address. He asked Mrs. Vail to come to White Plains and identify her, and she doesn't want to go, and neither does Mr. Vail. I suggested that he might want to ask you to send me."

Wolfe was scowling at Vail. He switched it to me. "Did she die by violence?"

"Mrs. Vail doesn't know. I've reported in full."

"Look," Vail said, "this is a hell of a thing." He was standing at the corner of my desk. "Good God. This is a real shocker. I suppose I ought to go myself."

"If it's Miss Utley," Wolfe said, "and if she died by violence, they'll ask you where you were last night. That would be routine."

"I'm not telling anyone where I was last night, not until Friday morning. Not even you."

"Then you'll be suspect. You and your wife should confer without delay. And if Mr. Goodwin goes to identify the body and it is Miss Utley, he will be asked about his association with her, when and where he has seen her. You know she was here yesterday?"

"Yes. My wife told me. But my God, he won't tell them about that, why she came here!"

Wolfe leaned back and shut his eyes. Vail started to say something, saw he wouldn't be heard, and stopped. He went to the red leather chair and sat, then got up again, walked halfway to the door, turned, and came back to Wolfe's desk and stood looking down at him.

Wolfe's eyes opened, and he straightened up. "Archie, get Mrs. Vail."

"I'm here," Vail said. "You can talk to me."

"You're not my client, Mr. Vail. Your wife is."

I was dialing. The number was in my head, where I had filed it when I looked it up Tuesday night. A female voice said, "Mrs. Vail's residence," and I said Nero Wolfe wanted to speak with Mrs. Vail. After a wait our client's voice came, "This is Althea Vail. Mr. Wolfe?" and I nodded to Wolfe and he took his phone. I stayed on, but I had to fight for it. Jimmy Vail came to take it away from me, reaching for it and getting his fingers on it, but I kept it against my ear and didn't hear what he said because I was listening to Wolfe.

"Good morning, madam. I was gratified to see your husband, as of course you were. The telephone call you received from White Plains puts a new problem, and I offer a suggestion. I understand that you prefer not to go to White Plains to see if the dead woman is Miss Utley. Is that correct?"

"Yes. Archie Goodwin said he would go."

Wolfe grunted. "Mr. Goodwin will always go. He is—uh—energetic. But there are difficulties. If it is Miss Utley, he will be asked when and where he last saw her, and when he says she came to my office yesterday he will be asked for particulars. If he gives them in full he will have to include the fact that when she left we, he and I, had formed a strong suspicion that she was implicated in the kidnaping of your husband, and then—"

"Dinah? She was implicated? That's ridiculous! Why did you suspect that?"

"I reserve that. I'll explain it later—or I won't. Then they'll demand full information about the kidnaping, not only from Mr. Goodwin and me, but from you and your husband, and they won't want to wait until Friday for it. That's the prob—"

"But why did you suspect *Dinah?*"

"That will have to wait. So I offer a suggestion. You gave me

checks for sixty thousand dollars. I told you I would refund a portion of it if your husband came back alive, since it covered the contingency that I might have to meet the commitment I made in that
published notice. I would prefer to keep it, but if I do I'll have to
earn it. My suggestion is that I send Mr. Goodwin to White Plains
to look at the body. If it is Miss Utley, he identifies it, he says that
he saw her for the first and last time when she came to my office
yesterday in connection with a confidential job you had hired me
for, and on instructions from me he refuses to give any further information. Also I engage that neither he nor I will disclose anything
whatever regarding your husband's kidnaping before eleven o'clock
Friday morning unless you give your consent. That will expose us
to inconvenience and possibly serious embarrassment, and I shall
not feel obliged to return any money to you. I will owe you nothing, and you will owe me nothing. That's my suggestion. I should
add, not to coerce you, merely to inform you, that if it isn't accepted
I can no longer withhold my knowledge of a capital crime, kidnaping. I'll have to inform the proper authority immediately."

"That's a threat. That's blackmail."

"Pfui. I've offered to incur a considerable risk for a moderate
fee. I withdraw my suggestion. I'll send you a check today. That
will end—"

"No! Don't hang up!" Nothing for five seconds. "I want to speak
to my husband."

"Very well." Wolfe looked around, then at me, and demanded,
"Where is he?"

I covered the transmitter. "Skipped. Right after you said we
suspected that Dinah was implicated. Gone. I heard the front door
close."

"I didn't." He returned to the phone. "Your husband has left,
Mrs. Vail, presumably to go to you. I didn't see him go. I'll send
you a check—"

"No!" Another silence, a little longer. "All right, send Archie
Goodwin. To White Plains."

"With the understanding that I proposed?"

"Yes. But I want to know why you thought Dinah was implicated. That's incredible!"

"To you, no doubt. It was merely a conjecture, possibly ill-grounded. Another time I may explain it, but not now. I must get Mr. Goodwin off. Permit me."

He hung up, and so did I. I got up and crossed to the hall, went to the front door to see that it was closed, opened the door to the front room and looked in, returned to the office, and told Wolfe, "He's gone. Not that I thought our client's husband would try any tricks, but he might have got confused and shut the door while he was still inside. Instructions?"

"Not necessary. You heard what I said to Mrs. Vail."

"Yeah, that's okay, the worst they can do is toss me in the jug, and what the hell, you're getting paid for it. But are we curious about anything? Do we care what happened to her, and when and where?"

"No. We are not concerned."

I headed for the hall, but at the door I turned. "You know," I said, "some day it may cost you something. You know damned well that we may have to be concerned and you may have to work, and it might be helpful for me to collect a few facts while they're still warm. But will you admit it? No. Why? Because you think I'm so—uh—energetic that I'll get the facts anyhow and have them available if and when you need them. For once I won't. If somebody wants to tell me no matter what, I'll say I'm not concerned."

I went and got my coat from the rack, no hat, let myself out, descended the seven steps to the sidewalk, walked to Tenth Avenue and around the corner to the garage, and got the 1961 Heron sedan which Wolfe owns and I drive.

CHAPTER 4

AT ONE-FIFTEEN P.M. Clark Hobart, District Attorney of Westchester County, narrowed his eyes at me and said, "You're dry behind the ears, Goodwin. You know what you're letting yourself
in for."

We were in his office at the Court House, a big corner room
with four windows. He was seated at his desk, every inch an elected
servant of the people, with a strong jaw, a keen eye, and big ears
that stuck out. My chair was at an end of the desk. In two chairs
in front of it were Captain Saunders of the State Police and a man
I had had contacts with before, Ben Dykes, head of the county detectives. Dykes had fattened some in the two years since I had last
seen him; what had been a crease was now a gully, giving him two
chins, and when he sat his belly lapped over his belt. But the word
was that he was still a fairly smart cop.

I met Hobart's eyes, straight but not belligerent. "I'd like to be
sure," I said, "that you've got it right. They reported to you before
I was brought in. I don't suppose they twisted it deliberately, I
know Ben Dykes wouldn't, but let's avoid any misunderstanding.
I looked at the corpse and identified it as Dinah Utley. Captain
Saunders asked me how well I had known her, and I said I had met
her only once, yesterday afternoon, but my identification was positive. Dykes asked where I had met her yesterday afternoon, and
I said at Nero Wolfe's office. He asked what she was there for, and
I said Mrs. Jimmy Vail had told her to come, at Mr. Wolfe's request, so he could ask her some questions in connection with a confidential matter which Mrs. Vail had hired him to investigate. He
asked me what the confidential matter was, and I—"

"And you refused to tell him."

I nodded. "That's the point. My refusal was qualified. I said I
was under instructions from Mr. Wolfe. If he would tell me where

the body had been found, and how and when and where she had died, with details, I would report to Mr. Wolfe, and if a crime had been committed he would decide whether it was reasonable to suppose that the crime was in any way connected with the matter Mrs. Vail had consulted him about. I hadn't quite finished when Captain Saunders broke in and said Dinah Utley had been murdered and I damned well would tell him then and there exactly what she had said to Mr. Wolfe and what he had said to her. I said I damned well wouldn't, and he said he had heard how tough I thought I was and he would take me where we wouldn't be disturbed and find out. Evidently he's the salt-of-the-earth type. Ben Dykes, who is just a cop, no hero, insisted on bringing me to you. If what I'm letting myself in for is being turned over to Captain Saunders, that would suit me fine. I have been thinking of going to a psychiatrist to find out how tough I am, and that would save me the trouble."

"I'll be glad to do you that favor," Saunders said. He moved his lips the minimum required to get the words out. Someone had probably told him that that showed you had power in reserve, and he had practiced it before a mirror.

"You're not being turned over," Hobart said. "I'm the chief law officer of this county. A crime *has* been committed. Dinah Utley was murdered. She was with you not many hours before she died, and as far as we know now, you were the last person to see her alive. Captain Saunders was fully justified in asking for the details of that interview. So am I."

I shook my head. "He didn't ask, he demanded. As for the crime, where and when? If a car ran over her this—"

"How do you know a car ran over her?" Saunders snapped.

I ignored him. "If a car ran over her this morning here on Main Street, and people who saw the driver say he was a dwarf with whiskers and one eye, I doubt if Mr. Wolfe will think his talk with her yesterday was relevant. Having seen the body, I assume that either a car ran over her or she was hit several times with a sledge-hammer, though there are other possibilities." I turned a hand over. "What the hell, Mr. Hobart. You know Mr. Wolfe knows the rules."

He nodded. "And I know how he abuses them—and you too.

Dinah Utley wasn't killed here on Main Street. Her body was found at ten o'clock this morning by two boys who should have been in school. It was in a ditch by a roadside, where it—"

"What road?"

"Iron Mine Road. Presumably it once led to an iron mine, but now it leads nowhere. It's narrow and rough, and it comes to a dead end about two miles from Route One Twenty-three. The body—"

"Where does it leave Route One Twenty-three?"

Saunders growled, in his throat, not parting his lips. He got ignored again.

"About two miles from where Route One Twenty-three leaves Route Thirty-five," Hobart said. "South of Ridgefield, not far from the state line. The body had been rolled into the ditch after death. The car that had run over her was there, about a hundred feet away up the road, headed into an opening to the woods. The registration for the car was in it, with the name Dinah Utley and the address Nine Ninety-four Fifth Avenue, New York twenty-eight. Also in it was her handbag, containing the usual items, some of them bearing her name. It has been established that it was that car that ran over her. Anything else?"

"When did she die?"

"Oh, of course. The limits are nine o'clock last evening and three o'clock this morning."

"Were there traces of another car?"

"Yes. One and possibly two, but on grass. The road's gravelly, and the grass is thick up to the gravel."

"Anyone who saw Dinah Utley or her car last night, or another car?"

"Not so far. The nearest house is nearly half a mile away, east, toward Route One Twenty-three, and that stretch of road is seldom traveled."

"Have you got any kind of a lead?"

"Yes. You. When a woman is murdered a few hours after she goes to see a private detective it's a fair assumption that the two events were connected and what she said to the detective is material. Were you present when she talked with Wolfe?"

"Yes. It's also a fair assumption that the detective is the best judge as to whether the two events were connected or not. As I said, Dinah Utley didn't come to see Mr. Wolfe on her own hook; she came because Mrs. Vail told her to, to give him some information about something Mrs. Vail wanted done." I got up. "Okay, you've told me what I can read in the paper in a couple of hours. I'll report to Mr. Wolfe and give you a ring."

"That's what you think." Saunders was on his feet. "Mr. Hobart, you know how important time is on a thing like this. You realize that if you let him go in twenty minutes he'll be out of your jurisdiction. You realize that he has information that if we get it now it might make all the difference."

I grinned at him. "Can you do twenty pushups? I can."

Ben Dykes told Hobart, "I'd like to ask him something," and Hobart told him to go ahead. Dykes turned to me. "There was an ad in the *Gazette* yesterday headed 'To Mr. Knapp' with Nero Wolfe's name at the bottom. Did that have anything to do with why Mrs. Vail told Dinah Utley to go to see Wolfe?"

The word that Dykes was still a fairly smart cop seemed to be based on facts. The grin I gave him was not the one I had given Saunders. "Sorry," I said, "but I'm under orders from the man I work for." I went to the District Attorney. "You know the score, Mr. Hobart. It would be stretching a point even to hold me for questioning as it stands now, and since I wouldn't answer the questions, and since Mr. Wolfe wouldn't talk on the phone or let anyone in the house until he gets my report, I suppose we'll have to let Captain Saunders go without. But of course it's your murder."

He had his head tilted back to frown at me. "You know the penalty," he said, "for obstructing justice." When I said, "Yes, sir," politely, he abruptly doubled his fists, bounced up out of his chair, and yelled, "Get the hell out of here!" As I turned to obey, Ben Dykes shook his head at me. I passed close enough to Saunders for him to stick out a foot and trip me, but he didn't.

Down on the sidewalk, I looked at my watch: 1:35. I walked three blocks to a place I knew about, called Mary Jane's, where someone makes chicken pie the way my Aunt Anna used to make it in Chillicothe, Ohio, with fluffy little dumplings; and as I went through a dish of it I considered the situation. There was no point in wasting money ringing Wolfe, since he wasn't concerned, and as for our client, there was no rush. I could call her after I reported to Wolfe. So, since I was already halfway there—well, a third of the way—why not take a look at Iron Mine Road? And maybe at the old iron mine if I could find it? If I kidnaped a man and wanted a place to keep him while I collected half a million bucks, I wouldn't ask anything better than an abandoned iron mine. I paid for the chicken and a piece of rhubarb pie, walked to the lot where I had parked the Heron, ransomed it, and headed for Hawthorne Circle. There I took the Saw Mill River Parkway, and at its end, at Katonah, I took Route 35 east. It was a bright sunny day, and I fully appreciate things like forsythia and trees starting to bud and cows in pastures as long as I have a car that I can depend on to get me back to town. Just short of Connecticut I turned right onto Route 123, glancing at my speedometer. When I had gone a mile and a half I started looking for Iron Mine Road, and in another two-tenths there it was.

After negotiating a mile of that road I wasn't so sure that the Heron would get me back to town. I met five cars in the mile, and for one of them I had to climb a bank and for another I had to back up fifty yards. There was no problem about spotting the scene of the crime when I finally reached it. There were eight cars strung along, blocking the road completely, none of them official. A dozen women and three or four men were standing at the roadside, at the edge of the ditch, and two men at the other side of the road were having a loud argument about who had dented whose fender. I didn't even bother to get out. To the north was thick woods, and to the south a steep rocky slope with a swamp at the bottom. I admit I was a little vague about what an abandoned iron mine should look like, but nothing in sight looked promising. I pushed the reverse button and started backing, with care, and eventually came to a spot with enough room to turn around. On the way to Route 123 I met three cars coming in.

Of the two decisions I made going back to town, I was aware of one of them at the time I made it, which was par. That one was to take my time, with half an eye on the landscape, to see how the country was making out with its spring chores, which was sensible, since I couldn't get to 35th Street before four o'clock and Wolfe would be up in the plant rooms, where he hates to be interrupted, especially when there's nothing stirring that he's concerned about. I made that decision before I reached Route 35.

I don't know when the other decision was made. I became aware of it when I found myself in the middle lane of the Thruway, hitting sixty-five. When I'm bound for New York from Westchester and my destination is on the West Side, I take the Saw Mill all the way; when my destination is on the East Side I leave it at Ardsley and get on the Thruway. And there I was on the Thruway, so obviously I was going somewhere on the East Side. Where? It took me nearly two seconds. I'll be damned, I told myself, I'm headed for our client's house to tell her I identified the body. Okay, that will save a dime, the cost of a phone call. And if her husband is there and they have any questions, I can answer them face to face, which is always more satisfactory. I rolled on, to the Major Deegan Expressway, the East River Drive, and the 96th Street exit.

It was ten minutes past four when, having found a space on 81st Street I could squeeze the Heron into, I entered the vestibule of the four-story stone mansion at 994 Fifth Avenue and pushed the button. The door was opened by a square-faced woman in uniform with a smudge on her cheek. I suppose the Tedder who had had the house built, Harold F.'s father, wouldn't have dreamed of letting that door be opened by a female, so it was just as well he wasn't around. She had a surprise for me, though she didn't know it. When I gave my name and said I wanted to see Mrs. Vail, she said Mrs. Vail was expecting me, and made room for me to enter. I shouldn't have been surprised to find once again that Wolfe thought he knew me as well as I thought I knew him, but I was. What had happened, of course, was that Mrs. Vail had phoned to ask if I had identified the body, and he had told her that I would stop at her house on the way back from White Plains, though that hadn't been mentioned by him or me. That was how well he thought he knew me. Some day he'll overdo it. As I have said, *I* hadn't known I was going to stop at her house until I found myself on the Thruway.

As the female door-opener took my coat, a tenor voice came

from above, "Who is it, Elga?" and Elga answered it, "It's Mr. Goodwin, Mr. Tedder," and the tenor called, "Come on up, Mr. Goodwin." I went and mounted the marble stairs, white, wide, and winding, and at the top there was Noel Tedder. I've mentioned that I had seen him a few times, but I had never met him. From hearsay he was a twenty-three-year-old brat who had had a try at three colleges but couldn't make it, who had been forced by his mother to stop climbing mountains because he had fallen off of one, and who had once landed a helicopter on second base at Yankee Stadium in the fifth inning of a ball game; but from my personal knowledge he was merely a broad-shouldered six-footer who didn't care how he dressed when he went to the theater or the Flamingo and who talked too loud after two drinks. The tenor voice was one of those mistakes that get made when the hands are being dealt.

He took me down a wide hall to an open door and motioned me in. I crossed the sill and stopped, thinking for a second I had crashed a party, but then I saw that only five of the people in the room were alive, the rest were bronze or stone, and I remembered a picture I had seen years ago of Harold F. Tedder's library. This was it. It was a big room, high-ceilinged, but it looked a little crowded with a dozen life-sized statues standing around here and there. If he liked company he sure had it. Mrs. Vail's voice came, "Over here, Mr. Goodwin," and I moved. The five live ones were in a group, more or less, at the far end, where there was a fireplace but no fire. As I approached, Mrs. Vail said, "Well?"

"It was Dinah Utley," I said.

"What—how—"

I glanced around. "I'm not intruding?"

"It's all right," Jimmy Vail said. He was standing with his back to the fireplace. "They know about it. My wife's daughter, Margot Tedder. Her brother, Ralph Purcell. Her attorney, Andrew Frost."

"They know about Nero Wolfe," Mrs. Vail said. "My children and my brother were asking questions, and we thought we had better tell them. Then when this—Dinah—and we'll be asked where we were last night . . . I decided my lawyer ought to know about it and about Nero Wolfe. It was Dinah?"

"Yes."

"She was run over by a car?" From Andrew Frost, the lawyer. He looked a little like the man of bronze who was standing behind his chair, Abraham Lincoln, but he had no beard and his hair was gray; and on his feet probably he wasn't quite as tall. Presumably he had learned how Dinah had died by phoning White Plains, or from a broadcast.

"She was run over by *her* car," I said.

"Her own car?"

I faced Mrs. Vail, who was sitting on a couch, slumped against cushions. "On behalf of Mr. Wolfe," I told her, "I owe you two pieces of information. One, I looked at the corpse and identified it as Dinah Utley. Two, I told the District Attorney that I saw her yesterday afternoon when she came to Mr. Wolfe's office in connection with a matter you had consulted him about. That's all. I refused to tell him what the matter was or anything about it. That's all I owe you, but if you want to know how and when and where Dinah died I'll throw that in. Do you want it?"

"Yes. First when."

"Between nine o'clock last evening and three o'clock this morning. That may be narrowed down later. It was murder, because her own car ran across her chest and was there, nosed into a roadside opening, when the body was found. There was a bruise on the side of her head; she was probably hit with something and knocked out before the car was run over her. Then the—"

I stopped because she had made a sound, call it a moan, and shut her eyes. "Do you have to be utterly brutal?" Margot Tedder asked. The daughter, a couple of years younger than her brother Noel, was at the other end of the couch. From hearsay, she was a pain in the neck who kept her chin up so she could look down her nose; from my personal knowledge, she was a nice slender specimen with real possibilities if she would round out a little and watch the corners of her mouth, and, seeing her walk or dance, you might have thought her hips were in a cast.

"I didn't do it," I told her. "I'm just telling it."

"You haven't said where," Jimmy Vail said. "Where was it?"

Mrs. Vail's eyes had opened, and I preferred to tell her, since she was the client. "Iron Mine Road. That's a narrow rocky lane off of Route One Twenty-three. Route One Twenty-three goes into Route Thirty-five seven miles east of Katonah, not far from the state line."

Her eyes had widened. "My God," she said, staring at me. "*They* killed her." She turned to Andrew Frost. "The kidnapers. They killed her." Back to me. "Then you were right, what Mr. Wolfe said about suspecting her. That's where—"

"Wait a minute, Althea," Frost commanded her. "I must speak with you privately. This is dangerous business, extremely dangerous. You should have told me Monday when you got that note. As your counselor, I instruct you to say nothing more to anyone until you have talked with me. And I don't— Where are you going?"

She had left the couch and was heading for the door. She said over her shoulder, "I'll be back," and kept going, on out. Jimmy moved. He went halfway to the door, stopped and stood, his back to us, and then came back to the fireplace. Ralph Purcell, Mrs. Vail's brother, said something to Frost and got no response. I had never seen Purcell and knew next to nothing of him, either hearsay or personal knowledge. Around fifty, take a couple of years either way, with not much hair left and a face as round as his sister's, he had a habit I had noticed: when someone started to say something he looked at someone else. If he was after an effect he got it; it made you want to say something to him and see if you could keep his eye.

Noel Tedder, who was leaning against George Washington, asked me, "What's this about suspecting her? Suspecting her of what?" The lawyer shook his head at him, and Margot said, "What's the difference now? She's dead." Purcell was looking at me, and I was deciding what to say to him and try to hold his eye when Mrs. Vail came in. She had an envelope in her hand. She came back to the couch, sat on the edge, and took papers from the envelope. Frost demanded, "What have you got there? Althea, I absolutely insist—"

"I don't care what you insist," she told him. "You're a good lawyer, Andy, Harold thought so and so do I, and I trust your advice on things you know about, you know I do, but this is different. I told you about it because you could tell me about the legal part of it, but now I don't need just *legal* advice, now that I know Dinah was killed there on Iron Mine Road. I think I need something more than legal advice, I think I need Nero Wolfe." She turned to me. "Would he come here? He wouldn't, would he?"

I shook my head. "He never leaves the house on business. If you want to see him he'll be available at six—"

"No. I don't feel like—no. I can tell you. Can't I?"

"Certainly." I got my notebook and pen from a pocket, went to a chair near the end of the couch, and sat.

She looked around. "I want you to hear it, all of you. You all knew Dinah. I'm sure you all thought of her as highly as I did—I don't mean you all liked her, that's not it, but you thought she was very competent and completely reliable. But apparently she —but wait till you hear it." She fingered in the papers, extracted one, handed it to me, and looked around again. "I've told you about the note I got Monday morning, saying they had Jimmy and I would get a phone call from Mr. Knapp. Nero Wolfe has it. And I've told you, haven't I—yes, I did—that when the phone call came Monday afternoon Dinah listened in and took it down. Later she typed it from her notes, and that's it. Read it aloud, Mr. Goodwin."

A glance had shown me that the typing was the same as the note, the same faint letters, but on a better grade of paper and a different size, 8½ by 11. I read it to them:

Mrs. Vail: This is Althea Vail. Are you—
Knapp: I'm Mr. Knapp. Did you get the note?
Mrs. Vail: Yes. This morning. Yes.
Knapp: Is anyone else on the wire?
Mrs. Vail: No. Of course not. The note said—
Knapp: Keep it strictly to yourself. You had better if you want to see your Jimmy again. Have you got the money?
Mrs. Vail: No, how could I? I only got the note—
Knapp: Get it. You've got until tomorrow. Get it and put it in a suitcase. Five hundred thousand dollars in used bills, nothing bigger than a hundred. You understand that?

MRS. VAIL: Yes, I understand. But where is my husband? Is he—

KNAPP: He's perfectly all right. Safe and sound, not a scratch on him. That's absolutely straight, Mrs. Vail. If you play it straight, you can count on us. Now listen. I don't want to talk long. Get the money and put it in a suitcase. Tomorrow evening, Tuesday, put the suitcase in the trunk of your blue sedan, and don't forget to make sure the trunk's locked. Take the Merritt Parkway. Leave it at the Westport exit, Route 33. You know Route 33?

MRS. VAIL: Yes.

KNAPP: Do you know where Fowler's Inn is?

MRS. VAIL: Yes.

KNAPP: Go to Fowler's Inn. Get there at ten o'clock tomorrow evening. Don't get there much before ten, and not any later than five after ten. Take a table on the left side and order a drink. You'll get a message. Understand?

MRS. VAIL: Yes. What kind of a message? How will I know—

KNAPP: You'll know. You're sure you understand?

MRS. VAIL: Yes. Fowler's Inn at ten o'clock tomorrow evening. But when—

KNAPP: Just do as you're told. That's all.

I looked up. "That's all."

"But my God, Mom," Noel Tedder blurted, "if you had told me!"

"Or me," Andrew Frost said grimly.

"Well?" Mrs. Vail demanded. "What could you have done? Jimmy's here, isn't he? He's here alive and well. I went to Nero Wolfe, I've told you about that, and what he did may have helped, I don't know and I don't care now."

"I think you were extremely wise," Margot Tedder said, "not to tell either of them. Mr. Frost would have tried to make you wait until he looked it up in the books. Noel would have gone to Fowler's Inn in disguise, probably with a false beard. You went, Mother? To Fowler's Inn?"

Mrs. Vail nodded. "I did exactly what he told me to. Of course Mr. Graham at the bank was suspicious—no, not suspicious, curious—and he wanted me to tell him what the money was for, but

I didn't. It was my money. I got to Fowler's Inn too early, and sat in the car until ten o'clock, and then went in. I tried not to show how nervous I was, but I suppose I did; I kept looking at my watch, and at twenty after ten I was called to the phone. It was in a booth. The voice sounded like the other one, Mr. Knapp, but he didn't say. He told me to look in the Manhattan phone book where Z begins, and hung up. I looked in the phone book, and there was a note. I have it." She extracted another sheet of paper and handed it to me. "Read it, Mr. Goodwin."

"Wait a minute." It was Jimmy Vail. He had moved and was standing looking down at his wife. "I think you'd better call a halt, Al. You and I had better have a talk. Telling Goodwin all this, telling Frost—it's not Friday yet."

She lifted a hand to touch his arm. "I have to, Jimmy. I *have* to, now that Dinah—my God, they killed her! Read it, Mr. Goodwin."

It was the same typing, and on the same cheap paper as the note that had come in the mail. I read it aloud.

> Leave immediately. Speak to no one. Go to car. Read the rest of this after you are in the car. Drive to Route 7 and turn right. Beyond Weston leave Route 7 on any byroad and turn off of it in a mile or so onto some other byroad. Do this, taking turns at random, for half an hour, then return to Route 7 and go towards Danbury. A mile beyond Branchville stop at The Fatted Calf, take a table and order a drink. You'll get a message.

"I'll take that," Jimmy Vail said. "And the other one." His hand was there for them. From his tone, it seemed likely that if I tried to argue that I wanted to show them to Wolfe I would lose the debate, so I got the texts in my notebook in shorthand. That wasn't really necessary, since after years of practice I can report long conversations verbatim, but with such documents as those it was desirable. Transferring typed text to shorthand was practically automatic, so my ears could take in what Mrs. Vail was saying:

"I did what the note said. I think a car was following me all the time, but I wasn't sure. I think I didn't want to know, I didn't want to be sure. The same thing happened at The Fatted Calf,

the same as Fowler's Inn. At ten minutes after eleven I was
called to the phone, and the same voice told me to look in the
phone book where U begins, and there was another note." She
handed it to me. "Read it."

Same typing, same paper. I read:

Leave immediately. Speak to no one. Read the rest of this
in the car. Continue on Route 7 to the intersection with Route
35. Turn left on Route 35, and continue on 35 through Ridgefield. Two miles beyond Ridgefield turn left onto Route 123.
Go 1.7 miles on Route 123 and turn right onto Iron Mine Road.
Go slow. When a car behind blinks its lights three times, stop.
The car will stop behind you. Get out and open the trunk. A
man will approach and say, "It's time for a Knapp," and you
will give him the suitcase. He will tell you what to do.

"He did," Mrs. Vail said. "He told me to drive straight back to
New York, here, without stopping. He told me not to tell anyone
anything until Jimmy came back or he would never come back. He
said he would be back within twenty-four hours. And he was! He
is! Thank God!" She put out a hand to touch her Jimmy, but had to
stretch because he was sticking with me to get the notes. I was
getting the last one in my notebook. The Tedder son and daughter were saying something, and so was Andrew Frost. Finishing
with my shorthand, I reached around Jimmy to hand the papers
to Mrs. Vail. He had a hand there, but I ignored it, and she took
them. She spoke to me.

"You see why I had to tell Nero Wolfe. Or you."

"I can guess," I told her. "Mr. Wolfe told you we suspected
that Dinah Utley was implicated in the kidnaping. Now I tell you
that her body was found on Iron Mine Road, at the spot where
you turned over the suitcase, or near there. That complicates your
problem when Westchester County comes to ask you about Dinah
Utley and why you had her go to see Mr. Wolfe, especially if you
and your husband still want to save it until Friday. Haven't they
been here yet?"

"No."

"They soon will be. As for Mr. Wolfe and me, we'll stand pat until eleven o'clock Friday morning. He made it eleven o'clock because that's when he comes down from the plant rooms. As for you and your husband, and now also your son and daughter and brother and lawyer, you'll have to decide for yourselves. It's risky to withhold information material to a murder, but if it's for self-protection from a real danger, if you think Mr. Knapp meant business when he told your husband he'd regret it if he or you spilled it before Friday, I doubt if you'll have any serious trouble. Is that what you want from Mr. Wolfe or me?"

"No." She had the papers back in the envelope and was clutching it. "Only partly that. I want to know why you thought Dinah was implicated."

"Naturally." I put the notebook back in my pocket. "You didn't see her there? At Iron Mine Road?"

"No, of course not."

"Not of course not, since she *was* there. Was the man alone in the car behind you?"

"I didn't see anyone else. It was dark. I wasn't—I wasn't caring if there was anyone else."

"What did the man look like?"

"I don't know. He had a coat and a hat pulled down, and his face was covered with something, all but his eyes."

"Who left first, him or you?"

"I did. He told me to. I had to go on up the road to find a place to turn around."

"Was his car still there when you came back past the spot?"

"Yes. He had it up against the bank so I could get by."

"Did you see any other car anywhere on that road?"

"No." She gestured impatiently. "What has this to do with Dinah?"

"Nothing," Noel Tedder said. "He's a detective. It's his nature. He's putting you through the wringer."

"I insist," Andrew Frost said emphatically, "that this is ill-advised. *Very* ill-advised. You're making a mistake, Althea. Don't you agree, Jimmy?"

Jimmy was back at the fireplace. "Yes," he said. "I agree."

"But Jimmy, you must see," she protested. "She was *there!* And they killed her! You must see I want to know why Nero Wolfe suspected her!" To me: "Why did he?"

I shook my head. "I only run errands. But you're welcome to a hint." I stood up. "That phone talk you had with Mr. Knapp Monday afternoon, that Dinah listened to and took down. May I see the machine she typed it on?"

The three men spoke at once. Jimmy Vail and Andrew Frost both said, "No!" and Noel Tedder said, "Didn't I tell you?" Mrs. Vail ignored them and asked, "Why?"

"I'll probably tell you after I see it. And I may have a suggestion to make. Is it here?"

"It's in my study." She arose. "Will you tell me why you suspected Dinah?"

"I'll either tell you or you'll have a healthy idea."

"All right, come with me." She moved, paying no attention to protests from the men. I followed her out and along the hall to a door frame where she pressed a button. The door of a do-it-yourself elevator slid open, and we entered. That elevator was a much newer and neater job than the one in Wolfe's house that took him up to his room or the roof. No noise or jiggle. When it stopped and the door opened, she stepped out and led the way down the hall, some narrower than the one below. The room we entered was much smaller than the Harold F. Tedder library. Inside, I stopped for a glance around—that's habit. Two desks, one large and one small, shelves with books and magazines, filing cabinet, a large wall mirror, a television set on a table, framed photographs. Mrs. Vail had crossed to the small desk. She turned and said, "It's not here! The typewriter."

I went to her. At the end of the desk was a typewriter stand on casters. There was nothing on it. She had turned again and was staring at it. There were only two questions worth asking, and I asked them.

"Is it always kept here, or is it sometimes taken to another room?"

"Never. It is kept here."

"When did you last see it here?"

"I don't—I'd have to think. I haven't been in here today, until just now, when I came to get this envelope. I didn't notice it was gone. Sometime yesterday—I'd have to think. I can't imagine . . ."

"Someone may have borrowed it." I went to the door and turned. "I'll report to Mr. Wolfe. If he has anything to say we'll ring you. The main thing is we'll stay put until Friday unless you—"

"But you're going to tell me why you suspected Dinah!"

"Not now. Find the typewriter, and we'll see." I left. As I went down the hall her voice followed me, but I kept going. I was in no mood for talk. I should never have mentioned the typewriter, since it had nothing to do with the job Wolfe had been paid for, but I had wanted to get a sample from it to take along. Noel Tedder had been right; I was a detective, and it was my nature. Nuts. Skipping the elevator, I took the stairs, three flights down, and when I reached the ground floor the square-faced female appeared through an arch. She got my coat and held it, and went and opened the door; and there entering the vestibule was Ben Dykes, head of the Westchester County detectives.

I said, "Hello there. Get stopped for speeding?"

He said, "I've been in the park feeding pigeons. I didn't want to butt in."

"That's the spirit. I fully appreciate it. May your tribe increase." I circled around him, on out, and headed for 81st Street, where I had left the car.

CHAPTER 5

AT SIX O'CLOCK, when the sound came of Wolfe's elevator descending, I was in my chair in the office, my feet up on the desk, my weight on the base of my spine, and my head back.

For twenty minutes I had been playing a guessing game, which was all it amounted to, since we had nothing to do but sit on it, and since I didn't have enough bones to make a skeleton, let alone meat. But some day all the details of the Jimmy Vail kidnaping, including the murder of Dinah Utley, would be uncovered, whether they got Mr. Knapp or not, and if I could dope it here and now with what little I had, and it turned out that I was right, I could pin a medal on myself. So I worked at it.

Question: Was Dinah Utley in on it?

Answer: Certainly. She typed the note that came by mail and those Mrs. Vail found in the phone books.

Q: Who took the typewriter?

A: Dinah Utley. When she learned that Mrs. Vail had gone to Nero Wolfe, and when I took her prints and asked about her fingers, she got leery and ditched the typewriter.

Q: Was she with the man who got the suitcase from Mrs. Vail?

A: No. She was in her car somewhere along Iron Mine Road, and when Mrs. Vail drove back out she drove on in. She wanted to be sure of getting her cut. The man who had got the suitcase, probably Mr. Knapp, didn't care for that and killed her.

Q: Was anyone at the Vail house in on it besides Dinah Utley?

A: Yes. Jimmy Vail. He kidnaped himself. He had another man in it too, because he wasn't Mr. Knapp on the phone; it would have been too risky trying to disguise his voice. But he might have been the man who got the suitcase and therefore the man who killed Dinah Utley. That disagrees with the "probably

Mr. Knapp" in the preceding answer, but we're not in court. Items: Jimmy scooted from this office when he heard Wolfe tell Mrs. Vail that we suspected Dinah Utley, he told her she'd better call a halt when she produced the notes she had got from the phone books, and he tried to take the notes from me. Also his reactions in general. Also his insisting on saving it until Friday.

Q: Why did he have Dinah in on it?

A: Pass. No bone. A dozen possible reasons.

Q: Wouldn't he have been a sap to have Dinah type the notes on that typewriter?

A: No. The state of mind Mrs. Vail would be in when she got the note by mail, he knew she wouldn't inspect the typing. When he got back he would destroy the notes. He would say he had promised Mr. Knapp he would and he was afraid not to. She had to use *some* typewriter, and buying or renting or borrowing one might have been riskier. Using that one and destroying the notes, there would be no risk at all. He wanted to take the notes from me.

Q: Could Ralph Purcell or Andrew Frost or Noel Tedder be Mr. Knapp?

A: No. Mrs. Vail knows their voices too well.

Q: Friday, if not sooner, Jimmy will have to open up. Where and how they took him, and kept him, and turned him loose. With the cops and the FBI both at him, won't he be sure to slip?

A: No. He'll say they blindfolded him and he doesn't know where they took him and kept him. Last night, early this morning, they took him somewhere blindfolded and turned him loose.

Q: Then how are they going to uncover it so you can check it with these guesses and get your medal? How would you?

I was working on that one when the sound of the elevator came. Wolfe entered, crossed to his desk, sat, and said, "Report?"

I took my feet down and pulled my spine up. "Yes, sir. It's Dinah Utley. I told District Attorney Clark Hobart that I had seen her yesterday afternoon when she came here in connection with a job Mrs. Vail had hired you to do. When he asked me what the job was it would have been rude just to tell him to go to hell, so I said that if he would tell me when and where and how Dinah

Utley had died, and if I relayed it to you, you would decide what
to do. Of course there's no point in relaying it, since you said
we don't care what happened to her and are not concerned. I have
informed Mrs. Vail and told her we'll stand pat until eleven a.m.
Friday."

I swiveled, pulled the typewriter around, inserted paper and
carbons, got the notebook from my pocket, and hit the keys. Perfect harmony. It helps a lot, with two people as much together as
he and I were, if they understand each other. He understood that
I was too strong-minded to add another word unless he told me
to, and I understood that he was too pigheaded to tell me to. Of
course I had to keep busy; I couldn't just sit and be strong-
minded. I typed the texts of the two notes and other jottings I had
made in my book, then went and opened the safe and got the note
Mr. Knapp had sent by mail. It seemed likely that Jimmy Vail
would be wanting it, and it was quite possible that developments
would make it desirable for us to have something to show someone. I clipped the note to the edge of my desk pad, propped the
pad against the back of a chair, got one of the cameras—the Tol-
lens, which I have better luck with—and took half a dozen shots.
All this time, of course, Wolfe was at his book, with no glance at
me. I had returned the note to the safe and put the camera away,
and was putting the film in a drawer, when the doorbell rang. I
went to the hall door for a look, turned, and told Wolfe, "Excuse
me for interrupting. Ben Dykes, head of the Westchester County
detectives. He was there this afternoon. He's a little fatter than
when you saw him some years ago at the home of James U. Sper-
ling near Chappaqua."

He finished a sentence before he turned his head. "Confound
it," he muttered. "Must I?"

"No. I can tell him we're not concerned. Of course in a week
or so they might get desperate and take us to White Plains on a
warrant."

"You haven't reported."

"I reported all you said you wanted."

"That's subdolous. Let him in."

As I went to the front I was making a mental note not to look up "subdolous." That trick of his, closing an argument by using a word he knew damn well I had never heard, was probably subdolous. I opened the door, told Dykes he had been expected as I took his coat and hat, which was true, and ushered him to the office. Three steps in, he stopped for a glance around. "Very nice," he said. "Nice work if you can get it. You don't remember me, Mr. Wolfe." Wolfe said he did remember him and told him to be seated, and Dykes went to the red leather chair.

"I didn't think it was necessary to get a local man to come along," he said, "since all I'm after is a little information. Goodwin has told you about Dinah Utley. When he was up there he was the last one who had seen her alive as far as we knew, him and you when she was here yesterday afternoon, but since then I've spoken with two people who had seen her after that. But you know how it is with a murder, you have to start somewhere, and that's what I'm doing, trying to get a start, and maybe you can help. Goodwin said Dinah Utley came here yesterday because Mrs. Vail told her to. Is that right?"

"Yes."

"Well, of course I'm not asking what Mrs. Vail wanted you to do for her, I understand that was confidential, and I'm only asking about Dinah Utley. I'm not even asking what you said to her, I'm only asking what she said to you. That may be important, since she was murdered just eight or nine hours after that. What did she say?"

A corner of Wolfe's mouth was up a little. "Admirable," he declared. "Competent and admirable."

Dykes got his notebook out. "She said that?"

"No. I say it. Your demand couldn't be better organized or better put. Admirable. You have the right to expect a comparable brevity and lucidity from me." He turned a hand over. "Mr. Dykes. I can't tell you what Miss Utley said to me yesterday without divulging what Mrs. Vail has told me in confidence. Of course that wasn't a privileged communication; I'm not a member of the bar, I'm a detective; and if what Mrs. Vail told me is material to your investigation of a murder I withhold it at my peril. The question, is it material, can be answered now only by me;

you can't answer it because you don't know what she told me. To my present knowledge the answer is no."

"You're withholding it?"

"Yes."

"You refuse to tell me what Dinah Utley said to you yesterday?"

"Yes."

"Or anything about what she came here for?"

"Yes."

Dykes stood up. "As you say, at your peril." He glanced around. "Nice place you've got here. Nice to see you again." He turned and headed for the door. I followed him out and down the hall. As I held his coat for him he said, "At your peril too, Goodwin, huh?" I thanked him for warning me as I gave him his hat, and asked him to give Captain Saunders my love.

When I returned to the office Wolfe had his book open again. Always he is part mule, but sometimes he is all mule. He still didn't know when or where or how Dinah Utley had died, and he knew I did know, and he had no idea how much or little risk he was running to earn the rest of that sixty grand, but by gum he wasn't going to budge. He wasn't going to admit that we cared what had happened to her because he had been childish enough to tell me we didn't.

At the dinner table, in between bites of deviled grilled lamb kidneys with a sauce he and Fritz had invented, he explained why it was that all you needed to know about any human society was what they ate. If you knew what they ate you could deduce everything else—culture, philosophy, morals, politics, everything. I enjoyed it because the kidneys were tender and tasty and that sauce is one of Fritz' best, but I wondered how you would make out if you tried to deduce everything about Wolfe by knowing what he had eaten in the past ten years. I decided you would deduce that he was dead.

After dinner I went out. Wednesday was poker night, and that Wednesday Saul Panzer was the host, at his one-man apartment on the top floor of a remodeled house on 38th Street between Lexington and Third. You'll meet Saul further on. If you've already met him you know why I would have liked to have an hour alone with him, to give him the picture and see if he agreed with me about Jimmy Vail. It was just as well I couldn't have the hour, because if Saul had agreed with me I would have had a personal problem; it would no longer have been just my private guess. Jimmy Vail was responsible for our holding it back until Friday, and if he had killed Dinah Utley he was making monkeys of us. Of course that would serve Wolfe right, but how about me? It affected my poker, with Saul right there, but four other men were there also so I couldn't tell him. Saul, who misses nothing, saw that I was off my game and made remarks about it. It didn't affect his game any. He usually wins, and that night he raked it in. When we quit at the usual deadline, two o'clock, he had more than a hundred bucks of my money, and I was in no mood to stay and confide in him as an old and trusted friend.

Thursday, the morning after a late session of hard, tight poker, I don't turn out until nine or nine-thirty unless something important is cooking, but that Thursday I found myself lying on my back with my eyes wide open before eight. It was getting on my nerves. I said aloud, "Goddam Jimmy Vail anyhow," swung my legs around, and got erect.

I like to walk. I liked to walk in woods and pastures when I was a kid in Ohio, and now I like to walk even more on Manhattan sidewalks. If you don't walk much you wouldn't know, but the angle you get on people and things when you're walking is absolutely different from the one you get when you're in a car or in anything else that does the moving for you. So after washing and shaving and dressing and eating breakfast and reading about Dinah Utley in the *Times,* nothing I didn't already know, I buzzed the plant rooms on the house phone to tell Wolfe I was going out on a personal errand and would be back by noon, and went.

Of course you don't learn anything about people in general by walking around taking them in; you only learn things about this one or that one. I learned something that morning about a girl in a gray checked suit who caught her heel in a grating on Second Avenue in the Eighties. No girl I had ever known would have done what she did. Maybe no other girl in the world would. But I shouldn't have got started about walking. I mentioned walking only to explain how it happened that at a quarter past eleven I entered a drugstore at the corner of 54th Street and Eighth Avenue, sat at the counter, and requested a glass of milk. As it was brought and I took a sip, a Broadway type came in and got on the stool next to me and said to the soda jerk, "Cuppa coffee, Sam. You heard about Jimmy Vail?"

"Where would I hear about Jimmy Vail?" Sam demanded, getting a cup. "All I hear here is step on it. What about Jimmy Vail?"

"He died. It was on the radio just now. Found him dead on the floor with a statue on top of him. You know I used to know Jimmy before he married a billion. Knew him well."

"I didn't know." Sam brought the coffee. "Too bad." A customer came to a stool down the line, and Sam moved.

I finished the glass of milk before I went to the phone booth. I may have gulped it some, but by God I finished it. I wasn't arranging my mind; there was nothing in it to arrange; I was just drinking milk. When I went to the phone booth I got out a dime and started my hand to the slot but pulled it back. Not good enough. A voice on a phone is all right up to a point, but I might decide to go beyond that point, and a little more walking might help. I returned the dime to my pocket, departed, walked seven blocks crosstown and ten blocks downtown, entered the marble lobby of a building, and took an elevator.

I gave the receptionist on the twentieth floor a nod and went on by. Lon Cohen's room, with his name on the door but no title, was two doors this side of the *Gazette*'s publisher's. I don't remember a time that I have ever entered it and he wasn't on the phone, and that time was no exception. He darted a glance at me and went on talking, and I took the chair at the end of his desk and noted that he showed no sign of being short on sleep, though he had left Saul's place the same time I had, a little after two. His little dark face was neat and smooth, and his dark brown, deep-set eyes were clear and keen. When he had finished on the phone he turned to me and shook his head.

"Sorry, I've banked it. I guess I could spare a ducat."

He had been the only winner last night besides Saul. "I wouldn't want to strap you," I said. "A dime would see me through the week. But first, what about Jimmy Vail?"

"Oh." He cocked his head. "Is Wolfe looking for a job, or has he got one?"

"Neither one. I'm interested personally. I was taking a walk and heard something. I could wait and buy a paper, but I'm curious. What about him?"

"He's dead."

"So I heard. How?"

"He was found—you know about the Harold F. Tedder library."

"Yeah. Statues."

"He was found there a little after nine o'clock this morning by his stepdaughter, Margot Tedder. On the floor, with Benjamin Franklin on him. Benjamin Franklin in bronze, a copy of the one in Philadelphia by John Thomas Macklin. That would be a beautiful picture, but I don't know if we got one. I can phone downstairs."

"No, thanks. How did Benjamin Franklin get on him?"

"If we only knew that and knew it first. You got any ideas?"

"No. What do you know?"

"Damn little. Nothing. I can phone downstairs and see if anything more is in, but I doubt it. We've got five men on it, but you know how the cops are, and the DA, when it's people in that bracket. They don't even snarl, they just button their lips."

"You must know something. Like how long he'd been dead."

"We don't. We will in time for the three-o'clock." The phone buzzed. He got it, said "Yes" twice and "No" four times, and returned to me. "Your turn, Archie. Your fee's showing, or Wolfe's fee is. Yesterday morning the body of Mrs. Vail's secretary is found in a ditch in Westchester. This morning the body of her husband is found in her library, and here you come—not on the phone, in person. So of course Wolfe has been hired by someone. When? Yesterday? About the secretary?"

I eyed him. "I could give you a whole front page."

"I'll settle for half. Don't pin me to the wall with your steely eyes. I'm sensitive. You know who killed the secretary."

"No. I thought I did, but not now. What I've got may break

any minute—or it may not. If I give it to you now you'll have to save it until I give the word—unless it breaks, of course. This is personal. Mr. Wolfe doesn't even know I'm here."

"Okay. I'll save it."

"You don't mean maybe."

"No. I'll save it unless it breaks."

"Then get pencil and paper. Jimmy Vail was expected home from the country Sunday night but didn't come. Monday morning Mrs. Vail got a note in the mail saying she could have him back for five hundred grand and she would get a phone call from Mr. Knapp. I have a photograph of the note, taken by me, and I may let you have a print if you'll help me mark a deck of cards so I can win my money back from Saul. How would you like to run a good picture of that note, exclusive?"

"I'd help you mark ten decks of cards. A hundred. Is this straight, Archie?"

"Yes."

"My God. That 'Knapp' is beautiful. How did he spell it?"

I spelled it. "He phoned Monday afternoon and told her to get the money, put it in a suitcase, put the suitcase in the trunk of her blue sedan, and Tuesday evening drive to Fowler's Inn on Route Thirty-three, arriving at ten o'clock. She did so. At Fowler's Inn she was called to the phone and was told, probably the same voice, to look in the phone book where Z begins. There was a note there giving instructions. I haven't—"

"Beautiful," Lon said. His pencil was moving fast.

"Not bad. Don't interrupt, I'm in a hurry. I haven't got a picture of that note, but I have the text, taken from the original by me. The notes were typewritten. Following the instructions, she drove around a while and got to The Fatted Calf around eleven o'clock. There she got another phone call and was told to look in the phone book where U begins. Another note, same typewriting—I have the text. More instructions. Following them, she took Route Seven to Route Thirty-five, Route Thirty-five to Route One Twenty-three, and Route One Twenty-three to Iron Mine Road, which is all rock and a yard wide. She turned into it. When a car—"

"Dinah Utley," Lon said. "The secretary. Her body was found on Iron Mine Road."

"Don't interrupt. When a car behind her blinked its lights she stopped and got out and got the suitcase from the trunk. A man with only his eyes uncovered came from the other car, took the suitcase, and told her to go straight home, stop nowhere, and say nothing, which she did. Around seven-thirty yesterday morning her husband phoned her from their place in the country and said the kidnapers had let him go in one piece and he would come to town as soon as he cleaned up and ate. He also said they had told him to keep the lid on for forty-eight hours or he would regret it, and he was going to and expected her to. I don't know exactly when he arrived at the house on Fifth Avenue, but it must have been around ten o'clock."

I stood up. "Okay, that's it. I've got to go. If your sheet prints even a hint of it before I give the word, I'll write a letter to the editor and feed your eyes to the cat. If and when I give the word, there is to be no mention of Nero Wolfe or me. If it breaks, about the kidnaping, before I give the word, you'll still be out in front with a lot of facts the others won't have. I'll be seeing you."

"Wait a minute!" Lon was up. "You know how hot this is. It could burn my ass to cinders."

"It sure could. Then you couldn't help me mark a deck."

"How solid is it?"

"It isn't. There's an alternative. Either it's good as gold, every word, or Mrs. Jimmy Vail is unquestionably a double-breasted liar and almost certainly a murderer. If the latter, she'll be in no position to burn even your ears, let alone your ass. If she killed Dinah Utley, who killed Jimmy? Benjamin Franklin?" I turned to go.

"Damn it, listen!" He had my arm. "Was Dinah Utley with Mrs. Vail Tuesday night in the blue sedan?"

"No. For either alternative, that's positive. Dinah's own car was there at Iron Mine Road. That's the crop for now, Lon. I just wanted to burn a bridge. You could ask questions for an hour, but I haven't got an hour."

I went. Out to the elevator, down to the lobby, out to the sidewalk; and I started walking again. A taxi wouldn't have been much quicker, and I preferred to be on my feet. Down Lexington Avenue to 35th Street, and crosstown to the old brownstone. I mounted the stoop, let myself in with my key, put my coat on a hanger, and went to the office. Wolfe was at his desk, pouring beer.

"Good afternoon," I said. "Did you turn on the radio for the twelve o'clock news?"

"Yes."

"Did it mention Jimmy Vail?"

"Yes."

I went to my desk and sat. "I dropped in so you could have the satisfaction of firing me face to face. I have disobeyed orders. I am disloyal. I have betrayed your trust. I just told Lon Cohen about the kidnaping of Jimmy Vail. Not for publication; he won't use it until I say he can. I didn't mention Mrs. Vail's hiring you. I kept you out of it. I'm not quitting, you're firing me, so I'm entitled to two months' severance pay."

He lifted the glass and drank. The idea is to drink when there is still an inch of foam so it will get on his lips and he can lick it off. He licked it off and put the glass down. "Is this flummery?" he demanded.

"No, sir. It's straight. If you want me to tell you why I did it, I will, but not as an excuse, just as information. Do you want it?"

"Yes."

"It was getting too hot. I knew too much that you didn't know. You wouldn't take what I had got at White Plains, and you knew darned well I had seen Mrs. Vail on my way back, and you wouldn't take what I had got there either. From what—"

"I did not refuse to listen to you."

"Nuts. You know as well as I do how it stood. You had said we didn't care what had happened to Dinah Utley and we were not concerned. Will it help to chew at that?"

"No."

"Okay. What I had got had made me decide that Jimmy had probably kidnaped himself, and he had killed Dinah Utley, and he was making monkeys of us. So I was stuck. I had to give in and say, please, Mr. Wolfe, put your book down for a while and kindly permit me to tell you what happened yesterday so you can decide what to do. When you came down at eleven o'clock. You know how I liked that. I wasn't going to sit here on my rump all morning looking forward to it, so I went for a walk, and at eighteen minutes past eleven I heard a man tell another man that Jimmy Vail had been found dead on the floor of the library, where I had been yesterday afternoon."

I paused for dramatic effect. "So where was I? If Homicide hadn't already learned that I had been there yesterday in conference with the whole damn family, they soon would. Cramer himself might already be here ringing the bell. When he asked me what I was doing there, if I told him, I would be ditching our commitment to Mrs. Vail, and if I didn't tell him, I would be in for a picnic and the least I could expect would be losing my license. It wouldn't help any to come and say, please, Mr. Wolfe, even if you're not concerned kindly permit me to tell you what has happened because I'm in a jam. What could you do? I had to handle it myself, and I did. I went and did something you had told me not to do. I told Lon Cohen about the kidnaping. Then I came and saw that Cramer or Stebbins wasn't here, since there was no police car out front, and entered. Now you fire me and I go. Fast. One will get you a thousand that no one will find me before eleven o'clock tomorrow morning, the deadline." I arose.

"Sit down," he growled.

"No. Cramer or Stebbins may be here any minute."

"He won't be admitted."

"They'll cover the house front and back and come back with a warrant." I moved.

"Stop!" he bellowed. "Very well," he said. "You leave me no choice. I concede that we care what happened to Miss Utley and we are concerned. Report in full."

"If I'm fired why should I report?"

"You are not fired. Confound you, report!"

"It's too late. I'd be interrupted. The doorbell might ring any second."

He glared at me, then turned his head to glare at the clock. He made fists of his hands and glared at them, then used them to push his chair back. He got up and headed for the door, and when he reached the hall he roared, "Fritz!" The door to the kitchen swung open, and Fritz appeared. Wolfe was moving to the front, to the rack. He got his coat off the hanger and turned.

"Are the mussels open?"

"No, sir. It's only—"

"Don't open them. Keep them. Archie and I are going out. We'll be back for lunch tomorrow. Keep the door bolted."

Fritz gawked. "But—but—" He was speechless.

"If anyone inquires, you can't tell him where we are, since you won't know." He found the armholes of the coat I had taken and was holding. "Lunch at the usual time tomorrow."

"But you must have a bag—"

"I'll manage. Tell Theodore. You know what a search warrant is. If a policeman comes with one admit him, and stay with him. Archie?"

I had my coat on and the door open. He crossed the sill, and as I followed I shut the door. As we descended the stoop I asked, "The car?" and he said no, and at the bottom he turned right, toward Ninth Avenue. But we didn't reach Ninth Avenue. Halfway there he turned right and started up a stoop of a brownstone the same size and color and age as his, but it had a vestibule. He had used his vestibule to enlarge the hall years ago. He pushed the button, and in a moment the door was opened by a dark-haired woman with fine frontage to whom we had sent orchids now and then for the past ten years. She was a little startled at sight of us.

"Why, Mr. Wolfe . . . Mr. Goodwin . . . come in. You want to see the doctor?"

We entered, and she closed the door. "Not professionally," Wolfe said. "And briefly. Here will do."

"Of course. Certainly." She was flustered. I had been there off and on, but Wolfe hadn't; Doc Vollmer had come to him when required. She went down the hall and opened a door and disappeared, and in a minute Vollmer came—a sad-looking little guy with lots of forehead and not much jaw. He had once taken twenty-two stitches in my side where a character with a knife had gone wide enough but not deep enough.

He approached. "Well, well! Come in, come in!"

"We have come to impose on you, Doctor," Wolfe said. "We need a room to sit in the rest of today and beds for tonight. We need enough food to sustain us until tomorrow. Can you oblige us?"

Vollmer wasn't startled; he was merely stunned. "Why—of course—you mean for you? You and Archie?"

"Yes. We expected a troublesome visitor, and we fled. By tomorrow he will be less troublesome. We want seclusion until then. If it would inconvenience you beyond tolerance . . ."

"No, of course not." He smiled. "I'm honored. I'm flattered. I'm afraid the food won't be quite . . . I have no Fritz. Will you need a phone in the room?"

"No, just the room."

"Then, if you'll excuse me—I have a patient in my office—"

He went back to the door and in, and in a couple of minutes the dark-haired woman, whose name was Helen Gillard, came out. She asked us to come with her, trying to sound as if it was perfectly natural for a couple of neighbors to drop in and request board and lodging, and led the way to the stairs. She took us up two flights and down a hall to the rear, and into a room with two windows and a big bed and walls covered with pictures of boats and baseball players and boys and girls. Bill Vollmer, whom I had once showed how to take fingerprints, was away at school. Helen asked, "Will you come down for lunch or shall I bring trays?"

"Later," Wolfe said. "Thank you. Mr. Goodwin will tell you."

"Can I bring you anything?"

Wolfe said no, and she went. She left the door open, and I went and closed it. We removed our coats, and I found hangers in a closet. Wolfe stood and looked around. It was hopeless. There were three chairs. The seats of two of them were about half as wide as his fanny, and the third one had arms and it would be a squeeze. He went to the bed, sat on the edge, took his shoes off, twisted around, stretched out with his head on the pillow, shut his eyes, and spoke.

"Report."

CHAPTER 6

AT 12:35 p.m. Friday, Inspector Cramer of Homicide West, seated in the red leather chair, took a mangled unlit cigar from his mouth and said, "I still want to know where you and Goodwin have been and what you've done the past twenty-four hours."

The only objection to telling him was that he would have gone or sent someone to check, and Doc Vollmer was a busy man, so it would have been a poor return for his hospitality. As for the hospitality, I had no kick coming, having been given a perfectly good bed in a spare room, but Wolfe had had a few difficulties. Books to read, but no chair upstairs big enough to take him, and he won't read lying down. No pajamas big enough for him, so he had to sleep in his underwear. Grub not bad enough to take credit for facing up to hardship, but not good enough to please the palate; only one brand of beer, and not his. Pillows too soft to use only one and too thick to use two. Towels either too little or too big. Soap that smelled like tuberoses (he said), and he uses geranium. He really bore up well for his first day and night away from home in more than a year; he was glum, of course, as you would be if you were forced to skedaddle, without stopping to take a toothbrush, by circumstances you weren't to blame for.

We had not phoned Fritz to find out if there had been any callers because we didn't know much about modern electronics, and who does? We knew tracing a phone call wasn't as simple as it used to be, but they might have a tame neutron or positron or some other tron that could camp inside Wolfe's number and tell where a call came from. For news there were the papers, Thursday evening and Friday morning. Not a word in the *Gazette* about kidnaping; Lon had kept it; and nothing in the *Times* Friday morning or on the radio at eleven o'clock. There was plenty about Jimmy Vail, but the main fact was still as I had got it from Lon:

Margot Tedder had entered the library at 9:05 Thursday morning and found him there on the floor underneath Benjamin Franklin. The bronze statue had flattened his chest.

Five people, not one, had last seen him alive Wednesday evening—his wife; her son and daughter, Noel and Margot Tedder; her brother, Ralph Purcell; and her attorney, Andrew Frost. They had all been in the library after dinner (subject of the family conference not mentioned), and shortly after ten o'clock Jimmy Vail, saying that he hadn't slept much for three days (reason not given), had stretched out on the couch and gone to sleep. He had still been there an hour later, sound asleep, when they broke it up and left. Noel and Margot Tedder and Ralph Purcell had gone up to bed, and Mrs. Vail and Andrew Frost had gone up to her study. Around midnight Frost had left, and Mrs. Vail had gone to bed. Evidently she too had been short on sleep, for she had still been in bed when her son and daughter came to her room Thursday morning to tell her about Jimmy.

Everyone in the house, of course including the servants, had known that Benjamin Franklin was wobbly. The *Gazette* had a piece by an expert about the different methods of fastening the bronze feet of a man to the base he stands on. He hadn't been permitted to examine the statue that had toppled onto Jimmy Vail, but he said the trouble couldn't have been a loose nut; his guess was that the bolt or bolts had had a flaw and had cracked at some time when the statue was being handled. It was quite possible, he said, that Jimmy Vail, half aroused from a deep sleep, on his way across the room to the door, had lost his balance and grabbed at the statue and pulled it down on him. I thought it was darned decent of the *Gazette* to run the piece. A good murder or suspicion of one will sell thousands of extra papers, and here they were promoting the idea that it had been accidental. They had got the picture Lon had said would be beautiful, of Benjamin Franklin on top of Jimmy Vail.

There were no quotes from any members of the family. Mrs. Vail was in bed under a doctor's care, inaccessible. Andrew Frost wasn't seeing reporters, but he had told the police that when he left the house around midnight, unescorted, he had not stopped at the library on his way out.

As I have said, there was nothing new on the radio at eleven o'clock Friday morning. At 11:10 I phoned Homicide West from Doc Vollmer's office downstairs—he was at the hospital—and told the desk man to tell Inspector Cramer that Nero Wolfe had some information for him regarding Jimmy Vail. At 11:13 I called the District Attorney's office at White Plains, got an assistant DA, and told him to tell Hobart that Wolfe had decided to answer any questions he might care to ask. At 11:18 I rang the *Gazette*, got Lon Cohen, and told him it was all his and would probably soon be everybody's, and he could even use our names as the source if he spelled them right. Of course he wanted more, but I hung up. At 11:24 we thanked Helen Gillard and asked her to thank the doctor for us, left the house, walked sixty yards to Wolfe's, found the door was bolted, pushed the button and were admitted by Fritz, and learned that Sergeant Purley Stebbins had come yesterday ten minutes after we left, and Inspector Cramer had come at six o'clock. No search warrant, but Cramer had phoned at 8:43 and again at 10:19. At the office door Wolfe asked about the mussels, and Fritz said they were in perfect condition. Wolfe was at his desk with his eyes closed, in the only chair that will really do, sitting and breathing, and I was at my desk opening the mail, when the doorbell rang and I went. It was Inspector Cramer, his rugged pink face a little pinker than normal and his burly shoulders hunched a little. When I let him in he didn't even give me an eye, but kept going, to the office, and as I followed, after closing the door, I heard him rasping.

"Where have you and Goodwin been since yesterday noon?"

Fifty minutes later, as I have said, at 12:35 p.m., he demanded, "I still want to know where you and Goodwin have been and what you've done the past twenty-four hours."

We had opened the bag. Most of the talking had been done by me because the whole world knows—well, six or eight people— that the only difference between me and a tape recorder is that you can ask me questions. And for some of it—the White Plains part and the session in the Harold F. Tedder library—Wolfe hadn't been present. We had handed over the note that had come in the mail, the original, and my transcriptions, carbons, of the other two notes and the telephone conversation between Mrs. Vail and Mr. Knapp. I did make a few improvements on Wolfe's phrasing, and mine too, by making it emphatic that the main point had been, first, to get Jimmy Vail back alive, and then to protect him and Mrs. Vail by keeping his promise to the kidnapers. Of course Cramer landed on that with both feet. Why had we gone on protecting Vail for twenty-four hours after he was dead? Obviously, so Wolfe could hang onto the money he already had in the bank. Withholding information vital to a murder investigation. Obstructing justice to earn a fee.

Wolfe snorted, and my feelings were hurt. There had still been Mrs. Vail to consider, and we hadn't known that Vail had been murdered. Did he? I had read an article by a statue expert which said that it could have been an accident. Wasn't it? Cramer didn't say, but he didn't have to; his being there was enough to show that it was open, though maybe not open-and-shut. He said we had of course seen the statement of the District Attorney's office in the morning paper that the apparent cause of Vail's death was the statue falling on him, that a final determination would be made when the autopsy had been completed, and that a thorough investigation was being made. Then he took the chewed unlit cigar from his mouth and said he still wanted to know where we had been the past twenty-four hours.

Wolfe would not be riled. He was back in his house, in his chair, the deadline was past, and the mussels would be ready in an hour. "As I told you," he said, "we knew we would be pestered and we decamped. Where is of no consequence. We did nothing and communicated with no one. At eleven this morning, when our obligation to Mrs. Vail had been fulfilled, Mr. Goodwin telephoned your office. You have no valid grievance. Even now you will not say that you're investigating a murder; you're trying to determine if one has been committed. A charge of obstructing justice couldn't possibly hold. Some of the questions you asked Mr. Goodwin indicated that you suspect him of trying to find the typewriter that was missing from Mrs. Vail's study. Nonsense. Since yesterday noon he has been trying to find nothing whatever, and neither have I. Our interest in the matter is ended. We have no further commitment to Mrs. Vail. We have no client. If she herself killed both Miss Utley and Mr. Vail, which seems unlikely but is not inconceivable, I owe her no service."

"She has paid you sixty thousand dollars."

"And by the terms of my employment I have earned it."

Cramer got up, came to my desk, and dropped the cigar in my wastebasket. That wasn't regular; usually he threw the cigar at it and missed. He went back and picked up his hat from the floor where he had dropped it and turned to Wolfe.

"I want a statement with nothing left out signed by you and Goodwin. At my office by four o'clock. The District Attorney's office will probably want to see Goodwin. It would suit me fine if they want you too."

"Not everything everybody said by four o'clock," I objected. "That would be a six-hour job."

"I want the substance. All details. You can omit White Plains, we've got that from them." He turned and tramped out. By the time I had followed him to the front, shut the door after him, and returned to the office, Wolfe had his book open. I finished opening the mail and put it on his desk and then pulled the typewriter around and got out paper and carbons. That would be a job, and it was water under the bridge, since we had no case and no client. Four carbons: one for Westchester, one for the Manhattan DA, and two for us. As I rolled the paper in Wolfe's voice came at my back.

"Dendrobium chrysotoxum for Miss Gillard and Laelia purpurata for Doctor Vollmer. Tomorrow."

"Right. And Sitassia readia for you and Transcriptum underwoodum for me." I hit the keys.

With time out for lunch and a shave and a clean shirt, it was five minutes past four when I left the house, walked to 34th and Eighth Avenue for a *Gazette,* and flagged a taxi. I had made it barely in time for Wolfe to sign it before he went up to the plant rooms, but there had been interruptions. Sergeant Purley Stebbins had phoned to tell me to take the statement to the DA's office instead of Homicide West. Ben Dykes had phoned and kept me on the wire fifteen minutes and had finally settled for an appointment with Wolfe at eleven-thirty Saturday morning. Reporters from three newspapers had called, two on the phone and one in person, and had been stalled. What had stung them was on the front page of the *Gazette,* which I perused as the taxi took me downtown—the first public notice of the kidnaping of Jimmy Vail and delivery of the ransom money by his wife. Of course it didn't have the big kick of a kidnaping story, the suspense about the fate of the victim, since Jimmy had come back safe and sound, but it had the added attraction of his death by violence in his own home some fifteen hours after he returned. There were pictures of Fowler's Inn and The Fatted Calf and Iron Mine Road. Lon had hung onto it, but he had taken steps. The mention of Wolfe and me was vague and sort of gave the impression that we knew about it because we knew everything, which wouldn't hurt a bit. It was the fattest scoop I had ever given Lon, and that wouldn't hurt either. When I got to 155 Leonard Street and was taken to the room of assistant DA Mandel, he greeted me by tapping the *Gazette* that was there on his desk and demanding, "When did you give them this?" I told him ten minutes after eleven this morning.

It didn't amount to much that time. I have had several conversations in that building that lasted more than six hours, one that lasted fourteen hours, and two that ended by my being locked up as a material witness. That day Mandel and two Homicide Bureau dicks let me go in less than two hours, partly because I had the signed statement with me, partly because they weren't officially interested in the kidnaping since that had been a Westchester job, and partly because they were by no means sure Jimmy Vail's death had been a homicide and if it wasn't that would be okay with them. A dick has enough grief dealing with riffraff, and he would prefer to have no part of Tedders and Vails. So after going through the routine motions for an hour and a half they shooed me out, and at a quarter past six I was paying a hackie in front of the old brownstone and climbing out. As my foot touched the sidewalk, someone grabbed my arm and pronounced my name, and I wheeled.

It was Noel Tedder. "Who the hell does this Nero Wolfe think he is?" he squeaked.

"It depends on his mood." I moved my arm, but he had a grip. "Let go of my arm, I might need it. Why, did he bounce you?"

"I haven't been in. First I was told through a crack to come back after six, and I did. Then I was told Wolfe was busy—'engaged,' he said. I asked for you and was told you were out and he didn't know when you'd be back. I said I'd come in and wait, and he said I wouldn't. What does it take, a passport?"

"Did you give your name?"

"Certainly."

"Did you say what you want to see him about?"

"No. I'll tell him."

"Not unless you tell me first. Not only is that the routine, but also he's had a hard day. There was no homemade blackberry jam for breakfast, he had to skip his morning turn with the orchids, a police inspector came and annoyed him, and he had to read a long statement and sign it. If you tell me what you want, there may be a chance. If you don't, it's hopeless."

"Out here?"

"We can sit on the stoop if you'd rather."

He turned his head to look at a man and woman who were passing. He needed a shave. He also needed either a haircut, a comb and brush, or a hat, and his plaid jacket and striped slacks could have stood a little pressing. When the man and woman were ten paces away his eyes came back to me.

"I've got a chance to make a pot but I can't do it alone. I don't even know how to start. My mother told me that if I can find the money she paid the kidnapers, or any part of it, I can have it. Half a million. I want Wolfe to help me. He can have a fifth of it for his share."

My brows were up. "When did your mother tell you that?"

"Wednesday evening."

"She may feel different about it now."

"No, she doesn't. I asked her this afternoon. She's not very—

she's in pretty bad shape—but I didn't think it would hurt to ask her. She said yes. She said she wouldn't want any of that money now anyhow."

My brows were still up. "The police know about the kidnaping. And the FBI."

"I don't know about the FBI. We told the police this morning."

"Dozens of trained men are on the job already. By tomorrow there'll be hundreds. Fat chance you'd have."

"Damn it, I know I wouldn't! That's why I've got to have Nero Wolfe! Isn't he better than they are?"

"That's a point." I was looking at another point. We had never taken a crack at that kind of problem, and if Wolfe could be pee-kayed into tackling it, it would be interesting to see how he went about it. It would also be interesting to collect his share if there was anything to share.

"I'll tell you," I said. "I doubt very much if Mr. Wolfe will touch it. He's not only eccentric, he hates to work, and he seldom takes a case on a contingent basis. But I'm willing to put it up to him. You may come inside to wait."

"If you can get inside," he squeaked. That tenor didn't fit his make-up at all.

"I can try," I said, and made for the stoop, and he followed me up. The chain-bolt was on, so I had to push the button. If Fritz, letting us in, was surprised to see me bringing a customer who had been turned away twice, he didn't show it. Fritz shows only what he thinks it is proper to show. I took Tedder to the front room and left him, and went to the office by way of the hall instead of the connecting door. Wolfe, at his desk, had the middle drawer open and was fingering in it. Counting caps of beer bottles to see how much he had gained on the week's quota by being away twenty-four hours. I waited to speak until he shut the drawer and looked up.

"Regards from Mandel. I didn't see the DA. They probably won't bother us again unless and until they have to decide that Jimmy Vail didn't die by accident, which they would hate to do. You have seen the *Gazette?*"

"Yes."

"Any comment?"

"No."

"Then I'm still not fired. I'm taking a leave of absence without pay. Say a month, but it may be more."

His lips tightened. He took a deep breath. "Are you bent on vexing me beyond endurance?"

"No, sir. I want to grab an opportunity. When I arrived just now Noel Tedder was there on the sidewalk, vexed beyond endurance because you wouldn't see him. His mother told him Wednesday that he could have the money she paid the kidnaper if he could find it and get it, and he came to offer you a one-fifth share to help him. Of course you wouldn't be interested now that you only take cases where all you have to do is put a notice in the paper, so I'm going to tell him I'll take it on myself. I took the liberty of putting him in the front room. I thought I ought to tell you first. Of course it's long odds, but if I got it, the whole pile, my cut would be a hundred grand and I could quit vexing you and open my own office, maybe with Saul Panzer for a partner, and we could—"

"Shut up!"

"Yes, sir. That will be one advantage, you won't have to bellow—"

"Shut up."

"Yes, sir."

He regarded me, not with affection. "So you expect to badger me into this fantastic gamble."

"You might take a minute out to look at it. It would be satisfactory to find something that ten thousand cops and FBI men will be looking for. And each year when you top the eighty-per-cent bracket you relax. I admit it's a big if, but if you raked this in and added it to what you've already collected this year, you could relax until winter, and it's not May yet. If you missed, you would only be out expenses. As for my badgering you, we have nothing on and nothing in prospect, and if I take a month off Fritz can dust your desk and empty the wastebasket and you can open the mail."

"That's bluster. You wouldn't."

"The hell I wouldn't."

He closed his eyes, probably to contemplate the rosy possibility of months and months with no work to do and no would-be customers admitted. In a minute he opened them and muttered, "Very well, bring him in."

CHAPTER 7

As NOEL TEDDER sat in the red leather chair and crossed his legs, showing blue and yellow socks beneath the striped slacks, Wolfe surveyed him. He had to adjust to the outfit. I have heard him say that men who wear conventional clothes are sheep, but I have also heard him say that men who wear unconventional clothes are popinjays. You can't win.

Tedder asked him if I had told him what he wanted, and Wolfe nodded. He spoke. "The most unpromising enterprise I have ever been asked to undertake, if Mr. Goodwin understood you and I understood him. Mrs. Vail, your mother, told you that if you recovered the money she paid to ransom her husband, you could keep it; and if I help you, you will pay me one-fifth of what we recover if we're successful, and nothing if we fail. Is that it?"

"That's it. Of course I—"

"If you please. When did your mother tell you that?"

"Wednesday evening. And again this afternoon. With Jimmy gone—my stepfather—I thought I'd better ask her."

"Wednesday evening, did she broach it or did you?"

"'Broach'?"

"Bring it up. Introduce the idea."

"I don't remember. Does that matter?"

"It may. If you suggested it a conjecture enters. That you knew where the money was and you wanted to get it in a manner that would entitle you—don't interrupt—entitle you to keep it. You come to me for help because you can't very well just go and get it and produce it. You will give me hints, cannily of course, and guided by them Mr. Goodwin, under my direction, will find the money. Even if your hints have made me smell a rat, I'll hold my nose and take my share. So who broached it, your mother or you?"

Tedder tittered. I don't want to give a false impression, especially since I have mentioned his tenor. Men do titter. "Jesus," he said, "that would be pups. That would be sharp. But how would I know where it is?"

"You would know where you put it Tuesday night after you or your confederate took it from your mother on Iron Mine Road."

"Huh?" He was squinting. "You've lost me. Say it again."

Wolfe wiggled a finger. "Mr. Tedder. You have come to me with an extraordinary proposal, and naturally my first question is what about you? Did you kidnap your stepfather?"

"Balls. He might have recognized me."

"Did you have a hand in the kidnaping? Yes or no."

"No. N, O, no." Tedder was still squinting. "Got a Bible?"

"That wouldn't establish it. If I assume your good faith, where are we? It would be witless to try to compete with the intricate and expert routine of the army of official investigators. If we start at all it must be from a point chosen by us and overlooked by them. Before I accept or decline your proposal I must know if you will agree with me on that point; and first of all I must ask, what if we find the money and your mother repudiates her engagement to let you keep it?"

"She won't."

"She might."

Tedder shook his head. "Four people besides me heard her say it—my sister Margot, her brother Ralph, Frost, the lawyer, and Jimmy. Of course Jimmy's dead."

"She still might. I must tell you that, if she does, my share will be legally collectible and I'll collect it."

"Sure, why not? You won't have to. My mother won't renege. What's the point I have to agree on?"

"It's a series of assumptions, and you may not like them. The first and basic one is that Mr. Vail's death was not an accident. He was murdered."

"Huh?" Tedder uncrossed his legs and sat up. "He pulled that goddam statue over on him."

"No." Wolfe was emphatic. "I concede that that's conceivable; it may even be sufficiently plausible for the police to accept it; but

I reject it. There is no implication in the published accounts that he was drunk. Was he?"

"No."

"Had he been drinking?"

"He had had a couple, not more. His usual, bourbon and water. He could handle half a dozen. He wasn't even started. He was just sleepy. He said he couldn't keep his eyes open and went to the couch."

"And later, after you and the others had gone— Did you turn the lights off when you left?"

"All but one. Mother said to leave one on."

"A good light?"

"Fairly good. A floor lamp by the wall."

"And he awoke enough to realize where he was, leave the couch, stand, and walk; and, losing his balance, he caught at the statue, which was insecure, and brought it down on him. It's possible, but I don't believe it. I do not believe that a man awake enough to walk would be so befuddled that he couldn't dodge a falling statue. Was it on a direct line from the couch to the door?"

"Not direct, but not far out." Tedder was squinting again. "You said murder. How? Was he so sound asleep that he didn't wake up when someone dragged him off the couch and over to the statue and pushed it over on him? Do you believe that?"

"No. He was drugged."

"The hell he was."

"He must have been. In one of his drinks. The handiest assumption is chloral hydrate, which is easily procured. In solution in an alcoholic beverage it has almost no taste. A moderate dose induces a deep sleep approaching coma. It decomposes rapidly and will not be detected by an autopsy unless it is performed within three or four hours after death, and even then the only reliable test is identification of urochloralic acid in the urine. That test is made only when chloral hydrate is specifically suspected, and with Mr. Vail I doubt if it was. I am not parading; I had this surmise yesterday and consulted a book."

He hadn't mentioned it to me; it would have been admitting that Jimmy Vail's death might possibly be of interest to us. We had several books on toxicology on the shelves, but he hadn't been here yesterday, so he must have found one when he was going over Doc Vollmer's shelves. I had had personal experience of chloral hydrate, having once been served a Mickey Finn by a woman named Dora Chapin. Two hours after I had swallowed it you could have rowed me out to Bedloe's Island and pushed the Statue of Liberty onto me and I wouldn't have batted an eye.

Wolfe was going on. "So that Mr. Vail was murdered with deliberation may properly be called a deduction, not an assumption. Not a final deduction, but a basic one, for it is the ground for my assumptions. Whether you like it or not, do you concur?"

"I don't know." Tedder's tongue showed between his lips. "Go on with your assumptions."

"They're purely tentative, to establish a starting point. But first another deduction, made three days ago, on Tuesday, by Mr. Goodwin and me. Dinah Utley, your mother's secretary, was implicated in the kidnaping, and not indirectly or passively. She had an active hand in it. Her death—"

"How do you know that?"

"By observed evidence and interpretation of it. I'll reserve it. I'm exposing my position, Mr. Tedder, because I have to if you're going to occupy it with me, but I need not reveal all the steps that have led to it. I'm taking your good faith as a working hypothesis, but there is still that conjecture—that you had a part in the kidnaping and you know where the money is. If so, it was an egregious blunder to come to me. I'll get my share of the money, and you'll get your share of doom. Do you want to withdraw before I commit myself to this mad gamble? Do you want to leave?"

"Hell no. You talk a lot and you talk big."

"I hope to the point—our starting point. I am almost there. Miss Utley was involved in the kidnaping and was murdered. Mr. Vail was the victim of the kidnaping and was murdered. My assumptions are, first, that both murders were consequential to the kidnaping operation; and second, that the person who killed Mr. Vail, with premeditation since he drugged him, being involved in the kidnaping, knows where the money is. He was present at the gathering at that house Wednesday evening. Therefore, if we are to find the money, our starting point is that house and its occupants. If you will proceed from that point with me, I'll accept your proposal."

Tedder was chewing his lip. "Jesus," he said. He chewed some more. "The way you put it . . . I guess I'm in over my head. You're saying one of them killed Jimmy—Uncle Ralph or Frost or my sister."

"Or your mother or you."

"Sure, we were there." He shook his head. "Holy Christ. My mother, that's crazy. Me, I liked Jimmy. He couldn't see me, but I liked him. Uncle Ralph—"

"That's irrelevant, Mr. Tedder. The murder resulted from the kidnaping—my assumption. The kidnaper wished him no harm and rendered him none; he only wanted the money. Logically that excludes your mother, but not you. There are several possibilities. For one, Miss Utley was killed because she demanded too large a share of the loot. For another, Mr. Vail was killed because he had learned that one of those present Wednesday evening was responsible for the kidnaping, and of course that wouldn't do. We ignore the mysterious Mr. Knapp perforce, because we don't know who or where he is. Presumably he was a confederate whose chief function was to make the phone calls, but he may also have got the money from your mother, since he spoke to her, and if he has bolted with it, we're done before we start. We could expose the murderer, to no profit, but that's all. I say 'we.' Is it 'we'? Do we proceed?"

"How?"

"First I would need to speak at length, separately, with those who were present Wednesday evening, beginning with you. You would have to bring them here, or send them, by some pretext—or some inducement, perhaps a share of the money. Then I'll see."

"Great. Just great. I ask them—my sister, for instance—to come and let you grill her to find out if she kidnaped Jimmy and then killed him. Great."

"You might manage to put it more tactfully."

"Yeah, I might." He leaned forward. "Look, Mr. Wolfe. Maybe you've got it right, your deductions and assumptions, and maybe not. If you have and you find the money, okay, I'll get mine and you'll get yours. I don't owe my uncle a damn thing, and God knows I don't owe that lawyer, Andrew Frost, anything. He talked my mother out of letting me have—oh, to hell with it. As for my sister, I'm not her keeper, repeat not—she can look out for herself. You try putting it to her tactfully and see what—"

The phone rang. I swiveled and got it. "Nero Wolfe's residence, Archie Goodwin speaking."

"This is Margot Tedder. I'd like to speak to Mr. Wolfe."

I told her to hold it and turned. "Margot Tedder wants to speak to you."

Noel made a noise. Wolfe frowned at his phone to remind it that he resents being summoned by it, no matter who, then reached for it. "Yes, Miss Tedder?"

"Nero Wolfe?"

"Yes."

"You never go anywhere, do you?"

"No."

"Then I'll have to come there. I'll come now."

"You won't be admitted. I'll be at dinner. Why do you wish to come?"

"I want you to help me do something."

"What?"

"I'd rather— Oh, it doesn't matter. About the money my mother gave the kidnapers. You know about that."

"Yes. What about it?"

"She has told me that if I can find it I can have it, and I want you to help me. We'll have to hurry. I'll come now. Your dinner can wait."

"I can't. More precisely, I won't. You may come at nine o'clock, not before. I'm busy. You will excuse me. I'm hanging up." He cradled the phone and turned. "Your sister says that her mother told her that if she finds the money paid to the kidnaper she can have it, and she is coming at nine o'clock to enlist my help. I'll tell her you have already engaged me. We have twenty minutes until my dinnertime. Where were you from eight o'clock Sunday evening until eight o'clock Wednesday morning?"

CHAPTER 8

A MAN'S TIME-AND-PLACE record as given by him may or may not prove anything, even if it doesn't check. There are a lot of people who wouldn't tell you exactly where they had been and what they had done between eight p.m. Sunday and eight a.m. Wednesday even if they hadn't kidnaped or murdered anybody. Wolfe, knowing how easy it is to frame an alibi, has seldom tried to crack one. In all the years I have been with him I haven't checked more than four or five. He has sometimes had Saul Panzer or Fred Durkin or Orrie Cather look into one, but not often. I put what Noel Tedder told him in my notebook, but I knew it wouldn't be checked unless developments nominated Noel for the tag. Besides, only one time and place was essential, either for Noel or for one of the others. It didn't have to be that he himself had snatched Jimmy Vail Sunday evening, or had helped to keep him wherever he had been kept, or had put notes in telephone books Tuesday evening, or had been at Iron Mine Road Tuesday night. The one essential time and place was the Harold F. Tedder library Wednesday evening, and we knew he had been there. They all had. The question had to be asked; if Noel had gone up in a balloon with six United States Senators Sunday morning and hadn't come down until Wednesday noon, he couldn't be expected to know where the money was, and that was the point. But I won't waste my space and your time reporting his whereabouts for those sixty hours.

More interesting was his reaction to the news that Margot was coming to see Wolfe. It fussed him more than anything Wolfe had said to him. When he said he didn't believe his mother had told her that, he had to squeeze it through his teeth. Evidently he had some strong feeling about his sister, and it wasn't brotherly love. Wolfe tried to ask him questions about Dinah Utley and her relations with Purcell and Frost and Margot, but got no usable answers.

Noel wanted to be damn sure that Wolfe wasn't going to let Margot talk him into switching to her. He even offered to bring Uncle Ralph that evening and Andrew Frost in the morning. When Fritz announced dinner he followed Wolfe to the dining-room door, and I had to take his arm and start him to the front.

Returning and entering the dining room, I found that Wolfe had pulled his chair out but hadn't sat. "A grotesque venture," he grunted. "Preposterous. Will that woman be punctual?"

"Probably not." I pulled my chair back. "She's not the punctual type."

"But she may be. You'll have to be at the phone with your coffee to get Saul and Fred and Orrie. In my room in the morning at eight, and in the office with you at nine." Fritz was there with the stuffed clams, and he sat and took the spoon and fork. He couldn't have sat before giving me instructions because that would have been talking business during a meal, and by heck a rule is a rule is a rule. As I helped myself to clams I held my breath, because if you smell them, mixed with shallots, chives, chervil, mushrooms, bread crumbs, sherry, and dry white wine, you take so many that you don't leave enough room for the duckling roasted in cider with Spanish sauce as revised by Wolfe and Fritz, leaving out the carrot and parsley and putting anchovies in. As I ate the clams I remarked to myself that we darned well had better find at least some leavings of the half a million, since Saul and Fred and Orrie came to twenty-five bucks an hour, plus expenses.

I don't know how Wolfe first got the notion that when I've had one good look at a woman and heard her speak, especially if she's under thirty, I can answer any question he wants to ask about her, but I know he still has it, chiefly on account of little items like my saying that Margot Tedder wouldn't be punctual. She was twenty-five minutes late. Of course if she had been on time I would have commented that she must need some ready cash quick. When you once get a reputation, or it gets you, you're stuck with it for good.

I have said that from hearsay she kept her chin up so she could look down her nose, and her manners when she entered the old brownstone didn't contradict it. Crossing the threshold, she gave me a nod for a butler, though I hadn't seen one at 994 Fifth Avenue, and when I took her to the office she stopped at the edge of the big rug, looked it over from side to side and end to end, and asked Wolfe, "Is that a Kazak?"

"No," he said. "Shirvan."

"You can't possibly appreciate it. Is it yours?"

"I doubt it. It was given to me in nineteen thirty-two, in Cairo, by a man to whom I had rendered a service, and I suspected he had stolen it in Kandahar. If it wasn't rightfully his, it isn't rightfully mine. But of course illegality of ownership does not extend indefinitely. If my possession of that rug were challenged by an heir of the Kandahar prince who once owned it, or by one of his wives or concubines, I would enter a defense. It would be a borderline case. After sufficient time legal ownership is undisputed. Your grandfather was a bandit; some of his forays were almost certainly actionable. But if a descendant of one of his victims tried to claim that fur thing you are wearing, she would be laughed at. I'm pleased that you recognize the quality of the rug, though only an ignoramus could mistake it for a Kazak. Kazaks have a long pile. You are Margot Tedder? I am Nero Wolfe." He pointed to the red leather chair. "Sit down and tell me what you want."

She had opened her mouth a couple of times to cut in on him, but Wolfe in full voice is not easy to interrupt, particularly if his eyes are pinning you. "I told you on the phone what I want," she said.

"You will please sit down, Miss Tedder. I like eyes at a level."

She glanced at me. The poor girl was stuck. She didn't want to sit down because he had ordered her to, but to stay on her feet would be silly. She compromised. One of the yellow chairs was at the end of my desk, and she came and sat on it. As I have said, when she walked you might have thought her hips were in a cast, but sitting she wasn't at all hard to look at.

"I didn't come," she said, "to listen to a lecture about legal ownership by a detective. You know what I came for. My mother paid you sixty thousand dollars for nothing. All you did was put that thing in the paper. For sixty thousand dollars you certainly ought to help me find the money my mother gave the kidnaper. That's more than ten per cent."

Wolfe grunted. "Twelve. That might be thought adequate. How would I go about it? Have you a suggestion?"

"Of course not. You would go about it the way any detective would. That's your business."

"Could I count on your cooperation?"

She frowned at him, her chin up. "How could I cooperate?"

He didn't frown back. Having put her in her place, he didn't mind if she didn't stay put. "That would depend on developments," he said. "Take a hypothesis. Do you know what a hypothesis is?"

"You're being impertinent."

"Not without provocation. You didn't know what a Shirvan is. The hypothesis: If I took the job you offer, I would want to begin by asking you some questions. For example, what were your relations with Dinah Utley?"

She stared. "What on earth has that got to do with finding the money?"

He nodded. "I thought so. You're under a misapprehension. You expected me to pit my wits and Mr. Goodwin's eyes and legs against the horde of official investigators who are combing the countryside and looking under every stone. Pfui. That would be infantile. I would have to approach it differently, and the best way—indeed, the only way—would be through Dinah Utley. You know that Mr. Goodwin and I suspected that she was implicated in the kidnaping; you heard your mother and Mr. Goodwin discuss it Wednesday afternoon. Now we don't suspect it; we know it. Therefore—"

"How do you know it? Because she was there and was killed?"

"Partly that, but there were other factors. She was here Tuesday afternoon. Therefore at least one of the kidnapers was someone with whom she had had contacts, and I would want to learn all I could about her. How well did you know her?"

"Why—she was my mother's secretary. She lived in the house, but she didn't regard herself as a servant. I thought my mother let her take too many liberties."

"What kind of liberties?"

"Different kinds. She ate with us. If we had people in for cocktails, she came in if she felt like it. If I asked her to do something, she might and she might not. You might have thought we were equals. You know, I must say, I think this is clever. Perhaps you *are* clever. I should have thought of this myself, about Dinah, only I really don't know much about her. She was there seven years, and I suppose she had friends of her own class, but I never saw them."

"Would your brother know more about her?"

"He might." She nodded. "Yes, I'm sure he would. He did things with her just to irritate me—like playing cards with her. Gin rummy in the library. You might have thought *they* were equals, and perhaps they should have been. Once he took her to a prizefight."

"That sounds promising. I would want to talk with him. I don't want to shock you, Miss Tedder, but the question should be asked. Is it conceivable that the kidnaping was a joint enterprise of Miss Utley and your brother? That your brother had a hand in it?"

"Good heavens." Her lips parted. She stared. "Of course it's conceivable. That's the second thing you've thought of that *I* should have thought of."

"Given time, undoubtedly you would have. Your emotions have interfered with your mental processes. We would—"

"But if he—Noel—then he knows where the money is! He *has* the money!"

"Not too fast, Miss Tedder. That's merely a surmise. We would have to consider all possibilities, all those who had frequent opportunity to see Miss Utley. I understand that your mother's brother, Ralph Purcell, lives in that house. Was he on good terms with her?"

She was only half listening. He had darned near lost her with his suggestion about Noel. I wouldn't have been surprised if she had bounced up, granting that a person of her class and with her hips could bounce, and gone to have it out with her brother. Wolfe saw he would have to repeat his question, and did so.

"Oh," she said, "he's on good terms with everybody, or he tries to be. He ran errands for Dinah, but of course he would. He runs errands for me too. He's all right, I like him, I really do, but he's so—oh, well. He just doesn't belong. He certainly wouldn't have anything to do with any kidnaping; he wouldn't have the nerve."

"But he was friendly enough with Miss Utley to make it plausible that he knows the names of her associates not of your class, and possibly has met some of them."

"Yes. No doubt of that. You won't have to talk with my brother. I'll talk with him."

"That would help. That was the sort of thing I had in mind when I asked if I could count on your cooperation. I believe I have named all those who had— No, there's another possibility. I saw in the newspaper the name of your mother's attorney—Frost, I think?"

"Yes. Andrew Frost."

"It might be that an attorney would have frequent contacts with a client's secretary, especially if he is also the client's business adviser. Did Mr. Frost see much of Miss Utley?"

"I suppose he did, but I don't know, after she came to work for my mother. Of course he saw her when she worked for him. She was his secretary. He let my mother take her. It was supposed to be a great favor, but he really did it for my father. My father died not long after that. My father was a true gentleman. I'd like to tell you something, I don't know why, if you'll promise not to repeat it. Do you promise?"

"Yes."

Her eyes came to me. "Do you?"

"Sure."

She went back to Wolfe. "My father told me once that his father was a bandit."

There you are. She was actually human.

Wolfe nodded. "Then I merely corroborated him. I am obliged to you, Miss Tedder. Manifestly, if I took the job you offer, I would need to speak with Mr. Purcell and Mr. Frost. I would also need to be informed about the gathering in the library of your home Wednesday evening. For example, I understand that drinks were served. Who served them?"

She frowned again. "Why? Why do you need to know that?"

"You conceded the possibility that I am clever. Any discussion in which Mr. Purcell and Mr. Frost and your brother took part may be informative. You say that Mr. Purcell likes to do errands. Did he serve the drinks?"

"No. The bar cart was there and we served ourselves, or someone—you know how it is. I think—yes, Uncle Ralph took brandy to Mr. Frost. My mother likes a champagne cobbler after dinner, and she mixes it herself. She poured me some champagne, but I didn't drink much."

"What did your brother have?"

"Champagne. He gulps it."

"And Mr. Vail?"

"I didn't notice, but probably bourbon and water. No matter how clever you are, this can't possibly mean anything. You're just trying to impress me." She glanced at her wristwatch. "Do you want to see my uncle first? He would come tonight if I tell him to."

"Not tonight." Wolfe cocked his head. "I'm not trying to impress you, but I have imposed on you. I must reject your demand, Miss Tedder—I shouldn't have called it an offer, since you have offered nothing. Your brother has. He was here this afternoon, and I have engaged with him to recover the money. My share will be one-fifth."

She was gawking. Of course a person of her class shouldn't gawk, but you can't blame her. A person of my class would have thrown something at him. "You're lying," she said. "You're trying to make me say you can have part of it. Of course one-fifth would be ridiculous. You already have more than enough from my mother, but I suppose, if you—very well, if you get it I'll give you ten thousand dollars. If you get *all* of it. Of course you'll have to do it, after everything I've told you."

Wolfe was slowly moving his head from side to side. "Amazing," he said. "How old are you?"

"I'm not a minor, if that's what you're thinking. I'm twenty-one."

"Amazing that a creature so obtuse could live so long without meeting disaster. I was at pains to make it clear that we were discussing a hypothesis, and the idea that you were being gulled never entered your mind. I don't know how a brain that is never used passes the time. It will be futile to try to browbeat your brother into deferring to you; I shall hold him to his engagement with me. I was not lying when I said that he anticipated you. He was here when you telephoned."

I suppose her father, Harold F. Tedder, was responsible for the way she took it. Naturally a true gentleman would teach his children never to argue with underlings. Since she couldn't very well order him to leave, his office and his house, there was only one thing to do, and she did it. She got up and walked out, stiff hips and all. She did it all right, too, no hurry and no prolonging it. I got to the hall ahead of her and had the door open when she reached the front, and she said thank you as she passed. Breeding will tell. I shut the door, bolted it for the night, returned to the office, and told Wolfe, "Taking candy from a baby."

He grunted and pushed his chair back. "An insupportable day. I'm going to my bed." He rose.

"What about Saul and Fred and Orrie?"

"The morning will do." He moved.

CHAPTER 9

SATURDAY MORNING I heard the seven-o'clock news on the radio in my room, and the eight-o'clock news on the radio in the kitchen. Saul and Fred and Orrie had come and had gone up to Wolfe's room. I was listening to the nine-o'clock news on the radio in the office when they came down. Ordinarily two or three times a day is often enough, but ordinarily I am not curious as to whether some dick or state cop or FBI hero has found half a million bucks, with or without a Mr. Knapp in illegal possession of it.

I had also read the morning paper. The DA's office was playing it safe on the death of Jimmy Vail. The cause of death had been Benjamin Franklin, definitely, and there was no evidence or information to indicate that it had not been an accident, but it was still under investigation. I doubted that last. The DA had to say it, to guard against the chance of something popping up, but I doubted if the five people who had last seen him alive were being pestered much.

There was no doubt at all that the kidnaping was being investigated. Since Jimmy had died before telling anyone how or where he had been snatched, or where and by whom he had been kept, or where he had been released, there was no lead at all. The caretaker of the country house near Katonah had been taken apart by a dozen experts, but he had stuck to it that Vail had left in his Thunderbird shortly after eight Sunday evening to drive back to town, and had returned in the Thunderbird about half past seven Wednesday morning, tired, mad, dirty, and hungry. He had told the caretaker nothing whatever. The theory was that the kidnapers had taken the Thunderbird and kept it wherever they had kept him, and, when they turned him loose, had let him have it to drive home in, which was a perfectly good theory, since they certainly wouldn't want to use it. It was being examined by a task force of scientists, for fingerprints, of course, and for where and how far it had been, and who and what had been in it. It was described both in the paper and on the radio, and shown on television, with the request that anyone who had seen it between Sunday evening and Wednesday morning should communicate immediately with the police, the Westchester DA, or the FBI.

Also described, but not shown on television, was the suitcase the money had been in: tan leather, 28 by 16 by 9, old and stained, scuffed a little, three brass clasps, one in the middle and one near each end. Mrs. Vail had taken it to the bank, where the money had been put in it, and the description had been supplied by the bank's vice-president. It was the property of Jimmy Vail—or had been.

The best prospect of some kind of a lead was finding someone who had been at Fowler's Inn or The Fatted Calf Tuesday evening and had seen one of the kidnapers. The man Mrs. Vail had given the suitcase to had had his face covered. It was assumed that a confederate had been present at both places to make sure that Mrs. Vail didn't show anyone the notes she got from the phone books. People at both places remembered seeing Mrs. Vail, and the cashier at Fowler's Inn had seen her go to the phone book and open it, but no one had been found who had seen anybody take a visible interest in her.

Funeral services for Jimmy Vail would be held at the Dunstan Chapel Saturday morning at eleven.

Thanks to Nero Wolfe and Archie Goodwin, though no one but Lon Cohen was thanking us, the murder of Dinah Utley was getting a big play both in print and on the air. Not only had her body been found at or near the spot where Mrs. Vail had delivered the suitcase, but also someone had leaked it, either in White Plains or in Manhattan, that she had been an accomplice in the kidnaping. So Cramer had bought the deduction Wolfe had made from the notes and had passed it on to Westchester, and when Ben Dykes came at eleven-thirty there would be some fancy explaining to do.

As I said, I was in the office listening to the nine-o'clock news when Saul and Fred and Orrie came down from Wolfe's room.

The kidnaping and murder items had been covered, so I switched it off and greeted them. If you wanted an operative for a tough job and were offered your pick of those three, never having seen or heard of them before, you would probably take Fred Durkin or Orrie Cather, and you would be wrong. Fred was big and broad, and looked solid and honest and was, but from the neck up he was a little too solid for situations that needed quick reactions. Orrie was tall and handsome and smart, and in any situation his reaction was speedy enough, but it might be the right reaction and it might not. Saul was small and wiry, with a long narrow face and a big nose. He always looked as if he would need a shave in another hour, he wore a cap instead of a hat, and his pants had always been pressed a week ago. But there wasn't an agency in New York that wouldn't have taken him on at the top figure if he hadn't preferred to free lance, and at ten dollars an hour he was a bargain for any job you could name.

"Six hundred three ways," Orrie said. "And I want a picture of Noel Tedder."

"I'll take one of Ralph Purcell," Fred said.

"So you're taking one apiece?" I went to the safe and squatted to twirl the knob. "The very best way to waste time and money. Foolproof. As for pictures, I only have newspaper shots."

"I'll get them from Lon," Saul said. "Mr. Wolfe says your credit's good with him."

"It sure is." I swung the safe door open and got the cash box. "Credit, hell. A truckload of pictures wouldn't make a dent in what he owes us. So you've got Andrew Frost?"

He said he had, and added that Wolfe had said that I would be in the office to receive reports. I had known that was coming. In a tough case it's nice to know that we have three good men on the job, even for chores as chancy as solo tailing, but the catch is that I have to sit there on the back of my lap to answer the phone and go to help if needed. I gave each of them two cees in used fives, tens, and twenties, made entries in the cash book, and supplied a few routine details, and they went. They had arrived at eight and it was then nine-thirty, so we were already out $37.50.

I was behind on the germination and blooming records, which I typed on cards from notes Wolfe brought down from the plant rooms, so after opening the mail I got the drawer from the cabinet and began entering items like "27 flks agar slp no fung sol B autoclaved 18 lbs 4/18/61." I was fully expecting a phone call from either Noel or Margot, or possibly their mother, but none had come by eleven, when Wolfe came down. There would be no calls now, since they would all be at the funeral services.

The session with Ben Dykes, who came at 11:40, ten minutes late, which I had thought would be fairly ticklish, wasn't bad at all. He didn't even hint at any peril to us, as far as he was concerned, though he mentioned that Hobart was considering whether we should be summoned and charged. What he wanted was information. He had seen our signed statement, and he knew what we had told Cramer and I had told Mandel, but he wanted more. So he laid off. Though he didn't say so, for him the point was that a kidnaper had collected half a million dollars right there in his county, and there was a chance that it was still in his county, stashed somewhere, and finding it would give him a lot of pleasure, not to mention profit. If at the same time he got a line on the murderer of Dinah Utley, okay, but that wasn't the main point. So he stayed for more than an hour, trying to find a crumb, some little thing that Mrs. Vail or Dinah Utley or Jimmy had said that might give him a trace of a scrap of a hint. When, going to the hall with him to let him out, I said Westchester was his and he and his men must know their way around, he said yeah, but the problem was to keep from being jostled or tramped on by the swarms of state cops and FBI supermen.

At one o'clock the radio had nothing new, and neither had we. Saul and Fred and Orrie had phoned in. They had all gone to the funeral, which was a big help. That's one of the fine features of tailing; wherever the subject leads you, you will follow. I once spent four hours tagging a guy up and down Fifth and Madison Avenues, using all the tricks and dodges I knew, and learned later that he had been trying to find a pair of gray suspenders with a yellow stripe.

It was one of those days. Shad roe again for lunch, this time larded with pork and baked in cream with an assortment of herbs. Every spring I get so fed up with shad roe that I wish to heaven fish would figure out some other way. Whales have. Around three o'clock, when we were back in the office, there was a development, if you don't care what you call it. The phone rang and it was Orrie Cather. He said his and Fred's subjects were together, so they were. He was in a booth at 54th and Lexington. Noel Tedder and Ralph Purcell had just entered a drugstore across the street. That was all. Ten seconds after I hung up it rang again. Noel Tedder. You couldn't beat that for a thrill to make your spine tingle: Fred and Orrie across the street, eagle-eyed, and the subject talking to me on the phone. He said he had persuaded Purcell to come and talk with Wolfe and he would be here in twenty minutes. I turned and asked Wolfe, and he looked at the clock and said of course not, and I turned back to the phone.

"Sorry, Mr. Tedder, Mr. Wolfe will be—"

"I knew it! My sister!"

"Not your sister. He turned her down, and the arrangement with you stands. But he'll be busy from four to six. Can Mr. Purcell come at six?"

"I'll see. Hold the wire." In half a minute: "Yes, he'll be there at six o'clock."

"Good." I hung up and swiveled. "Six o'clock. Wouldn't it be amusing if he gives us a hot lead and Fred and I hop on it—of course Fred will tail him here and be out front—and we're two hours late getting there and someone already has it? Just a lousy two hours."

Wolfe grunted. "You know quite well that if I permit exceptions to my schedule I soon will have no schedule. You would see to that."

I could have made at least a dozen comments, but what was the use? I turned to the typewriter and the cards. When he left for the plant rooms at 3:59 I turned on the radio. Nothing new. Again at five o'clock. Nothing new. When the *Gazette* came it had pictures of fourteen people who had been at Fowler's Inn or The Fatted Calf Tuesday evening, which showed what a newspaper that's on its toes can do to keep the public informed. I

was back at the typewriter when the doorbell rang at 5:55. I went
to the hall, saw Ralph Purcell through the one-way glass, and
stepped to the door and opened it, and he said apologetically,
"I guess I'm a little early," and offered a hand. I took it. What
the hell, it wouldn't be the first murderer I had shaken hands
with.

As I took his hat the elevator jolted to a stop at the bottom,
the door opened, and Wolfe emerged, three minutes ahead of
time because he likes to be in his chair when company comes.

Purcell went to him. "I'm Ralph Purcell, Mr. Wolfe." He had
a hand out. "I'm a great admirer of yours. I'm Mrs. Jimmy Vail's
brother."

Of course Wolfe had to take the hand, and when he does take
a hand, which is seldom, he really takes it. As we went to the
office Purcell was wiggling his fingers. Wolfe told him to take the
red leather chair, went to his, got his bulk arranged, and spoke.

"I assume Mr. Tedder has explained the situation to you?"

Purcell was looking at me. When I give Wolfe a report I am
supposed to include everything, and I usually do, and I had had
all the time there was Thursday afternoon at Doc Vollmer's, but I
had left out an item about Purcell. I had described him, of course—
round face like his sister's, a little pudgy, going bald—but I had
neglected to mention that when someone started to say something
he looked at someone else. I now learned that he didn't go so far
as to look at A when he was speaking to B. His eyes went to
Wolfe.

"Yes," he said, "Noel explained it, but I'm not sure—it seems
a little—"

"Perhaps I can elucidate it. What did he say?"

"He said you were going to find the money for him—the money
my sister paid the kidnaper. He asked me if I remembered that
my sister had told him he could have the money if he found it,
and of course I did. Then it seemed to be a little confused, but
maybe it was just confused in my mind. Something about you
wanted to ask me some questions because you thought one of
us might know something about it on account of Dinah, Dinah
Utley, and I thought he said something about one of us putting

something in Jimmy's drink, but when I asked about it he said you would explain that part of it."

So Noel had been fairly tactful after all, at least with Uncle Ralph.

Wolfe nodded. "It's a little complicated. The best— Why do you look at Mr. Goodwin when I speak?"

As Purcell's eyes left me a flush came to his cheeks. "It's a habit," he said, "a very bad habit."

"It is indeed."

"I know. You notice my eyes stick out?"

"Not flagrantly."

"Thank you, but they do. When I was a boy people said I stared. One person especially. She—" He stopped abruptly. In a moment he went on. "That was long ago, but that's why I do it. I only do it when someone starts speaking. After I talk a little I'm all right. I'm all right now."

"Then I'll proceed." Wolfe propped his elbows on the chair arms and joined his fingertips to make a tent. "You know that Miss Utley had a hand in the kidnaping."

"No, sir, I don't. I mean I don't know it, and I guess I don't believe it. I heard what my sister said to Mr. Goodwin and what he said to her, and that's all I know. The reason I don't believe it, kidnaping is so dangerous, if you get caught you don't stand any chance, and Dinah wasn't like that. She wasn't one to take big chances. I know that from how she played cards. Gin. She would hang onto a card she couldn't possibly use if she thought it might fill me. Of course everyone does that if you know it will, but she did it if she only thought it might. You see?"

Wolfe didn't, since he never plays cards, gin or anything else, but he nodded. "But you do take chances?"

"Oh, yes, I'm a born gambler. Three times my sister has staked me to some kind of wild idea I had—no, four—and none of them panned out. I'll bet on anything. When I have anything to bet with."

"Life needs some seasoning," Wolfe conceded. "As for Miss Utley, you are wrong. She was involved in the kidnaping. If I told you how that has been established to my satisfaction you would probably still be skeptical. But having come to indulge Mr. Tedder, now that you're here you might as well indulge me. If Miss Utley was involved, at least one of the kidnapers is someone she knew, and therefore I want information about her friends and acquaintances. I suppose you know them, some of them?"

"Well." Purcell shifted his weight in the chair. "Now, that's funny. Dinah's friends. Of course she had friends, she must have, but I don't really *know* any. She often went out evenings, movies and shows and so on, but I don't know who she went with. That's funny. I thought I knew her pretty well. Of course for acquaintances, she met a lot of people—"

The phone rang. I took it and got a familiar voice. "Archie? Fred. In a booth at the corner. Do I snatch a bite and come back or do I call it a day? I'm supposed to stay on him till he goes home. How long will he be there?"

"Hold it." I turned to Wolfe. "Fred. His subject has entered a building, a tumble-down dump that could be a den of vice. He wants instructions. Should he crash it?"

Wolfe shot me a mean glance. "Tell him to quit for the day and resume in the morning." To Purcell: "You were saying?"

But Uncle Ralph waited until I had relayed the order, hung up, and swiveled. Good manners, even if he didn't belong. "About Dinah's acquaintances," he said, "she met a lot of people there at the house, dinner guests and now and then a party, but that wouldn't be what you want. You want a different type, someone she might use for something dangerous like kidnaping."

"Or someone who might use her."

Purcell shook his head. "No, sir. I don't think Dinah would take a chance at kidnaping, but if she did she would be in charge. She would be the boss." He lifted a hand for a gesture. "I said I'm an admirer of yours, Mr. Wolfe, and I really meant it. A great admirer. I know you're never wrong about anything, and if you're sure Dinah was involved you must have a good reason. I thought I knew her pretty well, and naturally I'm curious, but of course if you're not telling anyone . . ."

"I have told someone." Wolfe regarded him. "I have told the police, and it will probably soon be public knowledge, so I may as well satisfy your curiosity. Miss Utley typed the notes—the one that your sister received in the mail and the two she found in telephone books. Indubitably."

No perceptible reaction. You might have thought Purcell hadn't heard. The only muscles that moved were the ones that blinked his eyelids as he kept focused on Wolfe. Then he said, "Thank you for telling me. That shows I'm not as big a ninny as some people think I am. I suspected something like that when they asked me if I knew who had taken the typewriter from my sister's study."

"The police asked you?"

"Yes. I didn't tell them, because I— Well, I didn't, but I'll tell you. I saw Dinah take it. Tuesday evening. Her car was parked in front, her own car, and I saw her take the typewriter out of the house, so she must have put it in the car."

"What time Tuesday evening?"

"I didn't notice, but it was before nine o'clock. It was about an hour after my sister had left in her car with the suitcase in it."

"How did you know the suitcase was in it?"

"I carried it out for her and put it in the trunk. I saw her with it upstairs and offered to take it. She didn't tell me where she was going, and I didn't ask her. I thought something was wrong, but I didn't know what. I thought she was probably going wherever Jimmy was. He had been gone since Sunday, and I didn't think he was at Katonah, and my sister hadn't told us where he was." Purcell shook his head. "So Dinah typed the notes, and so she took the typewriter. I've got to thank you for telling me. So you're right about her, and I thought I knew her. You know, I was playing gin with her a week ago Thursday—no, Friday—and of course she had it all planned then. That's hard to believe, but I guess I've got to believe it, and I can see why you want to know about her friends. If I could tell you I would. Is it all right to tell my sister about her typing the notes?"

"Your sister has probably already been told by the police." Wolfe palmed the chair arms. "You haven't been much help, Mr. Purcell, but you have been candid, and I appreciate it. Mr. Tedder should thank you, and no doubt he will. I needn't keep you longer."

"But you were going to explain about someone putting something in Jimmy's drink."

"So I was. Wednesday evening in the library. You were there."

"Yes."

"You served brandy to Mr. Frost."

"Yes, I believe I did. How did— Oh, Noel told you."

"No, his sister told me. I had the idea of trying to get from her who could, and who could not, have drugged Mr. Vail's drink, but abandoned it. Such an inquiry is nearly always futile; memories are too faulty and interests too tangled. The point is simple: Mr. Vail must have been drugged when he was pulled off the couch and across to the statue, therefore someone put something in his drink. That's the explanation."

The reaction to that was perceptible. Purcell stared, not blinking. "Pulled?" he asked. "You said pulled?"

"Yes."

"But he wasn't *pulled*. Unless you mean he pulled himself."

"No. He was unconscious. Someone pulled him across to the statue, to the desired spot, and pushed the statue over on him. I'm not going to elaborate on that, not now, to you; I mentioned it only because I felt I owed you an explanation of Mr. Tedder's remark about Mr. Vail's drink."

"But you're saying Jimmy was murdered."

"Yes."

"But the police don't say he was."

"No?"

"But you didn't tell Noel that."

"But I did."

"You told Noel Jimmy was murdered?"

"Yes."

"You don't know that. You can't."

"The word 'know' has various connotations. I have formed that conclusion."

"Then you didn't really—you don't care about Dinah Utley. You've been taking advantage of me." His cheeks were red.

"You've been making a fool of me." He got to his feet. "Noel should have told me. That wasn't fair. You should have told me too. I guess I *am* a fool." He turned and headed for the door.

I stayed in my chair. There are times when it's better to let a departing guest get his own hat and open the door for himself. When I heard it close I went to the hall to see that he had remembered to cross the sill before he shut it, then went back to my desk. Wolfe had straightened up and was making faces.

"If he's it," I said, "if he's *not* a fool, you might as well cross it off."

He made another face.

CHAPTER 10

I HAVE NEVER completely understood Wolfe's attitude on food and eating and probably never will. In some ways it's strictly personal. If Fritz presents a platter of broiled squabs and one of them is a little plumper or a more beautiful brown than the others, Wolfe cops it. If the supply of wild thyme honey from Greece is getting low, I am given to understand, through Fritz, that plain American honey on griddle cakes is quite acceptable. And so on. But it really pains him if I am out on a prolonged errand at mealtime because I may insult my palate with a drugstore sandwich, and, even worse, I may offend my stomach by leaving it empty. If there is reason to believe that a caller is hungry, even if it is someone whom he intends to take apart, he has Fritz bring a tray, and not scraps. As for interruptions at meals, for him there is absolutely nothing doing; when he is once in his chair at the table he leaves it only when the last bite of cheese or dessert is down. That's personal, but he has tried off and on to extend it to me, and he would if I would stand for it. The point is, does he hate to have my meal broken into because it interrupts his, or because it interrupts mine, or just on general principles? Search me.

Anyhow, he does. So when the phone rang while I was helping myself to another beef fillet, and Fritz answered it and came to say that Mrs. Vail wished to speak to Mr. Wolfe, and I pushed back my chair to go, Wolfe growled and glowered. He didn't tell me not to go, because he knew I would go anyway.

When I told our former client that Wolfe was at dinner and said he could call her back in half an hour, she said she wanted to see him. Now. I said okay, if she left in ten minutes he would be available when she arrived, and she said no, she couldn't come, she was worn out, and she sounded like it.

"That narrows it down," I told her, "if it's too private for the phone. Either I come there and get it and bring it back, or let it wait."

"It mustn't wait. Doesn't he *ever* go anywhere?"

"Not on business."

"Can you come now?"

I glanced at my wrist. "I can be there by nine o'clock. Will that do?"

She said she supposed it would have to, and I returned to the dining room and my place and asked Fritz to bring my coffee with my pie. The routine is back to the office for coffee because that's where the one and only chair is, and Wolfe's current book is there if I'm going out. When he had finished his pie and put his fork down, I said I was going to call on Mrs. Vail by request and asked for instructions.

He grunted. "Intelligence guided by experience. You know the situation. We owe her nothing."

I went. Having gone out to the stoop to feel the weather and decided I could survive without a coat, I walked to Eighth Avenue and got an uptown taxi. On the way uptown I looked it over. Wolfe's statement that I knew the situation left out something: I knew it from my angle, but not from his. He might already have made some deduction, not final; for instance, that Noel Tedder was a kidnaper, a murderer, and a liar. Or sister Margot, or Uncle Ralph. It wouldn't be the first time, or even the twentieth, that he had kept a deduction to himself.

Noel must have been waiting in the hall, for two seconds after I pushed the button he opened the door. He did own some regular clothes—a plain dark gray suit, white shirt, and gray tie, but of course he might have bought them for the funeral. He shut the door, turned to me, and demanded, "Why the hell did Wolfe tell Uncle Ralph that Jimmy was murdered?"

"You may have three guesses," I told him. "Mine is that he had to, since you had told Uncle Ralph that someone had put something in Jimmy's drink and Mr. Wolfe would explain it. Did you have to mention Jimmy's drink?"

"No. That slipped out. But what the hell, if Wolfe's so damn smart couldn't he have dodged it?"

"Sure he could. As for why he didn't, sometimes I know why he does a thing while he's doing it, sometimes I know an hour later, sometimes a week later, and sometimes never. Why, did Purcell tell your mother?"

"Certainly he did. There's hell to pay."

"All right, I'm the roving paymaster. Where is she?"

"What are you going to tell her?"

"I'll know when I hear myself. I play by ear. I told her I'd be here by nine o'clock, and it's five after."

He thought he had more to say, decided he hadn't, told me to come along, and led the way to the rear. I was looking forward to seeing the library again, especially if Benjamin Franklin was still there on the floor, but in the elevator he pushed the button marked 3. When it stopped I followed him out, along the hall, and into a room that one glance told me would suit my wife fine if I ever had a wife, which I probably wouldn't because she would probably want that kind of room. It was a big soft room—soft lights, soft grays and pinks, soft rug, soft drapes. I crossed the rug, after Noel, to where Mrs. Vail was flat in a big bed, most of her covered by a soft pink sheet that could have been silk, her head propped against a couple of soft pink pillows.

"You may go, Noel," she said.

She looked terrible. Of course any woman is something quite different if you see her without any make-up, but even allowing for that she still looked terrible. Her face was pasty, her cheeks sagged, and she was puffed up around the eyes. When Noel had gone, closing the door, she told me to sit down, and I moved a chair around.

"I don't know what good it will do, you coming," she said. "I want to ask Nero Wolfe what he means by this—this outrage. Telling my brother and my son that my husband was murdered. Can you tell me?"

I shook my head. "I can't tell you what he means by telling them. I assume you know why your son came to see him yesterday."

"Yes. To get him to help him find the money. When Noel asked me if he could have the money if he found it, I said yes. The money didn't matter; my husband was back. Now he's dead, and nothing matters. But he wasn't murdered."

So Noel had broached it. "Your son asked you again yesterday," I said, "and you said yes again. Didn't you?"

"I suppose I did. Nothing matters now, certainly that money doesn't— No, I'm wrong, something does matter. If you can't tell me why Nero Wolfe says my husband was murdered, then he will. If I have to go there, I will. I shouldn't, my doctor has ordered me to stay in bed, but I will."

I could see her tottering into the office supported by me, and Wolfe, after one look at her, getting up and marching out. He has done that more than once. "I can't tell you why Mr. Wolfe says it," I said, "but I can tell you why he thinks it." I might as well, since if I didn't Noel could. "Your husband was asleep on the couch when the rest of you left the room, leaving a light on. Right?"

"Yes."

"And the idea is that later he woke up, realized where he was, stood up, started for the door, lost his balance, grabbed at the statue, and pulled it down on him. Right?"

"Yes."

"That's what Mr. Wolfe won't take. He doesn't believe that a man awake enough to walk would be so befuddled that he couldn't dodge a falling statue. He realizes that he couldn't have been merely asleep when someone hauled him off the couch and over to the statue; he must have been unconscious. Since the autopsy found no sign that he had been slugged, he must have been doped. You had all been having drinks in the library, he had bourbon and water, so there had been opportunity to dope him. Therefore Mr. Wolfe deduces that he was murdered."

Her eyes were straight at me through the surrounding puffs. "That's absolutely ridiculous," she said.

I nodded. "Sure it is, to you. If Mr. Wolfe is right, then your daughter or your son or your brother or your lawyer, or you yourself, murdered Jimmy Vail. I think he's right, but I work for him. Granting that it wasn't you, you're up against a tough one. Naturally you would want whoever killed your husband to get what was coming to him, but naturally you wouldn't want your son or daughter or brother to get tagged for murder, and maybe not your lawyer. I admit that's tough, and I don't wonder that you say it's ridiculous. I wasn't trying to convince you of anything; I was just telling you why Mr. Wolfe thinks your husband was murdered. What else would you want to ask him if he was here?"

"I'd tell him he's a fool. A stupid fool."

"I'll deliver the message. What else?"

"I'd tell him that I have told my son that I'm taking back what I told him about the money, that he can have it if he finds it. He can't. I didn't know he would go to Nero Wolfe."

"You went to Nero Wolfe."

"That was different. I would have gone to the devil himself to get my husband back."

I gave my intelligence three seconds to be guided by experience before I spoke. "I'll deliver that message too," I said, "but I can tell you now what his reaction will be. He's stubborn and he's conceited, and he not only likes money, he needs it. Your son came to him and offered a deal, and he accepted it, and he won't let go just because you've changed your mind. If he can find that money he will, and he'll take his share. In my private opinion the chance of his finding it is about one in a million, but he won't stop trying. On the contrary. He's very sensitive. This attitude you're taking will make him try harder, and he might even do something peevish like writing a piece for a newspaper explaining why he has deduced that Jimmy Vail was murdered. That would be just like him. If you want some free advice, I suggest that you have your son in, here and now, and tell him you're *not* taking it back. I'll report it to Mr. Wolfe, and he'll decide if he wants to risk his time and money on a wild-goose chase."

It didn't work. As I spoke her lips kept getting tighter, and when I stopped she snapped, "He wouldn't get any share. Even if he found it. It's my money."

"That would be one for the lawyers. He would claim that his

agreement with your son was based on an agreement your son had with you, made before witnesses. It would be the kind of mix-up lawyers love; they can juggle it around for years."

"You may go," she said.

"Sure." I rose. "But you understand—"

"Get out!"

I can take a hint. I walked out, shutting the door behind me, and proceeded to the elevator. When I emerged on the ground floor, there was Noel. He came to me.

"What did she say?" he squeaked.

"This and that." I caught a glimpse of someone through an arch. "She's a little upset. How about a little walk? If there's a bar handy, I could buy you a drink, provided it's not champagne."

He twisted his neck to glance up the stairs, brought his face back to me, said, "That's an idea," and went and opened the door. I passed through and onto the sidewalk, and he joined me. I suggested Barney's, at 78th and Madison, and we turned downtown.

A booth in a bar and grill is not an ideal spot for a private conversation. You can see if there is anyone in the booth in front of you curious enough to listen in, but you have to leave the one behind to luck or keep interrupting to look back. Noel and I got a break at Barney's. As we entered, a couple was leaving the booth at the far end, and we grabbed it, and I had a wall behind me. A white apron came and removed glasses and gave the table a swipe, and we ordered.

"So it's off," Noel said. "You couldn't budge her." I had told him en route how it stood.

"Not an inch." I was regretful, even gloomy. "You know why I wanted to buy you a drink? Because I wanted one myself. That talk with your mother took me back, back years ago, in Ohio. *My* mother. How old are you?"

"Twenty-three."

"I was only seventeen, just out of high school. But of course the situation was different; it was easier for me than it would be for you. My mother wasn't wealthy like yours. I couldn't hit her for a hundred or a thousand or whatever I happened to need."

"Hell, neither can I. It's not that easy."

"It may not be easy, but the fact remains that she has it, and all you have to do is use the right approach. With me, with my mother, that wasn't the problem. She was a born female tyrant, and that was all there was to it. There wasn't a single goddam thing, big or little, that I could decide on my own. While your mother was talking I couldn't help thinking it was just too bad you couldn't do what I did."

The drinks came and we sampled them. Noel's sample was a gulp. "What did you do?" he asked.

"I told her to go to hell. One nice hot June day, the day after I graduated from high school, I told her to go to hell, and beat it. Of course I don't mean it literally, that it's too bad you can't do what I did. It's a different situation. You wouldn't have to. Now that Jimmy Vail's dead, you're the man of the house. All you'd have to do is just make it clear that you've got two feet of your own. Not in general terms like that, not just tell her to her face, 'Mother, I've got two feet of my own,' that wouldn't get you anywhere. It would have to be on a specific issue, and you couldn't ask for a better one than her taking back a definite promise she made you. That would be a beaut. You could tell her, 'Mother, you said I could have that money if I found it, and on the strength of that I made a deal with Nero Wolfe, and he'll hold me to it, and I'm going to hold you to it.'"

He took a swallow of gin and tonic. "She'd say it's her money."

"But it isn't. Not after what she told you before witnesses. She has given it to you, with only one condition attached, that you find it, and therefore it's a gift and you wouldn't have to pay tax on it. Granting that there's a slim chance of finding it, if we do find it you'll have four hundred thousand dollars in the till after you give Nero Wolfe his cut—no tax, no nothing. And even if we don't find it, you'll have let your mother know that you've got your own two feet, not by telling her so but by standing on them on a specific issue. There's another point, but we'll skip it."

"Why? What is it?"

I took a sip of scotch and soda. "It will be important only if Mr. Wolfe finds the money. If he does, one-fifth will be his, and don't think it won't. If your mother tries to keep him from getting it, or keeping it, the fur will fly, and some of it will be yours. If it gets to a court, you'll testify. For him."

"It wouldn't. It's not the money that's biting my mother, it's Jimmy. It's Wolfe's saying that Jimmy was murdered. Why the hell did he tell Uncle Ralph that?"

"He told you too."

"I had sense enough not to repeat it." He put his empty glass down. "Look, Goodwin, I don't give a damn. If Jimmy was murdered, someone that was there killed him, and I still don't give a damn. Of course it wasn't my mother, but even if it was, I'm not sure I'd give a damn even then. I'm supposed to be old enough to vote, but by God, the way I've had to knuckle under, you'd think I still wet the bed at night. You say I wouldn't have to do what you did, but if I had four hundred thousand dollars that's exactly what I'd do. I'd tell my mother to go to hell. I'm not as dumb as I look. I knew what I was doing Wednesday evening. I knew my mother was so glad her darling Jimmy was back she wouldn't stop to think, and I asked her about the money in front of witnesses, and I intended to go to Nero Wolfe the next morning, but the next morning Jimmy was dead, and that made it different. Now Wolfe has told Uncle Ralph Jimmy was murdered, I don't know why, and he has told my mother, and you tell me to show her I've got my own two feet. Balls. What if I haven't even got one foot?"

I signaled the white apron for refills. "Let's try something," I said and got out my notebook and pen and started writing. I dated a blank page at the top and wrote:

To Nero Wolfe: I hereby confirm the oral agreement we made yesterday. My mother, Mrs. Althea Vail, told me on Wednesday, April 26, and repeated on Friday, April 28, that if I find the $500,000 she gave a kidnaper on Tuesday, April 25, or any part of it, I may keep it for my own. Therefore that money belongs to me if I find it. I have engaged you to help me find it, and I have agreed that if you do find it, or any part of it, you are to keep one-fifth of the amount you find as payment for your services. I hereby confirm that agreement.

The refills had come, and I sampled mine as I read it over. Tearing the sheet out, I handed it to Noel and watched his face. He took his time, then looked up. "So what?"

"So you'd have a foot. I don't really expect you to sign it, I doubt if you have the nerve, you've knuckled under too long, but if you did sign it, you wouldn't have to tell your mother you were going to do so-and-so and stick to it. You could tell her you *had* done so-and-so, you had come here with me and talked it over and confirmed your agreement with Mr. Wolfe in writing. She couldn't send you to bed without any supper because you've already had your supper. Of course legally that thing isn't important, because you're already bound legally. Mr. Wolfe has a witness to his oral agreement with you. Me."

He started to read it over again, quit halfway, put his glass down, and extended his hand. "Give me that pen." I gave it to him, and he signed his name, pushed the paper across to me, picked up his glass, and raised it to eye level. "Excelsior! To freedom!" He put the glass to his mouth and drained it. A piece of ice slipped out and fell to the table, and he picked it up and threw it at the bartender across the room, missing by a yard. He shook his head, tittered, and asked me, "What did your mother do when you told her to go to hell?"

Since I had what I wanted, it would have suited me all right if we had been bounced, but apparently Noel was not a stranger at Barney's. The barkeep took no action beyond occasional glances in our direction to see if more ice was coming. Noel wanted to talk. The idea seemed to be that I had made a hero of him, and he wanted to know who or what had made a hero of me at the early age of seventeen. I was willing to spend another half-hour and another drink on him, but I suspected that he didn't want to go home until it was late enough for him to go to bed without stopping in his mother's room to say good night, and that might mean a couple of hours. So I began looking at my watch and worrying about being late for a date, and at ten o'clock I paid for the drinks and left him.

It was 10:26 when I mounted the stoop of the old brownstone and pushed the button. When Fritz opened the door he aimed a thumb to his rear, toward the office, signifying that there was company. I asked him who, and he told me in what he thinks is a whisper but is actually a kind of smothered croak, "Federal Bureau of Investigation." I told him, "Rub off all fingerprints and burn the papers," and went to the office.

You don't have to believe me, but I would have known after one look at him, even if Fritz hadn't told me. It's mostly the eyes and the jaw. An FBI man spends so much time pretending he's looking somewhere else that his eyes get confused; they're never quite sure it's okay to admit they're focused on you. His jaw is even worse off. It is given to understand that it belongs to a man who is intrepid, daring, dauntless, cool, long-headed, quick-witted, and hard as nails, but it is cautioned that he is also modest, polite, reserved, patient, bland, and never to be noticed in a crowd. No jaw on earth could handle that order. The only question is how often it will twitch, and sideways or up and down.

Wolfe said, "Mr. Goodwin. Mr. Draper."

Mr. Draper, having got to his feet, waited until my hand was unquestionably being offered, then extended his. Modest and reserved. His left hand went to a pocket, and I told him not to bother, but of course he did. An FBI man draws his credentials automatically, the way Paladin draws his gun. I glanced at it, not to hurt his feelings.

"Mr. Draper has been here a full hour," Wolfe said, with the accent on the "full." "He has a copy of the statement we signed, and he has asked many questions about details. He has covered the ground thoroughly, but he wanted to see you."

It looked like another full hour. I went to my desk and sat. Draper, back in the red leather chair, had his notebook out. "A few little questions, Mr. Goodwin," he said. "If you don't mind?"

"I like big ones better," I said, "but shoot."

"For the record," he said. "Of course you understand that; you're an experienced investigator. Mr. Wolfe says you left the house around half past six Tuesday evening, but he doesn't know when you returned. When did you?"

I permitted myself a grin, modest, polite, and bland. "Mr.

Draper," I said, "I appreciate the compliment. You think I may have tailed Mrs. Vail Tuesday night, against her wishes and with or without Mr. Wolfe's consent, and that I may even have got as far as Iron Mine Road without being spotted by one of the kidnapers. As you know, that would have been one for the books, a real honey, and I thank you for the compliment."

"You're welcome. When did you return?"

I gave it to him complete, from six-thirty until one o'clock, places, names, and times, going slow enough for him to get it down. When I finished he closed the notebook, then opened it again. "You drive a car, don't you?"

"Mr. Wolfe owns it, I drive it. Sixty-one Heron sedan."

"Where is it garaged?"

"Curran, Tenth Avenue between Thirty-fifth and Thirty-sixth."

"Did you use the car Tuesday night?"

"No. I believe I mentioned taxis."

"Yes. You understand, Mr. Goodwin, for the record." He pocketed the notebook, arose, and got his hat from the stand. "You've been very helpful, Mr. Wolfe. Thank you very much. I doubt if we'll bother you again." He turned and went. I didn't get up, because an FBI man moves fast and I would have had to jump to get ahead of him to open the door. When I heard it close I went to the hall for a look, came back, got from my pocket the paper Noel had signed, and handed it to Wolfe.

He read it and put it down. "This was called for?"

"It seemed to be desirable. Would you like a report?"

"Yes."

I sat down and gave it to him—verbatim, all but the last half-hour with Noel, which wasn't material. When I was through he picked up the paper, read it again, nodded, and said, "Satisfactory." He put it down. "When your mother was in New York for a week last year, and dined here twice, and you spent some time taking her around, I saw no trace of the animus you described to Mr. Tedder."

"Neither did I. If we find enough of that five hundred grand to make it worth telling about, and it gets printed and she reads it, she won't mind. She understands that in this job, working for you, the more lies the merrier, even one about her. By the way, in a letter I got last week she mentioned the chestnut croquettes again."

"Did you tell Fritz?"

"Sure. Anything for the morning?"

"No."

"Are Saul and Fred and Orrie still on?"

"Yes." He eyed me. "Archie. Your reply to Mr. Draper's question. Could he have had any other reason for asking it than the chronic suspicion of an inquisitor?"

"Certainly. They might have found the tire prints of your car at Iron Mine Road. I drove it there Wednesday."

"Don't dodge. You have friends who would lie for you without question, and you named some of them in your reply. One particularly. How much of your reply was fact?"

"All of it." I stood. "I'm going to bed. My ears are burning. First the FBI and now you. I wish I *had* tailed her, and Mr. Knapp with the suitcase; then we'd know where the cabbage is."

CHAPTER 11

IT'S ALWAYS POSSIBLE that people who invite me to the country for a weekend will get a break; there's a chance that there will be a development that will keep me in town, and they will neither have to put me up nor put up with me. The lucky ones that last weekend in April were a couple in Easthampton who had me booked for Friday evening to Monday morning. I have reported the developments of Friday and Saturday, and Sunday I had to stick around in case a call for reinforcements came from Saul or Fred or Orrie.

Wolfe's routine for Sunday is different. Theodore Horstmann, the orchid nurse, has the day off and goes to visit his married sister in Jersey, so there are no regular two-hour sessions in the plant rooms. Wolfe goes up once or twice to look around and do whatever chores the situation and the weather require, but there is no strict schedule. Usually he is down in the office by ten-thirty, at least the Sundays I am there, to settle down with the review-of-the-week section of the Sunday *Times,* which he goes right through.

From nine o'clock on that Sunday morning I was half expecting a call from Noel Tedder to tell me that he had issued his Declaration of Independence, one hero to another, but it hadn't come by the time I turned on the radio for the ten-o'clock news. Nor had there been any word from any of the tailers, but I was soon to know where Saul Panzer was. As I was turning the radio off the doorbell rang, and I went to the hall and saw Andrew Frost. So Saul was near enough to see the door opening, no matter how Frost had got there. I swung the door wide and said good morning.

It may be cheesy writing to say that Frost's expression and tone were frosty as he said he wanted to see Nero Wolfe, but it's good reporting. They were. It was possible that a factor was the probability that he would have to miss church, since he was dressed for it in a custom-made charcoal-gray topcoat and a forty-dollar homburg to match. I allowed him to enter, took the hat and coat, ushered him to the office, and buzzed the plant rooms on the house phone. When Wolfe's voice came, his usual testy "Yes?" and I told him Mr. Andrew Frost had come and had been admitted, he snapped, "Ten minutes," and hung up. When I told Frost he made a frosty little noise and gave me a frosty look. He didn't seem to look as much like Abraham Lincoln as he had Wednesday afternoon, but that may have been because I had never seen a picture of Lincoln simmering.

It was nearer fifteen minutes than ten when the sound came of the elevator, and Wolfe entered, a spray of Miltonia roezli in his left hand and the Sunday *Times* under his right arm. He takes his copy of the *Times* with him to the plant rooms so he won't have to stop off at his room on the way down to the office. Labor-saving device. He stopped at the corner of his desk to face the caller, said, "Mr. Frost? How do you do. I was expecting you," then put the flowers in the vase and the *Times* on the desk, and circled around to his chair.

Frost said distinctly, "You were not expecting me."

"But I was." Wolfe, seated, regarded him. "I invited you. I told Mr. Purcell that Mr. Vail was murdered, knowing that that would almost certainly bring you. I wished to see everyone who had been at that gathering Wednesday evening. You came, naturally, to remonstrate. Go ahead."

A muscle at the side of the lawyer's neck was twitching. "Are you saying," he demanded, "that you uttered that slander, knowing it was false, merely to coerce me to come here so you could see me?"

A corner of Wolfe's mouth went up a sixteenth of an inch. "That's quite a question. I uttered no slander, because what I said was true. I haven't coerced you; you are under no constraint; if you don't want to be here, go. Has Mr. Purcell told you what led me to the conclusion that Mr. Vail was murdered?"

"Yes. It's pure sophistry. The police and the District Attorney haven't formed that conclusion. It's false, fallacious, and defamatory, and it's actionable."

"Has the District Attorney made his final deduction and closed the inquiry?"

"Formally, no."

"Even if he does, that won't prove me wrong. He needs evidence that will convince a jury; I don't. I merely—"

"You'll need evidence if you persist in this slander and are made to answer for it."

"I doubt if I'll have to meet that contingency. I merely needed a starting point for a job I have undertaken, and I got it—my conclusion that Mr. Vail was murdered. I have no—"

"You have no job. You mean that fantastic scheme with Noel Tedder. That's off."

Wolfe turned his head. "Archie. That paper?"

I hadn't opened the safe, so I had to work the combination. I did so and got the paper from the shelf where I had put it before going up to bed. As I approached with it, Wolfe told me to give it to Frost. He took it, ran his eyes over it, and then read it word by word. When he looked up, Wolfe spoke.

"I'm not a counselor-at-law, Mr. Frost, but I have some knowledge of the validity of contracts. I'm confident that that paper binds Mrs. Vail as well as Mr. Tedder."

"When did he sign it?"

"Yesterday evening."

"It won't stand. He was tricked into signing it."

Wolfe turned. "Archie?"

"No tricks," I told Frost. "Ask him. He's fed up and wants to stand on his own two feet. I bought him three little drinks, but he was perfectly sober. There were witnesses."

"Witnesses where?"

"Barney's bar and grill, Seventy-eighth and Madison." I was still there by him, and I put out a hand. "May I have it, please?"

He took another look at it and handed it over. I went to the safe and put it back on the shelf and swung the door shut.

Wolfe was speaking. "I was about to say, Mr. Frost, that I have no intention of broadcasting my conclusion that Mr. Vail was murdered, or my reasons for it. I had to tell Mr. Tedder in order to explain my approach to our joint problem, and I told Mr. Purcell because I wanted to see you; he would of course tell his sister, and she would tell you. My purposes have been served. As for the murder, I am not—"

"There was no murder."

"That's *your* conclusion—or your delusion. I'm not bent on disturbing it. I am not a nemesis."

"Why did you want to see me?"

"When I know that one of a group of people has committed a murder, and possibly two murders, and I need to know which one, I like to look at them and hear them—"

"Then you *are* persisting in the slander. You're saying that you intend to identify one of the people there Wednesday evening as a murderer."

"Only to my satisfaction, for my private purpose. Perhaps my explanation has lost something on its way to you through Mr. Purcell and Mrs. Vail. No. I'm wrong. I explained fully to Mr. Tedder, but not to Mr. Purcell. Having deduced that Mr. Vail was murdered, I made two assumptions: that the murder was consequent to the kidnaping and therefore the murderer had been involved in the kidnaping, and that he or she knows who has the money and where it is or might be. So I needed to identify him and I had to see all of you. I had seen Mrs. Vail. I intend to find that money."

Frost was shaking his head, his lips compressed. "It's hard to believe. I know your reputation, but this is incredible. You wanted to see me so that, by looking at me and hearing me, you could decide if I was a kidnaper and a murderer? Preposterous!"

"It does seem a little overweening," Wolfe conceded, "but I didn't rely solely on my acumen." He turned. "Archie, bring Saul."

That shows you his opinion of Saul. Not "Archie, see if Saul is around." Frost was Saul's subject, so, since Frost was here, Saul was in the neighborhood. Of course it was my opinion too. I went to the front door and out to the stoop, descended two steps, stood, and beckoned to Manhattan, that part of it north of 35th Street. A passer-by turned his head to see who I was inviting, saw no one, and went on. I was expecting Saul to appear from behind one of the parked cars across the street, and I didn't see him until he was out of an areaway and on the sidewalk, on this side, thirty paces toward Tenth Avenue. He had figured that Frost would head west to get an uptown taxi, and undoubtedly he would. Reaching me, he asked, "Was I spotted?"

"You know damn well you weren't spotted. You're wanted. We need you for four-handed pinochle."

He came on up, and we entered and went to the office, Saul in front. Sticking his cap in his pocket, he crossed to Wolfe's desk with no glance at Frost and said, "Yes, sir?"

Wolfe turned to Frost. "This is Mr. Saul Panzer. He has been making inquiries about you since yesterday morning." Back to Saul: "Have you anything to add to your report on the phone last evening?"

Presumably after I had left to go to Mrs. Vail, Saul said, "Only one item, from a source I saw after I phoned. Last fall he bought a one-third interest in a new twelve-story apartment house on Eighty-third Street and Park Avenue."

"Briefly, some of the items you reported yesterday."

"He's a senior member of the firm of McDowell, Frost, Hovey, and Ulrich, One-twenty Broadway. Twenty-two names on the letterhead. He was co-chairman of the Committee of New York Lawyers for Nixon. Two years ago he gave his son a house in East Sixty-eighth Street for a wedding present. He's a director in at least twenty corporations—I don't think the list I got is complete. He was Harold F. Tedder's counsel for more than ten years. He has a house on Long Island, near Great Neck, thirty rooms and eleven acres. In nineteen fifty-four President Eisenhower—"

"That's enough." Wolfe turned. "As you see, Mr. Frost, I realize that my perspicacity is not infallible. Of course some of Mr. Panzer's items invite further inquiry—for example, is the estate on Long Island unencumbered? Is there a mortgage?"

Frost was no longer frosty; he was too near boiling. "This is unbelievable," he declared. He was close to sputtering. "You have actually paid this man to collect a dossier on me? To examine the possibility that I'm a kidnaper and murderer? Me?"

Wolfe nodded. "Certainly. You're a lawyer with wide experience; you know I could exclude no one who was there. Mr. Panzer is discreet and extremely competent; I'm sure he—"

The doorbell rang. I got up and went to the hall for a look, returned to my desk, scribbled "Cramer" on the scratch pad, tore off the sheet, and handed it to Wolfe. He glanced at it, closed his eyes, opened them in three seconds, and turned to Frost.

"Inspector Cramer of the police is at the door. If you would prefer not to—"

Frost's wires snapped. He jerked forward, his eyes blazing. "Damn you! *Damn* you! You phoned him!"

"I did not," Wolfe snapped. "He is uninvited and unexpected. I don't know why he's here. He deals only with death by violence. If he has heard of my conclusion that Mr. Vail was murdered, I don't know when or from whom. Not from Mr. Goodwin or me." The doorbell rang. "Do you want him to know you are here?"

"You're a liar! You're to blame—"

"Enough!" Wolfe hit the desk. "The situation is precisely as I have described it. Archie, admit Mr. Cramer. Do you want him to see you or not? Yes or no."

"No," Frost said, and left the chair. Wolfe told Saul to take him to the front room, and when Saul had gone to the connecting door and opened it, and Frost was moving, I went to admit the law. From the expression on Cramer's face I expected him to march on by to the office, but when I turned after shutting the door, he was there facing me.

"What were you doing with Noel Tedder last night?" he demanded.

"Don't snap my head off," I said. "I'd rather tell you before a witness. Mr. Wolfe will do." I walked to the office, entered, and told Wolfe, "He wants to know what I was doing with Noel Tedder last night. He didn't say please."

Cramer was at my elbow. "The day I say please to you," he growled, and went to the red leather chair, sat, and put his hat on the stand.

"I suppose," Wolfe said, "it's futile to complain. You have been a policeman so long, and have asked so many people so many impertinent questions, and so frequently have got answers to them, that it has become spontaneous. Have you any ground at all for expecting Mr. Goodwin to answer that one?"

"We might arrange a deal," I suggested. "I'll ask an impertinent question. Why have you got a tail on Noel Tedder if Jimmy Vail's death was an accident?"

"We haven't got a tail on him."

"Then how did you know he was with me?"

"A detective happened to see you with him on the street and followed you." Cramer turned to Wolfe. "Day before yesterday you refused to tell me where you and Goodwin had been for twenty-four hours. You said you had no further commitment to Mrs. Vail and you had no client. You repeated that in your signed statement. You did not repeat it to Draper of the FBI when he asked you last night. Your answer was evasive. That's not like you. I have never known you to hedge on a lie. Now this, Goodwin with Noel Tedder. You're not going to tell me that was just social. Are you?"

"No."

"Goodwin?"

"No."

"Then what was it?"

Wolfe shook his head. "You have a right to expect answers only to questions that are relevant to a crime. What crime are you investigating?"

"That's typical. That's you. I'm investigating the possibility that Jimmy Vail didn't die by accident."

"Then you aren't satisfied that he did."

"Satisfied, no. The District Attorney may be, I don't know, you can ask him. I say I have a right to expect Goodwin to answer that question. Or you."

Wolfe tilted his chair back, then his head, pursed his lips, and examined the ceiling. Cramer took a cigar from a pocket, rolled it between his palms, which was silly with a cigar that wasn't going to be lit, held it at an angle with his thumb and forefinger, frowning at it, and returned it to his pocket. Evidently he had asked it an impertinent question and it had refused to answer.

Wolfe let his chair come forward and said, "The paper, Archie."
I went to the safe and got it from the shelf and took it to him.
He put it on his desk pad and turned to Cramer.

"I think you have the notion that I have withheld information
from you on various occasions just to be contrary. I haven't. I
have reserved details only when I wanted them, at least temporarily, for my exclusive use, or when you have been excessively
offensive. Today you have been reasonably civil, though of course
not affable; imparting it will not make it less useful to me; and
if it furthers your investigation, though I confess I don't see how
it can, it will serve a double purpose." He picked up the paper. "I'll
read it. I won't hand it to you because you would probably say
it may be needed as evidence, which would be absurd, and pocket
it."

He read it, ending, "Signed by Noel Tedder. It isn't holograph;
Mr. Goodwin wrote it. I answered that question by Mr. Draper
ambiguously because if I had told him of my arrangement with
Mr. Tedder he would have kept me up all night, thinking that
I had some knowledge, at least an inkling, of where the money
might be found. I have no commitment to Mrs. Vail, but I do
have a client: Noel Tedder."

"Yeah." It came out hoarse, and Cramer cleared his throat.
He always gets a little hoarse when he talks with Wolfe, probably
a certain word or words sticking in his throat. "And either you
have some idea where the money is or this is a cover for something else. Does Mrs. Vail know about that agreement?"

"Yes."

"And that's what Goodwin and Tedder were discussing last
night?"

"Yes."

"What else were they discussing?"

Wolfe turned. "Archie?"

I shook my head. "Nothing. We touched on mothers some, his
and mine, but that was in connection with the agreement."

"So your question is answered," Wolfe told him. "I'm aware
that you'll pass it on to Mr. Draper, but he isn't here, and if he

comes he won't get in. We have given him all the information we possess about the kidnaping, with no reservations. I do have an idea where the money is, but it is based—"

"By God, you admit it."

"I state it. It's based on deductions and assumptions I have made, not on any evidence I'm withholding. That applies not only to the kidnaping and the whereabouts of the money, but also to the death of Mr. Vail. What would you say if I told you that I'm convinced that he was murdered, with premeditation, and that I think I know, I'm all but certain that I know, who killed him and why?"

"I'd say you were grandstanding. It wouldn't be the first time. I know you. God, do I know you! When you've really got something you don't say you're convinced and you're all but certain. You say you *know*. If you've got any evidence that he was murdered and that points to the murderer, I want it, and I want it now. Have you got any?"

"No."

"Then I'll leave you to your deductions and assumptions." He picked up his hat. "You're damn right I'll tell Draper." He rose. "But if he knew you as well as I do— Oh, nuts." He turned and marched out.

I stepped to the hall and saw him close the front door behind him, stepped back in, and asked Wolfe, "So you're all but certain? Do you know what 'grandstanding' means? Where did you get the idea—"

"Get Saul."

He snapped it. I went and opened the door to the front room and told Saul to come. As he entered, Wolfe spoke. "Mr. Frost has gone?"

Saul nodded. "He bent his ear for five minutes trying to hear you, found that he couldn't on account of the soundproofing, and left."

"I want Fred. If Mr. Purcell is at home, he will of course be nearby. Bring him as soon as possible." His eyes came to me. "Archie, I want Mr. Tedder, and Orrie with him. Also as soon as possible. Don't stop to tell Fritz about the door. I'll see that it's bolted."

"You want me back," Saul said.

"Yes. Go."

We went.

CHAPTER 12

IT WOULDN'T DO, of course, for me to ring the Vail house and get Noel and tell him Wolfe wanted to see him. One, he might not come without some fancy persuading. Two, Wolfe wanted Orrie too, and Orrie, tailing him, might possibly lose him on the way downtown. Three, Saul had to go there to get Fred, and the taxi fare is the same for two as for one. So we walked to Tenth Avenue and flagged a cab.

It was 11:23 of a sunny Sunday morning, nice and warm for the last of April, when we stopped at the curb in front of 994 Fifth Avenue, paid the hackie, and got out. When we're going on with the program, the method of getting in touch with a tail, understood by all of us, is a little complicated, but in that case it was simple. We merely raised an arm to wave at a squirrel in a tree in the park and started to stroll downtown. Before we had taken twenty steps Fred appeared from behind a parked car across the street and came over to us and said if we had come an hour sooner he could have gone to church.

"It would take more than church to square you," I told him. "Purcell hasn't shown?"

"No."

"What about Orrie?"

"His subject showed at ten fifty-one and led him away." Fred looked at Saul. "And yours came at eleven-fifteen in a cab and went in. So you got shook for once?"

"No," I said, "he got called off. Did Tedder ride or walk?"

"Walked. Turned east at Seventy-eighth Street. Orrie was keeping distance. Something happened? What's up?"

"God doesn't know, but Mr. Wolfe does. Everybody in for a conference." I turned to Saul. "If you and Fred go on down, you can read the Bible until I bring Tedder and Orrie. There are five versions in four different languages on the second shelf from the top near the left end. I'm thinking where to start looking for him. I think better when I talk."

"We can't help you think," Saul said, "because you know him and we don't, but we can help you look. Of course, if he wanted a taxi, it's Sunday and he could have got one here on Fifth, or if he thought he'd get one quicker on Madison he wouldn't have gone to Seventy-eighth to turn east. But if he has a car and it's garaged on Seventy-eighth, he—"

"No," Fred said. "Four cars garaged on Eighty-second Street. I've seen three of them." As I said, Fred was a little too solid for quick reactions, but give him time and he would collect a lot of miscellaneous information that might be useful.

"Okay," I said, "thanks a lot for doing my thinking. Now I know where he is, maybe. If you've thought wrong and he's not there, we might as well go back to Thirty-fifth Street and sing hymns until Orrie phones. Come along."

It was one chance in a thousand, but it was the only chance there was. I led them south to Seventy-eighth Street and east to Madison Avenue, halted in front of Barney's, and told them, "We might as well give Orrie the high sign first and have him join us. Then when I bring—"

"There he is," Saul said.

I turned. Orrie had emerged from a doorway across the street and was crossing the sidewalk. "All I need," I said, "is someone to do my thinking," and stepped to Barney's door and entered.

There was no one at the bar, since it was Sunday morning, and there weren't many at the tables or in the booths, but the top of a head was showing in the booth at the far end and I went to it. It was Noel, with a plate of roast turkey and trimmings in front of him, untouched, and a nearly empty glass in his hand. He looked up at me, blinked, and squeaked, "Well, for God's sake!"

I gave him a friendly grin, hero to hero. "This isn't luck," I said, "it's fate. When I learned you had gone out, it wasn't that I had a hunch, I just started to walk, and there I was in front of Barney's, and I came in, and here you are. Have you—uh—spoken to your mother?"

"No." He emptied the glass and put it down. "I was going to go up to her room right after breakfast, but then I thought I'd better wait. I thought I'd better kind of work up to it. I wanted to go over everything you said. So I came here to this booth where you said it. Sit down and oil your throat."

"Thanks, but I'm on an errand. You won't have to tell your mother you're big enough to shave; she knows it. Andrew Frost came to see Mr. Wolfe this morning, and Mr. Wolfe showed him the paper you signed, and Frost went to see your mother. He's there now."

"The hell he is. Holy Christ."

"And Mr. Wolfe sent me to bring you. I think he has an idea where the money is, but if so he didn't tell me; he wants to tell you. He said as soon as possible, which means now. You haven't touched your turkey."

"To hell with the turkey. Frost is with my mother?"

"Right."

"And Wolfe wants to see me?"

"Right."

He slid out of the booth and got erect. "Look. You see me?"

"I do."

"Am I standing on my own two feet?"

"You are."

"Check. Let's go."

The waiter was approaching, and as Noel didn't seem to see him, I asked him how much. He said four-twenty, and I gave him a fin and followed Noel to the door.

Outside, Saul had performed as usual. There were two taxis at the curb. The one in front was empty, and the trio were in the one in the rear. He had even arranged for a signal so the hackie wouldn't take the wrong passengers; as Noel and I crossed the sidewalk the horn of the cab in the rear let out a grunt.

When we stopped in front of the old brownstone at ten minutes past noon, and I paid the hackie and climbed out after Noel, the other taxi wasn't in sight. Saul again. He didn't know whether Wolfe wanted Noel to know that the whole army was mobilized, so he was hanging back to give us time to get inside. I had to ring, since the bolt was on. Fritz let us in, and I took Noel to the office. It had been just sixty-five minutes since Wolfe had told Saul and me to fetch. If I may say so, I would call that as soon as possible.

Wolfe did something remarkable: he left his chair and took two steps to offer Noel a hand. Either he was telling me that Noel was not a murderer, or he was telling Noel that he was with friends and since he could count on us we would expect to count on him. Of course Noel didn't appreciate it; a man who will some day be in the top bracket without trying has plenty of hands offered to him. He took the red leather chair and said, "Goodwin says you know where the money is."

"Correction," I objected. "I said I think he has an idea where it is."

Wolfe grunted. He eyed Noel. "The truth is somewhere between. I'm fairly certain. Call it a presumption. To test it we need your cooperation, your active assistance. Even with it, it may be difficult—"

The doorbell rang. I told Wolfe, "Three of my friends," and stood. "I'll put them in the front room."

"No," he said, "bring them."

So it was to be a family party. I went and let them in, told them they could come and sit with the quality if they would behave themselves, and followed them to the office. Wolfe greeted them and turned to the client. "Mr. Tedder, shake hands with Mr. Panzer. Mr. Durkin. Mr. Cather."

The very best corn. I had seldom seen him sink so low. I moved chairs up, and they sat. Wolfe's eyes took them in, left to right, then back to focus on Noel. "Time may be of vital importance, so I won't waste it. The money, all of it, half a million dollars in cash, is at your house in the country. If not in the house, it's on the premises."

"Jesus," Noel said.

"It would take all afternoon to explain fully all the circumstances that have led me to that conclusion, and I don't want to take even half an hour. You think I have sagacity, or you wouldn't have come to me with your problem. You'll accept that—"

"Wait a minute. How did the money get there?"

"Mr. Vail took it there. He took the suitcase from your mother at Iron Mine Road. You'll accept—"

"But my God, why did he—"

"Mr. Tedder. You could ask a thousand questions; I said it would take all afternoon. Do you want that money?"

"You're damn right I want it."

"Then take my conclusion on my word, tentatively at least. I say the money is there. Who is at that house now?"

"No one. Only the caretaker."

"No other servants?"

"No. We don't use it before the middle of May. Usually later."

"This is Sunday. Not on weekends?"

"We did when my father was alive, but not now. My mother says it's too cold until June."

"Mr. Vail went there last weekend. Saturday morning. What for?"

"To see about the roof and some other things. The caretaker said the roof was leaking."

"What's the caretaker's name?"

"Waller. Jake Waller."

"Are you on amicable terms with him?"

"Why, I guess so. Sure."

"A leaky roof should be attended to. How likely is it that your mother or sister or uncle will go there today to see to it?"

"My mother certainly won't. It's possible that my sister or my uncle will, but they haven't said anything about it so far as I know."

"Is the house locked up?"

"I suppose the doors are locked, yes."

"Have you a key?"

"Not now I haven't. I have one in the summer."

"Would the caretaker let you in?"

"Certainly he would. Why wouldn't he?"

Wolfe turned. "Archie. Will anyone be guarding that place? County or state or federal?"

I shook my head. "What for? Not unless someone has got to the same conclusion as you, which I doubt."

Back to Noel. "Mr. Tedder. I suggest that if you want that money you go there and get it. Now. Mr. Goodwin will drive my car. Mr. Panzer, Mr. Durkin, and Mr. Cather will go with you. They are competent, reliable, and experienced. My chef has prepared a hamper of food which you can eat on the way; it will be acceptable to your palate and your stomach. I have no suggestions as to your procedure when you get there; I didn't know Mr. Vail; you did. He returned to that house Wednesday morning with the suitcase in his car, and his time was rather limited. He wanted to act naturally, and naturally he would want to come to New York, where his wife was, without undue delay. According to the caretaker, in the published reports, he arrived about half past seven, and he left for New York around nine o'clock. Meanwhile he had bathed, shaved, changed his clothes, and eaten, so he hadn't spent much time on disposal of the suitcase; but it is highly likely that he had known on Saturday that he would bring it there for concealment and he had probably made preparations. You knew him and you must have some notion of how his mind worked, so ask yourself: where on those premises would he hide the suitcase? He anticipated no intensive search for it, since he thought it would never be suspected that he had got it and brought it there; what he had to make sure of was that it would not be accidentally discovered by a member of the family or a servant. I presume you know what the suitcase looked like?"

"Sure. Who doesn't?"

Wolfe nodded. "From the published descriptions. I think you may safely expect to find *that* suitcase. There was no reason for him to transfer the money to another container, and there was good reason not to; he would have had the added problem of disposing of the suitcase." Wolfe's head turned to take us in. "There it is, gentlemen, unless you have questions. If you have, let them be to the point. I wish you luck."

Noel squeaked, "I hope to God . . ." He let it hang.

"Yes, Mr. Tedder?"

"Nothing." Noel stood up. "Hell, what can I lose that I've got? Let's go."

I went to the kitchen to get the hamper.

CHAPTER 13

ABOUT TWO MILES northeast of Katonah you turn off the high-
way, right, pass between two stone pillars, proceed up the graveled
drive, an easy slope, winding, about four hundred yards, and there
is the house, old gray stone with high, steep roofs. At a guess, not
as many rooms as Frost's on Long Island—say twenty-five, maybe
less. Trees and other things with leaves, big and little, were all
around, and a lot of lawn, but although I can't qualify as an expert
I had the impression that they weren't getting quite enough attention. Saul eased the Heron to a stop a foot short of the bushes
that bordered a surfaced rectangle at the side of the house, and
we climbed out. He was at the wheel because at Hawthorne Circle
I had decided that I could use some of the contents of the hamper, which they had all been working on, and I don't like one-
handed driving.

Noel, in between bites of sturgeon or cheese or rhubarb tart,
or swallows of wine, had briefed us on the prospect and answered
questions. The house itself looked like the best bet. Not only was
there no likely spot in the stable, which no longer held horses, or
the kennels, which no longer held dogs, but also Jimmy would
have risked being seen by the caretaker if he had lugged a suitcase to one of them in the open. Nor was there any likely spot
in the garage, which was connected with the house. The only
other outbuilding was a six-room stone structure in the rear, living quarters for servants, occupied now only by the caretaker.
Something really fancy, like wrapping the suitcase in plastic and
burying it somewhere on the grounds, was of course out, with
the caretaker around. The house was the best bet, and not the
cellar, since there was no part of it that the caretaker might not
poke around in, or, later, if the suitcase was to stay put for a
while, a servant or even a member of the family.

As we climbed out a man appeared from around a corner—a tall, lanky specimen in a red wool shirt and dungarees who hadn't shaved for at least three days. As he caught sight of Noel he spoke. "Oh, it's you, Mr. Tedder?"

"On my own two feet," Noel said, meeting him and offering a hand. Either he believed in democracy or Wolfe had made it a habit. "How are you, Jake?"

"I'll make out if they don't trip me." Jake gave us a glance. "The roof, huh? We had a shower Friday and it leaked again. I phoned your mother."

"She's been . . . not so good."

Jake nodded. "Too bad about Mr. Vail. Terrible thing. You know they've been after me, but what could I tell 'em? For nearly a week all kinds of people drivin' in. I'm takin' no chances." His hand went to his hip pocket and came out with a gun, an old black Marley .32. He patted it. "Maybe I couldn't hit a rabbit, but I can scare 'em off." He put it back. "You want to see in your mother's room where it leaked?"

"Not today, Jake." Noel's squeak wasn't so squeaky; perhaps his voice was changing. "My mother may be out this week. These men are detectives from New York and they want to look around in the house. They think there may be something—I don't know exactly what. You know how detectives are. Is there a door open?"

Jake nodded. "The back door's open, the one off the kitchen. I cook and eat in the kitchen, better tools there. Your mother knows I do. Lucky I had bacon and eggs on hand when he came Wednesday morning. Terrible thing about him. I sure do know how detectives are, I do now." He looked at us. "No offense to you fellows."

Obviously one of us ought to say something, so I said, "We don't offend easy. We know how caretakers are too."

"I bet you do." He chuckled. "I just bet you do. You want me to help with anything, Mr. Tedder?"

"No, thanks. We'll make out. This way, Goodwin." Noel headed for the corner Jake had come from, and we followed.

To prove how competent and experienced we are I could describe the next forty minutes in detail, but it wouldn't help you any

more than it did us. We had learned from Noel that the possibilities were limited. Jimmy Vail had been a town man and had
never got intimate with this country place. His bedroom was the
only spot in the house he had had personal relations with, so we
tried that first, but after we had looked in the two closets and the
bottom drawer of a chest, then what? The bed was a big old walnut
thing with a canopy, and there was enough room under it for an
assortment of wardrobe trunks, but room was all there was.

We went all around, downstairs and up. We even spent ten
minutes in the cellar, most of it in a storage room where there were
some ancient pieces of luggage along with the other stuff. We
looked in the garage, which was big enough for five cars, and
there in a corner saw something that would have seemed promising if it hadn't been there in the open where anyone might have
lifted the lid—a big old-fashioned trunk. I did lift the lid and saw
something that took me back to my boyhood days in Ohio. But
a couple of cardboard boxes had held my two-year collection of
birds' eggs, and here were dozens of compartments, some with
one egg and some with two or three. I asked Noel if they were
his, and he said no, they had been his father's, and the trunk
held more than three hundred different kinds of eggs. I lifted the
tray out, and underneath it was another tray, not so many compartments but bigger eggs. Orrie came for a look and said, "Let's
take that. It may not be worth half a million, but it's worth something." I put the top tray back in and was shutting the lid when
I heard the sound of a car.

The garage doors were closed and the sound was faint, but I
have good ears. The parking area where we had left the Heron
was on this side of the house, but not in front of the garage. The
door we had come through was standing open—the door from the
garage to a back hall. I stepped to it quietly and poked my head
through, and in a moment heard a voice I had heard before.
Margot Tedder. She was asking Jake whose car that was. Then
Jake, telling her: her brother Noel and four detectives from New
York who were searching the house for something. Margot asked,
searching for what? Jake didn't know. Then Margot calling her

brother, a healthier yell than I thought she had in her: "Noel!
Noel!!"

Preferring the garage to the outdoors as a place for a conference, I sang out, "We're in the garage!" and turned and told Noel,
"It's your sister."

"I know it is. Damn her."

"I'll do the talking. Okay?"

"Like hell you will. She'll do the talking."

It's a pleasure to work with men who can tell time. Saul had
started to move when I called out that we were in the garage,
and Fred and Orrie a second later, and I had moved back from
the door, taking Noel with me. So when Margot appeared and
headed for Noel, with Jake right behind her, and Uncle Ralph
behind Jake, all my three colleagues had to do was take another
step or two and they were between the newcomers and the exit.
And both Saul and Orrie were only arm's length from Jake's
hip pocket. It's a real pleasure.

I was at Noel's side. As Margot approached she gave me a
withering glance, then switched it to Noel, stopped in front of
him, and said, "You utter idiot. Get out and take your gang with
you."

I said politely, "It's as much his house as yours, Miss Tedder,
and he got here first. What if he tells you to get out?"

She didn't hear me. "You heard me, Noel," she said. "Take
this scum and go."

"Go yourself," Noel said. "Go to hell."

She about-faced and started for the door. I raised my voice a
little. "Block it! Saul, you'd better get it."

"I have it," Saul said and raised his hand to show me the gun
he had lifted from Jake's pocket. Margot saw it and stopped. Fred
and Orrie had filled the doorway. Uncle Ralph made a noise.
Jake looked at Margot, then at Noel, and back at Margot. Saul
was back of him, and he didn't know he had been disarmed.

"You wouldn't shoot," Margot said scornfully, and I have to
admit there was no shake in her voice.

"No," I told her back, "he wouldn't shoot, but why should he?
Five against three, granting that you're one and Jake is with you.

As Jake told you, we're looking for something, and we haven't finished. Noel told you to go, but it would be better for you to stay here in the garage, all three of you, until we're through. One of you might use the phone, and we'd be interrupted. I don't—"

I stopped because she was moving. She went to the door, just short of Fred and Orrie, just not touching them, and said, "Get out of the way."

Orrie smiled at her. He thinks he knows how to smile at girls, and as a matter of fact he does. "We'd like to," he said, "but we're glued."

"I don't know how long we'll be," I told her, "but there's a stack of chairs there by the wall. Fred and Orrie, you—"

"Jake! Go and phone my mother!" Her voice still didn't shake, but it was a little shrill.

And by gum, Jake's hand went back to his hip pocket. I was almost sorry his gun was gone; it would have been interesting to see how he handled it. His jaw dropped, and he wheeled and saw it in Saul's hand. "It's all right," Saul said, "you'll get it back." Jake turned to Noel and said, "Fine lot you brought." He turned to Margot. "I guess I can't."

"You guess right," I told him. "Fred and Orrie, you stay here and keep the peace. Noel and Saul and I will look around some more. But it has occurred to me that I may have overlooked something. Wait till I see." I went to the corner where the big trunk was, lifted the lid, took out the top tray, and put it on the floor gently. Then I reached in and got the loops at the ends of the second tray and eased it up and out, and I damn near dropped it. There at the bottom of the trunk was an old tan leather suitcase. I took three seconds out to handle my controls, staring at it, then carefully put the tray on the floor to one side, straightened up, and said, "Come and take a look, Noel." He came and stooped over to see, then reached a hand in and heaved, and out it came. At that point I decided that he might really have two feet. I had expected him to squeak something like "Jesus Holy Christ what the hell," but he squeaked nothing. He just reached in and got it, put it on the floor, undid the clasps, and opened the lid; and there was the biggest conglomeration of engraved lettuce I had ever had the pleasure of looking at. I glanced around. Purcell was at my elbow, and Jake was at his elbow, and Saul was right behind them. Margot was approaching, hips stiff as ever. Noel, squatting, with a hand flattened out on top of the find, tilted his head back to look up at me and said, "I didn't believe him, but I thought I might as well come. How in the name of God did he know it was here?"

Orrie, still in the doorway with Fred, called over, "Damn it, have you got it?" Margot was saying something which I didn't bother to hear, and Purcell was making noises. I looked at my wrist; it's nice to know exactly what time you found half a million bucks. Eight minutes to three. I went and put the trays back in the trunk, gently and carefully, closed the lid, and came back. Noel was fastening the lid of the suitcase, paying no attention to what his sister was saying.

"Okay," I said, "we'll move. Saul and Noel will take it out to the car." I put out a hand to Saul. "The gun. I'll unload it and leave it on the kitchen table. Fred and Orrie will follow Saul and Noel. I'll stay in the kitchen to guard the phone until you have the car turned around and headed out. When you tap the horn I'll come. Miss Tedder, if you came to see about that leaky roof, don't neglect it just because we got in the way. As Mr. Wolfe remarked to your brother just this afternoon, a leaky roof should be attended to."

CHAPTER 14

WHEN THE DOORBELL rang at five minutes to six Monday afternoon I was in my chair in the office, leaning back, my feet up on the corner of the desk, looking at the headline on the front page of the *Gazette:*

VAIL RANSOM FOUND
$500,000 in Birds' Egg Trunk

With that second hot exclusive given to Lon Cohen in three days, our credit balance with him was colossal. The picture of the suitcase on page 3, with the lid open, had been taken by me. The article, which I had read twice, was okay. I was given a good play, and so was Wolfe, and Saul and Fred and Orrie were named. I had given Lon nothing about Margot or Uncle Ralph, but had mentioned Jake's gun. A gun improves any story.

The money was in the bank, but not the one it had come from. Noel had demonstrated that he was neither a piker nor a soft touch. When I had put the suitcase on the couch in the office, and he had opened it, and we had all gathered around to admire the contents, including Wolfe, he had taken out a couple of bundles of cees, counted off two grand and handed it to Orrie, then two grand to Fred, two to Saul, and five to me. Then he had asked Wolfe, "Do you want yours now?" and Wolfe had said it would have to be counted first since his share was a percentage; and Wolfe had gone to the kitchen to tell Fritz there would be four guests for dinner. It was then five o'clock, but at seven, just two hours later, Fritz had served us the kind of meal you read about. No shad roe.

The arrangement for the night was determined by two facts: one, there wasn't room in the safe; and two, Noel didn't want to take it home, which was understandable. So when bedtime came I got pajamas for him and took him up to the south room, which is above Wolfe's, checked the towel supply and turned the bed down, and took the suitcase up another flight to my room. It wouldn't go under my pillow, so I made room for it on the bed stand right against the pillow. We hadn't counted the money.

It was counted Monday morning in a little room at the Continental Bank and Trust Company on Lexington Avenue, where Wolfe has had his account for twenty years. Present were an assistant vice-president, two tellers, and Noel and me. Of course Noel and I were merely spectators. They started on it a little after ten, and it was a quarter past twelve when they declared finally and positively that the figure was $489,000. Noel took twenty twenties for pocket money; $100,000 was deposited in Wolfe's account; and an account was opened for Noel with a balance of $388,600. There would be no service charge, the assistant vice-president told Noel, with a banker's smile at his own hearty joke. We had said nothing about where it had come from, and he had asked no questions, since Wolfe was an old and valued customer, but he must have had a guess if he ever looked at a newspaper. Of course the *Gazette* wasn't out yet.

Noel and I shook hands in parting, out on the sidewalk. He took a taxi headed uptown. I didn't hear what he said to the hackie, but I gave myself five to one that he was going straight to 994 Fifth Avenue. A nice little bank balance in his own name is very good for a man's feet. I took a little walk to call on Lon Cohen.

I rather expected some kind of communication from Mrs. Vail or Andrew Frost before the day was out, but the afternoon went by without a peep. I also rather expected that Wolfe would put on a strutting act, his own special brand of strutting, explaining how simple it had been to dope out where the money was, but he didn't, and I wasn't going to pamper him by asking for it. I got back in time to dispose of the morning mail, which was skimpy, before lunch, and after lunch he finished his book and got another one from the shelf, and I got onto the germination and blooming records. There would soon be some new cards to add to the collection, with the bank balance where it now was.

When the doorbell rang at 5:55 and I took my feet down from the desk and went to see, there was Inspector Cramer.

That broke a precedent. Knowing Wolfe's schedule as he does, he may come at 11:01 or 6:01, but never at 5:55. Did it mean he wanted five minutes with me first? It didn't. When I let him in, all I got was a grunt as he went by, and when I joined him in the office he was in the red leather chair, his hat on the stand, his feet planted flat, and his jaw set. Not a word. I went to my chair, sat, planted my feet flat, and set my jaw. We were like that when Wolfe came in. As he passed the red leather chair he grunted, a perfect match for the grunt Cramer had given me. In his own chair, his bulk adjusted satisfactorily, he grunted again and asked, "How long have you been here?"

Cramer nodded. "So you can ride Goodwin for not telling you. Sure. You ride him, and he needles you. A damn good act. I've seen it often enough, so don't waste it on me. You lied to me yesterday morning. You said you had an idea where the money was. Nuts. You *knew* where it was. How did you know?"

Wolfe's brows were up. "Have you shifted from homicide to kidnaping?"

"No. If you knew where it was you knew who put it there. It must have been Jimmy Vail. He died Wednesday night. You told me yesterday that you had no evidence, either about the whereabouts of the money or Vail's death. That was a barefaced lie. You used the evidence about the money to get your paws on it. Now you're going to use the evidence about Vail's death to pounce on something else, probably more money. How many times have I sat here and yapped at you about withholding evidence or obstructing justice?"

"Twenty. Thirty."

"I'm not doing that now. This is different. I'm telling you that if the evidence you've got about Vail's death is evidence that he was murdered, and if you refuse to give it to me here and now, whatever it is I'll dig it up, I'll get it, and I'll hang an accomplice rap on you and Goodwin if it's the last thing I do this side of hell."

"Hhmmm," Wolfe said. He turned. "Archie. I have a good

memory, but yours is incomparable. Have we any shred of evidence regarding the death of Mr. Vail that Mr. Cramer lacks?"

I shook my head. "No, sir. He probably has a good deal, little details, that we lack." I turned to Cramer. "Look. I certainly know everything that Mr. Wolfe knows. But yesterday he not only told you that he was convinced that Vail was murdered, I'm with him on that, he also said he was all but certain that he knew who had killed him. I'm not. Certain, my eye. I'd have to pick it out of a hat."

"He didn't say that. That was a question."

Wolfe snorted. "A question only rhetorically. You said I was grandstanding—your word. Apparently you no longer think so, which isn't surprising, since I have found the money. In effect, you are now demanding that I do your interpreting for you."

"That's another lie. I am not."

"But you are." Wolfe turned a palm up. "Consider. As I told you yesterday, my conclusions about the whereabouts of the money and Mr. Vail's death were based on deductions and assumptions from the evidence at hand, and I have no evidence that you do not have. Yesterday you said you would leave me to my deductions and assumptions. Now you want them. You demand them, snarling a threat."

"You're twisting it around as usual. I didn't snarl."

"I'm clarifying it. I am under no necessity, either as a citizen or as a licensed detective, to share the product of my ratiocination with you. I am not obliged to describe the mental process by which I located the money and identified the murderer of Miss Utley and Mr. Vail. I may decide to do so, but it rests with my discretion. I shall consider it, and if and when—"

The doorbell rang. As I went to the hall I was considering whether it was Andrew Frost with a legal chip on his shoulder or some journalist after crumbs. It was neither. It was Ben Dykes of Westchester County and a stranger. It might or might not be desirable to let them join the party, so I only opened the door to the two-inch crack the chain permitted and spoke through it. "Back again?"

"With bells on," Dykes said.

"You're Archie Goodwin?" the stranger asked. He showed a buzzer, not Westchester. New York. "Open up."

"It's after office hours," I said. "Give me three good reasons why I should—"

"Take a look at the bells," Dykes said and stuck a paper through the crack.

I took it, unfolded it, and looked. Thoroughly. It was a little wordy and high-flown, but I got the idea. "Mr. Wolfe will want to see this," I said. "He's a great reader. Excuse me a minute." I went to the office, waited until Wolfe finished a sentence, and told him, "Sorry to interrupt. Ben Dykes from Westchester with a New York dick for an escort, and with this." I showed the paper. "A court order that Archie Goodwin is to be arrested and held on a charge of grand larceny. On a complaint by Mrs. Althea Vail. It's called a warrant." I turned to Cramer. "Got any more questions before I leave?"

He didn't even glance at me. His eyes were fastened on Wolfe, who had just said that he had identified a murderer. Wolfe put out a hand, and I gave him the paper, and he read it. "She's an imbecile," he declared. "Bring them in."

"We don't need Goodwin," Cramer said. "You'll have him out on bail in the morning."

"Bring them," Wolfe snapped.

I returned to the front, removed the chain, pulled the door open, invited them in, and was surprised to see that there were three of them. Presumably the third one had stayed at the foot of the steps as a reserve in case I started shooting. You've got to use tactics when you go for a gorilla. I soon discovered how wrong I was when they followed me to the office and the third one darted by me to Wolfe's desk, whipped a paper from a pocket, and shoved it at Wolfe. "For you," he said and wheeled and was going, but Ben Dykes caught his arm and demanded, "Who are you?"

"Jack Duffy, process server," he said and jerked loose and trotted out.

"A goddam paper boy," Dykes said disgustedly. I stepped to the hall, saw that he shut the door as he went, and stepped back in. Wolfe had picked up the document and was scowling at it. He read it through, let it fall to the desk, leaned back, closed his eyes, and pushed his lips out. In a moment he pulled them in, then out, in, out . . .

Dykes said, "All right, Goodwin, let's go." The New York dick had suddenly recognized Inspector Cramer and was trying to catch his eye so he could salute, but Cramer was staying at Wolfe. In a minute Wolfe opened his eyes, straightened up, and asked his expert on women, me, "Is she a lunatic?" He tapped the document. "This is a summons. She is suing me, not only for the money in the suitcase, but also to recover the fee she paid me."

"*That* hurts you," Cramer growled.

Wolfe regarded him. "Mr. Cramer. I have a proposal. I would prefer not to describe it for other ears, and I think you share that preference. It is within the discretion of the police to postpone service of a warrant of arrest if it is thought desirable. I suggest that you advise Mr. Dykes, who is accompanied by a member of your force, to wait until tomorrow noon to take Mr. Goodwin into custody. After they leave I'll make my proposal."

Cramer cocked his head and screwed his lips. He had to pretend to give it a hard look, but actually there was nothing to it. By now he knew darned well that Wolfe wasn't grandstanding. He spoke. "Dykes is from Westchester. He has a New York man with him for courtesy, but the arrest is up to him." His head turned. "What about it, Dykes? Would you have to phone White Plains?"

Dykes shook his head. "That wouldn't be necessary, Inspector. I'm supposed to use my head."

"All right, use it. You heard what Wolfe said. If it's just a stall, you can take Goodwin tomorrow."

Dykes hesitated. "If you don't mind, Inspector, I'd like to be able to say that you made it a request."

"Then say it. It's a request."

Dykes went to Wolfe's desk and picked up the warrant, then turned to me. "You won't leave the state, Goodwin."

I told him I wouldn't dream of it, and he headed out, followed by the dick, who never had got to salute Cramer. I got in front of them, wanting to be polite to a man who had postponed tossing me in the can, and let them out. When I returned to the office Wolfe was speaking.

". . . but I must first satisfy myself. As I told you, I have no evidence. Mr. Goodwin has already been served with a warrant, and I have been served with a summons, and I prefer not to expose myself to an action for libel."

"Nuts. Telling me privately, libel?"

"It's conceivable. But in candor, that's not the main point. I intend to take a certain step, and it's highly likely that if I told you what I have deduced and assumed you would make it extremely difficult for me to take it, if not impossible. You wouldn't dare to take it yourself because, like me, you would have no evidence. You'll hear from me, probably tonight, and by tomorrow noon at the latest."

Cramer was anything but pleased. "This is a hell of a proposal."

"It's the best I can do." Wolfe looked at the clock. "I would like to proceed."

"Sure you would." Cramer reached for his hat and put it on. "I should have let Dykes take Goodwin. I'd sleep better if I knew he was in a cell." He rose. "You'd have had to take your certain step anyway." He moved and, halfway to the door, turned. "If you call me tomorrow and say you've decided that your deductions and assumptions were wrong, God help you." He went. That time my going to see that the hall was empty when the door closed wasn't just routine; he might really have stayed inside to get a line on the certain step. As I stepped back in Wolfe snapped, "Get Mrs. Vail."

That wasn't so simple. First I got a female, and after some insisting I got Ralph Purcell. After more insisting he told me to hold the wire, and after a wait I had him again, saying that his sister wouldn't speak with Nero Wolfe or me either. I asked if he would give her a message, and he said yes, and I told him to tell her that Wolfe wanted to tell her how he had known the money was in the house. That did it. After another wait her voice came.

"This is Althea Vail. Nero Wolfe?"

He was at his phone. "Yes. I am prepared to tell you how I

knew where the money was, but it's possible that your telephone is tapped. I am also—"

"Why on earth would it be tapped?"

"The pervasive curiosity of the police. I am also prepared to tell you various other things. Examples: the name of the man to whom you gave the suitcase on Iron Mine Road; how I know that there was no Mr. Knapp; the reason why Mr. Vail had to be killed. I shall expect you at my office at nine o'clock this evening."

Silence. She hadn't hung up, but the silence lasted so long that I thought she had left the phone. So long that Wolfe finally asked, "Are you there, madam?"

"Yes." More silence, but after half a minute: "I'll come now."

"No. It will take some time and would run into the dinner hour. Nine o'clock."

"I'll be there." The connection went.

We hung up, and I turned to Wolfe. "What's all the hurry? You haven't got a single solitary scrap."

He was glaring at the phone and switched it to me. "I will not have you carted off to jail on a complaint by that silly wretch. It should be worth keeping. Is that thing in order?"

"I suppose so. It was the last time we used it."

"Test it."

I got up, slipped my hand in between my desk and the wall, and flipped a switch. Then I went and sat in the red leather chair and said in a fairly low voice, "Nero Wolfe is going to put on a charade, and let us hope he doesn't break a leg." I went to my desk and turned it off, then went to the kitchen, opened a cupboard door, did some manipulating, and flipped a switch, and in a few seconds my voice came out: "Nero Wofe is going to put on a charade, and let us hope he doesn't break a leg." I reached in and turned it off, returned to the office, and reported, "It's okay. Anything else?"

"Yes. That idiot may have a gun or a bomb or heaven knows what. Stay near her."

"Or she may have a lawyer."

"No. No indeed. She's not that big an idiot." He picked up the summons and scowled at it.

CHAPTER 15

SHE CAME AT 8:50, ten minutes ahead of time. I was getting Wolfe's okay on a change in the program when the doorbell rang. In order to stay near her I would have had to sit in one of the yellow chairs near the red leather chair, and I prefer to be at my desk, or I would have had to put her in one of the yellow chairs near me, and Wolfe prefers to have a caller in the red leather chair because the window is then at his back.

It was a pleasant May Day evening, and she had no wrap over her tailored suit, so the only problem was her handbag—a big black leather one with a trick clasp. I learned about the clasp when I tried to open it, after I had got it from her lap and taken it to my desk. Her reaction to my snatching it, which I did as soon as she was seated and had no hand on it, showed the condition of her nerves. She made no sound and no movement, but merely stared at me as I took it to my desk, and she said nothing while I fiddled with it, finding the trick clasp and opening it, and inspected the contents. Nothing in it seemed to be menacing, and when I went and put it back on her lap she had transferred the stare to Wolfe. I might have felt a little sorry for her if it hadn't been for the warrant that Ben Dykes would be back with at noon tomorrow. When you grab a woman's bag and open it and go through it, and all she does is sit and stare, she could certainly use a little sympathy.

There was no sympathy in Wolfe's expression as he regarded her. "This isn't an inquisition, Mrs. Vail," he said. "I have no questions to ask you. It will be a monologue, not a tête-à-tête, and it will be prolonged. I advise you to say nothing whatever."

"I wouldn't answer any questions if you did ask them," she said. Her voice was good enough. "You said there was no Mr. Knapp. That's crazy."

"Not as crazy as your invention of him." Wolfe leaned back. "This will be easier to follow if I begin in the middle. Mr. Goodwin has told you how I reached the conclusion that your husband was murdered. That didn't help much unless I could identify the murderer, and as a first step I needed to see those who were at that gathering Wednesday evening. Let's take them in the order in which I saw them.

"First, your son. When he came to hire me to find the money for him I suggested the possibility that he had had a hand in the kidnaping and knew where the money was, that he couldn't very well just go and get it, and that he intended to supply hints that would lead to its discovery by me—or by Mr. Goodwin. When I made that suggestion at the beginning of our conversation, I thought it was a real possibility, but by the time our talk ended I had discarded it. For such a finesse a subtle and agile mind would be needed, and also a ready tongue. Such a witling as your son couldn't possibly have conceived it, much less execute it. So he had come to me in good faith; he hadn't been involved in the kidnaping; he didn't know where the money was; and he hadn't killed Mr. Vail."

"You said you would tell me how you knew there was no Mr. Knapp."

"That will come in its place. Second, your daughter. But you may not know even now what led Mr. Goodwin and me to suspect that Dinah Utley was a party to the kidnaping. Do you?"

"No."

"Your brother hasn't told you?"

"No."

"Nor the police?"

"No."

"The note that came in the mail. It had been typed by her. I won't elucidate that; this will take long enough without such details. When Mr. Goodwin saw that the other two notes which you had found in telephone books—I know now, of course, that they were not in the books, you had them with you and went to the books and pretended to find them—when Mr. Goodwin saw that they too had been typed by her, the suspicion became a conclusion. And ten minutes' talk with your daughter made it manifest that it was quite impossible that she had been allied with Dinah Utley in any kind of enterprise, let alone one as ambitious and hazardous as kidnaping. Your daughter is a vulgarian, a dunce, and a snob. Also she had come to demand that I find the money for her, but even without that it was plain that she, like her brother, had not been involved in the kidnaping; she didn't know where the money was; and she hadn't killed Mr. Vail.

"Third, your brother. From Mr. Goodwin's report of his behavior Wednesday afternoon, or rather, his lack of behavior, his silence, I had tentatively marked him as the one who most needed watching. After twenty minutes with him, him in the chair you are in now, I had to conclude that it was impossible. You know his habit of looking at A when B starts to speak."

"Yes."

"His explanation of that habit was enough. A man with a reaction so hopelessly out of control cannot have effective and sustained control over any of his faculties. He would never trust himself to undertake an operation that required audacity, ingenuity, and mettle. There were many other indications. His parting words were 'I guess I *am* a fool,' and he meant them. Patently he was not the man.

"Fourth, Andrew Frost. As you know, he came yesterday morning, but I learned nothing from that interview. There was nothing in his words or tone or manner to challenge the possibility that he was the culprit, and, except for you, that was the only possibility that remained. But through an assistant I had already learned enough about him to exclude him—his record, his position in his profession and in society, his financial status. That didn't exclude him as a possible murderer, but it was inconceivable that he had been involved in the kidnaping. He would have had to conspire with at least two others, Miss Utley and Mr. Knapp, and probably more, with the only objective in view a share of the loot, and therefore he would have been at their mercy, in mortal danger indefinitely. What if one of his confederates had been caught and had talked? To suppose that such a man had incurred such a risk for such a return? No."

Wolfe shook his head. "No. Therefore it was you. You had been a party to the kidnaping, you had killed Dinah Utley, and you had killed your husband. I reached that conclusion at ten o'clock Saturday evening, but I wanted to see Mr. Frost before I acted on it. It was barely possible that after talking with him I would reconsider my decision about him. I didn't. Will you have some refreshment? A drink? Coffee?"

No reply. No movement.

"Tell me if you want something. I'll have some beer." He pushed a button and leaned back again. "Also before I acted on it I had to examine it. I had to satisfy myself that no fact and no factor known to me rendered it untenable; and first came motive. What conceivable reason could you have had for getting half a million dollars in cash from your bank and going through that elaborate rigmarole to deliver it to a masked man at an isolated spot on a country road at midnight, other than your ostensible reason? Please bear in mind, Mrs. Vail, that from here on I am not reporting; I am only telling you how I satisfied myself. If in this instance or that I chose the wrong alternative you may correct me, but I still advise you to say nothing."

I never saw advice better followed. She had a good opportunity to speak, for Fritz came with beer, and Wolfe poured, but she didn't take advantage of it. He waited for the foam to sink to the proper level, then lifted the glass and drank.

He leaned back. "I found only one acceptable answer. The man you delivered the suitcase to was your husband. He probably was masked, for both you and he gave meticulous attention to detail throughout the operation. Very well; why? What were you accomplishing? You were establishing the fact that you had suffered a loss of half a million dollars, and that fact would net you ninety-one per cent of the half a million, since you would deduct it as a casualty on your income-tax report. I haven't inquired as to whether such a casualty would be deductible, and I don't suppose you did; probably you merely assumed that it would be. If your income for the year would be less than half a million, no matter; you could carry the loss back for three previous years and forward for five future years. Well worth the effort, surely."

He came forward to drink, then back again. "Other facts and factors. Why did you and your husband bring Dinah Utley into it? You couldn't plan it to your satisfaction without her. Take one detail, the phone call from Mr. Knapp. You wanted no doubt whatever in any quarter that the kidnaping was genuine, and you thought there must be a phone call. Mr. Vail couldn't make it, for even if he disguised his voice it might be recognized. It would be simpler and safer to use Miss Utley, your trusted employee, than to have some man, no matter who, make the call. Of course the call was never made. Miss Utley not only typed the notes; she also typed the transcript of the supposed conversation on the phone. I presume her reward was to be a modest share of the booty.

"Was it you or your husband who conceived the notion— No. I said I would ask you no questions. All the same, it's an interesting point, which of you thought of coming to me, since that was what led to disaster. No doubt it seemed to be an excellent stroke in your elaborate plans to achieve verisimilitude; not only coming to me but also the hocus-pocus about getting here; ten thousand dollars wasn't much to pay for establishing that you were desperately concerned for your husband's safety. You couldn't foresee that I would insist on seeing your secretary, but when I made that demand your check was already on my desk, and you didn't dare take it back merely because I wished to speak with Miss Utley. Nor could you foresee that I would propose a step that would expose me to the risk of an extended and expensive operation, and that I would demand an additional sum as insurance against possible loss. You didn't like that at all. Your teeth bit into your lip as you wrote the check, but you had to. Fifty thousand dollars makes a substantial hole in half a million, but you had made it so clear that nothing mattered but your husband's safety, certainly money didn't, that you couldn't very well refuse."

He poured beer, drank when the foam was right, and went on. "I don't know if you regretted that you had come to me when you left, but you certainly did later, when Miss Utley returned after seeing me. As I said, I'm not reporting, I'm telling you how I satisfied myself. I got an inkling of Miss Utley's temperament and character when she was here, and more than an inkling from what your brother told me about her. From questions Mr. Goodwin and I asked her, and from our taking her fingerprints, she became apprehensive. She feared that you had somehow aroused my suspicion, that I suspected her, and that I might disclose the fraud; and when she returned she tried to persuade you to give it up. You wouldn't. All the preliminaries had been performed; you had the money in the suitcase; you had given me sixty thousand dollars; all that remained was the consummation. You tried to remove Miss Utley's fears, to convince her that there was no danger of exposure, and you thought you succeeded, but you didn't.

"Shortly before eight o'clock you left in your car with the suitcase in the trunk, not knowing that, instead of subsiding, Miss Utley's alarm had grown. An hour after your departure she took the typewriter from the house, put it in her car, and drove to the country. Here there are alternatives; either is acceptable; I prefer this one: after disposing of the typewriter she intended to go to where Mr. Vail was in hiding, arriving before he left for the rendezvous with you, describe the situation, and insist that the project be abandoned. But something intervened, probably the difficulty of disposing of the typewriter unseen in a spot where it would surely never be found, and to see Mr. Vail she had to go to Iron Mine Road, which had been named in one of the notes she had typed."

Wolfe drank beer. "Some of what I have said is conjectural, but this is not. Miss Utley got to Iron Mine Road before you did. When you and your husband arrived, you in your car and he in his, she told him of her fears and insisted that the project must be abandoned. He didn't agree. He didn't stay long to debate it; he was supposed to be concealed somewhere by kidnapers, and even in that secluded spot there was a possibility that someone might come along. He put the suitcase in his car and drove off, leaving it to you to deal with her, and you tried to, but she wouldn't be persuaded. She may have demanded a large share of the half a million to offset the risk, but I doubt it. From what your brother said of her it's more likely that she was filled with dismay. Either she made it plain that she would wreck the project by disclosing it, or you were convinced that she intended to. Infuriated, you assaulted her. You hit her on the head with something—a handy rock?—and as she lay unconscious you got in her car and ran it over her, nosed the car into an opening, dragged the body to the ditch and rolled it in, got in your car, and drove away. If, ignoring my advice to say nothing, you ask why I say that you, not Mr. Vail, killed her, I repeat that I had to satisfy myself. If he killed her, why was he killed the next day? There was no tenable answer.

"To satisfy myself it wasn't necessary to supply answers to all relevant questions. For example, where was your husband from Sunday evening to Wednesday morning? I don't know and need not bother to guess, but since other details were carefully and thoroughly planned I assume that one was too. It had to be some spot where both he and his car could be effectively concealed, especially in the daytime. Of course you had to know where it was, since something might happen that would make it necessary to alter the plan. No doubt you and he chose the spot with great care and deliberation. Wherever it was, probably it lacked the convenience of a telephone, so he had to get to one Tuesday evening in order to make the calls to Fowler's Inn and The Fatted Calf, but that was after dark, and of course that detail too was prudently contrived.

"For another example of questions that can be left open, why did you tell your son he could have the money if he found it? Why not? Knowing yourself where it was, you knew he wouldn't find it. Still another example, why did you and your husband insist on keeping silent about the kidnaping for forty-eight hours after he returned home? A good guess is that you wanted enough time to pass to make sure that no trail had been left, but it doesn't have to be verified for my satisfaction. Regarding any known fact or factor I need only establish that it doesn't contradict my deduction—my final deduction, that you killed your husband. As for his coming to see me Wednesday morning, posthaste after his return, it would have been surprising if he hadn't. He wanted to learn how much ground there was, if any, for Miss Utley's fears; what he learned, over the telephone from you, was that she was dead; and he departed, again posthaste, to go to you.

"He knew, of course, that you had killed Dinah Utley, and you were completely at his mercy. He couldn't expose you as a murderer without divulging his own complicity in preparations for a swindle, but the swindle hadn't been consummated; there would be no swindle until the deduction had been made on your income-tax return and you and he had signed it. Meanwhile he had a cogent threat, and he used it. He demanded the entire half a million for himself. You were in a pickle. After all the planning, all the exertion, all the painstaking, all the zeal, even after your desperate resort to murder, you were to get nothing. That was not to be borne. Jimmy Vail must die."

A noise came from her, but it wasn't a word; it was merely the kind of involuntary noise that is squeezed out by a blow or a sting. Wolfe went on. "You planned it with the care and foresight you had so admirably demonstrated in planning the kidnaping. You needed a drug, and since you assuredly wouldn't take the risk of procuring one in haste, you must have had one in your possession —probably chloral hydrate, since you may plausibly have had it in some mixture in your medicine cabinet, but that's another question I may leave open. Either luck was with you Wednesday evening, or you knew him so well that you could safely calculate that when drowsiness overtook him from the drug you had put in his drink he would lie on the couch instead of going to his room. For the rest you needed no luck. After Mr. Frost left you went down to the library, found your husband in a coma as you had a right to expect, dragged him across to the desired spot, and toppled the statue on him. With your marked talent for detail, undoubtedly you took his feet. Shoes dragged along a floor will leave telltale marks, even on a rug, but a head and shoulders won't. Certainly you didn't leave it to luck whether the statue would land where you wanted it. You wiggled it to learn its direction of least resistance. Evidently the thump wasn't heard, because the inmates were all in upper rooms; and the statue didn't hit the floor, the main impact was on your husband's chest, and it would have been more of a crunch than a thump."

Wolfe straightened up, took in air through his nose as far down as it could go, and let it out through his mouth. His eyes narrowed at her. "Mrs. Vail," he said, "I confess that I am not without animus. I have been provoked by the suit you have served against me, and by your complaint against Mr. Goodwin, subjecting him to arrest on a criminal charge. But even so I would hesitate to upbraid you on moral grounds for the fraud you conceived and tried to execute. Millions of your fellow citizens will cheat on their income tax this year. Nor would I reproach you without qualification for killing Miss Utley; you did it in the instant heat of uncontrollable passion. But killing your husband is another matter. That was planned and premeditated and ruthlessly executed; and for a sordid end. Merely for money. You killed him in cold blood because he was going to deprive you of the fruit of your swindle. That, I submit, was execrable. That would be condemned even by—"

"That's not true," she said. It barely got out through her tight throat, and she repeated it. "That's not true!"

"I advised you to say nothing, madam. That would be condemned even—"

"But it's not true! It wasn't the money!" She was gripping the chair arms. "He could have had the money. I told him he could. He wouldn't. It was Dinah. He was going to leave me because I had—because of Dinah. That was why—it wasn't the money."

"I prefer it that he demanded the money."

"No!"

"He threatened to expose you as a murderer?"

"No. He said he wouldn't. But he was going to leave me, and I loved him." Her mouth worked, and her fingers clawed at the chair arms, scratching at the leather. "I loved him, and he was going to leave me."

"And of course that might mean your exposure." Wolfe's voice was low, down almost to a murmur. "Away from you, no longer enjoying your bounty, there was no telling what he might

do. So he had to die. I offer you my apology. I concede that your
end was not sordid, that you were in mortal danger. Did you try
to gull him, did you deny that you had killed Dinah Utley?"

"No, he knew I had." She made fists. "I was insane, I must
have been. You're right, I knew what would happen if he left
me, but that wasn't it. I must have been insane. Later that night
I went down to the library again and stayed there with him until—"
She jerked up straight. "What am I saying? What did I say?"

"Enough." Not a murmur. "You said what I expected you
to say when I accused you of killing your husband merely for
money. That was absurd, but no more absurd than your attack
on Mr. Goodwin and me after we found the money. You intended,
of course, to put the onus on your deceased husband—to have it
inferred that he had arranged the kidnaping to get the money for
himself, with Dinah Utley as an accomplice, that he had killed
her, and possibly even that he had killed himself through fear or
remorse, though that would be rather farfetched—a man would
hardly choose that method of committing suicide. But you should
have known that you would arouse—"

He stopped because his audience was walking out on him.
When she shifted her feet to get up, her bag slipped to the floor,
and I went and picked it up and handed it to her and followed
her out. Having circled around her in the hall to get in front, I
had the door open by the time she reached it, and I went out to
the stoop to watch her go down the steps. If she went home and
finished up the chloral hydrate, that would be her funeral, but I
didn't want her stumbling and breaking her neck on our premises.
She wasn't any too steady, but she made it to the sidewalk and
turned right, and I went back in.

Going to the kitchen, I got the tape and the playback from the
cupboard and took them to the office. Wolfe sat and scowled at
me as I got things ready, switched it on, ran it through to what
might be the spot, and turned on the sound. Wolfe's voice came.

". . . in the instant heat of uncontrollable passion. But killing
your husband is another matter. That was planned and premeditated and ruthlessly executed; and for a sordid end. Merely for
money. You killed him in cold blood because he was going to

deprive you of the fruit of your swindle. That, I submit, was execrable. That would be condemned even by—"

"That's not true. That's not true!"

"I advised you to say nothing, madam. That would be condemned even—"

"But it's not true! It wasn't the money! He could have had the money. I told him he could. He wouldn't. It was Dinah. He was going to leave me because I had—because of Dinah. That was why—it wasn't the money."

It went on to the end, good and clear, as it should have been, since that installation had cost twelve hundred smackers. As I turned it off Wolfe said, "Satisfactory. Take it to Mr. Cramer."

"Now?"

"Yes. That wretch may be dead within the hour. If he isn't at his office, have him summoned. I don't want him storming in here tomorrow to bark at me for delaying delivery of a confession of a murderer."

I reached for the tape.

CHAPTER 16

SHE NOT ONLY wasn't dead within the hour; she's not dead yet.
That was three months ago, and last week a jury of eight men
and four women stayed hung for fifty-two hours and then gave
up. It stood seven for conviction of first-degree murder and five
for acquittal. Whether this report gets published or not depends on
the jury at the second trial. If it hangs too, or acquits, this script
will have to go into a locked drawer in my room, with several
others to keep it company.

If you care about whether I took another trip to White Plains,
I did—Tuesday noon, escorted by Ben Dykes. By then Mrs. Vail
had been taken to the District Attorney's office, but everyone
was too busy to worry about me. I was out on bail by five o'clock,
but I had had my fingerprints taken for the nineteenth time. It
took a week before the charge was quashed, and the cost of the
bail cut Wolfe's hundred grand down to $99,925. Even so, I'm
having plenty of time to go for walks, getting angles on people
and things. Having reached that bracket by the first of May, Wolfe
relaxed and has stayed relaxed. If you offered him ten thousand
bucks to detect who swiped your hat at a cocktail party yesterday
he wouldn't even bother to glare at you.